"America's leading source of self-help legal information." ★★★★
—YAHOO!

LEGAL INFORMATION ONLINE ANYTIME
24 hours a day

www.nolo.com

AT THE NOLO.COM SELF-HELP LAW CENTER, YOU'LL FIND

- Nolo's comprehensive Legal Encyclopedia filled with plain-English information on a variety of legal topics
- Nolo's Law Dictionary—legal terms <u>without</u> the legalese
- Auntie Nolo—if you've got questions, Auntie's got answers
- The Law Store—over 200 self-help legal products including Downloadable Software, Books, Form Kits and eGuides
- Legal and product updates
- Frequently Asked Questions
- NoloBriefs, our free monthly email newsletter
- Legal Research Center, for access to state and federal statutes
- Our ever-popular lawyer jokes

Quality LAW BOOKS & SOFTWARE FOR EVERYONE

Nolo's user-friendly products are consistently first-rate. Here's why:

- A dozen in-house legal editors, working with highly skilled authors, ensure that our products are accurate, up-to-date and easy to use
- We continually update every book and software program to keep up with changes in the law
- Our commitment to a more democratic legal system informs all of our work
- We appreciate & listen to your feedback. Please fill out and return the card at the back of this book.

OUR "NO-HASSLE" GUARANTEE

Return anything you buy directly from Nolo for any reason and we'll cheerfully refund your purchase price. No ifs, ands or buts.

Read This First

The information in this book is as up to date and accurate as we can make it. But it's important to realize that the law changes frequently, as do fees, forms, and procedures. If you handle your own legal matters, it's up to you to be sure that all information you use—including the information in this book—is accurate. Here are some suggestions to help you:

First, make sure you've got the most recent edition of this book. To learn whether a later edition is available, check the edition number on the book's spine and then go to Nolo's online Law Store at www.nolo.com or call Nolo's Customer Service Department at 800-728-3555.

Next, even if you have a current edition, you need to be sure it's fully up to date. The law can change overnight. At www.nolo.com, we post notices of major legal and practical changes that affect the latest edition of a book. To check for updates, find your book in the Law Store on Nolo's website (you can use the "A to Z Product List" and click the book's title). If you see an "Updates" link on the left side of the page, click it. If you don't see a link, that means we haven't posted any updates. (But check back regularly.)

Finally, we believe accurate and current legal information should help you solve many of your own legal problems on a cost-efficient basis. But this text is not a substitute for personalized advice from a knowledgeable lawyer. If you want the help of a trained professional, consult an attorney licensed to practice in your state.

6th edition

How to Form a Nonprofit Corporation

by Attorney Anthony Mancuso

NOLO

SIXTH EDITION	SEPTEMBER 2004
Editor	DIANA FITZPATRICK
Illustrations	MARI STEIN
Cover Design	TONI IHARA
Book Design	TERRI HEARSH
CD-ROM Preparation	ANDRÉ ZIVKOVICH
Index	BAYSIDE INDEXING SERVICE
Proofreading	ROBERT WELLS
Printing	CONSOLIDATED PRINTERS, INC.

Mancuso, Anthony.
    How to form a nonprofit corporation / by Anthony Mancuso. — 6th ed.
      p. cm.
    Includes index.
    ISBN 1-4133-0039-1
    1. Nonprofit organizations—Law and legislation—United States—Popular works. 2.
Incorporation--United States--Popular works. I. Title

KF1388.Z9M36 2004
346.73'064--dc22

                                                          2004044891

For information on bulk purchases or corporate premium sales, please contact the Special Sales
Department. For academic sales or textbook adoptions, ask for Academic Sales. Call 800-955-4775
or write to Nolo at 950 Parker Street, Berkeley, CA 94710.

About the Author

Tony Mancuso is a California attorney and the author of Nolo's best-selling corporate law series, including *Incorporate Your Business* and Nolo's *LLC Maker* software. Tony authored Nolo's *The Corporate Minutes Book* and *Your Limited Liability Company: An Operating Manual*, national titles on holding meetings, preparing and maintaining corporate and LLC records, and taking care of important ongoing corporate and LLC legal and tax business. He is also the author of *The California Nonprofit Corporation Handbook* that shows California incorporators how to handle the specific forms and procedures to form a nonprofit corporation in California. Tony is a jazz guitarist and a licensed helicopter pilot.

Table of Contents

Introduction

Part I: How Nonprofit Corporations Work

1 Is Nonprofit Incorporation Right for You?

2 Legal Rights and Duties of Incorporators, Directors, Officers, Employees, and Members

Part II: Incorporating Your Nonprofit

7 Prepare Your Bylaws

8 Apply for Your Federal 501(c)(3) Tax Exemption

9 Final Steps in Organizing Your Nonprofit Corporation

10 After Your Corporation Is Organized

11 Lawyers and Accountants

Appendix A:

How to Use the CD-ROM

Appendix B:

State Sheets

Appendix C:

Forms and Publications on CD-ROM

Appendix D:

Information and Tear-Out Forms

Index

Introduction

*I*nterest in forming nonprofit corporations is on the rise. All sorts of groups—artists, musicians, and dancers; people active in conservation, education, and health issues; organizations devoted to ethnic and community services, women's rights, help for the homeless, and countless other concerns—wish to organize their efforts as nonprofit corporations. These groups have an enormous dedication to doing good work amid challenging fiscal and social conditions and to helping others improve their lives and communities. Understandably, there is often little time, money, or enthusiasm for attending to legal and tax formalities. But bypassing these steps could be a mistake.

This book gives groups like yours the information and tools necessary to deal with legal and tax technicalities and obtain the substantial benefits available to nonprofits. Specifically, this book gives you:

- background information, specific line-by-line instructions, and sample language necessary to prepare the Internal Revenue Code Section 501(c)(3) federal tax exemption application

- a step-by-step guide to preparing the legal paperwork necessary to form a nonprofit corporation in each state. This paperwork includes articles of incorporation, bylaws, and the minutes of the board of directors' meeting with sample language you can use to complete most of the clauses found in your official state articles form.

- State Sheets in Appendix B containing each state's basic incorporation requirements. We refer you to this state-specific information when we explain how

to fill in an official or tear-out incorporation form.

The legal documents and tax forms necessary to form your corporation are provided both in tear-out form and on CD-ROM. Instructions on how to use the forms on the CD-ROM are in Appendix A.

We have also included chapters to help you understand the legal, tax, and practical issues and areas of concern for ongoing nonprofit operations. Steps to take after you have completed your incorporation papers, including ongoing legal and tax filing formalities, are also covered.

Finally, because many incorporators will follow our suggestion to consult a legal and tax professional during the incorporation process, we include a chapter on how to find a lawyer and an accountant with nonprofit experience who will charge reasonable fees for their services. Because many incorporators will wish to look up some of the law themselves, this chapter also includes basic information on how to do your own self-help legal research.

A. Why Form a Nonprofit Corporation?

Often the reason for forming a nonprofit corporation is simple—being organized as a tax-exempt nonprofit corporation is a common requirement for obtaining grant funds from government agencies and private foundations. There are also important federal, state, and local income, property, sales, excise, and other tax exemptions available to nonprofit corporations. In addition, only tax-exempt nonprofit organizations provide donors with the incentive of an individual tax deduction for contributions made to the organization. There are additional benefits available to tax-exempt nonprofit corporations such as low-cost nonprofit mailing, advertising, and purchasing rates as well as other private and governmental discounts and preferences.

In addition, nonprofits, like all other product or service providers, need to protect their members, officers, and directors against possible lawsuits and potential liability for the nonprofit's activities and operations. Incorporating gives directors, officers, and members a valuable form of legal protection from personal liability for claims brought against the corporation. Lawsuits against the nonprofit can only reach the corporate assets, not the bank accounts, houses, or other property owned by the individuals who manage, work for, or participate as members of the corporation.

Many people who form nonprofit corporations also feel that the act of setting up the corporation is itself beneficial. Why? Because preparing the standard paperwork necessary to organize a nonprofit corporation makes you deal with important organizational issues that might otherwise be ignored in a more informal setting. For example, when drafting corporate articles, bylaws, and tax-exemption applications, you must define the nonprofit purpose of your group, describe your fundraising program, project expected sources of support, determine whether you will adopt a formal membership structure, specify the qualifications and procedures for selecting your board of directors, officers, and members, and attend to a number of other matters. Thinking now about how you'll handle these issues will be particularly valuable later, when clarity of purpose and procedure will help you meet the countless fiscal and program challenges that you'll encounter.

In sum, organizing as a nonprofit corporation can be a handy means of attracting tax-exempt and tax-deductible support and, at the same time, obtaining certain benefits and protections available to corporations in general. There are certain restrictions that come with the territory, however, that are discussed in more detail below.

Nonprofit Corporations Can Make a Profit

"Nonprofit" does not mean literally that you cannot make a profit. Under the federal tax law and state corporate statutes, as long as your corporation is organized and operated for a recognized nonprofit purpose, it can take in more money than it expends in conducting its activities. A nonprofit may use its tax-free profits for its operating expenses (including salaries for officers, directors, and employees) or for the benefit of its organization. What it cannot do under IRC § 501(c)(3) is distribute any of the profits for the benefit of its officers, directors, or employees (as dividends, for example).

B. Nonprofit Status Isn't for Everyone

Forming a nonprofit corporation is a lot of work, both at the beginning and as an ongoing proposition. Lots of groups who "do good works" can operate just fine as unincorporated associations. If your group does not generate a surplus (does not make a taxable profit), does not need to attract tax deductible contributions, does not need to apply for public or private grant monies, and does not need to provide its officers, directors, personnel, or members with protection against being sued, it may decide it's best, at least for the present, not to form a tax-exempt nonprofit corporation. (Chapter 1, Section B, explains the benefits of nonprofit status in detail.)

Many commercial and noncommercial enterprises furnish services and products that provide an educational or charitable benefit to the public, such as booksellers, self-help centers, and associations offering training courses and instructional seminars. A surprising number of these groups could qualify for nonprofit status under federal and state law—but not all choose to do so. Operating as a tax-exempt nonprofit involves some significant trade-offs. For example, most nonprofits must comply with the following rules and restrictions:

- Nonprofits may not distribute profits or other private benefits to directors, officers, members, or staff (although reasonable salaries and standard employment benefits are allowed).
- Income from sources unrelated to the tax-exempt purposes of the group must not be substantial.

- The assets of the organization must be dedicated to its tax-exempt purpose. This means that if and when the group dissolves, any remaining assets must be distributed to another tax-exempt 501(c)(3) organization.

Because of the rules and restrictions applicable to nonprofits, many organizations that could qualify for tax-exempt status under Section 501(c)(3) decide not to.

C. Organizations That Can Use This Book

This book provides the information, forms, and instructions needed to form the most common types of nonprofit corporations—ones organized under Section 501(c)(3) of the Internal Revenue Code. Section 501(c)(3) is the catch-all category for nonprofit tax-exempt status. These groups must be organized for religious, charitable, scientific, literary, or educational purposes. (These purposes are explained in more detail in Chapters 1 and 3.) Most groups seeking nonprofit status will use this part of the Internal Revenue Code to obtain tax-exempt status.

There are other kinds of nonprofit activity that can qualify for nonprofit status, including groups organized for a civic, patriotic, political, recreational, or social purpose. These groups, however, must qualify under a different section of the Internal Revenue Code (not Section 501(c)(3)). If this describes your group, you will not be able to complete the incorporation process using this book. (See Chapter 1 for more information on these non-501(c)(3) groups and where these groups can go for help.)

Please scan the entire book at least once before you make decisions and fill out papers. It is not difficult to organize a nonprofit corporation, but many of the corporate and tax laws are picky or technical—often both—and you should get an overview of the whole subject before getting down to details. The Incorporation Checklist included in Appendix D and on the CD-ROM provides an overview of the material in this book and a checklist for completing the steps involved in forming a nonprofit corporation.

References to IRS Articles and Materials

Throughout the book, there are references to IRS articles and materials included on the CD-ROM that comes with this book. Some of this material includes articles and information made available by the IRS on its website as part of its Exempt Organizations Continuing Professional Education Technical Instruction Program, which regularly publishes articles for tax-exempt organizations. The IRS has the following statement on its website regarding this material: "These materials were designed specifically for training purposes only. Under no circumstances should the contents be used or cited as authority for setting or sustaining a technical position."

In other words, use this material to learn about IRS tax issues, but don't expect to be able to rely on it if you end up in a dispute with the IRS. Nolo includes this material on the CD-ROM as a convenience to the reader and as an alternative to directing you to an IRS website link to this material. This material is taken from the exempt organization tax law training articles available from the IRS website at www.irs.gov/charities/index.html. If you are interested in one of the issues, you should check the IRS website for any updated articles or information on your topic.

If you are forming a nonprofit in California. If you plan to incorporate your nonprofit in California and want additional information about incorporating there—for example, line-by-line instructions for completing California's special state income tax exemption application (California, unlike most other states, uses its own state tax exemption application process), see *How to Form a Nonprofit Corporation in California*, by Anthony Mancuso (Nolo).

Icons Used in This Book

 Tells you when you can skip information that doesn't apply in your situation.

 A caution that you need to slow down and consider potential problems.

 Alerts you to important tips.

 Tells you when we believe you need the advice of an expert—either an attorney or tax advisor.

 Refers you to additional sources of information about the particular issue or topic discussed in the text.

 Shows you where in the book to turn for more information on a particular issue or topic discussed in the text.

Points the way to forms and other materials included on the CD-ROM at the back of the book.

Refers you to the State Sheets in Appendix B, where you will find each state's rules for nonprofit corporations.

Refers you to IRS publications.

We have enjoyed assembling and explaining this incorporation material. We hope it helps you with the legal and tax formalities necessary to incorporate your organization and brings you closer to attaining your nonprofit goals. Best of Luck! ∎

Part I

How Nonprofit Corporations Work

Chapter 1

Is Nonprofit Incorporation Right for You?

Deciding to form a nonprofit corporation will be a big step for you and the members of your group. It will involve more paperwork and government forms, on both the state and federal level, than anyone will like; and you'll have to conduct your business within the legal framework of various state and federal laws. Fortunately, there are big payoffs to all this work and attention, including the ability to attract donors and grant funds, obtain real and personal property tax exemptions and special nonprofit mailing rates, avoid corporate income taxes, and shield officers and directors from legal liability. Before starting down the path of nonprofit incorporation, however, you'll want to learn a little more about who can form a nonprofit and the consequences of doing so. In this chapter, we'll explain:

- the kinds of groups that can—and can't—form a nonprofit using this book (Section A)
- the benefits you'll enjoy as a nonprofit—and some of the disadvantages to choosing this route (Sections B and C)
- how nonprofits can raise start-up funds and earn money, should they wish to do so (Section D)
- the process you'll go through (following the instructions in this book) to incorporate and obtain your tax-exempt status (Section E), and
- for those considering incorporating in another state, considerations to bear in mind before doing so (Section F).

In the following sections, we occasionally refer to your State Sheet to find a particular legal rule in your state. You can find the State Sheets in Appendix B.

A. Is Your Group a Nonprofit That Can Use This Book?

For-profit corporations can usually be formed for "any lawful purpose" under state statutes. Nonprofit corporations, on the other hand, generally must be established to accomplish one or more specific purposes that benefit either the public at large, a segment of the community, or a particular membership. While it may be easy for your group to incorporate as a nonprofit in your state, this is only the first hurdle. The next important step is to obtain tax-exempt status under state and federal tax statutes. To do this, your group must meet specific purpose requirements contained in state and federal tax statutes.

This book has been written specifically for nonprofits that want to qualify for federal income tax exemption under Section 501(c)(3) of the Internal Revenue Code. This means that your nonprofit corporation must be formed for religious, charitable, scientific, literary, and/or educational purposes. There are other types of groups—labor unions, chambers of commerce, social and recreational clubs, fraternal societies, credit unions, farmers' co-ops, and legal service organizations, to name a few—that may be eligible for tax-exempt status under other sections of the Internal Revenue Code. (See "Special Nonprofit Tax-Exempt Organizations," in Appendix D, for a list of organizations that can qualify for tax-exempt status under a subsection of 501(c) other than Subsection 3). These groups often have more leeway to provide direct financial benefits to their members, but they don't receive the same tax benefits as a 501(c)(3) group. If you are planning on forming one of these non-501(c)(3) nonprofits, this book can help acquaint you with the process of forming a nonprofit. It will not, however, guide you step-by-step through the process of preparing articles of incorporation and bylaws for your group or the tax exemption applications you will need for your nonprofit.

If your group falls within one of the 501(c)(3) purposes, however, you can rest assured that this book will help you step-by-step through the process of incorporating and obtaining tax-exempt status. First, we'll help you create your corporate entity by showing you how to prepare and file articles of incorporation that meet your state's corporate law requirements. Then we'll show you how to obtain your state and federal nonprofit income tax exemptions for Section 501(c)(3) tax-exempt status.

Corporation Basics

You don't have to understand all there is to know about corporations in order to follow this book or form your nonprofit. But there are a few basic concepts you'll want to have under your belt as we go through the process. Here they are, with special emphasis on any differences between for-profit corporations and nonprofits.

- **A corporation is a separate legal entity.** A corporation is a legal entity that allows a group of people to pool energy, time, and money for profit or nonprofit activities. It acquires legal existence after its founders comply with their state's incorporation procedures and formalities. The law treats a corporation as a separate "person," distinct from the people who own, manage, or operate it. The corporation can enter into contracts, incur debts, and pay taxes. Corporations are either for-profit (business corporations) or nonprofits.

- **For-profit, or business, corporations versus nonprofits.** Business corporations can be formed for any legal purpose. They can issue shares of stock to investors in return for money or property, or services performed for the corporation. Shareholders receive a return on their investment if dividends are paid or if, upon dissolution of the cor-

poration, any corporate assets remain to be divided among the shareholders after payment of all creditors. Nonprofits, on the other hand, generally cannot issue shares of stock or pay dividends under state law (unless they are some type of hybrid such as consumer or producer co-ops). The federal tax code also prohibits 501(c)(3) tax-exempt nonprofit corporations from paying dividends or profits to their members or other individuals. When a 501(c)(3) tax-exempt nonprofit corporation dissolves, it must distribute its remaining assets to another tax-exempt nonprofit group.

- **In-state and out-of-state corporations.** Corporations formed in a particular state are known as "domestic" corporations in their state. Corporations formed in other states, even if physically present and engaging in activities in a state, are called "foreign" corporations in that state. For example, a corporation formed in California is a domestic corporation as far as California is concerned, but a foreign corporation when considered by other states. Section F, below, gives more information on deciding whether to incorporate in a particular state.

B. Benefits of the Nonprofit Corporation

Now that you understand that this book is intended for nonprofit corporations organized for religious, charitable, scientific, literary, and/or educational purposes that want to qualify for a tax exemption under Section 501(c)(3) of the Internal Revenue Code (and hopefully your nonprofit is among them), let's look at the benefits you'll enjoy as a 501(c)(3) tax-exempt nonprofit corporation. The relative importance of each of the following benefits will vary from group to group, but at least one of them should be very significant for your organization.

If you finish this section and conclude that nothing here is very important for your group, you'll want to consider whether it makes sense to incorporate at all. Many groups accomplish their nonprofit purposes just fine as unincorporated nonprofit associations, without formal organizational paperwork or written operational rules. If you can continue to accomplish your nonprofit purposes and goals informally, you may be happier staying small.

1. Tax Exemptions

Nonprofit corporations are eligible for state and federal exemptions from payment of corporate income taxes, as well as other tax exemptions and benefits. At federal corporate tax rates of 15% on the first $50,000 of taxable income, 25% on the next $25,000 and 34% and higher on income over $75,000, it goes without saying—at least if you expect to earn a substantial amount of money (from services, exhibits, or performances, for ex-

ample)—that you'll want to apply for an exemption. In states with a corporate income tax, a state income tax exemption is equally attractive, as are local county, real, and personal property tax exemptions. Chapters 3, 4, and 5 cover tax exemptions in detail.

Get the help of a competent tax advisor as soon as you decide to incorporate. Make sure you choose someone experienced in the special field of nonprofit bookkeeping and reporting. Ask the advisor to help you (especially your treasurer) set up a good record keeping system, which you can use to prepare your annual federal and state nonprofit tax forms and reports. Have the tax helper periodically review the system to be sure that you are maintaining your financial records properly and have filed your tax forms on time.

2. Receiving Public and Private Donations

One of the primary reasons for becoming a 501(c)(3) nonprofit corporation is that it increases your ability to attract and receive public and private grant funds and donations.

- **Public sources.** Tax-exempt government foundations (like the National Endowment for the Arts or Humanities, the Corporation for Public Broadcasting, or the National Satellite Program Development Fund) as well as private foundations and charities (such as the Ford Foundation, the United Way, or the American Cancer Society) are usually required by their own operating rules and federal tax regulations to donate their funds only to 501(c)(3) tax-exempt organizations.

- **Individual private** donors can claim personal federal income tax deductions for contributions made to 501(c)(3) tax-exempt groups. At death, a complete federal estate tax exemption is available for bequests made to 501(c)(3) groups.

In short, if you plan to ask people to give you significant amounts of money in furtherance of your nonprofit purpose, you need to demonstrate to your donors that you have 501(c)(3) tax-exempt status.

3. Protection From Personal Liability

Protecting the members of your group from personal liability is one of the main reasons for forming a corporation (either profit or nonprofit). Once you're incorporated, directors or trustees, officers, employees, and members of a corporation usually won't be personally liable for corporate debts or liabilities, including unpaid organizational debts and unsatisfied lawsuit judgments against the organization, as they normally would be if they conducted their affairs without incorporating. Creditors can go after only corporate assets to satisfy liabilities incurred by the corporation—not the personal assets (car, home, or bank accounts) of the people who manage, work for, or volunteer to help the nonprofit corporation.

EXAMPLE: A member of the audience sued a nonprofit symphony orchestra when the patron fell during a concert, claiming that the symphony (which also owned the concert hall) provided an unsafe ramp. The patron won a judgment that exceeded the orchestra's insurance policy limits. The amount of the judgment in excess of insurance is a debt of the corporation, but not of its individual directors, members, managers, or officers. By contrast, had the orchestra been an unincorporated association of musicians, the principals of the unincorporated group could be held personally liable for the excess judgment amount.

In a few situations, however, people involved with a nonprofit corporation may be personally liable for the corporation's liabilities. Here are some major areas of potential personal liability:

- **Taxes.** State and federal governments can hold the corporate employee who is responsible for reporting and paying corporate taxes personally liable for any unpaid taxes, penalties, and interest due for failure to pay taxes or file necessary returns (for example, the treasurer if the nonprofit board has given this officer full authority to pay all taxes as they become due). With proper planning, your nonprofit corporation should be tax exempt, but you still have to file federal and state informational returns and annual reports to the secretary of state and state attorney general, as well as pay employee withholding and other payroll taxes and taxes on income unrelated to your nonprofit purposes. IRS penalties for delinquent tax payments and returns are substantial, so keep this exception to limited liability in mind—particularly if you will be the treasurer or a board member who specifically approves the payment of taxes on behalf of your corporation.

- **Dues.** Members of a nonprofit corporation are personally liable for any membership fees and dues they owe the corporation. In most cases, this is a minor obligation since dues are normally set at modest amounts.

- **Violations of statutory duties.** Corporate directors are legally required to act responsibly (not recklessly) when managing the corporation. They may be held personally financially liable if they fail to act responsibly. Personal liability of this sort is the exception, not the rule. Generally, as long as directors attend meetings and carry out corporate responsibilities conscientiously, they should have little to worry about—the corporate limited liability shield insulates directors from all but the most reckless and irresponsible decisions.

- **Intermingling funds or other business dealings.** A nonprofit corporation must act so that its separate existence is clear and respected. If it mixes up corporate funds with the personal funds of those in charge, fails to follow legal formalities (such as failing to operate according to bylaws, hold director meetings, or keep minutes of meetings) or risks financial liability without sufficient backup in cash or other assets, a court may disregard the corporate entity and hold the principals responsible for debts and other liabilities of the corporation. In legalese, this is known as "piercing the corporate veil." Piercing the veil is the exception, not the rule, and only happens when a court decides that it is necessary to prevent a gross injustice or fraud perpetuated by the founders or principals of a corporation.

- **Private foundation managers.** If the nonprofit corporation is classified as a private foundation, foundation managers can be held personally liable for federal excise taxes associated with certain prohibited transactions. They may also be held personally liable for penalties and interest charged for failing to file certain tax returns or pay required excise taxes. (As explained in Chapter 4, Section C, a private foundation is a 501(c)(3) corporation that does not qualify as a public charity—you'll see that most 501(c)(3) nonprofits qualify as public charities and are not subject to the private foundation requirements).

- **Loans.** When a nonprofit corporation takes a loan to cover its operating costs or buys property subject to a mortgage, banks and commercial lending institutions sometimes insist on the personal guarantee of its directors or officers. If the directors or officers agree to personally guarantee the loan or mortgage, the protection that they would normally enjoy as a result of their organization's corporate status goes away. It is somewhat unusual for nonprofit directors or officers to sign a personal guarantee. Obviously, if they do, they will be liable to repay the loan if the corporation cannot do so.

4. Separate and Perpetual Legal Existence

A corporation is a legal entity that is separate from the people who work for it. Again, one benefit of this separate existence is that corporate liabilities are not the liabilities of the managers, officers, or members of the corporation (known as the corporate characteristic of "limited liability"). Another benefit is that this corporate legal person is, in a sense, immortal; the nonprofit corporation continues to exist as a legal entity despite changes in management or other corporate personnel caused by the resignation, removal, or death of the people associated with it. It may, of course, be dissolved or drastically affected by the loss of key people, but its inherent perpetual existence makes it more likely that the group's activities will continue, an attractive feature to the private or public donor who prefers funding activities that are organized to operate over the long term.

5. Employee Benefits

Another benefit of the nonprofit corporation is that its principals can also be employees and, therefore, eligible for employee fringe benefits not generally available to the workers in unincorporated organizations. These benefits include group term life insurance, accident and health insurance, reimbursement of medical expenses, and coverage by an approved corporate employee pension or retirement income plan.

6. Formality and Structure

The formal corporate documents—the articles, bylaws, minutes of meetings, and board resolutions—that you'll prepare as a nonprofit will actually be quite useful to your organization. They'll outline the group's purposes, embody its operating rules, and provide structure and procedures for decision making and dispute resolution. This is important for any collective activity, but for nonprofit groups it is vital, especially if the board includes members of the community with diverse interests and viewpoints. Without the clear-cut delegation of authority and specific operating rules in the articles and bylaws, running the organization might be a divisive, if not futile, affair.

7. Miscellaneous Benefits

Additional advantages are available to nonprofits that engage in particular types of activities or operations. These benefits can be helpful, and in some cases are critical, to the success of a nonprofit organization. Here are examples of some of the benefits available to certain types of tax-exempt nonprofits.

- Your nonprofit may qualify for exemptions from county real and personal property taxes.
- 501(c)(3) organizations receive lower postal rates on third-class bulk mailings.
- Many publications offer cheaper classified advertising rates to nonprofit organizations.
- Nonprofits are the exclusive beneficiaries of free radio and television public

service announcements (PSAs) provided by local media outlets.

- Many stores offer lower membership rates to nonprofit employees.

- Nonprofit employees are often eligible to participate in job training, student intern, work-study, and other federal, state, and local employment incentive programs (where salaries are paid substantially out of federal and state funds).

- 501(c)(3) performing arts groups are qualified to participate in the performance programs sponsored by federally supported colleges and universities.

- Certain 501(c)(3) educational organizations are eligible for a tax refund for gasoline expenses (for example, in running school buses).

Does Incorporation Make Sense for Your Group?

A senior citizens botany club began as an informal organization. Initially, six members took a monthly nature walk to study and photograph regional flora. Everyone chipped in to buy gas for whoever drove to the hike's starting point. Recently, however, membership increased to 15 and the group decided to collect dues from members to pay the increased expenses—gas money, guidebooks, maps, and club T-shirts—associated with more frequent field trips. To avoid mixing club monies with personal funds, a treasurer was designated to open a bank account on behalf of the organization. Several people suggest that it is time to incorporate the club.

Does incorporation make sense at this time? Probably not. There is no new pressing need to adopt the corporate form or to obtain formal recognition as a tax-exempt nonprofit. Most banks will allow an unincorporated group without a federal Employer Identification Number or IRS tax exemption to open up a non-interest-bearing account. However, should the club decide to seek funding and contributions to spearhead a drive to save open space in the community, it might be a good idea to incorporate.

C. The Disadvantages of Going Nonprofit

If your group has come together for 501(c)(3) tax-exempt purposes, and if reading about the benefits of becoming a nonprofit above prompted a "Wow! We would really like to be able to do *that!*" then chances are you've decided to tackle the rules and forms necessary to establish your status as a legal nonprofit. Before jumping in, however, take a minute to read the following descriptions of some of the hurdles and work you'll encounter along the way, especially if you have been operating informally (and successfully) without financial or employee record keeping or controls. If any of the following appear insurmountable to you, think again about incorporating.

1. Official Paperwork

One disadvantage in forming any corporation is the red tape and paperwork. You'll begin by preparing initial incorporation documents (articles of incorporation, bylaws, and minutes of first meeting of the board of directors). Although this book will show you how to prepare your own incorporation forms and bylaws with a minimum of time and trouble, the process will still take you a few hours. You and your compatriots must be prepared for some old-fashioned hard work.

After you've set up your corporation, you'll need to file annual tax and reporting returns with the state (the state tax or revenue office and the attorney general) as well as the Internal Revenue Service. Also, you will need to regularly prepare minutes of on-

going corporate meetings, and, occasionally, forms for amending articles and bylaws. The annual tax reporting forms will require the implementation of an organized bookkeeping system plus the help of an experienced nonprofit tax advisor as explained below. Fortunately, keeping minutes of these meetings is not all that difficult to do once someone volunteers for the task (typically the person you appoint as corporate secretary). Sample forms for amending nonprofit articles are usually available from the state corporate filing office online (see the State Sheets in Appendix B for the website address of your state's corporate filing office).

Annual nonprofit tax and information returns do present a challenge to a new group unfamiliar with state tax reporting forms and requirements. Other record keeping and reporting chores, such as double-entry accounting procedures and payroll tax withholding and reporting, can be equally daunting. At least at the start, most nonprofits rely on the experience of a tax advisor, bookkeeper, or other legal or tax specialist on the board or in the community to help them set up their books and establish a system for preparing tax forms on time. See Chapter 11 for recommendations on finding legal and tax professionals for your nonprofit.

2. Incorporation Costs and Fees

For nonprofit incorporators unwilling to do the job themselves, a main disadvantage of incorporating a nonprofit organization is the cost of paying an attorney to prepare the incorporation forms and tax exemption applications. Putting some time and effort into understanding the material in this book can help you eliminate this disadvantage, leaving you with only the actual cost of incorporation. Including the typical $150 federal tax exemption application fee, total fees to incorporate are approximately $200–$250. (Costs are $350 higher for nonprofits that anticipate gross receipts of more than $10,000. These groups pay a $500, rather than a $150, federal tax exemption application fee.)

3. Time and Energy Needed to Run the Nonprofit

When a group decides to incorporate, the legal decision is often part of a broader decision to increase not just the structure, but the overall scope, scale, and visibility of the nonprofit. With a larger, more accountable organization come a number of new tasks: setting up and balancing books and bank accounts, depositing and reporting payroll taxes, and meeting with an accountant to extract and report year-end figures for annual informational returns. Although these financial, payroll, and tax concerns are not exclusively corporate chores, you'll find that most unincorporated nonprofits keep a low employment, tax, and financial profile and get by with minimum attention to legal and tax formalities.

> **EXAMPLE:** A women's health collective operates as an unincorporated nonprofit organization. It keeps an office open a few days a week where people stop by to read and exchange information on community and women's health issues. The two founders donate their time and the office space and pay operating costs

(such as phone, utilities, and photocopying) that aren't covered by contributions from visitors. The organization has never made a profit, there is no payroll, and tax returns have never been filed. There is a minimum of paperwork and record keeping.

The founders could decide to continue this way indefinitely. However, the founders want to expand the activities and revenues of the collective. They decide to form a 501(c)(3) nonprofit corporation in order to be eligible for tax-deductible contributions and grant funds from the city, and to qualify the group to employ student interns and work-study students. This will require them to prepare and file articles of incorporation and a federal corporate income tax exemption application. They must select an initial board of directors and prepare organizational bylaws and formal written minutes of the first board of directors' meeting.

After incorporation, the group holds regular board meetings documented with written minutes, sets up and uses a double-entry bookkeeping system, implements regular federal and state payroll and tax procedures and controls, files exempt organization tax returns each year, and expands its operations. A full-time staff person is assigned to handle the increased paperwork and bookkeeping chores brought about by the change in structure and increased operations of the organization.

This example highlights what should be one of the first things you consider before you decide to incorporate: Make sure that you and your coworkers can put in the extra time and effort that an incorporated nonprofit organization will require. If the extra work would overwhelm or overtax your current resources, we suggest you hold off on your incorporation until you get the extra help you need to accomplish this task smoothly (or at least more easily).

4. Restrictions on Paying Directors and Officers

As a matter of state corporation law and the tax-exemption requirements, nonprofits are restricted in how they deal with their directors, officers, and members. None of the gains, profits, or dividends of the corporation can go to individuals associated with the corporation, including directors, officers, and those defined as members in the corporation's articles or bylaws. State self-dealing rules apply as well, regulating action by the board of directors if a director has a financial interest in a transaction.

Officers and staff can be paid a reasonable salary for work they do for the corporation. State laws often provide for this type of compensation, and even if nothing is specified, it is permissible. Directors can also be paid for their expenses and time for attending director meetings. In all cases, however, these payments should be reasonable. Lavish payments or undeserved payouts characterized as "salaries" or "compensation" can be challenged by the IRS and can lead to penalties and even a loss of tax exemption (see Chapter 3, Section C).

5. Restrictions Upon Dissolution

One of the requirements for the 501(c)(3) tax exemption is that upon dissolution of the corporation, any assets remaining after the corporation's debts and liabilities are paid must go to another tax-exempt nonprofit, not to members of the former corporation.

6. Restrictions on Your Political Activities

Section 501(c)(3) of the Internal Revenue Code establishes a number of restrictions and limitations that apply to nonprofits. Here, we discuss a limitation that may be very significant to some groups—the limitation on your political activities. Specifically, your organization may not participate in political campaigns for or against candidates for public office, and cannot substantially engage in legislative or grassroots political activities except as permitted under federal tax regulations (for more on this, see Chapter 3, Section C).

> **EXAMPLE:** Society for a Saner World, Inc., has as one of its primary objectives lobbying hard to pass federal and local legislation that seeks to lessen societal dependency on fossil fuels. Since a substantial portion of the group's efforts will consist of legislative lobbying, the group's 501(c)(3) tax exemption probably will be denied by the IRS. Instead, the group should seek a tax-exemption under IRC § 501(c)(4) as a social welfare group, which is not limited in the amount of lobbying the group can undertake. Of course, the benefits of 501(c)(4) tax ex-

emption are fewer too—contributions to the group are not tax-deductible and grant funds will be more difficult to obtain—see "Special Nonprofit Tax-Exempt Organizations," in Appendix D.

7. Oversight by the Attorney General

Each state's attorney general has broad power to oversee the operations of 501(c)(3) nonprofits. The attorney general can take the corporation to court to make sure it complies with the state corporation law. This usually doesn't happen, however, unless an organization commits a serious offense (such as the founders diverting contributions for their personal use) and the organization is on the state attorney general's enforcement division radar (through a complaint filed by a disgruntled group or member of the public who feels aggrieved by the nonprofit's actions or policies).

Religious 501(c)(3) nonprofit corporations have wider flexibility in managing their internal affairs. A state attorney general is less likely to step in and sue a religious nonprofit to enforce compliance with state corporate laws, except in the most extreme and unusual cases of fraud or misappropriation by the principals of a religious-purpose nonprofit.

D. How Nonprofits Raise, Spend, and Make Money

Most nonprofits need to deal with money—indeed, being able to attract donations is a prime reason for choosing nonprofit status. Nonprofits can also make money. "Nonprofit" does not literally mean that a nonprofit corporation cannot make a profit. Under federal tax law and state law, as long as your nonprofit is organized and operating for a recognized nonprofit purpose, it can take in more money than it spends in conducting its activities. This section explains how nonprofits raise initial funds and how they make money on an ongoing basis.

1. Initial Fundraising

Under state corporate statutes, a nonprofit corporation is not legally required to have a specified amount of money in the corporate bank account before commencing operations. This is fortunate, of course, because many beginning nonprofits start out on a "shoestring" of meager public and private support.

So, where will your seed money come from? As you know, nonprofit corporations cannot issue shares, nor can they provide investment incentives, such as a return on capital through the payment of dividends to investors, benefactors, or participants in the corporation (see "Corporation Basics" at the beginning of this chapter). Nonprofits have their own means and methods of obtaining start-up funds. Obviously, the most common method is to obtain revenue in the form of contributions, grants, and dues from the people, organizations, and governmental agencies that support the nonprofit's purpose and goals. Also, if you are incorporating an existing organization, the organization's assets are usually transferred to the new corporation—these assets may include the cash reserves of an unincorporated group, which can help your corporation begin operations.

You can also borrow start-up funds from a bank, although for newly formed corporations a bank will usually require that incorporators secure the loan with their personal assets—a pledge most nonprofit directors are understandably reluctant to make.

Often, of course, nonprofits receive initial and ongoing revenues from services or activities provided in the pursuit of their exempt purposes (ticket sales, payments for art lessons or dance courses, school tuition, or clinic charges). Section 501(c)(3) nonprofits are allowed to earn this type of revenue under federal and state tax laws and still maintain their tax-exempt status.

2. Making Money From Related Activities

Many nonprofits make money while they further the goals of the organization. The nonprofit can use this tax-exempt revenue to pay for operating expenses (including reasonable salaries) and to further its nonprofit purposes. For example, an organization dedicated to the identification and preservation of shore birds might advertise a bird watching and counting hike for which they charge a fee; the group could then use the proceeds to fund their bird rescue operations. What it cannot do with the money, however, is distribute it for the benefit of officers, directors, or employees of the corporation (as the payment of a patronage dividend, for example).

EXAMPLE: Friends of the Library, Inc., is a 501(c)(3) nonprofit organized to encourage literary appreciation in the community and to raise money for the support and improvement of the public library. It makes a profit from its sold-out lecture series featuring famous authors and from its annual sale of donated books. Friends can use this tax-exempt profit for its own operating expenses, including salaries for officers and employees, or to benefit the library.

3. Making Money From Unrelated Activities (Unrelated Income)

Nonprofits can also make money in ways unrelated to their nonprofit purpose. Often this income is essential to the survival of the nonprofit group. This unrelated income, however, is usually taxed as unrelated business income under state and federal corporate income tax rules. While earning money this way is permissible, it's best not to let unrelated business activities reach the point where you start to look more like a for-profit business than a nonprofit one. This can happen if the unrelated income-generating activities are absorbing a substantial amount of staff time, requiring additional paid staff or volunteers, or producing more income than your exempt-purpose activities. If the unrelated revenue or activities of your tax-exempt nonprofit reach a substantial level, the IRS can decide to revoke the group's 501(c)(3) tax-exemption—a result your nonprofit will no doubt wish to avoid (for more information, see Chapter 3, Section C).

EXAMPLE: Many thousands of books are donated to Friends of the Library for its annual book sale, one of its major fundraising events. Although the sale is always highly successful, thousands of books are left over. Friends decides to sell the more valuable books by advertising in the rare and out-of-print books classified sections in various magazines. The response is overwhelming; soon, there are six employees cataloguing books. In addition, Friends begins a business purchasing books from other dealers and reselling them to the public. Such a situation could attract attention from the IRS and prompt it to reconsider Friends' 501(c)(3) tax-exempt status.

4. Making Money from "Passive" Sources

Although it's not typical for the average non-profit, a nonprofit corporation can make money from "passive" sources such as rents, royalties, interest, and investments. This income is nontaxable in some cases.

E. Your Path to Nonprofit Status

Nonprofit organizations first obtain nonprofit corporate status with the state corporate filing office—usually the corporations division of the secretary of state's office. This is a simple formality accomplished by filing articles of incorporation. Then they go on to obtain a corporate income tax exemption with the Internal Revenue Service. Once the IRS exemp-

tion is obtained, a copy of the federal tax exemption determination letter is filed with the state tax or revenue office. This automatically qualifies the nonprofit for a state corporate income tax exemption. In a few states, you must apply for the state nonprofit corporate income tax exemption.

In sum, your path to nonprofit status is a usually a two-step process—first you incorporate with the state, then you apply for tax-exempt recognition from the IRS. When you're done with this book, you'll have completed each of these steps, plus additional follow-up steps to make sure your corporation is off to a good legal and tax start.

F. Where Should You Incorporate?

Corporations formed in a particular state are known in that state as "domestic" corporations. When viewed from outside that state, these corporations are considered "foreign." A foreign corporation that plans to engage in a regular or repeated pattern of activity in another state must qualify to do business there by obtaining a certificate of authority from the secretary of state. For example, a corporation formed in Nevada that intends to do regular business in California is a foreign corporation in California, and must qualify with the California Secretary of State.

Incorporators who plan to operate in another state besides their home state might wonder whether it makes sense to incorporate in that other state. Maybe the incorporation fees or corporate taxes are lower than those in the home state or the nonprofit statutes are more flexible. Then, the reasoning goes, one could qualify the corporation in the home state as a foreign corporation. As tempting as this end run may appear, it's usually not worth it. This section explains why, and also advises you of out-of-state activities that you can engage in without worrying about qualifying in another state.

1. Qualifying as a Foreign Corporation in Your Home State Will Cost You More

The process of qualifying a foreign corporation to operate in your home state takes about as much time and expense as incorporating a domestic corporation in your home state. This means that you will pay more to incorporate out-of-state since you must pay the regular home state qualification fees plus out-of-state incorporation fees.

2. Two Sets of Tax Exemptions

Your corporation will still be subject to taxation in each state in which it earns or derives income or funds. If the state of incorporation, which we here assume is a "foreign" state, imposes a corporate income tax, then the nonprofit corporation will need to file for and obtain two state corporate tax exemptions— one for its home state (the state where the corporation will be active and qualify to do business) and one for the foreign state of incorporation. Similarly, double sales, property, and other state tax exemptions may often be necessary or appropriate.

3. Two Sets of State Laws

Your out-of-state corporation will still be subject to many of the laws that affect corporations in your home state. Many state corporate statutes that apply to domestic corporations also apply to foreign corporations.

4. Out-of-State Activities Below the Radar

For the above reasons, most readers who flirt with the idea of incorporating in a state other than their home state would be well advised to skip it. This doesn't mean, however, that you'll have to trim all of your activities to stay within your home state. Fortunately, there are many things nonprofits can do as a foreign corporation in another state without obtaining a certificate of authority from the secretary of that state. Here are some activities that can be done in most states without qualifying to do business there:

- maintaining, defending, or settling any legal action or administrative proceeding, including securing or collecting debts, and enforcing property rights
- holding meetings of corporate directors or of the membership and distributing information to members
- maintaining bank accounts and making grants of funds
- making sales through independent contractors and engaging in interstate or foreign commerce
- conducting a so-called "isolated transaction" that is completed within 30 days and is not one of a series of similar transactions, and

- exercising powers as an executor, administrator, or trustee, as long as none of the activities required of the position amounts to transacting business.

5. When Out-of-State Incorporation Makes Sense

There may be a few of you for whom incorporation in another state makes sense. If you plan to set up a multistate nonprofit with corporate offices and activities in more than one state (a tristate environmental fund for example), you may want to consider incorporating in the state that offers the greatest legal, tax, and practical advantages. To help you decide where to incorporate, you can refer to the information contained in the State Sheets in Appendix B. For further information on state-by-state differences, go online to each state's corporate filing office website (the website address for each state's filing office is listed in Appendix B). Another approach is to check a nonprofit resource center library. For nonprofit library resources online, type "nonprofit resource libraries" into your search engine—you'll find a host of online libraries at your disposal. An experienced nonprofit lawyer or consultant can also help you determine which state is the most convenient and least costly to use as the legal home for your new nonprofit corporation. ■

Chapter 2

Legal Rights and Duties of Incorporators, Directors, Officers, Employees, and Members

*E*ven though a corporation is a legal person capable of making contracts, incurring liabilities, and engaging in other activities, it still needs real people to act on its behalf to carry out its activities. These people decide to incorporate, select those who will be responsible for running the organization, and actually manage and carry out the nonprofit's goals and activities.

This chapter explains the rights and responsibilities of those in your group who will organize and operate your nonprofit corporation. These incorporators, directors, officers, members, and employees have separate legal rights and responsibilities. Later, after your nonprofit is up and running, you may want to refer back to this chapter if you have questions regarding the powers and duties of these important people.

A. Incorporators and Their Role as Promoters

An incorporator is the person (or persons) who signs and delivers the articles of incorporation to the secretary of state for filing. In practice, the incorporator is often selected from among the people who serve as the initial directors of the corporation. Once the corporation is formed, the incorporator's legal role is finished. Attorneys often serve as the incorporator for a corporation. Because you are doing the paperwork yourself with the help of this book, you won't need to pay a lawyer to act as your incorporator—one or more of your founders can act as the incorporator(s) of your nonprofit.

During the organizational phase, it's not unusual for an incorporator to become a "promoter" of the corporation. An incorporator's promotional activities can quickly go beyond enthusiastic talk about the organization. Promotional activities may involve obtaining money, property, personnel, and whatever else it takes to get the nonprofit corporation started. Arranging for a loan or renting office space will require signatures and promises—to repay the loan and pay the rent. But will the newly formed corporation automatically become responsible? Future directors may hesitate to join a new organization that is saddled already by contracts negotiated by an eager (but perhaps naive) promoter. The promoters themselves will naturally be nervous that they'll be personally responsible if the incorporation plans go awry. And what about the third parties—they may not be inclined to do business with promoters unless they are assured that there will be a responsible party at the other end. After explaining in Section 1, below, how a promoter must approach every transaction—with the corporation's best interests in mind—we'll show you how to address the concerns of the eventual directors, the promoters themselves, and the third parties with whom they do business.

1. A Promoter Must Act With the Corporation's Best Interests in Mind

When an incorporator acts as a promoter, she is considered by law to be its fiduciary. This legal jargon simply means she has a duty to act in the best interests of the corporation,

Ways to Reassure Potential Officers and Directors

Before you start looking for people to help run your nonprofit, take a moment for a reality check: Many potential helpers will hesitate to become involved because they've read in the press about a few notorious, high-visibility lawsuits where nonprofit directors have been held personally liable for misconduct by executives of the nonprofit (for example, the executive of a large, public membership nonprofit misappropriates program funds to buy a yacht or high-priced apartment for personal use). On a more down-to-earth level, a potential treasurer for your nonprofit may hesitate to serve if he thinks he'll be personally responsible for the organization's tax reporting penalties or a potential director may be worried about being personally sued by a fired employee of the nonprofit. Fortunately, these types of personal liability are extremely rare. Most nonprofits should be able to assure potential director and officer candidates that the nonprofit will be run accountably and sensibly without undue risk of tax or legal liability for the directors.

One obvious way to reassure candidates is to purchase directors' and officers' liability insurance from an insurance broker who handles nonprofit corporate insurance (called "D & O errors and omissions insurance"). This type of insurance, however, is expensive and usually beyond the reach of newly-formed small nonprofits. Also, D & O coverage often excludes the sorts of potential liabilities that your directors and officers may be worried about (personal injury and other types of legal tort actions, claims of illegality, or intentional misconduct and the like). If you decide to investigate the cost of D & O insurance, you will want to make sure to go over the areas of coverage and exclusion in the policy very carefully before you buy in.

State legislators recognize that nonprofits often can't afford D & O liability insurance with adequate claim coverage, and many states have enacted nonprofit law provisions that help limit *volunteer* directors' and officers' exposure to liability. State laws also often require corporations to indemnify (advance or pay back) a director for legal expenses incurred in a lawsuit under certain conditions. These laws can provide added comfort to people considering serving as a nonprofit corporation director or officer. If you want more information about the laws in your state, browse your state's nonprofit laws online (see your State Sheet in Appendix B for the URL) or consult with a nonprofit lawyer in your state. Again, we believe the best and most practical way to reassure directors and officers to hitch their wagon to your nonprofit organization's star is to be able to show them that you will operate your nonprofit fairly, responsibly, and safely without undue risk of lawsuits by employees or complaints by the public.

and must make full disclosure of any personal interest and potential benefits she may derive from business transacted for the nonprofit.

> **EXAMPLE:** When the incorporator/promoter arranges to sell property she owns to the nonprofit corporation, she must disclose to the nonprofit's board of directors both her ownership interest in the property and any gain she stands to make on the sale.

2. Directors Must Ratify a Promoter's Actions

Most of the time, a nonprofit corporation will not be bound by an incorporator's preincorporation contract with a third party unless the board of directors ratifies the contract or the corporation accepts the benefits of the contract. For example, if a nonprofit board votes to ratify the lease signed by an incorporator before the date of incorporation, the corporation will be bound to honor the lease. Similarly, if the nonprofit moves into its new offices and conducts business there, their actions will constitute a ratification and the nonprofit will be bound.

3. Promoters Can Avoid Personal Liability

Fortunately, if promoters carefully draft documents—such as any loan papers and leases—they can avoid the risk of personal liability in the event that the corporation doesn't ratify the deal (or if the corporation never comes

into being). Incorporators will not be personally liable for these contracts if they sign in the name of a proposed corporation, not in their individual name, clearly inform the third party that the corporation does not yet exist and may never come into existence, and tell the third party that even if it does come into existence, it may not ratify the contract.

4. Convincing Third Parties to Do Business With a Promoter

As you might imagine, a cautious third party may balk at doing business with an individual whose yet-to-be-formed nonprofit may repudiate the deal. One way to provide some assurance to a third party is for an incorporator to bind himself personally to the contract—in essence, become a guarantor for the loan, lease, or other contract. Understandably, few incorporators will be able or willing to put their personal finances on the line, unless they are absolutely sure that the corporation will in fact be formed and will ratify the deal. The other solution is to incorporate quickly—which you can do with the help of this book!

> **EXAMPLE:** An incorporator/promoter enters into an agreement to lease office space for its organization. Six months later, the organization obtains nonprofit corporate status. The newly formed nonprofit is not bound by the lease agreement unless its board of directors ratifies the agreement or the organization used the office space during the preincorporation period.

B. Directors

Directors meet collectively as the board of directors, and are responsible—legally, financially, and morally—for the management and operation of your nonprofit corporation.

Check the State Sheets for your state's requirements for directors. The State Sheets in Appendix B show the number of directors required in each state and list any additional director qualifications, such as age and residency. Because directors may need to sign contracts and other legal documents, they should be at least of the age of majority in your state (usually 18).

Before we discuss legalities and state law requirements, let's look at an overriding practical concern: how to select the best directors for your organization.

1. Selecting Directors

Choosing directors is one of the most important decisions you will make when organizing your nonprofit. Here are some important things to consider that will help you make the best possible choice for your organization.

a. Commitment to Your Nonprofit's Purpose

Your directors are a crucial link between your organization and its supporters and benefactors. Make sure that the members of the community that you plan to serve will see your directors as credible and competent representatives of your group and its nonprofit goals. Their status and integrity will be crucial to encouraging and protecting public trust in your organization, and their connections will be vital to attracting recognition, clients, donations, and other support.

- Consider members of the communities you will serve who have a proven commitment to the goals of your organization. There may be more than one community that you'll want to consider. For example, your draw may be local (city, county, or state), regional, or national. If you are an environmental group concerned with issues in the southern part of the state, you have both a geographic community (people in the area) and a community of interest (environmentalists generally). Your board should reflect a cross section of interested and competent people from both of these communities.

- Look for people with contacts and real-world knowledge and experience in the specific area of your nonprofit's interest. If you are starting a new private school or health clinic, someone familiar with your state's educational or public health bureaucracy would be a big help.

- If your organization is set up to do "good works" that will benefit a particular group, don't overlook the value of including a member of that recipient group. You may learn important things about your mission and get valuable "buy in" from the beneficiaries of your hard work.

b. Business Knowledge and Expertise

Directors' responsibilities include developing and overseeing organizational policies and goals, budgeting, fundraising, and disbursing a group's funds. The board of directors may hire an administrator or executive director to supervise staff and daily operations, or it may supervise them directly. Either way, your board of directors should be a practical-minded group with strong managerial, technical, and financial skills. In making your selection, try to find people with the following skills and experience:

- **Fundraising experience.** While many large nonprofits have a staff fundraiser, smaller groups often can benefit from the advice of an experienced board member.
- **Experience managing money.** A professional accountant or someone with expertise in record keeping and budgeting can be a godsend. Many nonprofits get into difficulty because their record keeping and reporting techniques aren't adequate to produce the information required by the federal and state governments. Many are simply inattentive to financial responsibilities, such as paying withholding taxes or accounting properly for public or private grant monies.
- **Useful practical skills.** Do you need the professional expertise of a doctor, lawyer, or architect; or operational assistance in areas such as public relations, marketing, or publishing? If so, make finding one of these professionals a high priority during your board search.

Public Officials Are a Good Choice

The IRS likes to see that you have a representative (and financially disinterested) governing body that reflects a range of public interests, not simply the personal interests of a small number of donors. In fact, IRS Form 1023 (*Application for Recognition of Exemption*) specifically asks if any of your directors have been selected because they are either public officials or appointed by public officials. While it's by no means required, the presence of a sympathetic public official on your board can enhance its credibility with both the IRS and the community.

c. Avoid Conflicts of Interest

When selecting board members, you may need to inquire about, or at least consider, a prospective member's agenda or motives for joining the board. Obviously, people who want to join for personal benefit rather than for the benefit of the organization or the public should not be asked to serve. This doesn't mean that everyone with a remote or potential conflict of interest should be automatically disqualified. It does mean that any slight or possible conflict of interest should be fully recognized and discussed. If the conflict is limited, the director may be able to serve constructively if he refrains from voting on certain issues.

d. Develop a Realistic Job Description

Your board of directors should be prepared to put time and energy into the organization. Make sure every prospective director has a realistic and clear understanding of what the job entails. Before you contact prospective candidates, we suggest that you prepare a job description that specifies at least the following:

- the scope of the nonprofit's proposed activities and programs
- board member responsibilities and time commitments (expected frequency and length of board meetings, extra duties that may be assigned to directors), and
- the rewards of serving on your board (such as the satisfaction of working on behalf of a cause you care about or the experience of community service).

A clear and comprehensive job description will help with decision making and will also help avoid future misunderstandings with board members over what is expected of them.

e. Train Your New Directors

The organizers of a nonprofit corporation often need to give initial directors orientation and training about the nonprofit's operations and activities. This training should continue so that board members can handle ongoing operational issues as well. For example, if your nonprofit corporation is organized to provide health care services, board members may need to learn city, state, and federal program requirements that impact your operations, and should get regular updates on changes made to these rules and regulations.

Choose the right number of directors.
You'll want enough to ensure a wide basis of support (particularly with respect to fundraising), but not so many as to impede efficiency in the board's operation. Boards with between nine and 15 directors often work well.

2. Paying Your Directors

Nonprofit directors usually serve without compensation. We believe this is generally wise. Having nonprofit directors serve without pay reinforces one of the important legal and ethical distinctions of the nonprofit corporation: Unlike its for-profit counterpart, its assets are used to promote its goals, not for the private enrichment of its incorporators, directors, agents, members, or employees.

If you compensate directors, do so at a reasonable rate, related to the actual performance of services and established in advance by a board resolution. Most nonprofits reimburse directors only for necessary expenses incurred in performing director duties, such as travel expenses—typically a gas or mileage allowance—to attend board meetings. Sometimes directors are paid a set fee for attending meetings. In most cases, however, director compensation is minimal or nominal, if it is paid at all.

3. Term of Office

The term of office for directors is usually specified in the corporation's bylaws. Some states set a maximum term for directors (typically one year) only if the term is not specified in the articles or bylaws; other states specify a maximum term in all cases.

The State Sheets show each state's rules on how long a director may serve. If it's allowed in your state, we suggest a three-year term for directors. This will let you get the most of what a director has to contribute and ensure continuity in operations. In return, the director will get the satisfaction of long-term service and hopefully will see some goals fulfilled.

Staggered Elections for Board Members

In the interest of continuity, staggered elections of board members may be a good idea. For example, rather than replacing the entire board at each annual election, you may wish to reelect 1/3 of the board members each year to serve a three-year term. To start this staggered system out with a 15-member board—five of the initial directors would serve for one year, five for two years, and the remaining five for the full three-year term. At each annual reelection, 1/3 of the board would be elected to serve three-year terms.

4. Quorum Rules

For the board of directors to take action at a meeting, a specified number of directors of the corporation—called a quorum—must be present. Generally, state nonprofit statutes require a majority quorum. This means that a

majority of the full board must be present to hold a meeting. Some states allow the quorum requirement for board action to be lower.

Check your state's director quorum requirements. The State Sheets list the quorum requirements for each state.

Director Action by Written Consent or Conference Call

Your board of directors doesn't necessarily have to meet, in person, to take action affecting the corporation. Many states authorize directors to take action by written consent or by a conference telephone hookup. In some states, the directors must consent unanimously, in writing, to this procedure; in others, only the number of directors needed to pass the resolution (normally a majority of a quorum) must consent. If you're interested in having your board take action without a meeting, check your state's nonprofit corporation law. Look for a section titled "Action by Written Consent" in the part dealing with "Directors."

5. Voting Rules

Once a quorum is present at a meeting, a specified number of votes is needed to pass a board resolution. Unless otherwise stated in the articles or bylaws, a resolution must be passed by a majority vote of the directors present at a meeting where there is a quorum. In some cases, the votes of interested directors cannot be counted. This is discussed more in Section 9 below.

> **EXAMPLE:** The bylaws of a corporation with ten board members specify that a quorum consists of a majority of the board and that action by the board can be taken by a majority of the directors present. This means that a quorum of at least six people (a majority of the ten-person board) must be present to hold a board meeting and, at the very least, four votes (a majority of the six members present at a meeting) are required to pass a resolution. If eight of the ten directors attend the meeting, action must be approved by at least five votes—a majority of those present at the meeting.

If a quorum is present initially at a meeting and one or more board members leaves, action can often still be taken even if you lose your quorum. As long you can still obtain the number of votes that represents a majority of the required quorum stated in the bylaws, the board normally can take action even though a quorum is no longer present at the meeting (this is known as the "initial quorum rule"). Going back to the example above, in a ten-director board, the required quorum for board action is six directors (a majority of the ten) and at least four votes (a majority of those present) are needed to take board action. Under the initial-quorum rule, two directors can leave the meeting and the four remaining votes will still be sufficient to pass a

resolution. Why? Because a quorum was initially present and four board members, representing a majority of the required quorum of six, can vote to pass a resolution.

6. Executive Committees

The board of directors can delegate some or even a significant part of the board's duties to an executive committee, usually consisting of two or more directors. This arrangement is often used when some directors are more involved in running and managing the nonprofit's affairs and business than others.

The State Sheets indicate how many directors must be appointed to an executive committee in each state.

Even the passive directors, however, should still keep an eye on what their more active colleagues are up to and actively participate in regular meetings of the full board. To encourage passive directors to stay involved, courts have held the full board responsible for the actions of the executive committee.

Fortunately, keeping the full board abreast of executive committee actions isn't very difficult. The full board should receive regular, timely minutes of executive committee meetings and should review and, if necessary, reconsider important executive committee decisions at each regularly scheduled meeting of the full board. The full board should retain the power to override decisions of the executive committee.

Under state law, there are certain actions that can't be delegated to an executive committee. Typically, an executive committee cannot be given authority to do one or more of the following:

- approve action that requires approval by the membership
- fill vacancies on the board or other committees
- fix directors' compensation
- alter bylaws, or
- use corporate funds to support a nominee to the board after more people have been nominated than can be elected.

Don't confuse this special executive committee of directors with other corporate committees. The board typically appoints several specialized committees to keep track of and report on corporate operations and programs. These committees act as working groups that are more manageable in size and help make better use of the board's time and its members' talents. They may include finance, personnel, buildings and grounds, new projects, fundraising, or other committees. These committees, often consisting of a mix of directors, officers and paid staff, do not normally have the power to take legal action on behalf of the corporation; their purpose is to report and make recommendations to the full board or the executive committee.

EXAMPLE: The board of directors appoints a finance committee charged with overseeing the organization's fundraising, budgeting, expenditures, and bookkeeping. The corporation's treasurer chairs the committee. Periodically, this committee makes financial recommendations to the full board. The board could also appoint a personnel committee to establish hiring and employment policies and to interview candidates for important positions. A plans and programs committee might be selected to put together the overall action plan for accomplishing the goals of the organization. Any action taken based on a committee's report or recommendation would be subject to approval by the board.

7. Directors' Duty of Care

Corporate directors and officers have a legal duty to act responsibly and in the best interests of the corporation—this is called their statutory "duty of care." The statutes defining this phrase use general, imprecise legal terms that are not very helpful in understanding what exactly it means. As a result, the meaning of the term has developed over time as judges and juries, faced with lawsuits, decide whether a director's acts did (or did not) live up to the duty of care. Fortunately, most of it boils down to common sense, as the following discussions show.

a. Personal Liability for Directors' Acts

In general, you shouldn't be overly concerned about the prospect of personal liability for your directors. Broadly speaking, courts are reluctant to hold nonprofit directors personally liable, except in the clearest cases of dereliction of duty or misuse of corporate funds or property. In the rare cases when liability is found, the penalties are usually not onerous or punitive—typically, the court orders directors to repay the losses their actions caused.

Ordinary negligence or poor judgment is usually not enough to show a director breached his duty of care. Instead, there generally must be some type of fraudulent or grossly negligent behavior. *Volunteer* directors and executive officers of nonprofits enjoy extra protection from personal liability. These personal immunity laws are discussed in detail in Section 11, below.

> EXAMPLE: A committee of the nonprofit advises the board of an unsafe condition on the corporation's property. The committee recommends certain remedial actions to get rid of the problem. If the board fails to implement any remedial measures or otherwise take steps to deal with the problem, a court could hold the directors personally liable for any ensuing damage or injuries.

Although the risk of being held personally liable is small, there are some things a director can and should do to minimize the risk of personal liability. Most importantly, all directors, whether active participants or casual community observers, should attend board meetings and stay informed of, and participate in, all major board decisions. If the board makes a woefully wrong headed or ill-advised decision that leads to monetary damages, the best defense for any board member is a "No" vote recorded in the corporate minutes.

Also, all boards should try to get an experienced financial manager on their board or use the services of a prudent accountant who demands regular audited financial statements of the group's books. Legalities aside, what is most likely to put nonprofit directors at risk of personal liability is bad financial management, such as failing to pay taxes, not keeping proper records of how much money is collected and how it is disbursed, and commingling funds, either directors' personal funds with corporate funds or mixing restricted with nonrestricted funds.

b.   Reliance on Regular Business Reports: A Safe Haven

To help directors accomplish their managerial duties, state law as well as IRS regulations and procedures often allow directors to rely on information from reliable, competent sources within the corporation (officers, committees, and supervisory staff), or on outside professional sources (lawyers, accountants, and investment advisors). If this information later turns out to be faulty or incorrect, the directors will not be held personally liable for any decision made in reliance on the information, unless the directors had good reason to question and look beyond the information presented to the board and failed to do so.

For example, if a nonprofit's treasurer tells the board that the organization has sufficient cash to meet ongoing payroll tax requirements, and the report seems reasonable (perhaps because the nonprofit has a budget surplus), the IRS will probably find that the individual board members were entitled to rely on the treasurer's report, even if there is not enough money to pay the taxes. However, if the board knows or should have known that the nonprofit is having a difficult time paying its bills despite reports to the contrary by the treasurer, and the board does not direct the treasurer to make sure to set money aside to pay payroll taxes, the IRS may try to hold board members personally liable for unpaid taxes.

c. Investment Decisions Involving Corporate Assets

Directors of 501(c)(3) nonprofit corporations must use more caution when making investment decisions than when they decide routine business matters. That's because when they make investment decisions involving corporate funds, directors usually have an added duty of care under state nonprofit law to avoid speculation and protect those funds—a stricter standard of care than the normal standard discussed above. A typical phrasing of this stricter standard of care, known as the directors' fiduciary duty to the corporation, is that the directors must "avoid speculation, looking instead to the permanent disposition of the funds, considering the probable income, as well as the probable safety of the corporation's capital." (California Corporations Code, § 5240(b)(1).)

> **EXAMPLE:** The treasurer of a performing arts group tells the group's directors that the group has a hefty surplus of funds because of its recent road tour. The board decides to invest this money in a stable asset mutual fund rather than one of several high-risk equity funds that reported double-digit declines in the last several quarters. If challenged by the state attorney general or a complaining member, the directors should be able to show that they've met their fiduciary duty to the corporation—they attempted to preserve the capital of the corporation by investing in a stable fund with a predictable positive return track record rather than a riskier fund that was more likely to lose money.

8. Directors Must Be Loyal

A director has a duty of loyalty to the corporation. In most states, this is commonly understood to mean that the director must give the corporation a right of first refusal on business opportunities that he becomes aware of in his capacity as director. If the corporation fails to take advantage of the opportunity after full disclosure, or if the corporation clearly would not be interested in the opportunity, the director can take advantage of the opportunity himself.

> **EXAMPLE:** Bob is a volunteer director on the board of Help Hospices, a nonprofit hospice and shelter organization. He agrees to shop around for a low-rent location in a reasonably safe neighborhood for the next nonprofit hospice site. He learns of three low-rent locations, one of which would also be ideal as a low-cost rental studio for his son who wants to move out of his parents' house as soon as possible. Bob reports all three locations to the board, and tells them that he plans

to apply for a lease in his son's name on one of the rental units only if the board decides that it is not interested in leasing the space for nonprofit purposes. This type of specific disclosure is exactly what is required for Bob to meet his duty of loyalty to the nonprofit. Bob can apply for the lease for his son if the board gives him the go-ahead after deciding the non-profit is not interested in leasing the space for itself.

9. How to Avoid Self-Dealing

Directors must guard against unauthorized self-dealing—that is, involving the corpora-tion in any transaction in which the director has a material, or significant, financial interest without proper approval. The self-dealing rules and proper approval requirements can arise in many different types of transactions, including the purchase or sale of corporate property, the investment of corporate funds, or the payment of corporate fees or compen-sation.

The nonprofit corporation laws of most states include special rules for validating self-interested director decisions of this sort. In most cases, the interest of the director must be disclosed prior to voting and only disinter-ested members of the board may vote on the proposal.

> **EXAMPLE:** A board votes to authorize the corporation to lease or buy property owned by a director, or to purchase ser-vices or goods from another corporation

in which a director owns a substantial amount of stock. Either of these could be considered a prohibited self-dealing trans-action if not properly disclosed and ap-proved, because a director has a material financial interest in each transaction and neither falls within one of the specific statutory exceptions.

Directors Who Serve on Two Boards

It's not uncommon for one director to serve on multiple boards, be they nonprofit or for-profit corporations. Suppose your non-profit and another corporation share a di-rector and are contemplating a business deal. What must your nonprofit do to avoid running afoul of the rules against self-deal-ing?

If the common director has no material financial interest in the transaction, includ-ing stock ownership in the other corpora-tion, technically speaking this transaction won't involve self-dealing because there is no financially interested director. It can be approved by normal board action, as long as the contract or transaction is just and reasonable to the corporation at the time it is authorized, approved, or ratified. To be on the safe side, however, these transac-tions should be approved after full disclo-sure of all the facts and without counting the vote of the common director who sits on both boards.

See a lawyer if you have questions about self-dealing. If your board plans to approve a self-dealing transaction, we recommend you check first with an experienced nonprofit lawyer to take a close look at the board approval rules contained in your state's Nonprofit Corporation Law.

10. Loans and Guarantees

Most states expressly prohibit nonprofits from making or guaranteeing a loan to a director, or require approval by special disclosure or voting rules. Because of the strict rules prohibiting individuals involved with a nonprofit's operations from personally benefiting from the nonprofit, it's easy to see why a loan to a director from tax-exempt funds over which he or she exercises control might appear questionable. As with self-dealing discussed above, we suggest that you carefully review your state's nonprofit statutes before considering approval of loans or guarantees to directors—and, as always, ask a nonprofit lawyer for advice if you have questions.

11. Director Indemnification and Insurance

In addition to director and officer immunity statutes, all but nine states have director indemnification laws. These laws require a corporation to indemnify (reimburse) a director for legal expenses incurred as a result of acts done on behalf of the corporation, if the director is successful in the legal proceeding.

Directors' (and officers') liability coverage (also called acts and omissions coverage) is, of course, one way to insulate directors from possible personal liability for their actions on behalf of the corporation. This type of insurance, however, is normally priced far beyond the reach of the average small nonprofit organization. Rather than worrying about trying to obtain this kind of coverage, it often makes more sense to do everything possible to minimize potential risks that might arise in the pursuit of your nonprofit purposes.

For example, try to make sure that employees perform their work in a safe manner and that anyone required to perform skilled tasks is properly trained and licensed. In addition, the corporation should obtain specific coverage for any likely risks: motor vehicle insurance to cover drivers of corporate vehicles, general commercial liability insurance to cover the group's premises, and so on.

C. Officers

Most states require a nonprofit corporation to have a president, a secretary, and a treasurer. A vice president may be required or optional under state statutes. Typically, officers are selected from the board of directors. In a majority of states, one person can hold two or more offices. However, even those states that allow one person to hold multiple offices specifically prohibit one person from serving simultaneously as both the president and secretary of the corporation.

The State Sheets list the required officer positions and the rules for filling these positions in each state.

1. Duties and Responsibilities

The powers, duties, and responsibilities of officers are specified in the corporation's articles or bylaws, or by resolution of the board of directors. Generally, officers are in charge of supervising and implementing the day-to-day business of the corporation. This authority does not usually include the authority to enter into major business transactions, such as the mortgage or sale of corporate property. These kinds of major transactions are left to the board of directors. If the board wants the officers to have the power to make one or more major business decisions, special authority should be delegated by board resolution.

Officers have a duty to act honestly and in the best interests of the corporation. Officers are considered agents of the corporation and can subject the corporation to liability for their negligent or intentional acts if their acts cause damage and are performed in the scope of their employment.

2. Officers May Bind the Corporation

Generally, the actions and transactions of an officer are legally binding on the corporation. A third party is entitled to rely on the apparent authority of an officer and can require the corporation to honor a deal, regardless of whether the officer was actually empowered by the board to enter into the transaction. To avoid confusion, if you delegate a special task to an officer outside the realm of the officer's normal duties, it's best to have your board pass a resolution granting the officer special authority to enter into the transaction on behalf of the corporation.

And, of course, any action taken by an officer on behalf of a corporation will be binding if the corporation accepts the benefits of the transaction or if the board ratifies the action, regardless of whether or not the officer had the legal authority to act on the corporation's behalf.

3. Compensation of Officers

Officers can receive reasonable compensation for services they perform for a nonprofit corporation. It is appropriate to pay officers who have day-to-day operational authority, and not to pay the officers who limit themselves to presiding over the board of directors or making overall nonprofit policy decisions. In smaller nonprofits, it is more common for officers and directors to also assume staff positions and be paid for performing these operational tasks.

> **EXAMPLE:** In a larger nonprofit organization, a paid executive director or medical director (these are staff positions, not board of director posts) might oversee routine operations of a medical clinic, and the paid principal or administrator (also staff positions) will do the same for a private school. However, in a smaller nonprofit, the corporate president or other officer may assume these salaried tasks.

Don't count interested director's vote when setting compensation of directors and officers. If you decide to pay a salary to an officer who is also a member of the board of directors, we recommend that you have your board approve the salary without counting the vote of the interested director, even though your state's law may allow board members to vote on their own compensation. This may help avoid a claim of a conflict of interest or apparent unfairness. And public and private grant programs may condition their funding on your acceptance of their own conflict of interest regulations, which often forbid the corporation from paying a salary to any member of the board or any officer of the corporation.

4. Loans, Guarantees, and Immunity Laws

Loans and guarantees to nonprofit officers are either prohibited or very strictly regulated, as they are with directors (see Section B, above). Officers have a duty to act honestly and in the best interests of the corporation. Officers can be insured or indemnified against personal liabilities, and they can benefit from the same immunity statutes that relieve volunteer, and in some states paid, directors from personal liability for monetary damages.

D. Employees

Employees of nonprofit corporations work for and under the supervision of the corporation and are paid a salary in return for their services. Paid directors and officers are considered employees for purposes of individual income tax withholding, Social Security, state unemployment, and other payroll taxes the employer must pay. Employees have the usual duties to report and pay their taxes, and the usual personal liability for failing to do so.

1. Employee Immunity

Employees are generally not personally liable for any financial loss their acts or omissions may cause to the corporation or to outsiders, as long as they are acting within the course and scope of their employment. If the harm is done to outsiders, it is the corporation, not the employees, which must assume the burden of paying for the loss.

Employees may be personally liable for taxes. An important exception to the rule of employee nonliability concerns the employee whose duty it is to report or pay federal or state corporate or employment taxes. The responsible employee (or officer or director) can be held personally liable for failure to report or pay such taxes. The IRS may take a broad view as to who is "responsible" for such duties—see Chapter 10, Section B.

2. Employee Compensation

Salaries paid to officers or regular employees should be reasonable and given in return for services actually performed. A reasonable salary is one roughly equal to that received by employees rendering similar services elsewhere. If salaries are unreasonably high, they are apt to be treated as a simple distribution of net corporate earnings and could jeopardize the nonprofit's tax-exempt status. Nonprofits should avoid paying discretionary bonuses at the end of a good year—this may look like a payment from the earnings and profits of the corporation, a no-no for nonprofits. In reality, since the pay scale for nonprofit personnel is usually lower than that of their for-profit counterparts, most of this cautionary advice shouldn't be needed.

3. Employee Benefits

Among the major advantages associated with being an employee of a corporation are the employment benefits it can provide, such as corporate pension plans, corporate medical expense reimbursement plans, and corporate group accident, health, life, and disability insurance. Generally, amounts the corporation pays to provide these benefits (such as the payment of insurance premiums by the corporation) are not included in the employee's individual gross income and therefore are not taxed to the employee. Also, the benefits themselves (such as insurance proceeds) are often not taxed when the employee receives them. These corporate employee benefits can sometimes be an important collateral reason for forming a nonprofit corporation. They are often more favorable than those allowed noncorporate employees.

The nonprofit itself enjoys a tax break when offering benefits in certain situations. Benefits are deductible by a nonprofit corporation if taxes are owed by the corporation in connection with an activity that uses the services of these employees. For example, if a nonprofit generates $20,000 in gross revenue unrelated to its exempt purposes, but pays

wages of $10,000 plus benefits of $5,000 to generate this income, its net unrelated business income is reduced to $5,000.

Nonprofits may also establish profit-sharing plans and similar arrangements (see IRC § 401(a)(27)). However, tax-exempt nonprofits may not set up 401(k) plans (see IRC § 401(k)(4)(B)). For information on setting up qualified employee plans and other benefits, consult your tax advisor or a benefit plan specialist.

E. Membership Nonprofits

If a nonprofit corporation establishes a formal membership structure in its articles of incorporation or bylaws, then members of the corporation will be granted basic rights to participate in the affairs and future of the nonprofit corporation. We refer to members who are given these special legal rights as "formal members."

It is optional for a nonprofit corporation to have formal members with legal voting rights. To avoid the problems (including the paperwork and expense) of having to put elections of directors and other major corporate decisions to a vote of the members, most nonprofits choose not to have formal membership structures.

Not having formal members is organizationally simpler than adopting a formal membership structure because only the directors are legally entitled to participate in the operation of the corporation. People interested in a nonmembership nonprofit, although they may play fundamental advisory roles, need not be notified nor allowed to vote for directors or approve changes to the corporation's articles or bylaws. Normally this works well—since most people become involved in nonprofit organizations out of interest in the group's activities and purposes, or in some cases because they receive attendance privileges or discounts to nonprofit events or programs, not because they wish to participate in the legal affairs of the corporation.

Interested people who work with a nonprofit corporation to help it achieve its goals (and who may pay annual dues or fees) but are not formal members are often called "supporters," "patrons," "contributors," or "advisors." For example, a patron may be issued an "informal" museum membership that entitles the person to free admissions, participation in educational programs and events, use of a special facility, or attendance at exhibition previews, but does not give the person any say as a formal (legal) member in the museum's operation and management. We discuss the decision to set up (or do without) a formal membership structure and show you how to adopt membership or non-membership bylaws in Chapter 7.

1. Classes of Membership

If you decide to set up a formal membership structure, you may establish different classes of membership, such as voting and nonvoting membership classes. If so, the rights, privileges, restrictions, and obligations associated with each class of membership must normally be stated in the articles of incorporation. (Again, most smaller corporations are better off without a formal membership structure and won't choose this option.)

2. Membership Quorum and Voting Rules

Most states allow nonprofits to set their own quorum requirement for members' meetings in the articles or bylaws. If the corporation does not adopt a membership quorum provision, state statutes typically set a quorum for members' meetings at a low percentage of the full membership. Other states specify a limit (such as one-third of the membership) below which the quorum cannot be set in any case. Some states simply say that a quorum is the actual number of voting members that attend the meeting (under this circularly phrased rule, a meeting of members can always be held if one or more members show up for the meeting).

Despite this flexibility under state statutes, many membership nonprofits will wish to set the members' quorum requirement at a majority (or some higher percentage) of the voting membership to ensure that representational meetings are attended by a sufficient cross section of the voting membership.

The State Sheets indicate the membership quorum rules for each state.

Use proxy voting with large membership groups. Larger membership nonprofits rarely call and hold meetings of membership with the expectation that members will attend and vote at the meeting in person. Instead, membership proxies (written votes) are usually solicited by mail well in advance of the meeting. The corporate secretary tallies and reports these votes at the membership meeting. The main business of the membership—the reelection of the board—is usually accomplished through this proxy-by-mail procedure (or by relying on a specific nomination and balloting by mail procedure authorized by the state's nonprofit corporation statutes).

Our membership provisions provide a simple membership balloting procedure that allows members to elect directors and transact other business by mail without a meeting.

Unless the articles or bylaws state otherwise, each member is entitled to cast one vote on any matter submitted for approval to the members. Again, it's possible to have several classes of membership with different voting rights attached to each membership.

Formal Membership Rights in a Nonprofit Corporation

A formal (legally recognized) member of a nonprofit corporation is usually entitled, under the state's nonprofit corporation law, to vote on the following matters:

- election and removal of directors
- amendment of articles and bylaws
- approval of merger or consolidation with another corporation
- election to wind up or dissolve the corporation
- sale of corporate assets, and
- approval of a transaction involving an interested director or officer.

Chapter 3

Requirements for Section 501(c)(3) Tax Exemption

orporations, like individuals, are normally subject to federal and state income taxation. One reason to establish a nonprofit corporation is to obtain an exemption from corporate income taxes. Exemption is not automatic—a corporation must apply and show that it is in compliance with nonprofit exemption requirements to receive it. This chapter focuses on the basic federal tax exemption available to nonprofits under Section 501(c)(3) of the Internal Revenue Code and what is required to obtain tax-exempt status under this provision. In later chapters, we discuss the state exemption (which is very similar to the federal exemption) and also take you line by line through the federal tax exemption application.

You'll notice in going through the material in this chapter that many IRS tax exemption requirements are broad and seemingly applicable to a wide range of activities, both commercial and noncommercial. In fact, many commercial organizations are engaged in activities that could qualify for 501(c)(3) tax-exempt status. For example, there are for-profit scientific organizations that perform research that could qualify as 501(c)(3) scientific research. Similarly, many commercial publishing houses publish educational materials that could qualify the organization for 501(c)(3) status.

So why do only certain organizations obtain tax-exempt status? Because a corporation must choose to apply for tax-exempt status from the IRS. Many organizations that might be eligible for 501(c)(3) status prefer to operate as commercial enterprises because they do not want to be subject to the money-making, profit distribution, and other restrictions applicable to nonprofits. (See Chapter 1 for a discussion of these restrictions). By defining and organizing your activities as eligible for 501(c)(3) status and then seeking tax-exempt status from the IRS, you distinguish your organization from similar commercial endeavors.

A. Section 501(c)(3) Organizational Test

Under Section 501(c)(3) of the Internal Revenue Code, groups organized and operated exclusively for charitable, religious, scientific, literary, and educational purposes can obtain an exemption from the payment of federal income taxes. The articles of incorporation of a 501(c)(3) corporation must limit the group's corporate purposes to one or more of the allowable 501(c)(3) purposes and must not empower it to engage (other than as an insubstantial part of its activities) in activities that don't further one or more of these tax-exempt purposes. This formal requirement is known as the 501(c)(3) organizational test.

A group can engage in more than one 501(c)(3) tax-exempt activity. For example, a group's activities can be characterized as charitable and educational, such as a school for blind or physically handicapped children.

A nonprofit cannot, however, engage simultaneously in a 501(c)(3) exempt purpose activity and an activity that is exempt under a different subsection of Section 501(c). Thus, a group cannot be formed for educational *and* social or recreational purposes because social and recreational groups are exempt under Section 501(c)(7) of the Internal Revenue Code (see Chapter 1, Section A, for a discussion of non-501(c)(3) tax-exempt groups). As a practical matter, this problem rarely occurs because the non-501(c)(3) subsections are custom-tailored to specific types of organizations, such as war veterans' organizations and cemetery companies.

B. Valid Purposes Under Section 501(c)(3)

Now let's take a closer look at the most common 501(c)(3) purposes—charitable, religious, scientific, literary, and educational—and the requirements for each of these purposes. In addition to the valid purpose requirements discussed in this section, there are other general requirements that all 501(c)(3) groups must comply with to obtain 510(c)(3) status. These other requirements are discussed below in Section C.

Humane Societies and Sports Organizations

There are other, less commonly used exemptions available under Section 501(c)(3) that we do not cover in this book. For example, groups organized to prevent cruelty to children or animals, or to foster national or international amateur sports competitions can claim a tax exemption under Section 501(c)(3). However, these groups must meet narrowly defined 501(c)(3) requirements, and, for humane societies, special state requirements. See IRS Publication 557 for specifics on each of these special 501(c)(3) groups and contact your state attorney general's office for special incorporation requirements for humane societies.

1. Charitable Purposes

The charitable purpose exemption is the broadest, most all-encompassing exemption under Section 501(c)(3). Not surprisingly, it is also the most commonly used exemption.

a. Benefit to the Public

The word "charitable" as used in Section 501(c)(3) is broadly defined to mean "providing services beneficial to the public interest." In fact, other 501(c)(3) purpose groups—educational, religious, and scientific groups—are often also considered charitable in nature because their activities usually benefit the public. Even groups not directly engaged in a religious, educational, or scientific activity, but whose activities indirectly benefit or promote a 501(c)(3) purpose can qualify as a 501(c)(3) charitable-purpose group.

Groups that seek to promote the welfare of specific groups of people in the community (handicapped or elderly persons or members of a particular ethnic group) or groups that seek to advance other exempt activities (environmental or educational) will generally be considered organized for charitable purposes because these activities benefit the public at large and are charitable in nature.

Groups that advance religion, even if they do not have a strictly religious purpose or function, are often considered charitable purpose organizations under Section 501(c)(3). The IRS reasons that the advancement of religion is itself a charitable purpose. Examples of some of these charitable purpose groups include:

- **Monthly Newspaper:** A group that published and distributed a monthly newspaper with church news of interdenominational interest was held to accomplish a charitable purpose because it contributed to the advancement of religion.

- **Coffeehouse:** A nonprofit organization formed by local churches to operate a supervised facility known as a coffeehouse was found to have a valid 501(c)(3) charitable purpose because it advanced religion and education by bringing together college-age people with church leaders, educators, and leaders from the business community for discussions and counseling on religion, current events, social, and vocational problems.

- **Genealogical Research:** An organization formed to compile genealogical research data on its family members to perform religious observances in accordance with the precepts of their faith was held to advance religion and be a charitable organization under 501(c)(3).

- **Missionary Assistance:** A missionary group established to provide temporary low-cost housing and related services for missionary families on furlough in the United States from their assignments abroad was held to be a charitable purpose organization under Section 501(c)(3).

Other examples of activities and purposes that have met the IRS organizational test for charitable purpose (and possibly another 501(c)(3) purpose as well) include:

- relief of the poor, distressed, or underprivileged
- advancement of education or science
- erection or maintenance of public buildings, monuments, or works
- lessening the burdens of government
- lessening neighborhood tensions
- elimination of prejudice and discrimination
- promotion and development of the arts
- defense of human and civil rights secured by law
- providing facilities and services to senior citizens
- maintaining a charitable hospital
- providing a community fund to support family relief and service agencies in the community
- providing loans for charitable or educational purposes, and
- maintaining a public-interest law firm.

b. Class or Group of Beneficiaries

A charitable organization must be set up to benefit an indefinite class of people, not particular persons. The number of beneficiaries can be relatively small as long as the benefited class is open and the beneficiaries of the group are not specifically identified.

EXAMPLE 1: A charitable nonprofit corporation cannot be established under Section 501(c)(3) to benefit Jeffrey Smith, an impoverished individual. But Jeffrey Smith can be selected as a beneficiary of a 501(c)(3) charitable group whose purpose is to benefit needy individuals in a particular community (as long as he is a member of that community).

EXAMPLE 2: A foundation that awards scholarships solely to undergraduate members of a designated fraternity was found to be a valid charitable organization under 501(c)(3), even though the number of members in the benefited group is small.

The following groups, all charitable in nature and benefiting a defined but indefinite group of people, were found to be valid charitable purpose organizations under Section 501(c)(3):

- an organization formed to build new housing and renovate existing housing for sale to low-income families on long-term, low-payment plans
- a day care center for children of needy, working parents
- a group created to market the cooking and needlework of needy women
- a self-help housing program for low-income families
- homes for the aged where the organization satisfies the special needs of an aged person for housing, health care, and financial security. (The requirements for housing and health care will be satisfied if the organization is committed to housing residents who become unable to pay and if services are provided at the lowest possible cost.)
- an organization that takes care of patients' nonmedical needs (reading, writing letters, and so on) in a privately owned hospital
- an organization that provides emergency and rescue services for stranded, injured, or lost persons

- a drug crisis center and a telephone hotline for persons with drug problems, and
- a legal aid society offering free legal services to indigent persons.

Health care nonprofits, whether hospitals or less formal, noninstitutional health care facilities or programs, can qualify as charitable 501(c)(3) organizations. However, the IRS is particularly concerned about conflicts of interest and business dealings between doctors who do work for the nonprofit and also rent space or have other commercial dealings with the nonprofit. The IRS recommends that the health care nonprofit form a community board and have conflict of interest provisions in their bylaws.

For additional information on tax issues related to health care organizations and for a sample community board and conflict of interest policy promulgated by the IRS, see the following files on the CD-ROM included at the back of this book:

- *Tax-Exempt Health Care Organizations Community Board and Conflicts of Interest Policy*
- *Tax-Exempt Health Care Organizations Revised Conflicts of Interest Policy.*

c. Services Need Not Be Free

Section 501(c)(3) charitable organizations are not required to offer services or products free or at cost. Nevertheless, doing so, or at least providing services at a substantial discount from the going commercial rate, can help convince the IRS of your group's bona fide charitable intentions. Charging full retail prices for services or products does not usually demonstrate a benefit to the public.

Other restrictions applicable to a nonprofit's ability to make money are discussed in Section C.

2. Religious Purposes

For Section 501(c)(3) purposes, religious purpose groups can be either a loosely defined religious organization that practices or promotes religious beliefs in some way or a formal institutional church. Groups formed to advance religion often qualify as charitable purpose organizations under Section 501(c)(3) (see Section 1, above).

a. Qualifying as a Religious Organization

Traditionally, the IRS and the courts have been reluctant to question the validity or sincerity of religious beliefs or practices held by a group trying to establish itself as a religious purpose organization. As long as the organization's beliefs appear to be "truly and sincerely held" and their related practices and rituals are not illegal or against public policy, the IRS generally does not challenge the validity of the religious tenets or practices. However, the IRS will question the nature and extent of religious activities (as opposed to religious beliefs) if they do not appear to foster religious worship or advance a religious purpose, or if they appear commercial in nature.

> **EXAMPLE:** A group that holds weekly meetings and publishes material celebrating the divine presence in all natural phenomena should qualify as a religious purpose group. However, an organization that sells a large volume of literature to the general public, some of which has little or no connection to the religious beliefs held by the organization, could be regarded by the IRS as a regular trade or business, not as a tax-exempt religious organization.

A religious group need not profess belief in a supreme being to qualify as a religious organization under Section 501(c)(3).

Religious corporations also have the widest flexibility in managing their internal affairs.

b. Qualifying as a Church

You can also qualify under the 501(c)(3) religious purpose category as a church, but doing so is more difficult than simply qualifying as a 501(c)(3) religious organization. One of the advantages of qualifying as a church is that a church automatically qualifies for 501(c)(3) *public charity status*—a status that all 501(c)(3) groups want to obtain, as we explain later in Chapter 4.

The Internal Revenue Service has developed a guide designed to assist churches and clergy in complying with the religious purpose requirement of the Internal Revenue Code. The publication is intended to be a user-friendly compilation, set forth in question-and-answer format. A copy of this guide, IRS Publication 1828, Tax Guide for Churches and Other Religious Organizations, is available from the Internal Revenue Service website at www.irs-.gov/pub/irs-pdf/p1828.pdf. Most church and religious-purpose groups will find the information in this publication extremely helpful when preparing their federal exemption application (see Chapter 8).

Under IRS rulings, a religious organization should have the following characteristics to qualify as a church (not all are necessary but the more the better):

- a recognized creed or form of worship
- a definite and distinct ecclesiastical government
- a formal code of doctrine and discipline
- a distinct religious history
- a membership not associated with any other church or denomination
- a complete organization of ordained ministers
- a literature of its own
- established places of worship
- regular congregations, and
- regular religious services.

Courts have used similar criteria to determine whether or not a religious organization qualifies as a church. In one case, the court looked for the presence of the following "church" factors:

- services held on a regular basis
- ordained ministers or other representatives
- a record of the performance of marriage, other ceremonies, and sacraments
- a place of worship
- some support required from members
- formal operations, and
- satisfaction of all other requirements of federal tax law for religious organizations.

All religious purpose groups that claim church status must complete a special IRS schedule with specific questions on some of the church characteristics listed above. We discuss this tax application and the special IRS schedule for churches in Chapter 8.

Traditional churches, synagogues, associations, or conventions of churches (and religious orders or organizations that are an integral part of a church and engaged in carrying out its functions) can qualify as 501(c)(3) churches without difficulty. Less traditional and less formal religious organizations may have a harder time. These groups often have to answer additional questions to convince the IRS that they qualify as tax-exempt churches.

Some churches stand a greater chance of being audited by the IRS than others. Not surprisingly, the IRS is more likely to examine and question groups that promise members substantial tax benefits for organizing their households as tax-deductible church organizations.

3. Scientific Purposes

Groups that engage in scientific research carried on in the public interest are also eligible for tax-exempt status under 501(c)(3). Under IRS regulations, research incidental to commercial or industrial operations (such as the normal inspection or testing of materials or products, or the design or construction of equipment and buildings) does not qualify as a scientific purpose under Section 501(c)(3). In an IRS case involving a pharmaceutical company, the company's clinical testing of drugs was held not to be "scientific" under Section 501(c)(3) because the clinical testing in question was incidental to the pharmaceutical company's commercial operations.

Generally, research is considered in the public interest if the results (including any patents, copyrights, processes, or formulas) are made available to the public; that is, the scientific research must be published for others to study and use. Research is also considered in the public interest if it is performed for the United States or a state, county, or city government, or if it is conducted to accomplish one of the following purposes:

- to aid in the scientific education of college or university students
- to discover a cure for a disease, or
- to aid a community or region by attracting new industry, or by encouraging the development or retention of an existing industry.

EXAMPLE: An organization was formed by a group of physicians specializing in heart defects to research the causes and treatment of cardiac and cardiovascular conditions and diseases. The physicians practiced medicine in a private practice facility that was separate and apart from the organization's research facility, which was used exclusively for the research program. Although some patients from the physicians' private practice were accepted for the research program, they were selected on the same criteria as other patients. The IRS found that the physician's research group met the scientific purpose organizational test for Section 501(c)(3) purposes.

If you are applying for a scientific exemption under Section 501(c)(3), your federal exemption application (covered in Chapter 8) should show that your organization is conducting public interest research and you should provide the following information:

- an explanation of the nature of the research
- a description of past and present research projects
- how and by whom research projects are determined and selected, and
- who will retain ownership or control of any patents, copyrights, processes, or formulas resulting from the research.

For a list of the specific information the IRS requires from scientific groups, see IRS Publication 557, page 14.

4. Literary Purposes

This is a seldom-used Section 501(c)(3) category because most literary purpose nonprofits are classified as educational by the IRS. Nevertheless, valid 501(c)(3) literary purposes include traditional literary efforts, such as publishing, distribution, and book sales. These activities must be directed toward promoting the public interest as opposed to engaging in a commercial literary enterprise or serving the interests of particular individuals (such as the proprietors of a publishing house). Generally, this means that literary material must be available to the general public and must pertain to the betterment of the community.

A combination of factors helps distinguish public interest publishing from private publishing. If you publish materials that are clearly educational and make them available to the public at cost, or at least below standard commercial rates, then you might qualify as a 501(c)(3) literary purpose organization. However, if your material seems aimed primarily at a commercial market and is sold at standard rates through regular commercial channels, chances are that your literary organization will be viewed by the IRS as a regular business enterprise ineligible for a 501(c)(3) tax exemption. For example, publishing textbooks at standard rates will probably not qualify as a tax-exempt literary purpose under Section 501(c)(3) because the activity is more private than public in nature. On the other hand, publishing material to promote highway safety or the education of handicapped children is likely to qualify as a bona fide 501(c)(3) literary purpose.

> **EXAMPLE:** A publishing house that only published books related to esoteric Eastern philosophical thought applied for 501(c)(3) literary exemption. Their books were sold commercially but at modest prices. The IRS granted the tax exemption after requesting and reviewing the manuscript for the nonprofit's first publication. The IRS found that the material was sufficiently specialized to render it noncommercial in nature.

5. Educational Purposes

The type of educational activities that qualify as educational purpose under 501(c)(3) are broad, encompassing instruction both for self-development and for the benefit of the community. The IRS allows advocacy of a particular intellectual position or viewpoint if there is a "sufficiently full and fair exposition of pertinent facts to permit an individual or the public to form an independent opinion or conclusion. However, mere presentation of unsupported opinion is not (considered) educational."

If a group takes political positions, it may not qualify for an exemption (see discussion on political activities in Section C). An educational group that publishes a newsletter with a balanced analysis of issues, or at least with some room devoted to debate or presentation of opposing opinions, should qualify as a 501(c)(3) educational purpose group. If its newsletter is simply devoted to espousing one side of an issue, platform, or agenda, the educational purpose tax exemption may not be granted.

Examples of activities that qualify as educational purpose include:

- publishing public interest educational materials
- conducting public discussion groups, forums, panels, lectures, and workshops
- offering a correspondence course or a course that uses other media such as television or radio
- operating a museum, zoo, planetarium, symphony, orchestra, or performance group
- serving an educational institution, such as a college bookstore, alumni association, or athletic organization, or
- publishing educational newsletters, pamphlets, books, or other material.

See the CD-ROM file *Education, Propaganda, and the Methodology Test,* for guidelines used by the IRS and courts to determine if a nonprofit qualifies as an educational purpose organization under Section 501(c)(3).

a. Formal School Not Necessary

To qualify as a 501(c)(3) educational organization, a group does not need to provide instruction in traditional school subjects or organize as a formal school facility with a regular faculty, established curriculum, and a regularly enrolled student body.

⚠️ **You may need formal school attributes for other reasons.** People setting up nontraditional schools should remember that although they do not need a regular faculty, full-time students, or even a fixed curriculum to qualify for a 501(c)(3) educational purpose tax exemption, as a practical matter, they may need some or all of these things to qualify for state or federal support, participate in federal student loan programs, and obtain accreditation.

b. Child Care Centers

Providing child care outside the home qualifies as a 501(c)(3) educational purpose under special provisions contained in Internal Revenue Code Section 501(k) if:

- the care enables parent(s) to be employed, and
- the child care services are available to the general public.

A child care facility that gives enrollment preference to children of employees of a specific employer, however, will not be considered a 501(c)(3) educational purpose organization.

c. Private School Nondiscrimination Requirements

If you set up a 501(c)(3) private school, you must include a nondiscrimination statement in your bylaws and publicize this statement to the community served by the school. This statement must make it clear that the school does not discriminate against students or applicants on the basis of race, color, or national or ethnic origin.

Here is a sample statement taken from IRS *Revenue Procedure* 75-50:

NOTICE OF NONDISCRIMINATORY POLICY AS TO STUDENTS

The M school admits students of any race, color, national and ethnic origin to all the rights, privileges, programs, and activities generally accorded or made available to students at the school. It does not discriminate on the basis of race, color, national and ethnic origin in administration of its educational policies, admissions policies, scholarship, and loan programs, and athletic and other school-administered programs.

📖 Additional information on the history and status of 501(c)(3) private school nondiscrimination requirements is on the IRS website (www.irs.gov), in a tax topic update titled Private School Update. For further information on IRS private school antidiscrimination rules and procedures, see *IRS Revenue Procedure 75-50* and IRS Publication 557.

The CD-ROM at the back of this book contains the following related IRS material:

- *Tax-Exempt Status for Your Organization*
- *Private School Update*
- *IRS Revenue Procedure 75-50.*

C. Other Requirements for 501(c)(3) Groups

In addition to being organized primarily for one or more allowable tax-exempt purposes, a nonprofit must not engage in other activities that conflict or substantially interfere with its valid 501(c)(3) purposes. This section discusses some of the requirements that keep a 501(c)(3) from straying too far from its exempt-purpose activities.

1. Unrelated Business Activities

To obtain 501(c)(3) status, a corporation cannot substantially engage in activities unrelated to the group's tax-exempt purposes. Or, put differently, your nonprofit corporation can conduct activities not directly related to its exempt purpose as long as these activities don't represent a substantial portion of your total activities. Some unrelated activity is allowed because as a practical matter, most nonprofits need to do some unrelated business to survive. For example, a nonprofit dance group might rent unused portions of its studio space to an outside group for storage. Another nonprofit might invest surplus funds to augment its income.

Most groups need not be overly concerned with this limitation unless activities unrelated to exempt purposes start to involve a significant amount of the group's energy or time, or if these activities produce "substantial" income. If the activities are themselves nonprofit, they should be included in the organization's exempt purposes and classified as related activities. The IRS keeps an eye out for tax-exempt groups that regularly engage in profit-making businesses with little or no connection to their exempt purposes (a church running a trucking company). Business activities necessary to further the group's exempt purposes, such as hiring and paying employees and paying rent for space used for the group's exempt purpose, are considered related activities.

Most new nonprofits work full time simply tending to their exempt purposes and do not explore unrelated moneymaking activities until later, if at all. However, if you plan to engage in unrelated business from the start, be careful. It's hard to pin down exactly when these activities become substantial enough to jeopardize the corporation's tax-exempt status. Also, income derived from unrelated business activities is subject to federal and state corporate income tax, even if it is not substantial enough to affect the group's 501(c)(3) tax-exempt status.

For more information on the federal unrelated business income tax that applies to nonprofit 501(c)(3) groups, see the CD-ROM file *UBIT: Current Developments*.

2. Limitation on Profits and Benefits

A 501(c)(3) nonprofit corporation cannot be organized or operated to benefit individuals associated with the corporation (directors, officers, or members) or other persons or entities related to, or controlled by, these individuals (such as another corporation controlled by a director). In tax language, this limitation is known as the "prohibition on private inurement" and means that 501(c)(3) groups can't pay profits to, or otherwise benefit, private interests.

Two specific 501(c)(3) requirements implement this prohibition on self-inurement:

- no part of the net earnings of the corporation can be distributed to individuals associated with the corporation, and
- upon dissolution, the assets of a 501(c)(3) group must be irrevocably dedicated to another tax-exempt group.

These federal tax exemption requirements often are mirrored in the state's nonprofit corporation law. Note that the IRS and state law allow a nonprofit to pay reasonable salaries to directors, officers, employees, or agents for services rendered in furtherance of the corporation's tax-exempt purposes.

a. Excess Benefit Rules

In recent years, the IRS has adopted strict rules and regulations regarding the payment of money, benefits, or property to nonprofit directors, officers, sponsors, donors, and others associated with the nonprofit. The main purpose for these rules, called the "excess benefit rules," is to make sure nonprofit organizations do not pay out lavish benefits or skim off program funds to line the pockets or serve the private interests of individuals associated with the nonprofit. The excess benefit rules are also called the IRS "intermediate sanctions," a euphemism that is meant to have an appropriately harsh ring. These rules are contained in Section 4958 of the Internal Revenue Code and Section 53.4958 of the IRS Regulations.

The excess benefit rules apply to individuals associated with 501(c)(3) nonprofit public charities. (As explained more fully in Chapter 4, in all likelihood you will be forming a public charity nonprofit.) The individuals subject to the rules include nonprofit directors, officers, and trustees as well as major sponsors, donors, or anyone else in a position to exercise substantial influence over the affairs of the nonprofit. The rules also apply to family members and entities owned by any of the individuals subject to the rules.

Under the rules, an "excessive benefit transaction" is any transaction where the nonprofit gives cash, property, or anything of value to a recipient that exceeds the value of the services performed by the recipient (or the value of any other cash, property, or thing of value given to the nonprofit by the recipient). If a nonprofit pays $100 to an officer who has contributed $75 worth of services, the excess benefit is $25. Of course, the IRS is looking for much bigger numbers, sometimes in the realm of thousands, or hundreds of thousands of dollars worth of extra benefits paid from the nonprofit coffers to directors, officers, consultants, sponsors, and donors.

The remedy, as you might guess, is a tax that must be paid by both the recipient of the excess benefit as well as the nonprofit managers (the directors and executive officers) who approved the excess benefit transaction. The recipient of the excess benefit can be assessed a 25% tax on the excess benefit, and the manager or managers who approved it can be assessed a 10% tax, with a limit on a manager's liability capped at $10,000 per transaction. A director must object to the transaction to be excluded from those considered to have approved it—silence or abstention at a board meeting that results in the excess benefit payment is not a defense. The recipient must repay or return the excess benefit to the nonprofit or the recipient will be charged an additional 200% tax. The message is clear—if you receive an undeserved benefit from your nonprofit, expect a substantial financial slap on the wrist, plus a whopping big penalty if you don't return the benefit to the nonprofit.

The IRS regulations add detail about the scope and operation of the excess benefit rules. For example, "disqualified persons" is broadly defined to include all sorts of people paid by or associated with the nonprofit organization. Excess salaries, contract payments, benefits, privileges, goods, services, or anything else of value paid or provided to almost anyone associated with your nonprofit can potentially trigger the excess benefit tax rules.

The regulations also contain a "safe harbor" provision for deals or decisions that provide an economic benefit to a director, officer, contractor, or other key nonprofit person. To qualify for the protection of the safe harbor rule, a number of conditions must be met, including:

- disinterested members of the board or committee must approve the transaction in advance
- the decision must be based on "comparability" data reviewed and relied on by the board that shows the property is transferred at fair market value or compensation is paid at a rate similar to that paid by other organizations for comparable services, and
- the decision must be documented in the corporate records at the time the transaction is approved.

Falling within the safe harbor provision creates a presumption that your deal or decision was fair. The IRS can rebut this presumption if it obtains evidence to the contrary.

The excess benefit rules are complex and, if you really need to dig into them, you may need the help of a nonprofit legal or tax specialist. We recommend, however, for everyone involved with a nonprofit to have your nonprofit antennae tuned to this issue whenever your organization decides to provide an economic benefit to a person, organization, or business entity. Think about these rules whenever your board, or a committee of your board, decides to set or increase salaries, enter into contracts, or approve deals with individuals or other organizations. If you think the IRS could possibly raise the issue of economic fairness in relation to the deal, then take a look at the excess benefit rules (or have your legal or tax adviser do so) to make sure you are on a solid footing. After reviewing the rules, if you think you may be on the outside edges of what's permissible, the best course is probably to not do the deal or cut back the economic benefit to a point where you feel safe. If you want to go forward in the face of uncertainty and reduce your risk, then comply with the safe harbor provision. Take these rules seriously, and include compliance with the rules as an integral part of your due diligence procedures when advising your board on the legal and tax constraints that apply to their decision making. The last thing you want to have happen is to subject board members, officers, contractors, sponsors, donors, and others who deal with your nonprofit to the prospect of having to pay back money or the value of benefits previously paid out or provided by your nonprofit plus very hefty taxes, interest, and penalties.

If you are interested in reading more information about these rules, you can use the CD-ROM files listed below.

The CD ROM at the back of this book contains the following files with information on the excess benefit rules and regulations.

- This file contains IRC Section 4958
- This file contains the IRS regulations promulgated under Section 4958
- *Intermediate Sanctions (IRC 4958) Update.*

b. Conflict of Interest Provisions

One way for a nonprofit to show the IRS, its members, sponsors, and donors that it is serious about not paying out special benefits to directors, officers, and other nonprofit insiders is for the group to include a conflict of interest policy in its bylaws. At a minimum, this policy should require disinterested board member approval for any deal or decision that financially benefits a director or officer of the nonprofit. Approval for this type of transaction should be allowed only if, after full disclosure about who will be benefited and how, the disinterested directors (or a disinterested committee of the board) determines that the corporation can't get a more advantageous deal elsewhere and the deal is fair to the corporation. Of course, you could adopt a stricter policy and only allow transactions that financially benefit an officer or director if it furthers your organization's exempt purposes. Or, you could decide to prohibit these types of transactions altogether unless they involve standard business matters, such as the approval of salaries to officers and remuneration of expenses to directors for attending meetings.

Any conflict of interest provision that you include in your bylaws would supplement (not supersede) state law rules regarding self-dealing by directors of a nonprofit. These self-dealing rules also regulate transactions that financially benefit directors of a nonprofit and have similar requirements for disclosure of financial self-interest, approval of decisions by a disinterested board, and a finding of fairness to the nonprofit.

The IRS has promulgated a sample conflicts of interest policy for Section 501(c)(3) health care organizations that can also be used as a model for other 501(c)(3) nonprofits. It is included (with updates) in the CD-ROM files listed below. Although the IRS doesn't require nonprofits to adopt this type of policy, having one in place can help show anyone interested in your organization that you are serious about operating your organization for the benefit of your nonprofit programs, not for the interests of insiders.

See the following files for a sample IRS conflicts of interest policy that you can adapt for use by your nonprofit.

- *Tax-Exempt Health Care Organizations Community Board and Conflicts of Interest Policy*
- *Tax-Exempt Health Care Organizations Revised Conflicts of Interest Policy.*

3. Limitation on Political Activities

A 501(c)(3) corporation is prohibited from participating in any political campaigns for or against any candidate for public office. Participation in or contributions to political campaigns can result in the revocation of 501(c)(3) tax-exempt status and the assessment of special excise taxes against the organization and its managers. (See Internal Revenue Code §§ 4955, 6852, and 7409.)

a. Voter Education Activities

Section 501(c)(3) groups can conduct certain voter education activities if they are done in a nonpartisan manner (see IRS Revenue Ruling 78-248). If you want to engage in this type of political activity, we recommend you consult an attorney. Your organization can request an IRS letter ruling on its voter education activities by writing to the address listed in IRS Publication 557, Chapter 3, "Political Activity."

For information on restrictions on political candidate campaign activity by 501(c)(3) organizations, see *Election Year Issues,* in the CD-ROM. It also contains information about other laws and restrictions applicable to political campaign nonprofits—non-501(c)(3) groups organized primarily to support or oppose political candidates under Internal Revenue Code § 527.

b. Influencing Legislation

Section 501(c)(3) organizations are prohibited from acting to influence legislation, "except to an insubstantial degree." In the past, courts have found that spending more than 5% of an organization's budget, time, or effort on political activity was "substantial." More recently, courts have tended to look at the individual facts of each case. Generally, if a nonprofit corporation contacts, or urges the public to contact, members of a legislative body, or if it advocates the adoption or rejection of legislation, the IRS considers it to be acting to influence legislation.

Lobbying to influence legislation also includes:

- any attempt to affect the opinions of the general public or a segment of the public, and
- communication with any member or employee of a legislative body, or with any government official or employee who might participate in the formulation of legislation.

However, lobbying to influence legislation does not include:

- making available the results of nonpartisan analysis, study, or research
- providing technical advice or assistance to a government body, or to its committee or other subdivision, in response to a written request from it, where such advice would otherwise constitute the influencing of legislation
- appearing before, or communicating with, any legislative body with respect to a possible decision that might affect the organization's existence, powers,

tax-exempt status, or the deductibility of contributions to it, or

- communicating with a government official or employee, other than for the purpose of influencing legislation.

Also excluded from the definition of lobbying efforts are communications between an organization and its members about legislation (or proposed legislation) of direct interest to the organization and the members, unless these communications directly encourage members to influence legislation.

EXAMPLE: A Housing Information Exchange keeps its members informed of proposed legislation affecting low-income renters. This should not be considered legislative lobbying activity unless members are urged to contact their political representatives in support of, or in opposition to, the proposed legislation.

In determining whether a group's legislative activities are substantial in scope, the IRS looks at the amount of time, money, or effort the group spends on legislative lobbying. If they are substantial in relation to other activities, 501(c)(3) tax status might be revoked and, again, special excise taxes can be levied against the organization and its managers. See IRC § 4912.

Political Expenditures Test

Under the political expenditures test in IRC § 501(h), limitations are imposed on two types of political activities: lobbying expenditures and grassroots expenditures. Lobbying expenditures are those made for the purpose of influencing legislation, while grassroots expenditures are those made to influence public opinion.

For examples of these two types of activities, see IRS Publication 557, the "Lobbying Expenditures" section. The monetary limits are different for each of the categories and the formulas for computing them are somewhat complicated.

If your 501(c)(3) nonprofit elects the political expenditures test, you must file IRS Form 5768, *Election-Revocation of Election by an Eligible Section 501(c)(3) Organization to Make Expenditures to Influence Legislation*, within the tax year in which you wish the election to be effective. This election is also available under similar rules at the state level. A copy of this form is included on the CD-ROM provided with this book.

c. The Alternative Political Expenditures Test

Since it is impossible to know ahead of time how the IRS will assess the "substantiality" of a group's legislative activity, the IRC allows 501(c)(3) public charities (most 501(c)(3) groups will qualify as public charities—see Chapter 4) to elect an alternative "expenditures test" to measure permissible legislative activity. Under this test, a group may spend up to 20% of the first $500,000 of its annual expenditures on lobbying, 15% of the next $500,000, 10% of the next $500,000, and 5% of its expenditures beyond that, up to a total limit of $1 million each year.

Some groups can't use the political expenditures test. This expenditures test and its provisions for lobbying and grassroots expenditures are not available to churches, an integrated auxiliary of a church, a member of an affiliated group of organizations that includes a church, or to private foundations.

If your nonprofit corporation plans to do considerable lobbying activity, mostly by unpaid volunteers, then electing the expenditures test might be a good idea. Why? Because the minimal outlay of money to engage in these activities will probably keep you under the applicable expenditure limits. If you didn't make this election, your 501(c)(3) tax exemption might be placed in jeopardy if the IRS considers your political activities to be a substantial part of your overall purposes and program.

If you plan to engage in more than a minimum amount of political lobbying or legislative efforts, you need to decide whether it is to your advantage to elect the expenditures test based on the facts of your situation. If you find that these alternative political expenditures rules are still too restrictive, you might consider forming a social welfare organization or civic league under Section 501(c)(4) of the Internal Revenue Code—this exemption requires a different federal exemption appli-

cation, IRS Form 1024, and does not carry with it all the attractive benefits of 501(c)(3) status (access to grant funds, tax deductible contributions, etc.). See Chapter 1, Section A, and IRS Publication 557 for further information on 501(c)(4) organizations.

Additional limitations for certain groups. Federally funded groups may be subject to even more stringent political expenditure tests than those discussed here (for example, political activity and expenditure restrictions imposed by the federal Office of Management and Budget).

For a thorough discussion of the rules that apply to lobbying activities by 501(c)(3) organizations and detailed information on the Section 501(h) political expenditures test election, see *Lobbying Issues,* in the CD-ROM.

d. Political Action Organizations

The IRS can also challenge a 501(c)(3) group's political activities by finding that it is an action organization: One so involved in political activities that it is not organized exclusively for a 501(c)(3) tax-exempt purpose. Under these circumstances the IRS can revoke the organization's tax-exempt status. Intervention in political campaigns or substantial attempts to influence legislation, as discussed above, are grounds for applying this sanction. In addition, if a group has the following two characteristics, it will be classified as an action organization and lose its 501(c)(3) status:

1. Its main or primary objective or objectives—not incidental or secondary objectives—may be attained only by legislation or defeat of proposed legislation, and

2. It advocates or campaigns for the attainment of such objectives rather than engaging in nonpartisan analysis, study, or research and making the results available to the public.

In determining whether a group has these characteristics, the IRS looks at the surrounding facts and circumstances, including the group's articles and activities, and its organizational and operational structure.

The point here is to be careful not to state your exempt purposes in such a way that they seem only attainable by political action. Even if you indicate that your activities will not be substantially involved with legislative or lobbying efforts, the IRS may decide otherwise and invoke this special classification to deny or rescind 501(c)(3) status.

If the IRS classifies a group as an action organization, the group can still qualify as a social welfare group under 501(c)(4).

EXAMPLE: A group that has a primary purpose of "reforming the judicial system in the United States" will likely sound like a political action organization to the IRS, because this sounds like a political goal that must be accomplished mostly by political means. However, if the group rephrases its primary purpose as "educating the public on the efficacy of mediation, arbitration, and other alternative nonjudicial dispute resolution mechanisms," it stands a better chance of having the IRS approve its application, even if it lists some political activity as incidental to its primary educational purpose.

Watch for new Federal Election Commission (FEC) rules. Pending federal rules would subject politically active nonprofits to the Federal Election Campaign Act (FECA) rules, restrictions, and reporting requirements. The new rules, which could be crippling for even moderately active political organizations, could apply to your politically active nonprofit, even if you don't participate directly in federal political candidate campaigns and only provide and discuss political issue information that treats political parties or candidates. Stay tuned to this issue and possible federal legislation in this area that could impact your nonprofit's political issues program (if you have one). To follow developments, check the FEC website at www.fec.gov.

D. Information for Specific Questions About Your Group's Activities

Even after reading through this chapter, you might still have some questions about whether your specific nonprofit activities meet the IRS definition of educational, charitable, or religious purposes under Section 501(c)(3) of the Internal Revenue Code. Or, after you take a closer look at Chapter 4, you might wonder whether your nonprofit can qualify for special public charity treatment as a "school" or "church."

Answers to these types of questions used to be left to the expertise of highly paid lawyers and tax professionals—this is no longer true. It is remarkably easy to find out more about how the IRS might look at your nonprofit organization when it reviews your tax exemption application. The IRS website disseminates most of the material necessary to answer many technical questions as long as you are persistent enough to search the site thoroughly and uncover the material. Specifically, IRS publications and regulations, as well as the technical manuals the IRS examiners use when reviewing tax exemption applications, are available online.

This chapter refers to special IRS training materials from the IRS website and includes this material on the CD-ROM that accompanies this book. We describe how each of these articles helps explain and illustrate a specific issue related to obtaining and maintaining a 501(c)(3) tax exemption. There is a lot more helpful material on the IRS website and we encourage you to browse it to learn as much as you'd like about nonprofit organization tax issues.

Here is one way to search the IRS site for nonprofit tax exemption answers:

Go to the main page of the IRS website at www.irs.gov and click the Charities and Nonprofit link on the left side of the page. The left panel of the page contains a table of contents, extra resources, and special nonprofit tax topics, plus a link to additional topics. The right panel of the page contains specific links to current nonprofit tax developments. If you don't find what you're looking for, type in a word or phrase in the Search IRS Site For box at the top of the page. The word or phrase should succinctly describe your question.

You can also try to find your topic by clicking on the Site Map link that appears at the top of most of the site's Web pages. You should see a list of links for Charities and Nonprofits, which you can use to navigate

through the site to find the material you're looking for.

Another more advanced approach is to click the Site Map link at the top of the Web page, then click the Internal Revenue Manual listed under the Tax Professionals heading. This link takes you to a table that lists different sections of the internal IRS procedures manual used by IRS examiners and field agents. It contains a wealth of technical material about IRS procedures, rulings, and policies. Part 7 is the main area of interest for nonprofit groups applying for their 501(c)(3) tax exemption. Select this link, then scroll down the heading list until you see the heading, "7.25 Exempt Organizations Determinations Manual." Click on the link under this heading to "7.25.3, Religious, Charitable, Educational, Etc., Organizations." This chapter contains examples of groups that have and have not qualified under each of the 501(c)(3) tax-exempt purposes. Also see the earlier link in the headings list to "7.81 Exempt Organizations Examination Guidelines Handbook." Chapter 3 of this Handbook contains checklists of questions used by IRS examiners to determine if a nonprofit organization qualifies under 501(c)(3).

If you want to learn even more, you can examine any IRS rulings and cases that you uncover in your website search. Rulings are compiled in *IRS Cumulative Bulletins*, the most recent of which are available for browsing on the IRS website. Click the Site Map link at the top of any IRS site Web page, then select IRS Resources under the Tax Professionals heading. Scroll down and select the Internal Revenue Bulletins link. Then select the volume for the year when the ruling was issued and scroll through the beginning table of contents to find the page where the ruling begins (the first two numbers of a ruling indicate its year—for example, Ruling 93-10 was issued in 1993, so you would look at the *Bulletin* for 1993 to find the text of the ruling). Most years have more than one *Bulletin* volume, and some rulings are placed in the next year's volume. It takes persistence to track down rulings, but they can be enormously helpful in understanding why the IRS accepted or rejected a nonprofit organization's application for a 501(c)(3) tax exemption. You'll have to go to a law library to read unposted rulings and tax cases—this is easy to do, just more time-consuming (see Chapter 11).

For an in-depth discussion and analysis of the requirements that apply to each type of 501(c)(3) nonprofit, supplemented annually with the latest IRS and court rulings in each area, see *The Law of Tax-Exempt Organizations*, by Bruce R. Hopkins, (John Wiley & Sons, New York, N.Y.). ■

Chapter 4

Public Charities and Private Foundations

*I*n this chapter, we explain why it is not enough to simply obtain your 501(c)(3) tax-exempt status—you also need to be recognized as a 501(c)(3) public charity. Getting this extra recognition is essential to make your life as a nonprofit easier to manage. Even though the last thing you may be interested in at this point is delving into more tax technicalities, it will help you enormously to have a general understanding of the distinction between public charity and private foundation tax status before you do your federal tax exemption application. You will understand the importance of some of the most technical questions on the application and you'll know how to answer questions to show you qualify for public charity tax status.

We help you get through this information by explaining the different public charity classifications and requirements in plain English. You don't need to master this material. In fact, many nonprofits let the IRS decide which public charity category works for them. For now, simply read through the information to get a general understanding of the concepts. You can come back to this chapter when you do your federal tax exemption application and reread the sections that apply to you.

Throughout this chapter, we refer to the Internal Revenue Code sections that apply to the different public charity classifications. You don't need to pay attention to these section references. They will be useful later as a reference when you prepare your federal tax exemption application.

A. The Importance of Public Charity Status

The IRS classifies all 501(c)(3) tax-exempt nonprofit corporations as either private foundations or public charities. Initially, most 501(c)(3) corporations are presumed to be private foundations. It's extremely important to understand that your group, too, will initially be viewed as a private foundation. The problem with this classification is that private foundations are subject to strict operating rules and regulations that don't apply to groups classified as public charities. You'll want to get yourself out from under this presumption because, like most 501(c)(3) groups, you would probably find it impossible to operate under the rules and restrictions imposed on private foundations. To overcome this presumption, you must show on your federal 501(c)(3) tax exemption application that you qualify as a public charity.

A few special groups are not presumed to be private foundations and do not have to apply for public charity status—the same groups that are not required to file a 501(c)(3) tax exemption application. We think it's foolhardy in most cases not to apply for, and obtain, official notification from the IRS that you are a public charity. (For a discussion of this issue, see Chapter 8, Section B.)

B. How to Qualify for Public Charity Status

As explained above, almost all 501(c)(3) nonprofits want to overcome the private foundation presumption and establish themselves as a public charity. There are three basic ways to do this:

- **Form one of the types of nonprofits that automatically qualify.** Particular types of nonprofit organizations, such as churches, schools, or hospitals, automatically qualify for public charity status because of the nature of their activities.

EXAMPLE: A church that maintains a facility for religious worship would most easily obtain automatic public charity status. A church qualifies for recognition as a public charity because of the nature of its activities rather than its sources of support.

- **Derive most of your support from the public.** If your group receives support primarily from individual contributions, government, or other public sources, you can qualify for public charity status as a publicly supported organization.

EXAMPLE: An organization formed to operate a center for rehabilitation, counseling, or similar services, that plans to carry on a broad-based solicitation program and depend primarily on government grants, corporate contributions, and individual donations, would most likely seek public charity status as a publicly supported organization.

- **Receive most of your revenue from activities related to your tax-exempt purposes.** If your group receives most of its revenue from activities related to its

tax-exempt purposes, you can qualify under a special public charity support test that applies to many smaller nonprofits.

EXAMPLE: An arts group deriving most of its income from exempt-purpose activities (lessons, performances, and renting studio facilities to other arts groups) would probably choose the support test. This public charity test, unlike those that apply to publicly supported organizations, allows groups to count income derived from the performance of their exempt purposes as qualified support.

For additional information on the rules that apply to each of the three public charity tests, see the file, *Public Charity or Private Foundation Status Issues under IRC §§ 509(a)(1)-(4), 4942(j)(3), and 507*, on the CD-ROM included at the back of this book. For information on the public charity requirements associated with each type of automatically recognized public charity (churches, schools, hospitals, and others), see the section titled, "Public Charity or Private Foundation Status Issues under IRC §§ 509(a)(1)-(4), 4942(j)(3), and 507." For information on the public charity test we call the public support test, see the section titled, " Publicly Supported Organizations Described in IRC §§ 509(a)(1) and 170(b)(1)(A)(vi)." For information on the public charity test we call the exempt-activities support test, see the section titled, "Publicly Supported Organizations Described in IRC § 509(a)(2)."

You Can Let the IRS Decide Your Public Charity Classification

It's sometimes hard to figure out whether your organization will meet the public support test discussed below in Section B2 or the exempt activities test discussed in Section B4 below. To make this decision, an organization must second-guess future sources of support and tackle quite a few tax technicalities. Fortunately, if you have doubts, the IRS will help. Simply check a box on the federal tax exemption application and the IRS will decide this question for you based upon the financial and program information you submit with your application.

For the specifics on making this election, see the Chapter 9 instructions to Part III, Line 9(j), of the federal tax exemption application.

1. Automatic Public Charity Status

The IRS automatically recognizes certain 501(c)(3) groups as public charities because they perform particular services or engage in certain charitable activities. The following groups automatically qualify:

a. Churches

Religious purpose groups that qualify as churches for 501(c)(3) tax exemption purposes also automatically qualify as a public charity. (IRC §§ 509(a)(1) and 170(b)(1)(A)(i).) Qualifying as a church under Section 501(c)(3) is more difficult than qualifying as a 501(c)(3) religious purpose organization. To qualify as a church, the organization must have the institutional and formal characteristics of a church. (See Chapter 3, Section B2.) If your religious-purpose 501(c)(3) group does not qualify as a church, it can still qualify for public charity status under one of the other public charity tests described below.

b. Schools

Certain educational institutions that have the institutional attributes of a school automatically qualify as public charities. (IRC §§ 509(a)(1) and 170(b)(1)(A)(ii).) Generally, these are educational organizations whose primary function is to present formal instruction. These schools usually have a regular faculty and curriculum, a regularly enrolled body of students, and a place where their educational activities are carried on.

This school category for automatic public charity recognition is geared towards primary or secondary preparatory or high schools, and colleges and universities with regularly enrolled student bodies. The farther an educational group strays from the institutional criteria mentioned above, the harder it will be to qualify as a public charity. This doesn't mean that less structured educational institutions can't automatically qualify for public charity status as schools, it just may be more difficult. Nontraditional groups have a better chance of obtaining automatic public charity status if they have some conventional institutional attributes, such as regional accreditation and a state-approved curriculum. If your educational-purpose 501(c)(3) group does not fall within this school category for automatic recognition, it can still qualify for public charity status under one of the other tests described in Sections B2 and B4, below.

c. Hospitals and Medical Research Organizations

Nonprofit health care groups that operate charitable hospitals or facilities and whose main function is to provide hospital or medical care, medical education, or medical research automatically qualify as public charities. (IRC §§ 509(a)(1) and 170(b)(1)(A)(iii).) These charitable hospitals generally have the following characteristics:

- doctors selected from the community at large who are part of the courtesy staff
- a community-oriented board of directors
- emergency room facilities available on a community-access basis
- admission of at least some patients without charge (on a charitable basis)
- nondiscrimination with respect to all admissions (particularly Medicare or Medicaid patients), and
- a medical training and research program that benefits the community.

Other 501(c)(3) health care organizations, such as rehabilitation groups, outpatient clinics, community mental health programs, or drug treatment centers, can qualify as hospitals if their principal purpose is to provide hospital or medical care. A health organization that uses consultation services of certified medical personnel such as doctors and nurses will have an easier time meeting the hospital criteria. The IRS does not, however, recognize convalescent homes, homes for children or the aged, or institutions that provide vocational training for the handicapped as fitting within this public charity category.

Medical education and research organizations do not qualify under these IRC sections unless they actively provide on-site medical or hospital care to patients as an integral part of their functions. Medical research groups must also be directly and continuously active in medical research with a hospital, and this research must be the organization's principal purpose.

Hospitals and other tax-exempt health care organizations may want to adopt a community board and a conflict of interest policy in their bylaws. For more information on this topic, see the following files on the CD-ROM included at the back of this book:

- *Tax-Exempt Health Care Organizations Community Board and Conflicts of Interest Policy*
- *Tax-Exempt Health Care Organizations Revised Conflicts of Interest Policy.*

d. Public Safety Organizations

Groups organized and operated exclusively for public safety testing automatically qualify for public charity status. Generally, these organizations test consumer products to determine their fitness for use by the general public. (IRC § 509(a)(4).)

e. Government Organizations

Certain government organizations operated for the benefit of a college or university automatically qualify as public charities. (IRC §§ 509(a)(1) and 170(b)(1)(A)(iv).) Also, government units (described in IRC § 170(c)(1)) that receive gifts or contributions for public purposes qualify as public charities. (IRC §§ 509(a)(1) and 170(b)(1)(A)(v).) You won't be forming a government corporation, but we mention these organizations because they are included in the list of public charities on the federal tax exemption application form.

f. Supporting Organizations

Organizations operated solely for the benefit of, or in connection with, one or more of the above organizations, or those described in Sections B2 or B4 below (publicly supported groups or groups that meet the exempt activities support test), are also automatically classified as public charities (except those that benefit a public safety organization). (IRC § 509(a)(3).)

For further information on organizations listed above, see IRS Publication 557, *Tax Exempt Status for Your Organization*, "Section 509(a)(1) Organizations." For supporting organizations, see Publication 557, "Section 509(a)(3) Organizations."

2. Public Support Test

To be classified as a publicly supported public charity, a group must regularly solicit funds from the general community. It must normally receive money from government agencies and/or from a number of different private contributors or agencies. (IRC §§ 509(a)(1) and 170(b)(1)(A)(vi).) The term "normally" has a special meaning in this context that is explained below. We call this public charity test the "public support" test because the main requirement is that the organization must receive a substantial portion of its funds from broad-based public support sources.

In general, museums, libraries, and community centers that promote the arts should qualify under this public charity test if they rely on broad-based support from individual members of the community or from various public and private sources. Organizations that expect to rely primarily on a few private sources or occasional large grants to fund their operations will probably not meet the requirements of this section. This support test is difficult for small, grassroots groups to meet because income from the performance of tax-exempt purposes does not count as qualifying public support income—a source of support commonly relied upon by these groups.

To determine whether your group qualifies as a publicly supported public charity, you will need to do some basic math and understand some technical rules. Try not to get overwhelmed or discouraged by this technical material. For now, you can simply read through the information to get a sense of the basic criteria for this test and whether or not you might qualify. You can revisit anything that might seem applicable to you later when you fill in your federal tax exemption application.

More importantly, you may decide to let the IRS figure out which public support test works for you. In most cases, unless you know your nonprofit easily fits within the automatic public charity classification discussed in Section B1, above, the best and easiest approach is to let the IRS decide whether the public support test (covered here in Section B2) or the exempt activities support test (discussed in Section B4 below) works for your nonprofit. After all, the technical staff on the IRS Exempt Organizations Determinations staff knows this material inside out. Why not use their expertise and let them apply the public charity support tests to your group's past and projected sources of public support which you will disclose in your federal tax exemption application.

For more detailed information on qualifying as a public charity using the public support test, see IRS Publication 557 (included on the CD-ROM, which is at the back of the book), *Tax Exempt Status for Your Organization*, "Publicly Supported Organizations."

a. How Much Public Support Do You Need?

The IRS will usually consider an organization qualified under the public support test if it meets one of the following tests:

- The group normally receives at least 1/3 of its total support from governmental units, from contributions made directly or indirectly by the general public, or from a combination of the two (including contributions from other publicly supported organizations), or
- The organization receives at least 1/10 of its support from these sources *and* meets an additional "attraction of public support" requirement (we discuss the attraction of public support test in Section 3, below).

We call this 1/3 or 1/10 figure "public support." To keep your percentage high enough, you'll want the IRS to classify as much of your income as possible as public support (the numerator amount), and keep your total support figure (the denominator amount) as low as possible. This will make your final percentage of public support as high as possible. Of course, the IRS has many rules, and exceptions to the rules, to define "public support" and "total support." We provide a guide to the basic technical terms used below.

Some basic math must be used to estimate your organization's percentage of support. As we explain later, only certain types of support can be included in the numerator of the fraction—the support funds classified as qualified public support. The denominator of the fraction includes the organization's total support, which includes most sources of support received by the nonprofit. You will want as much support as possible to show up in the numerator as qualified public support. If some support received by the nonprofit does not qualify as public support, then it is better to have the support also excluded from the total support. This will keep the excluded support from reducing your public support percentage, since both the numerator and denominator will be left intact.

Advance and Definitive Rulings

There are two ways to request public charity status if you are seeking it: either under the public support test (covered in Section B2) or under the exempt activities support test (covered in Section B4).

If your organization has been operating for one tax year consisting of at least eight months at the time you complete your federal exemption application, you can ask for a definitive ruling on your public charity status. The IRS will use the past support received by the group to determine if it qualifies as a publicly supported organization.

Existing groups can, and new groups must, request an advance ruling on their public charity status. If your expected sources of support seem likely to qualify you under either the public support test or the exempt activities support test, the IRS will grant you one of these tentative rulings. Later, at the end of an advance ruling period consisting of the corporation's first five tax years, the IRS will give a definitive ruling. If the group's public support during the advance ruling period satisfies the support requirements of the appropriate public charity test, the organization will qualify as a public charity.

In granting advance rulings under the public support test, the IRS always looks to see if your organization will meet the attraction of public support factors (discussed in Section 3, below) whether you plan to meet the 1/3 or 1/10 public support test.

For further information on definitive and advance public charity ruling requests, see Chapter 8.

b. What Is Public Support?

Qualified public support (support included in the numerator of the fraction) includes funds from private and public agencies as well as contributions from corporate and individual donors. However, the IRS limits how much qualified support your group can receive from one individual or corporation. Also, some membership fees can be included as qualified support. We discuss these special rules in more detail below.

c. What Does "Normally" Mean?

An organization must "normally" receive either 1/3 or 1/10 of its total support from public support sources. This means that one tax year won't make or break your chances of meeting the test—the IRS bases its decision on four years' cumulative receipts. Your organization will meet either the 1/3 or 1/10 support test for both its current and the following tax year if, during the four tax years before its current tax year, its cumulative public support equals 1/3 or 1/10 of its cumulative total support.

> **EXAMPLE:** Open Range, Inc., is a nonprofit organization for medical research on the healthful effects of organic cattle ranching. ORI's cumulative total support was $60,000 for 1996 through 2000, and its cumulative public support was $25,000. The organization will, therefore, be considered a publicly supported public charity for 2000 and the following tax year. This remains true even if, for one or more of the previous four years, public support did not equal 1/3 of the total support—it's the cumulative total that counts.

d. What Is a "Government Unit"?

Money received from a "government unit" is considered public support. Government units include federal or state governmental agencies, county and city agencies, and so on. The most common example of governmental support is a federal or state grant.

e. The 2% Limit Rule

Direct or indirect contributions from the general public are considered public support. Indirect contributions include grants from private trusts or agencies also funded by contributions from the general public, such as grants from Community Chest or the United Fund.

However, there is a major restriction applicable to these contributions. The total contributions from one individual, trust, or corporation made during the preceding four tax years can be counted only to the extent that they do not exceed 2% of the corporation's total support for those four years. Contributions from government units, publicly supported organizations, and unusual grants are not subject to this 2% limit. These exceptions are discussed below.

> **EXAMPLE:** If your total support over the previous four-year period was $60,000, then only $1,200 (2% of $60,000) contributed by any one person, private agency, or other source can count as public support.

Note that the total amount of any one contribution, even if it exceeds this 2%, four-year limitation, is included in the corporation's total support. Paradoxically, therefore, large contributions from an individual or private agency can have a disastrous effect on your status as a publicly supported charity. You get to include such contributions as public support only to the extent of 2% of the previous four years' total income, but the total income figure is increased by the full amount of the contribution. This makes it more difficult for you to meet the 1/3 or 1/10 public support requirement.

EXAMPLE: On Your Toes, a ballet troupe, received the following contributions from 2000 through 2003:

2000	$10,000	from individual X
2001	20,000	from individual Y
2002	60,000	from Z Community Chest
2003	10,000	as an additional contribution from individual X
	$100,000	Total Support

All support for the four-year period is from contributions, direct or indirect, from the general public. However, in view of the 2% limit, On Your Toes will have trouble maintaining its publicly supported public charity status. While all contributions count toward total support, only $2,000 (2% x $100,000) from any one contributor counts as public support.

Therefore, the troupe's public support for this period is only $6,000 ($2,000 from each contributor, X, Y, and Z), which falls

$4,000 short of the minimum 1/10 public support requirement.

Now, suppose On Your Toes received $2,000 each from 50 contributors over the four-year period. It still has $100,000 total support, but because no one contributor gave more than 2% of the four years' total support, it can count the entire $100,000 as public support.

Increase your chances of qualifying as a publicly supported public charity. One way to do this is to solicit smaller contributions through a broad-based fundraising program and don't rely constantly on the same major sources. This way, you'll beat the 2% limit and have a better chance of qualifying contributions as public support.

f.   Exceptions to the 2% Limit Rule

There are two major exceptions to the 2% limit.

(i)   Money From Government Units or Publicly Supported Organizations

Contributions received from a government unit or other publicly supported organization are not subject to the 2% limit, except those specifically earmarked for your organization by the original donor.

EXAMPLE: Ebeneezer Sax gives $1 million to National Public Music, a national government foundation that promotes musical arts. NPM then gives your organization the million dollars as a grant. If Sax made the contribution to NPM on the condition that the foundation give it to your organization, it is considered earmarked for you and the 2% limit applies. If not, the limit doesn't apply—and you can count the whole donation as public support.

Except for earmarked contributions or grants, you can rely on large contributions or grants from specific government agencies or other publicly supported organizations every year, since all such contributions will be counted as public support.

(ii) Money From "Unusual Grants"

Another major exception to the 2% limit is for "unusual grants" from the private or public sector. A grant is unusual if it:

- is attracted by the publicly supported nature of your organization
- is unusual—this means you don't regularly rely on the particular grant and it is an unexpectedly large amount, and
- would, because of its large size, adversely affect the publicly supported status of your organization (as we've seen, because of the 2% limit, large grants can cause trouble).

If a grant qualifies as an unusual grant, you can exclude the grant funds from both your public support and total support figures for the year in which they are given.

EXAMPLE: The National Museum of Computer Memorabilia, Inc., is a nonprofit corporation that operates a museum of computers and artificial intelligence memorabilia. The years 2000 through 2002 are difficult ones and the museum raises very little money. But in 2003 the organization receives an unexpected windfall grant. A look at the receipts for 2000 to 2003 helps illustrate the importance of the unusual grant exception. All amounts are individual contributions from the general public unless indicated otherwise:

2000	$1,000	from A
	1,000	from B
2001	1,000	from C
2002	1,000	from D
	1,000	from E
2003	100,000	from Z, a private grant agency
	$105,000	Total Receipts

Assume that the 2003 grant qualifies as an unusual grant. The total support computation for the four-year period would be:

2000	$1,000	from A
	1,000	from B
2001	1,000	fro C
2002	1,000	from D
	1,000	rom E
2003	0	the $100,000 grant drops out from total support
	$5,000	Total Support

Because the total support is $5,000, the museum can only count a maximum of 2% times $5,000, or $100, received from any one individual during this period as public support. Therefore, the public support computation for this period looks like this:

2000	$100	from A
	100	from B
2001	100	from C
2002	100	from D
	100	from E
2003	0	the $100,000 contribution also drops out from the public support computation
	$500	Total Public Support

The museum meets the 10% support test because total public support of $500 equals 10% of the total support of $5,000 received over the four-year period. If the organization also meets the attraction of public support requirement (which must be met by groups whose public support is less than 1/3 of total support), it will qualify as a publicly supported public charity for 2003 and 2004.

If the $100,000 contribution did not qualify as an unusual grant, the nonprofit would not meet the 10% public support test. Total support would equal total receipts of $105,000; a maximum of 2% times $105,000, or $2,100, from each individual and the grant agency would be classified as public support. Public support received over the four-year period would consist of $1,000 from individuals A, B, C, D, and E and the maximum allowable sum of $2,100 from the grant agency, for a total public support figure of $7,100. The percentage of public support for the four-year period would equal $7,100 divided by $105,000, or less than 7%, and the group would not qualify as a publicly supported public charity in 2003. Again, you can see how a large grant can hurt you if it does not qualify as an unusual grant.

g. Membership Fees as Public Support

Membership fees are considered public support as long as the member does not receive something valuable in return, such as admissions, merchandise, or the use of facilities or services. If a member does receive direct benefits in exchange for fees, the fees are not considered public support. These fees are, however, always included in the total support computation.

h. What's Not Public Support?

We've already mentioned some sources of support that are excluded because of special circumstances (they exceed the 2% limit or are paid by members in return for something of value). There are additional types of support that are never included as public support. The following types of income are not considered public support and, in some cases, are also not included in the total support figure (in which case they would drop entirely from the percentage of 1/3 or 1/10 support calculation).

(i) Unrelated Activities and Investment
Net income from activities unrelated to exempt purposes as well as "gross investment

income," which includes rents, dividends, royalties, and returns on investments, are not considered public support. Both these types of income are added to the total support figure (they stay in the denominator of your 1/3 or 1/10 support calculation).

(ii) Sales of Assets or Performing Tax-Exempt Activity

The following types of income are not considered as public support or part of total support (as with unusual grants, they drop out of both computations):

- **Gains from selling a capital asset.** Generally, capital assets are property owned by the corporation for use in its activities. Note that capital assets do not include any business inventory or resale merchandise, business accounts or notes receivable, or real property used in a trade or business. Gains from selling these noncapital asset items are characterized as "gross investment income" and are not considered public support, but are added to the total support figure.
- **Receipts from performing tax-exempt purposes.** Examples include money received from admissions to performances of a tax-exempt symphony, fees for classes given by a dance studio, and tuition, or other charges paid for attending seminars, lectures, or classes given by an exempt educational organization.

Since we're dealing with tax laws, you'd probably expect at least one complicating exception. Here it is. If your organization relies primarily on gross receipts from activities re-

lated to its exempt purposes (such as an educational nonprofit that receives most of its support from class tuition), this exempt-purpose income will *not* be considered public support. Instead it will be computed in total support (so it will decrease your percentage of support calculation by making the fraction smaller). If your group falls in this category, it will probably not be able to qualify as a publicly supported public charity and should attempt to qualify under the public charity exempt activities support test discussed in Section B4 below.

3. Attraction of Public Support Test

Groups that can't meet the 1/3 public support requirements can qualify for public charity status if they receive at least 1/10 of their total support from qualified public income sources and meet the additional "attraction of public support" requirement. Only groups trying to qualify for public charity status using the 1/10 (as opposed to 1/3) public support requirements must satisfy this attraction of public support test. The IRS considers a number of factors in determining whether a group meets the test. Only Factor 1, below, must be met; none of the other factors are required.

The IRS looks favorably on organizations that meet one or more of the attraction of public support factors listed below. Meeting as many of these factors as possible will not only help you obtain public charity status, it also shows that you satisfy the basic 501(c)(3) tax-exempt status requirements—namely, that your nonprofit is organized and operated in the public interest and has broad-based community support and participation. Finally, if you request an advance ruling to see if your organization meets the public support test, the IRS will decide whether you meet the attraction of public support requirement, regardless of whether you expect to meet the 1/3 or the 1/10 public support percentage (see "Advance and Definitive Rulings," in Section B2, above).

a. Factor 1. Continuous Solicitation of Funds Program

Your group must continually attract new public or governmental support. You will meet this requirement if you maintain a continuous program for soliciting money from the general public, community, or membership—or if you solicit support from governmental agencies, churches, schools, or hospitals that also qualify as public charities (see Section B1 above). Although this factor concerns broad-based support, the IRS allows new groups to limit initial campaigns to seeking "seed" money from a select number of the most promising agencies or people.

b. Factor 2. Percentage of Financial Support

At least 10% of your group's total support must come from the public. However, the greater the percentage of public support, the better. Remember that if your public support amounts to 1/3 or more, you do not have to meet the attraction of public support factors listed in this section.

c. Factor 3. Support From a Representative Number of People

If your group gets most of its money from government agencies or from a broad cross section of people as opposed to one particular individual or a group with a special interest in your activities, it will more likely meet the attraction of public support requirement.

d. Factor 4. Representative Governing Body

A nonprofit corporation whose governing body represents broad public interests, rather than the personal interest of a limited number of donors, is considered favorably by the IRS. The IRS is more likely to treat an organization's governing body as representative if it includes:

- public officials
- people selected by public officials
- people recognized as experts in the organization's area of operations
- community leaders or others representing a cross section of community views and interests (such as members of the clergy, teachers, and civic leaders), or
- for membership organizations, people elected under the corporate articles or bylaws by a broad-based membership.

e. Factor 5. Availability of Public Facilities or Services

If an organization continuously provides facilities or services to the general public, the IRS will consider this favorably. These facilities and services might include a museum open to the public, an orchestra that gives public performances, a group that distributes educational literature to the public, or an old-age home that provides nursing or other services to low-income members of the community.

f. Factor 6. Additional Factors

Corporations are also more likely to meet the attraction of public support requirement if:

- members of the public with special knowledge or expertise (such as public officials, or civic or community leaders) participate in or sponsor programs
- the organization maintains a program to do charitable work in the community (such as job development or low-income housing rehabilitation), or
- the organization gets a significant portion of its funds from another public charity or a governmental agency to which it is, in some way, held accountable as a condition of the grant, contract, or contribution.

g. Factor 7. Additional Factors for Membership Groups Only

A membership organization is more likely to meet the attraction of public support requirement if:

- the solicitation for dues-paying members attempts to enroll a substantial number of people in the community or area, or in a particular profession or field of special interest

- membership dues are affordable to a broad cross section of the interested public, or
- the organization's activities are likely to appeal to people with some broad common interest or purpose—such as musical activities in the case of an orchestra or different forms of dance in the case of a dance studio.

4. Exempt Activities Support Test

Don't worry if your Section 501(c)(3) group does not qualify as a public charity either automatically (Section B1) or through the 1/3 or 1/10 public support test described above (Section B2). There is another way to qualify as a public charity. The exempt activities support test is likely to meet your needs if your 501(c)(3) group intends to derive income from performing exempt-purpose activities and services (IRC § 509(a)(2)).

Although IRS publications sometimes include groups that meet the support test described in this section as "publicly supported organizations," we do not. For us, publicly supported organizations are those that qualify under the public support test described above in Section B2 of this chapter. We use the term "exempt activities support test" to describe this test.

For more detailed information on this public charity category, see IRS Publication 557, *Tax Exempt Status for Your Organization*, "509(a)(2) Organizations."

Let the IRS do the work for you. You can let the IRS do the hard part of deciding how each of the special rules described below applies to your group's anticipated sources of financial support. We show you how to check a box on the federal exemption application to do this. For now, just read through this material and you can come back to a particular section if you need to later when you fill in your IRS tax exemption application.

a.   What Type of Support Qualifies and How Much Do You Need?

To qualify under the exempt activities public charity support test, a 501(c)(3) nonprofit organization must meet two requirements:

1. The organization must normally receive more than 1/3 of its total support in each tax year as qualified public support. Qualified public support is support from any of the following sources:
   - gifts, grants, contributions, or membership fees, and
   - gross receipts from admissions, selling merchandise, performing services, or providing facilities in an activity related to the exempt purposes of the nonprofit organization.

2. The organization also must normally not receive more than 1/3 of its annual support from unrelated trades or businesses or gross investment income. Gross investment income includes rent from unrelated sources, interest, dividends, and royalties—sources of support far removed from the activities of most small nonprofit organizations. However, it does not include any taxes you pay on income from unrelated businesses or activities—these amounts are deducted before the 1/3 figure is calculated.

Again, the most important aspect of this test, and the one that makes it appropriate for many 501(c)(3) groups, is that it allows the 1/3 qualified public support amount to include the group's receipts from performing its exempt purposes. Hence, this public charity classification is appropriate for many self-sustaining nonprofits that raise income from their tax-exempt activities, such as performing arts groups, schools, and other educational-purpose organizations, and nonprofit service organizations. School tuition, admissions to concerts or plays, or payments for classes at a pottery studio count as qualified public support under this public charity test.

b.   Support Must Be From Permitted Sources

Qualified public support under this test must come from permitted sources including:
- individuals
- government agencies, and
- other 501(c)(3) public charities—generally, those that qualify as public charities under one of the tests described in Sections B1 or B2 above.

Permitted sources do not include disqualified persons—people who would be considered disqualified if the organization were classified as a private foundation. These include substantial contributors, the organization's founders, and certain related persons (for a discussion of disqualified persons, see "Who Are Disqualified Persons?" in Chapter 9, Section C).

c. Membership Fees and Dues Get Special Treatment

Dues paid to provide support for or to participate in the nonprofit organization, or in return for services or facilities provided only to members, are considered valid membership dues and can be counted in full as qualified public support. On the other hand, fees or dues paid in return for a discount on products or services provided to the public, or in return for some other monetary benefit, are not valid membership fees. However, these payments can still be counted as qualified public support if the fee entitles the member to special rates for exempt-purpose activities—in which case the payments would qualify as receipts related to the group's exempt purposes, but the payments may be subject to the 1% or $5,000 limitation discussed in Subsection d below.

EXAMPLE: People pay $50 to become members of All Thumbs, a nonprofit group dedicated to rebuilding interest in the unitar, a near-extinct one-stringed guitar-like musical instrument. All Thumbs' members are allowed $50 worth of reduced rate passes to all unitar concerts nationwide. Although these fees can't be counted as valid membership fees because they are paid in return for an equivalent monetary benefit (a $50 discount at unitar concerts), they still count as receipts related to the performance of the group's exempt purposes (putting on these concerts is an exempt purpose and activity of the group). Therefore, the fees can be counted by the organization as

qualified public support (we assume the fees paid by each individual do not exceed the 1% or $5,000 limitation that applies to exempt-purpose receipts as discussed in Subsection d, below).

Are You Selling Services or Information That the Federal Government Offers for Free?

If your nonprofit plans to sell services or information, check to see if the same service or information is readily available free (or for a nominal fee) from the federal government. If so, you may need to tell potential clients and customers of this alternate source. This rule applies to all tax-exempt nonprofits (including any 501(c)(3) organization, whether classified as a public charity or private foundation). (IRC § 6711.) Failure to comply with this disclosure requirement can result in a substantial fine. For further information on these disclosure requirements, see IRS Publication 557.

d. The 1% or $5,000 Limit for Exempt-Purpose Income

There is one major limitation on the amount of income from exempt-purpose activities that can be included in the 1/3 qualified public support figure. In any tax year, receipts from individuals or government units from the performance of exempt-purpose services that exceed $5,000 or 1% of the organization's total support for the year, whichever is greater, must be excluded from the organization's qualified public support figure. This limitation applies only to exempt-purpose receipts and not to gifts, grants, contributions, or membership fees received by the organization.

> **EXAMPLE:** Van-Go is a visual arts group that makes art available to people around the nation by toting it around in specially marked vans. In 2002, Van-Go derives $30,000 total support from the sale of paintings. The funds are receipts related to the performance of the group's exempt purposes. Any amount over $5,000 paid by any one individual cannot be included in computing its qualified public support for the year, although the full amount is included in total support. Of course, if Van-Go's total support for any year is more than $500,000, then the limitation on individual contributions will be 1% of the year's total support, since this figure exceeds $5,000.

e. Some Gifts Are Gross Receipts

When someone gives money or property without getting anything of value in return, we think of it as a gift or contribution. But when people give a nonprofit money or property in return for admissions, merchandise, services performed, or facilities furnished to the contributor, these aren't gifts. They are considered gross receipts from exempt-purpose activities and are subject to the $5,000 or 1% limitation.

> **EXAMPLE:** At its annual fundraising drive, the National Cormorant Preservation League rewards $100 contributors with a book containing color prints of cormorants. The book normally retails for $25. Only $75 of each contribution is considered a gift; the remaining $25 payments are classified as gross receipts from the performance of the group's exempt purposes and are subject to the $5,000 or 1% limitation.

f. Some Grants Are Gross Receipts

It is sometimes hard to distinguish money received as a grant from exempt-purpose gross receipts. The IRS rule is that when the granting agency gets some economic or physical benefit in return for its grant, such as a service, facility, or product, the grant is classified as gross receipts related to the exempt activities of the nonprofit organization. This means that the funds will be subject to the 1% or $5,000 limitation that applies to exempt-purpose receipts. Money contributed to benefit the public will be treated as bona fide grants by the IRS, not as exempt-purpose receipts. This type of bona fide grant is not subject to the 1% or $5,000 limitation.

> **EXAMPLE 1:** A pharmaceutical company, Amalgamated Mortar & Pestle, provides a research grant to a nonprofit scientific and medical research organization, Safer Sciences, Inc. The company specifies that the nonprofit must use the grant to develop a more reliable childproof cap for prescription drug containers (the results

of the nonprofit research will be shared with the commercial company). The money is treated as receipts received by Safer Sciences in carrying out its exempt purposes and is subject to the $5,000 or 1% limitation.

EXAMPLE 2: Safer Sciences gets a grant from the federal Centers for Disease Control to build a better petri dish for epidemiological research. Since the money is used to benefit the public, the full amount will be included in the nonprofit organization's qualified public support figure.

g. Unusual Grants Drop Out of the Percentage of Support Computation

To be included as qualified support (in the numerator of the support fraction), the support must be from permitted sources. Disqualified persons include founders, directors, or executive officers of the nonprofit. A large grant from one of these sources could undermine the ability of the nonprofit to qualify under this public charity test.

To avoid this result for nonprofits that would otherwise qualify under the exempt activities support test, "unusual grants" are ignored—that is, they drop out of both the numerator and denominator of the support calculation. (There is a similar exclusion for unusual grants under the public support test discussed in Section B2, above.) A grant will be classified as unusual if the source of the grant is not regularly relied on or actively sought out by the nonprofit as part of its sup-

port outreach program and if certain other conditions are met. If you want to learn more about these "unusual grant" requirements for groups that qualify as a public charity under the exempt-activities support test, see IRS Publication 557 (included on the CD-ROM).

h. Rents Related to Exempt Purposes Are Not Gross Investment Income

Rents received from people or groups whose activities in the rented premises are related to the group's exempt purpose are generally not considered gross investment income. This is a good thing. Why? Remember: Under this public charity test, the organization must normally not receive more than 1/3 of its total support from unrelated trades or businesses or from gross investment income.

EXAMPLE: Good Crafts, Inc., a studio that provides facilities for public education in historic crafts, rents a portion of its premises to an instructor who teaches stained glass classes. This rent would probably not fall into the gross investment income category. However, if the tenant's activities in the leased premises was not related to the nonprofit's purposes, then the rent would be included as gross investment income and, if all the unrelated and investment income of the nonprofit exceeded 1/3 of its total support, the nonprofit could lose its public charity status under the exempt activities support test.

Keep this exception in mind if your group owns or rents premises with extra space. It may be important to rent (or sublease, if you are renting, too) to another person or group whose activities are directly related to your exempt purposes. (If you're renting, be sure the terms of your lease allow you to sublease; most of the time, you'll need your landlord's permission.)

When to consult a tax expert. If you plan to supplement your support with income from activities unrelated to your exempt purposes (as more and more nonprofits must), check with your tax advisor. You'll want to make sure this additional income will not exceed 1/3 of your total support and jeopardize your ability to qualify under this public charity category.

i.   There's That Word "Normally" Again

To qualify as a public charity under the support test, groups must "normally" meet the 1/3 qualified support requirements set forth in Section 2 above. As with publicly supported organizations, this means that the IRS looks at the total amount of support over the previous four-year period to decide if the organization qualifies as a public charity for the current and the following tax year. (See Section 2c above.)

You can qualify under a definitive or advance ruling. Like the publicly supported public charities discussed earlier, the groups discussed here can qualify for public charity status under a definitive or advance ruling. For further information on advance and de-finitive rulings, see "Advance and Definitive Rulings," in Section B2 above, and Chapter 8.

C. Private Foundations

Initially, the IRS will classify your 501(c)(3) corporation as a private foundation. As we mentioned at the beginning of this chapter, almost all nonprofits will want to overcome this presumption and establish themselves as a public charity instead. Because you are probably interested in public charity status, you can skip this section or read through it quickly if you want learn about private foundations and the operating limitations and restrictions applicable to them. If you want to form a private foundation, you can use this book as an introduction to the subject, but you will probably also need the help of a nonprofit lawyer or tax specialist with experience setting up private foundations. The rules that apply to private foundations are very complicated and the penalties for not obeying the rules are stiff.

1.   Background

Broadly speaking, the reason that private foundations are subject to strict operating limitations and special taxes, while public charities are not, is to counter tax abuse schemes by wealthy individuals and families. Before the existence of private foundation restrictions, a person with a lot of money could set up his own 501(c)(3) tax-exempt organization (such as The Jonathan Smith Foundation) with a high-sounding purpose (to wipe out the potato bug in Northern Louisiana).

The potato bugs, though, were never in any danger, because the real purpose of the foundation was to hire all of Jonathan Smith's relatives and friends down to the third generation. Instead of leaving the money in a will and paying heavy estate taxes, William Smith neatly transferred money to the next generation tax free by use of a tax-exempt foundation that just happened to hire all of his relatives.

To prevent schemes such as this, Congress enacted the private foundation operating restrictions, special excise taxes, and other private foundation disincentives discussed in the next section.

2. Operating Restrictions

Private foundations must comply with operating restrictions and detailed rules, including:

- restrictions on self-dealing between private foundations and their substantial contributors and other disqualified persons
- requirements that the foundation annually distribute its net income for charitable purposes
- limitations on holdings in private businesses
- provisions that investments must not jeopardize the carrying out of the group's 501(c)(3) tax-exempt purposes, and
- provisions to assure that expenditures further the group's exempt purposes.

Violations of these provisions result in substantial excise taxes and penalties against the private foundation and, in some cases, against its managers, major contributors, and certain related persons. Keeping track of and

meeting these restrictions is unworkable for the average 501(c)(3) group, which is the main reason why you'll want to avoid being classified by the IRS as a private foundation.

To learn more about private foundation excise taxes, see IRS Publication 578, *Tax Information for Private Foundations and Foundation Managers* (included on the CD-ROM at the back of this book).

3. Limitation on Deductibility of Contributions

Generally, a donor can take personal income tax deductions for individual contributions to private foundations of up to only 30% of the donor's adjusted gross income. Donations to public charities, on the other hand, are generally deductible up to 50% of the donor's adjusted gross income.

Of course, the overwhelming number of individual contributors do not contribute an amount even close to the 30% limit, so this limitation is not very important. The real question of importance to contributors is whether you are a qualified 501(c)(3) organization so that charitable contributions to your group are tax deductible.

For more on IRS rules about deduction limitations. IRS Publication 526, Charitable Contributions, discusses the rules limiting deductions to private foundations (called 30% limit organizations) and public charities (50% limit organizations), including special rules that apply to donations of real estate, securities, and certain types of tangible personal property. 501(c)(3) organizations (both public charities and private foundations) and other qualified groups eligible to receive tax-deductible charitable contributions are listed in IRS Publication 78, Cumulative List of Organizations.

4. Special Types of Private Foundations

The IRS recognizes two special types of private foundations that have some of the advantages of public charities: private operating, and private nonoperating foundations. We mention them briefly below because they are included in IRS nonprofit tax publications and forms. Few readers will be interested in forming either of these special organizations.

a. Private Operating Foundations

To qualify as a private operating foundation, the organization generally must distribute most of its income to tax-exempt activities and must meet one of three special tests (an assets, support, or endowment test). This special type of 501(c)(3) private foundation enjoys a few benefits not granted to regular private foundations, including the following:

- **More generous deductions for donors.** As with public charities, individual donors can deduct up to 50% of adjusted gross income for contributions to the organization.
- **Extended time to distribute funds.** The organization can receive grants from a private foundation without having to distribute the funds received within one year (and these funds can be treated as "qualifying distributions" by the donating private foundation).
- **No excise tax.** The private foundation excise tax on net investment income does not apply.

All other private foundation restrictions and excise taxes apply to private operating foundations.

For additional information on the rules that apply to private operating foundations, see the file, *Public Charity or Private Foundation Status Issues under IRC §§ 509(a)(1)-(4), 4942(j)(3), and 507*, on the CD-ROM included at the back of this book. See the section titled, "IRC 4942(j)(3)—Private Operating Foundations."

b. Private Nonoperating Foundations

This special type of private foundation is one that either:

- distributes all the contributions it receives to public charities and private operating foundations (discussed just above) each year, or
- pools its contributions into a common trust fund and distributes the income and funds to public charities.

Individual contributors to private nonoperating foundations can deduct 50% of their donations. However, the organization is subject to all excise taxes and operating restrictions applicable to regular private foundations. ■

Chapter 5

Other Tax Benefits and Reporting Requirements

*I*n this chapter we discuss additional federal tax issues that affect non-profits, such as the deductibility of contributions made to 501(c)(3) nonprofits and what happens if a 501(c)(3) makes money from activities not related to its tax-exempt purposes. We also cover nonprofit tax benefits and tax and nontax requirements that apply to 501(c)(3) nonprofits under state law.

A. Federal and State Tax Deductions for Contributions

A donor (corporate or individual) can claim a personal federal income tax deduction for contributions made to a 501(c)(3) tax-exempt organization. These contributions are called "charitable contributions." Generally, states follow the federal tax deductibility rules for charitable contributions made to nonprofit corporations.

Corporations can make deductible charitable contributions of up to 10% of their annual taxable income. Individuals can deduct up to 50% of their adjusted gross income in any year for contributions made to 501(c)(3) public charities and to some types of 501(c)(3) private foundations, as explained in Chapter 4. Donations to most types of private foundations are limited to 30% of an individual's adjusted gross income in each year.

1. What Can Be Deducted

A donor can deduct the following types of contributions:

- **Cash.**
- **Property.** Generally, donors can deduct the fair market (resale) value of donated property. Technical rules apply to gifts of appreciated property (property that has increased in value) that may require donors to decrease the deduction they take for donating appreciated property—see IRS Publication 526, *Charitable Contributions*, "Giving Property That Has Increased In Value."
- **Unreimbursed car expenses.** These include the cost of gas and oil incurred by the donor while performing services for the nonprofit organization.
- **Unreimbursed travel expenses.** These include expenses incurred by the donor while away from home and performing services for the nonprofit organization, such as the cost of transportation, meals, and lodging.

2. What Cannot Be Deducted

Certain types of gifts cannot be deducted as charitable contributions. Nondeductible gifts include:

- **The value of volunteer services.** For example, if you normally are paid $40 per hour for bookkeeping work, and you volunteer ten hours of your time to a nonprofit to help them prepare their annual financial statements, you cannot claim a charitable deduction for the value of your time donated to the nonprofit (you can't claim a charitable deduction of $400).
- **The right to use property.** If you rent out office space for $1,000 per month

and allow a nonprofit to use 1/10 of the total space for a small office, you cannot claim a charitable deduction of $100 per month for letting the nonprofit use the space for free.

- **Contributions to political parties.** These contributions, however, can be taken as a tax credit, subject to dollar and percentage limitations.
- **Direct contributions to needy individuals.**
- **Tuition.** Even amounts designated as "donations," which must be paid in addition to tuition as a condition of enrollment, are not deductible.
- **Dues paid to labor unions.**
- **The cost of raffle, bingo, or lottery tickets, or other games of chance.**
- **Child care costs paid while performing services for a nonprofit organization.**

3. Donations That Can Be Partially Deducted

Contributions that a nonprofit receives in return for a service, product, or other benefit (such as membership fees paid in return for special membership incentives or promotional products, or "donations" charged for attending a performance) are only partially deductible. Donors may deduct for these only to the extent that the value of the contribution exceeds the fair market value of the service, product, or benefit received by the donor.

EXAMPLE: If a member of a 501(c)(3) organization pays a $30 membership fee and receives a record album that sells for $30, nothing is deductible. But if a $20 product is given in return for the $30 payment, $10 of the fee paid is a bona fide donation and may be deducted by the member as a charitable contribution.

501(c)(3) nonprofit groups should always clearly state the dollar amount that is deductible when receiving contributions, donations, or membership fees in return for providing a service, product, discount, or other benefit to the donor.

4. Reporting Requirements

Individuals can claim deductions for charitable contributions by itemizing the gifts on IRS Schedule A and filing this form with their annual 1040 income tax return. IRS rules require donors to obtain receipts for all charitable contributions claimed on their tax returns. Receipts must describe the contribution and show the value of any goods or services received from the nonprofit by the donor as part of the transaction. See IRS publications mentioned below for more information on how to prepare donor receipts for your organization.

Both donors and the nonprofit must do a bit more when a donation is worth more than $500. If a donor claims a deduction on Schedule A totaling more than $500 but not more than $5,000 for contributions of property, he must complete and attach Section A of Form 8283 to his income tax return. Section B of the form must be completed and submitted for any item, or group of items, with a claimed deduction on Schedule A exceeding $5,000 (the nonprofit organization completes a portion of this form). A written appraisal of the property reported on Section B must also be obtained and kept with the donor's income tax records. If the nonprofit organization sells this property within two years of the gift, it must file IRS Form 8282 and send the donor a copy of this form.

The IRS requirements for deducting and reporting charitable contributions change from year to year. For current information, see IRS Publication 526, Charitable Contributions. For information on valuing gifts, see IRS Publication 561, Determining the Value of Donated Property. For additional information, see IRS Publication 1391, Deductibility of Payments Made to Charities Conducting Fund-Raising Events.

B. Federal Estate and Gift Tax Exemptions

Gifts made as part of an individual's estate plan (through a will or trust document) can be an important source of contributions for 501(c)(3) nonprofits. When the individual dies, the 501(c)(3) organization receives the money and the money is excluded from the taxable estate of the individual.

The tax savings for the donor can be enormous, since taxable estates can be taxed at a rate as high as 55%. This maximum tax rate is scheduled to gradually decline to 45%, until the estate tax is repealed in its entirety in 2010 (see Warning icon, below). Only estates that are quite large enjoy this tax savings, however, because all estates receive an automatic tax credit that is quite significant. By

2009, the amount of the automatic tax credit for estates will be $3.5 million. Nevertheless, more and more people are realizing that their estate may be big enough to get hit with an estate tax. This is particularly true of people who own real estate in large urban centers where real estate values have kept going up. Many people are motivated, therefore, to engage in estate planning, including making charitable gifts to nonprofit organizations.

The repeal of the estate tax "sunsets" at the end of 2010. This double negative means that the estate tax repeal is temporary, unless Congress renews it or takes some other action on it. So, unless Congress votes to make the repeal permanent, the estate tax will be reinstated in 2011. Keep in touch with your tax advisor and check the IRS website at www.irs.gov for the latest changes.

Traditionally, colleges and universities and larger environmental and health organizations have actively solicited estate charitable giving by providing information to members and donors about estate planning and the benefits of charitable bequests. Increasingly, smaller nonprofits are starting to understand the game and are pursuing similar strategies in their fundraising efforts. If you understand how charitable giving affects the donor's taxes, you'll be better able to persuade potential donors to give to your cause.

An individual does not pay taxes on gifts made during his lifetime. However, gifts to an individual (who isn't the giver's spouse) or to a nonqualified organization will reduce the donor's unified estate and gift tax credit to the extent the gifts exceed $11,000 in one calendar year. For example, a $12,000 gift to a struggling writer, who will use the money to support himself while he writes the great American novel, will not be taxed to you. But the excess of $1,000 will be counted as part of your estate tax credit. On the other hand, gifts made to a 501(c)(3) nonprofit (even if they exceed $11,000) do not reduce this federal and estate gift tax credit. Tax-wise, you might be better off giving the money to a literary nonprofit that, in turn, gives grants to promising writers (unfortunately, you could not earmark the money for a particular writer, as explained in Chapter 3, Section B1).

For further information on federal and state estate and gift taxes and individual estate planning techniques, see *Plan Your Estate*, by Denis Clifford and Cora Jordan (Nolo).

C. Federal Unrelated Business Income Tax

All tax-exempt nonprofit corporations, whether private foundations or public charities, may have to pay tax on income derived from activities unrelated to their exempt pur-

poses. The first $1,000 of unrelated business income is not taxed. After that, the normal federal corporate tax rate applies: 15% on the first $50,000 of taxable corporate income; 25% on the next $25,000; and 34% on taxable income over $75,000 (with a 5% surtax on taxable income between $100,000 and $335,000). Higher corporate tax rates (35% and an interim 38% surtax) apply to corporate taxable incomes over $10 million dollars.

Be careful with unrelated income. As explained in Chapter 3, Section C1, if unrelated income is substantial, it may jeopardize the organization's 501(c)(3) tax exemption.

For past history and current developments in the federal treatment of an exempt organization's unrelated business income tax, see the disk file, *UBIT: Current Developments*, contained on the CD-ROM included at the back of this book.

1. Activities That Are Taxed

Unrelated business income comes from activities that are not directly related to a group's exempt purposes. An unrelated trade or business is one that is regularly carried on and not substantially related to a nonprofit group's exempt purposes. It is irrelevant that the organization uses the profits to conduct its exempt-purpose activities.

EXAMPLE 1: Enviro-Home Institute is a 501(c)(3) nonprofit organized to educate the public about environmentally sound home design and home construction techniques. Enviro-Home develops a model home kit that applies its ideas of appropriate environmental construction and is very successful in selling the kit. The IRS considers this unrelated business income because it is not directly related to the educational purposes of the organization.

EXAMPLE 2: A halfway house that offers room, board, therapy, and counseling to recently released prison inmates also operates a furniture shop to provide full-time employment for its residents. This is not an unrelated trade or business because the shop directly benefits the residents (even though it also produces income).

2. Activities That Are Not Taxed

A number of activities are specifically excluded from the definition of "unrelated trades or businesses." These include activities in which nearly all work is done by volunteers, and those that:

- are carried on by 501(c)(3) tax-exempt organizations primarily for the benefit of members, students, patients, officers, or employees (such as a hospital gift shop for patients or employees)
- involve the sale of mostly donated merchandise, such as thrift shops
- consist of the exchange or rental of lists of donors or members
- involve the distribution of low-cost items, such as stamps or mailing labels worth less than $5, in the course of soliciting funds, and

- involve sponsoring trade shows by 501(c)(3) groups—this exclusion extends to the exempt organization's suppliers, who may educate trade show attendees on new developments or products related to the organization's exempt activities.

Some of these exceptions have been hotly contested by commercial business interests at congressional hearings. The primary objection is that nonprofits receive an unfair advantage by being allowed to engage, tax free, in activities that compete with their for-profit counterparts. Expect more hearings and future developments in this volatile area of nonprofit tax law.

Also excluded from this tax is income not derived from services (termed "gross investment income" in the Internal Revenue Code). Remember, this tax applies to unrelated activities, not necessarily to unrelated income. Examples of nontaxable income include:

- dividends, interest, and royalties
- rent from land, buildings, furniture, and equipment (some forms of rent are taxed if the rental property was purchased or improved subject to a mortgage, or if the rental income is based on the profits earned by the tenant), and
- gains or losses from the sale or exchange of property.

See Section 512(b) of the Internal Revenue Code for the complete list of these untaxed sources of income and the exceptions that exist for certain items.

It is often difficult to predict whether the IRS will tax an activity or income as unrelated business. Furthermore, IRS regulations and rulings and U.S. Tax Court decisions contain a number of rules classifying specific activities as unrelated businesses that are subject to tax. In short, you should do more research or consult a tax specialist if you plan to engage in activities or derive income from sources not directly related to your exempt purposes. Please note, this isn't the same thing as saying you shouldn't engage in an unrelated activity—many nonprofits must engage in commercial businesses unrelated to their exempt purposes to survive. But to avoid jeopardizing your 501(c)(3) tax-exempt status and to understand the tax effects of engaging in unrelated business, you simply need good tax advice.

D. State Corporate Income Tax Exemptions

Most states have a corporate income tax, but nonprofit groups are eligible to apply for an exemption in all cases. Fortunately, in the overwhelming majority of states, there is little or nothing to do, as state authorities will rely on your federal 501(c)(3) exemption determination as proof that you are also entitled to a state corporate income tax exemption.

In about half the states, a nonprofit corporation that has received its federal exemption is automatically exempt from state corporate income taxes. A few states exempt nonprofits if they file nonprofit articles with the secretary of state (obtaining a federal tax exemption is not necessary to obtain the state tax exemption).

Approximately one-third of the states require you to notify the department of revenue or complete a separate exemption application, but their decision is based on the federal determination. Finally, only a handful of states make an independent evaluation of nonprofit purposes, activities, and financial statements to determine whether to grant an exemption.

The State Sheets show the method your state uses to grant a corporate income tax exemption to nonprofit organizations.

Generally, a corporation that has filed for its federal tax exemption need not pay state corporate income taxes prior to receiving a federal determination, which can take a few months or more in special cases. If the federal application is denied—and the state exemption determination is based upon obtaining the federal exemption—the corporation may have to pay the state income taxes it would have paid as a for-profit corporation while the application was pending.

Even if your organization receives a state tax exemption, it may still be required to file an informational tax return yearly. For forms and information about exemption requirements, contact the tax agency listed on your State Sheet. It may take considerable patience and persistence to get all the tax information you need—some states' exempt organization tax units are small and understaffed.

Also keep in mind that just as at the federal level, there are state taxes on unrelated business income generated by a regular activity that has nothing to do with your exempt purposes. If you will have unrelated business income, you might wish to see a tax accountant in your state to be certain about your state corporate tax liabilities and necessary state filings.

Don't forget about state unrelated business income taxes. Like the IRS, each state with a corporate income tax scheme normally will assess regular state corporate income tax on income earned by a nonprofit within the state from activities that are unrelated to the nonprofit's tax-exempt purposes. Your state tax office can provide the specific details of your state's unrelated business income tax—see your State Sheet in Appendix B for the website address of your state's tax office.

E. Other State Taxes

Each state imposes additional taxes that may apply to your nonprofit activities and operations. In many cases, your tax-exempt 501(c)(3) can apply for an exemption from one or more of these additional taxes.

Most states have enacted a sales tax. Some states exempt nonprofits from payment when purchasing goods. Only a few exempt nonprofits from collecting sales tax when selling goods, and then only under restricted circumstances, such as fundraising events—bake sales, crafts fairs, benefit dinners, or performances, for example—that take place occasionally during the year.

In addition, a nonprofit corporation may be eligible to apply for exemption from state and local use, excise, and property taxes, hotel and meal taxes, and business license fees.

The materials you receive from the secretary of state should include a listing of state tax agencies. Contact these agencies to learn more about your tax responsibilities—and exemption possibilities.

Some States Require an Advance Tax Payment

In a small number of states, incorporators must make a franchise tax, trust fund, or other advance payment when filing nonprofit articles of incorporation with the secretary of state. Check with your state tax agency by going to its online website, listed in the State Sheets in Appendix B.

F. State Solicitation Regulations

Fundraising is a way of life for most nonprofit organizations, which must depend either on public or private grants, or on contributions solicited from the general public, for all operating funds. This activity—solicitation of contributions from the general public by a 501(c)(3) public charity—is regulated by most states.

Generally, state regulation of charitable solicitations is meant to serve two purposes:

- to curb fundraising abuses by monitoring the people involved and their activities, and
- to give the public access to information on how much an organization spends to raise whatever ultimately goes into funding its charitable, educational, religious, or other nonprofit purposes.

A majority of states require groups that solicit within the state to register, usually with the attorney general. Most of these states also require the registration of paid fundraisers and solicitors, both the people who administer the programs and those who go door-to-door or use the telephone or other media to solicit money. A registration fee, a bond, or both may also be required for solicitors, ranging from as little as $15 to $800 or more.

The U.S. Supreme Court has decided several cases affecting how much information solicitors must disclose about their methods of solicitation and what happens to the money they collect. At present, states may require professional solicitors to tell prospective donors where to check for financial information on their campaigns, including what percentage of the money collected actually goes to charity, but fundraisers needn't submit scripts of their pitches to the state for review.

In addition to solicitor regulation, many states have detailed contribution reporting requirements, and demand information on the amount spent (on paid solicitors, advertising and promotion, mailings, and so on) to raise the total amount solicited. The organization may have to be supply this information either annually or for each individual fundraising campaign.

While large scale fundraising operations—those that use telemarketing and massive direct mail solicitation—are the targets of these regulations, all organizations must comply with these rules. Find out what your obligations are by checking with your city government. At the state level, the attorney general's office is usually in charge of solicitation registration; if not, find out from your secretary of state what registration and reporting requirements, if any, you must meet.

Regulation of charitable solicitation is currently an active area of both legislation and litigation. At the federal level, Congress has proposed putting multistate nonprofit fundraising activities under Federal Trade Commission (FTC) regulation, and thereby under federal court jurisdiction; single-state efforts would remain under state and local jurisdiction. Many state legislatures have also enacted laws or tightened existing ones regulating charitable solicitation.

Exceptions to State Solicitation Regulations

Typically, grants, unrestricted gifts, bona fide membership fees, and payments for goods and services not received in connection with a solicitation are exempted from state solicitation rules and regulations.

G. State Nonprofit Corporate Report Requirements

Nonprofit corporations in most states must periodically file reports with the secretary of state, in effect reregistering their existence. Generally this is an annual report, but in a few states a report is required less frequently.

The State Sheet lists the corporate report requirements for each state. You can find these sheets in Appendix B.

The contents of the state corporate report—generally submitted on a form supplied by the secretary of state—vary. Most states want only a simple recital of minimal information to confirm that a corporation is still operating, under the same name, at the same address, and for the purposes stated in its articles of incorporation. Sometimes the names and addresses of directors and/or officers must be included, and the report must be signed by one of these people. Many states also collect a filing fee with the annual report.

A few states, however, require more detailed financial and other information, such as:

- a disclosure of salaries, loans, guarantees, and other payments or benefits made to or conferred on directors and officers

- the amount of money invested in real or personal property in the state, or

- a complete financial statement listing all assets and liabilities, revenues and receipts, and expenses and disbursements (except for the smallest nonprofits; your accountant or treasurer should prepare a balance sheet and income statement at least annually).

Each state has its own filing date or period; you can get this information from your secretary of state. Although completing the corporate report is a mere formality in most states, requiring the submission of very little information, compliance is important. Failing to file may, in some cases, result in the imposition of a fine and the suspension of corporate powers by the secretary of state. ■

Part II

Incorporating Your Nonprofit

Chapter 6

Choose a Name and File Your Articles of Incorporation

This chapter shows you how to form your nonprofit corporation in a sequence of small, manageable steps. Fortunately, most incorporation steps are relatively easy and straightforward. For the most part, you will fill in blanks on standard incorporation forms based on information you already have at your fingertips. Take your time and relax—you'll be surprised at how easy it all is when you follow our instructions one step at a time.

Forming your corporation will be the first step you take to obtain nonprofit status. Your corporation must be in existence when you apply for your state and federal tax exemptions. We recommend, however, that before you file your articles, you read through and prepare some of the other documents required later in the process, such as your bylaws and tax exemption applications. That way you'll know what is required to complete the process before you form your corporation. (See discussion in Section H1, below).

Because the content and format of certain corporate documents differ from state to state, it's essential that you contact your secretary of state or other corporate official to obtain official incorporation forms and information. We show you how to do this. To help you complete your incorporation forms as required by your state's nonprofit corporation law, we list the incorporation form requirements for each state in the State Sheets included in Appendix B (referred to as the State Sheets throughout this book). In addition, we provide sample clauses, forms, and information designed to show you how to use this state-specific information to prepare your nonprofit incorporation forms.

As you begin the process of forming your corporation, we suggest that you use the tear-out Incorporation Checklist in Appendix D (or, access the checklist file on the CD-ROM) to chart your way through the incorporation steps in Chapters 6 through 10. This will help you keep track of where you are and can greatly simplify the incorporation process for you.

Nonprofit Nomenclature

Different states use different words in their nonprofit statutes, regulations, and bureaucracies. We have tried to use the most common terms to describe nonprofit forms, procedures, and officials. For example, we refer to the charter document used to form the nonprofit corporation as the articles of incorporation. In some states, this document is given another name such as the certificate of incorporation. Similarly, we refer to the office that handles corporate filings as the secretary of state's office—this is the official designation used in most states for this function. Just keep in mind that your state may occasionally use different corporate terminology than we use in the text.

A. Order Materials From Your Secretary of State

To get started, contact your secretary of state to obtain nonprofit incorporation information and materials.

Many states supply materials such as:

- a nonprofit articles of incorporation form with instructions for filling it in, and
- nonprofit corporation statutes that contain the technical requirements for organizing and operating a nonprofit corporation in your state. You may need to refer to these statutes when completing your articles of incorporation and corporate bylaws. Some states don't supply the statutes free, but tell you how to obtain them for a fee. The fee, if charged, is usually modest and worth paying to have this valuable reference material on hand.

Where to find your state's nonprofit laws. In most states, the nonprofit laws are contained in a separate nonprofit statute or act. In a few states, the nonprofit laws are mixed in with, and can be obtained as part of, the state's regular business corporation act or law.

- a fee schedule showing current charges for filing, copying, and certifying various corporate forms
- forms and instructions to check corporate name availability and reserve a corporate name, and
- forms and instructions for post-incorporation procedures. These may include materials to amend articles, change the corporation's registered office or registered agent, or register an assumed corporate name (one which is different from the corporate name shown in the incorporation papers).

To Order Your Nonprofit Material

Check your state's website (using the URL (address) in the State Sheets). The site probably has everything you need online.

You may prefer to call your secretary of state instead. If so, the phone number of the corporations division or similar office in your state is listed on your State Sheet.

In Appendix D and on the CD-ROM, we provide an incorporation contact letter that you can use to request specific information on forming a nonprofit corporation in your state. The secretary of state information on your State Sheet lists the name and address of the corporate filings office in your state. Complete the letter by typing the name of your corporate filings office in the salutation of the letter. Then type your name, address, and telephone number in the box at the bottom. Enclose a stamped, self-addressed envelope, and mail the letter to your corporate filing office.

B. Choose a Corporate Name

Your first step in forming your corporation is to choose a name that you like and one that also meets the requirements of state law. The state corporate filing office (typically the secretary of state) will approve your corporate name when you file your articles of incorporation. As explained more below, you can check name availability and reserve a corporate name before you file your articles.

Keeping or Changing Your Name

If you are incorporating an existing organization, you may want to use your current name as your corporate name, particularly if it has become associated with your group, its activities, fundraising efforts, products, or services. Many new corporations do this by simply adding "Inc." to their old name (for example, The World Betterment Fund decides to incorporate as The World Betterment Fund, Inc.). Using your old name is not required, however. If you have been thinking about a new name for your organization, this is your chance to change it.

---

1. The Importance of Your Corporate Name

As a practical matter, your corporate name is one of your most important assets. It represents the goodwill of your organization. We don't use the term "goodwill" here in any legal, accounting, or tax sense; rather, your name is significant because people in the community, grant agencies, other nonprofits, and those with whom you do business will identify your nonprofit primarily by its name.

For this reason, as well as to avoid having to print new stationery, change promotional literature, or create new logos, you should pick a name you'll be happy with for a long time.

2. Corporate Name Legal Requirements

Let's look at the basic legal name requirements for nonprofit corporations applicable in most states.

a. Your Name Must Be Unique

Your proposed corporate name (the name stated in your articles of incorporation) must not be the same as, or confusingly similar to, a name already on file with the secretary of state.

The list of names maintained by the secretaries of state includes:

- existing corporations formed in your state
- out-of-state corporations qualified to do business in your state
- names reserved for use by individuals planning to incorporate in your state (name reservation periods vary from 30 to 120 days and often can be renewed at least once)
- names registered in your state by out-of-state corporations, and
- in some states, names registered as trademarks or service marks and those registered as assumed corporate names (we discuss these special types of business names below).

In deciding whether a corporate name is too similar to one already on file, the secretary's office will usually only look at similarities between the names themselves, not at similarities in the types and locations of the businesses using the names. If you attempt to form a corporation with a name that is similar in sound or wording to the name of another corporation on the corporate name list, the secretary's office may reject your name and return your articles of incorporation to you.

> **EXAMPLE:** Your proposed corporate name is Open Spaces Society, Inc. If another corporation has filed the name Open Spaces International, Inc., with the secretary of state, your name will probably be rejected as too similar.

b. Corporate Designator Requirements

In many states, your corporate name must include a corporate designator, such as Incorporated, Corporation, Company, Limited, or one of their abbreviations.

Although corporate designators are typically included at the end of a corporate name (The Foundation for Health, Incorporated), the designator may generally be placed anywhere in your corporate name (The Incorporated Healthcare Foundation).

See the corporate name section of your State Sheet shown in Appendix B to determine whether your state requires a corporate designator in your name.

c. Prohibited Names

The statutes of various states forbid the use of specific words in the name of a nonprofit corporation. Mostly, prohibited names are those associated with specialized business, nonprofit, professional or governmental entities, or corporations. Try to avoid names from each of these categories—here are several examples of specialized corporate names whose use is limited by state laws:

Accounting	Insurance
Attorney	Physician
Banking	Reserve
Cooperative	Trust
Engineering	United States
Federal	

Of course, if you are forming a specialized nonprofit corporation, such as a consumers' or producers' cooperative or a nonprofit organization named "Solar Engineering Data Sciences" that collects research on solar engineering, you may be entitled to use one of these special words in your corporate name.

d. Using Two Names and Changing Your Name

If you want to adopt a formal corporate name in your articles that's different than the one you have used (or plan to use) to identify your nonprofit organization, you can do so. You'll need to file a fictitious business name statement (also known as an assumed business name statement or a dba statement in some states) with the local county clerk.

You can also change your corporate name after you've filed your articles. After making sure that the new name is available for use (as explained further below), you can amend your articles and file the amendment with the secretary of state.

⚠ **Having your name approved by the corporate filing office when you file your articles of incorporation does not guarantee that you will have the absolute legal right to use that name.** As explained in more detail in Section E, below, another organization or business may already be using the name as its business name or may be using it as a trademark or service mark. If someone else is using the name, they may be able to prevent you from using it, depending on their location, type of business, and other circumstances. We show you how to do some checking on your own to be relatively sure that no one else has a prior claim to your proposed corporate name based on trademark or service mark.

3. Practical Suggestions When Selecting a Name

Now that we've looked at the basic legal requirements related to your choice of a corporate name, here are some practical suggestions to help you do it.

a. Use Common Nonprofit Terms in Your Name

There are a number of words that broadly suggest 501(c)(3) nonprofit purposes or activities. Choosing one of these names can simplify the task of finding the right name for your organization and will alert others to the nonprofit nature of your corporate activities. Here are just a few:

Aid	Human
American	Humane
Appreciation	Institute
Assistance	International
Association	Learning
Benefit	Literary
Betterment	Mission
Care	Music
Center	Orchestra
Charitable	Organization
Coalition	Philanthropic
Community	Philharmonic
Congress	Program
Conservation	Project
Consortium	Protection
Council	Public
Cultural	Refuge
Education	Relief
Educational	Religious
Environmental	Research
Exchange	Resource
Fellowship	Scholarship
Foundation	Scientific
Friends	Service
Fund	Shelter
Health	Social
Help	Society
Heritage	Study
Home	Troupe
Hope	Voluntary
Hospice	Welfare
Hospital	

b. Names to Avoid

When selecting a corporate name, we suggest you avoid, or use with caution, the types of words described and listed below. Of course, there are exceptions. If one of these words relates to your particular nonprofit purposes or activities, it may make sense to use the word in your name.

Avoid words that, taken together, signify a profit-making business or venture, such as Booksellers Corporation, Jeff Baxter & Company, Commercial Products Inc., or Entrepreneurial Services Corp.

Avoid words that describe or are related to special types of nonprofit organizations (those that are tax exempt under provisions of the IRC other than Section 501(c)(3)), such as Business League, Chamber of Commerce, Civic League, Hobby, Recreational or Social Club, Labor, Agricultural or Horticultural Organization, Political Action Organization, Real Estate Board, or Trade Group.

For a complete listing of these special tax-exempt nonprofit groups and a brief description of each group, see "Special Nonprofit Tax-Exempt Organizations," in Appendix D.

EXAMPLE: The name Westbrook Social Club, Inc., would clearly identify a social club, tax exempt under IRC § 501(c)(7). For this reason, you shouldn't use this type of name for your 501(c)(3) nonprofit. However, The Social Consciousness Society might be an appropriate name for a 501(c)(3) educational-purpose organization. Also, although The Trade Betterment League of Pottersville would identify a 501(c)(6) business league and The Millbrae Civic Betterment League a 501(c)(4) civic league, The Philanthropic League of Castlemont might be a suitable name for a 501(c)(3) charitable giving group.

Avoid words or abbreviations associated with nationally known nonprofit causes, organizations, programs, or trademarks. You can bet that the well-known group has taken steps to protect its name as a trademark or service mark. Steer clear of the names in "These Names Are Already Taken," below.

These Names Are Already Taken

Here is a small sampling of some well-known—and off-limits—nonprofit names and abbreviations:

AAA

American Red Cross

American Ballet Theatre or ABT

American Conservatory Theatre or ACT

Audubon

Blue Cross

Blue Shield

Environmental Defense Fund

National Geographic

National Public Radio or NPR

Sierra Club

Public Broadcasting System or PBS

Avoid words with special symbols or punctuation that might confuse the secretary of state's computer name-search software, such as: @ # $ % ^ & * () + ? and > or <.

c. Pick a Descriptive Name

It's often a good idea to pick a name that clearly reflects your purposes or activities (for example, Downtown Ballet Theater, Inc.; Good Health Society, Ltd.; Endangered Fish

Protection League, Inc.). Doing this allows potential members, donors, beneficiaries, and others to easily locate and identify you. More fanciful names (The Wave Project, Inc., Serendipity Unlimited Inc.) are usually less advisable because it might take a while for people to figure out what they stand for, although occasionally their uniqueness can provide better identification over the long term.

> EXAMPLE: Although the name Northern Counties Feline Shelter, Inc., will alert people at the start to the charitable purposes of the nonprofit group, Cats' Cradle, Inc., may stay with people longer once they are familiar with the activities of the organization.

d. Limit Your Name Geographically or Regionally

If you use general or descriptive terms in your name, you may need to further qualify it by geographic or regional descriptions to avoid conflicts or public confusion.

> EXAMPLE 1: Your proposed name is The Philharmonic Society, Inc. Your secretary of state rejects this name as too close to a number of philharmonic orchestras on file. You refile using the proposed name, The Philharmonic Society of East Creek, and your name is accepted.

> EXAMPLE 2: Suppose you are incorporating the AIDS Support Group, Inc. Even if this name does not conflict with the name of another corporation on file in your

state, it is an excellent idea to limit or qualify the name to avoid confusion by the public with other groups in other parts of the country that share the same purposes or goals. You could do this by changing the name to the AIDS Support Group of Middleville.

e. Choose a New Name Instead of Trying to Distinguish Yourself

Instead of trying to distinguish your proposed name from another established group by using a regional or other identifier, it's usually better to choose a new and different name if the public is still likely to confuse your group with the other group.

> EXAMPLE: Your proposed nonprofit name is The Park School, Inc. If another corporation (specializing in a nationwide network of apprentice training colleges) is already listed with the name Park Training Schools, your secretary of state may reject your name as too similar.

You may be able to limit your name and make it acceptable (The Park Street School of Westmont, Inc.) but this may not be a good idea for two reasons: First, members of the public who have heard of the Park Training Schools might think that your school is simply a Westmont affiliate of the national training program. Second, you might still be infringing the trademark rights of the national group (they may have registered their name as a state or federal trademark).

C. Check Name Availability

The secretary of state will reject your articles of incorporation if the name you've chosen for your corporation is not available. Any name already being used by another corporation on file with the secretary of state's office is considered unavailable. To avoid having your articles rejected, it's often wise to check if the name you want is available before you try to file your articles.

1. Check Online or by Phone

In many states, you can check corporate name availability online by going to the state filing office website listed in your State Sheet in Appendix B, or you can call the main number of the corporate filings office listed on your State Sheet and ask to speak to someone in the corporate name availability section.

If your proposed corporate name is not the same as or similar to an existing name listed online, you may decide it's safe to go ahead and file your articles without formally checking name availability or reserving your name with the secretary of state. If you discover a match to your proposed name, and the corporation is still active (the name search tells you whether the corporation is active or not), you need to look for another name. If you discover a similar corporate name, the secretary of state may find that it is too similar to your proposed name to let you use it. The only way to tell whether the secretary of state will allow you to use a name that is similar to an existing corporate name is to do a formal name availability check or try to re-

serve the name (see Section E, below). If the secretary of state reports that the name is not available or won't reserve it for your use, you know the name was too similar to the existing corporation's name.

2. Check by Mail

A few states will not advise you of the availability of a proposed corporate name over the phone—your secretary of state website should indicate if you live in one of these states. If you do, you can usually check by mail, although there may be a small charge for checking each name. To request a corporate name check by mail, you can send a letter to your secretary of state. Check your secretary of state's website to see if a name availability inquiry letter is available to fill in online, print, and mail in. Shown below is a sample letter with special instructions keyed to the circled numbers.

Name Availability Letter

Date:_____

(Name and address of Secretary of State office from your

State Sheet in Appendix B)

_____

_____

Re: Corporate Name Availability

Please advise if the following proposed corporate names, listed in order of preference, are available for corporate use:

(first choice for corporate name) ❶_____

(second choice for corporate name)_____

(third choice for corporate name)_____

(fourth choice for corporate name)_____

Enclosed is a stamped, self-addressed envelope for your reply. My name, address, and phone number are included below if you wish to contact me regarding this request.

[I enclose a check for $_____ in payment of the fee for checking the availability of the above names.]❷

Name: _____

Address: _____

Phone: _____

Thank you for your assistance.

_____(your signature)_____

Special Instructions

❶ Your secretary of state website will indicate whether you can check the availability of more than one name. If so, list your proposed names in order of preference here.

❷ If there is a fee for checking the availability of one or more names by mail, type and complete this bracketed sentence on the tear-out letter.

The CD-ROM includes a copy of the Name Availability Letter form and a blank, tear-out copy is in Appendix D.

Don't use an LLC name for your corporation. Even though the corporate filing office may let you use a corporate name that conflicts with an LLC name, we advise against doing this. To avoid legal disputes, it's best to stay clear of any business name (whether a corporate, LLC, or unincorporated business name) that is the same as or similar to your proposed corporate name. The fact that an LLC name has a different ending than your corporate name (for example, "Racafrax, LLC" and you want to use "Racafrax" as your corporate name) does not mean you will be allowed to use your proposed name. If the names are substantially similar, a court may stop you from using your proposed name, even if you use it for a corporation and the competing business name is used by an LLC.

Check your state's accepted payment methods. A few secretaries of state require payment by money order or certified check only. Check your state website to see if there are special payment requirements in your state.

Do You Want to Bypass Name Checking Procedures?

Even if your proposed corporate name is available when you check with the secretary of state, this does not guarantee that your name will be available when you later file your articles of incorporation. For this reason, you may wish to dispense with a written name availability check and attempt to reserve your corporate name, as explained below, or file your articles and hope that your name is available for use.

Filing your articles without preliminary name checking or reservation makes sense if your state offers an expedited (24-hour) filing procedure for a small additional fee—you'll know in a day or two if your proposed name is available and if your articles were filed. Of course, if your state allows you to check a proposed corporate name over the phone, we suggest you take the time to do this in all cases.

D. What to Do When There's a Name Conflict

If using your proposed name is crucial to you and the secretary of state's office tells you that it is too similar to an existing corporate name already on file, there are a few things you can do, explained below.

1. Appeal the Decision

You can ask the corporate filing office's legal counsel to review the staff's determination regarding your name's acceptability. This will involve filing a written request, and you may decide to seek the help of a lawyer. Here's why: The legal question of whether or not a name is so close to another name so as to cause confusion to the public is a difficult one, and involves looking at a number of criteria contained in court decisions. Factors such as the nature of each trade name user's business (the term "trade name" simply means a name used in conjunction with the operation of a trade or business), the geographical proximity of the two businesses, and other factors work together in ways that are difficult to predict. We cover trade name issues in more detail below but, for now, we simply note that if you do get into this sort of debate, you will probably want to see a lawyer who is versed in the complexities of trade name or trademark law or do some additional reading on your own.

2. Get Permission

An obvious resolution would be to obtain the written consent of the other corporation. Sometimes, profit corporations that have registered a name similar to the proposed name of a nonprofit corporation will be willing to allow the nonprofit corporation to use the similar name. We think this is too much trouble. Besides, most businesses jealously guard their name, and it is unlikely any business or organization will let you ride on the coattails of their existing name. If you are told your proposed corporate name is too similar to another name, we recommend you move on and choose another name that is available for your use.

3. Pick Another Name

You may decide that it's simpler (and less trouble all the way around) to pick another name for your nonprofit corporation. We usually recommend this approach.

⚠️ **A name check is just a preliminary indication of the availability of your proposed corporate name.** Don't order your stationery, cards, or office signs, until the secretary of state has formally accepted your name by approving a Reservation of Corporate Name or filing your articles of incorporation.

E. Reserve Your Corporate Name

Most states allow you to reserve an available corporate name with the secretary of state. During the reservation period, only you may file articles with this name or a similar name. The reservation period and the fees vary. In many states, you can renew your reservation if you don't get around to filing your articles during the first reservation period.

Once you have decided on a corporate name and established its availability, it makes sense to reserve it if you will not be filing your articles immediately, because:

- available corporate names are becoming hard to find, particularly in states with a lot of corporate filing activity, and

- reserving a name allows you to hold on to it while you complete your initial paperwork.

To reserve a corporate name, follow the instructions on your secretary of state website—most states provide an online Reservation of Name form, which you can download.

If you have no information, call the corporations filings office of your secretary of state listed on your State Sheet and ask for instructions. If the secretary does not provide a form, you can use the reservation of corporate name letter shown below.

Application for Reservation of Corporate Name

Date:_____

(Name and address of secretary of state office from your

_State Sheet in Appendix B)_____

_____

_____

Re: Corporate Name Reservation

Please reserve the following corporate name for my use for the allowable period specified under the state's corporation statutes.

_(your proposed corporate name)_____

I enclose the required payment of $_____fee_____. My name, address, and phone number are included below if you wish to contact me regarding this request.

Name: _____

Address: _____

Phone: _____

Thank you for your assistance.

_(your signature)_____

The CD-ROM includes a copy of the Application for Reservation of Corporate Name form and Appendix D includes a blank, tear-out copy.

The person that signs the letter must also sign the articles. Make sure that the person signing this reservation letter will be available to sign articles of incorporation on behalf of your organization—the corporate name is reserved for this person's use only.

Reservation fees are subject to change. To be sure the fee amounts are correct, call your secretary of state's office or check current fee information at your state's website.

F. Perform a Name Search

Approval by the secretary of state's office doesn't necessarily mean that you have the legal right to use a name; it simply means that your name does not conflict with that of another corporation already on file with the secretary of state and that you are presumed to have the legal right to use it within your state. Another organization (corporate or noncorporate, profit or nonprofit) may, in fact, already have the legal right to use this same name as a federal or state trademark or service mark used to identify their goods or services. Most secretaries of state do not even check their own state trademark/service mark registration lists to see if your proposed corporate name is available; none check the federal trademark register. Also, another organization may already be presumed to have the

legal right to the name in a particular county if they are using it as a tradename (as the name of their business or organization) and have filed an assumed (or fictitious) business name statement with their county clerk. The secretaries of state of many states do not register or check assumed names, even assumed corporate names—this is most often done at the county level.

1. Who Needs to Do a Name Search

In many circumstances, you will know that your name is unique and unlikely to infringe on another organization's name. This would probably be the case, for example, if you called your group the Sumner County Crisis Hotline, or the Southern Wisconsin Medieval Music Society. By qualifying your name this way, you know that you are the only nonprofit in your area using the name. However, in some circumstances you may be less sure of your right to use a name. For example, the names Legal Rights for All or The Society to Cure Lyme Disease may be in use by a group in any part of the country.

2. Who Gets to Use a Name

The basic rule is that the ultimate right to use a particular name will usually be decided based on who was first in time to actually use the name in connection with a particular trade, business, activity, service, or product. In deciding who has the right to a name, the similarity of the types of businesses or organizations and their geographical proximity are usually taken into account.

3. Do Your Own Search

Below we list self-help name checking procedures you may want to use to be more certain that your proposed corporate name is unique. Do these name search procedures before you file your articles. Obviously, you can't be 100% certain—you can't possibly check all names in use by all other groups. However, you can check obvious sources likely to expose names similar to the one you wish to use. Here are some places to start.

- **State and county assumed business name files:** Your secretary of state website should indicate whether assumed (or fictitious) corporate names (different from the name a corporation uses in its articles) are registered with your secretary of state's office, at the county level, or both. If they are registered at the state level, call the assumed name section at the secretary of state's office and ask whether your proposed corporate name is the same as or similar to a registered assumed (or fictitious) corporate name. Also, call your local county clerk's office to ask how you can check assumed business name filings—in most states, noncorporate assumed or fictitious business name statements, or "doing business as" (dba) statements, are filed with the county clerk's office. In most cases, you will have to go in and check the assumed business name files in person—it takes just a few minutes to do this.
- **State trademarks and service marks:** Call the trademark section of your secretary

of state's office and ask if your proposed corporate name is the same as or similar to trademarks and service marks registered with the state (some offices may ask for a written request and a small fee before performing this search).

- **Directories:** Check major metropolitan phone book listings, nonprofit directories, business and trade directories, and other directories to see if another company or group is using a name similar to your proposed corporate name. Large public libraries keep phone directories for many major cities throughout the country, as well as trade and nonprofit directories. A local nonprofit resource center or business branch of a public library may have a special collection of nonprofit research materials—check these first for listings of local and national nonprofits. One commonly consulted national directory of nonprofit names is the *Encyclopedia of Associations* published by Gale Research Company.
- **The Federal Trademark Register:** If your name is the type that might be used to market a service or product or to identify a business activity of your nonprofit corporation, you should check federal trademarks and service marks. You can check the Federal Trademark Register for free at www.uspto.gov. You can also go to a large public library or special business and government library in your area that carries the *Federal Trademark Register*, which lists trademark and service mark names

broken into categories of goods and services.

- **Internet databases:** Most of the business name listings mentioned above, including Yellow Page listings, business directory databases, and the federal and state trademark registers, are available as part of several commercial computer databases. For example, the federal and state registers can be accessed through the TrademarkScan® service (go to http://library.dialog.com /bluesheets/html/bl0226.html for subscription information). Subscription databases charge fees for your research time (unlike the www.uspto.gov site which is free).

4. Outside Help

Of course, if you wish to go farther in your name search, you can pay a private records search company to check various databases and name listings. Alternatively, or in conjunction with your own efforts or search procedures, you can pay a trademark lawyer to oversee or undertake these searches for you (or to render a legal opinion if your search turns up a similar name). Most organizers of smaller nonprofits, particularly those who believe that a specialized or locally based name is not likely to conflict with anyone else's name, will not feel the need to do this and will be content to undertake the more modest self-help search procedures mentioned above.

5. The Consequences of Using Another's Name

To avoid problems, we suggest using the name selection techniques discussed in Section B, above, and performing the kind of commonsense checking described earlier. Disputes involving trade names, trademarks, and service marks tend to arise in the private, commercial sector. It is unlikely that your nonprofit will wish to market products and services as aggressively as a regular commercial concern and thereby run afoul of another business's trademark or service mark (you'd also be jeopardizing your tax-exempt status by engaging in a substantial amount of commercial activity). Nonetheless, as a matter of common sense, and to avoid legal disputes later on, you should do your best to avoid names already in use by other profit and nonprofit organizations, or in use as trademarks or service marks.

Legal remedies for violation of trade name or trademark rights vary under federal and state laws and court decisions. Most of the time, the business with the prior claim to the name can sue to enjoin (stop) you from using your name or can force you to change it. The court may also award the prior owner money damages for loss of sales or goodwill caused by your use of the name. If you violate a trademark or service mark registered with the U.S. Patent and Trademark Office, the court may award treble damages (three times the actual money damages suffered as a result of the infringement), any profits you make from using the name, and court costs; and may order that the goods with the offending labels or marks to be confiscated and destroyed.

EXAMPLE: A company called Foul Weather Gearheads has been in business for ten years selling foul weather gear such as rain slicks and hip boots via catalogues and the Internet. For the first seven to eight years, Foul Weather averaged gross annual sales of approximately $2 million. Another company, calling itself Rainy Day Gearheads, starts selling competing products and Foul Weather's gross revenues slip by about 25% over the next two years. If Foul Weather can prove that the Rainy Day Gearheads trademark likely caused customer confusion which resulted in Foul Weather's decrease in sales, Foul Weather can recover its lost profits. Or, if prior to the infringement, Foul Weather had registered its name on the Principal Trademark Register maintained by the U.S. Patent and Trademark Office, it could choose to go after Rainy Day's profits (instead of recovering its own losses), attorneys' fees, and treble damages.

For further information, see *Patent, Copyright & Trademark—An Intellectual Property Desk Reference*, by Stephen Elias and Richard Stim (Nolo).

G. Protect Your Name

Once you have filed your articles of incorporation, you may want to take some additional steps to protect your name against later users. For example, if your name is also used to identify your products or services, you may wish to register it with your state of incorporation and the United States Patent and Trademark Office as a trademark or service mark. You may also want to register in other states if you plan to conduct operations there.

Federal registration costs $200. You can register your name if:

- you have actually used the name in interstate commerce (that is, in two or more states) in connection with the marketing of goods or services, or
- you intend to use the name in interstate commerce in connection with the marketing of goods or services.

If you specify the second ground in your trademark application, you must file an affidavit (sworn statement) within six months stating that the name has been placed in actual use—and pay an additional $100. This six-month period may be extended for additional six-month periods (at a fee of $100 for each extension), up to a total extension of two and one-half years. To obtain these extensions, you have to convince the Patent and Trademark Office that you have good cause for delaying your use of the name. Because trademark application procedures are relatively simple and inexpensive, you may wish to tackle this task yourself—your local county law library should have practice guides available to help you handle state and federal trademark and service mark filing formalities.

Applying for a Federal Trademark

To apply for a federal trademark, go to the website of the Patent and Trademark Office (PTO) at www.uspto.gov and download a trademark application. Fill out the form following the instructions. A month or so after mailing the form, you should hear from the PTO. If there are any problems, you will receive a written list of questions together with the telephone number of a trademark examiner. The examiner should be able to address any questions and issues you can't handle yourself and should help you finalize your application without undue difficulty or delay.

H. Prepare Your Articles of Incorporation

The next step in organizing your nonprofit corporation is to prepare articles of incorporation. This is your primary incorporation document—your corporation comes into existence on the date you file your articles with your secretary of state. You must complete this step before you send in your federal tax exemption application because the IRS requires a filed copy of your articles with your tax exemption application.

1. Check Your Materials

Most secretaries of state provide sample or ready-to-use forms for articles of incorporation that meet the statutory requirements. You can download these forms from the website listed in your State Sheet. Before you do anything else, check the materials available online. Here's what you can expect to find:

- **Sample forms and instructions.** Many secretaries of state provide a sample articles form with instructions. You will need to retype your final form using the format and content of the sample form.
- **Ready-to-use articles.** Some states provide a form that you can print, fill in, and file with the secretary of state. Instructions for filling in the blanks are often provided on the printed form.
- **Links to nonprofit statutes.** Most state websites provide a link to the state's nonprofit corporation laws. We list these links (if available) in your State Sheet.
- **Filing checklist.** Some websites include a checklist showing both the filing requirements and some common reasons for rejection of articles. This information can help you comply with some of the less obvious substantive and formal requirements of the secretary of state's office (such as whether you can show a P.O. box as an address, how to properly sign and acknowledge the form, how much space to leave at the top of the first page for the secretary's file stamp, and so on).

 If your state website does not provide everything you need, call the office at the telephone number listed in the State Sheets.

Typical Secretary of State Guidelines for Retyping Articles

- Write all text in English (no foreign language characters, punctuation, or diacritical marks).
- Type your responses to blank items (or retype your form) using a black ink ribbon. Some secretaries may allow hand-printed responses—check your secretary of state's instructions.
- Use letter-sized (8 1/2" x 11") paper.
- Fasten pages with staples, not rivet-type fasteners.
- Make sure all typing and signatures (and any hand-printed responses) are of sufficient contrast to be legibly photocopied by the secretary's office; black ink is usually specified.

2. Complete Your Articles

The basic clauses various states require in articles of incorporation are similar. By fol-

lowing the material below and referring to the specific instructions for preparing articles provided by your secretary of state, you should be able to prepare your form without undue difficulty. Here are some hints to make this job easier:

- Scan this information to get a general idea of the various types of clauses and provisions traditionally included in standard articles of incorporation. This information will help you understand the specific form and instructions provided by your secretary of state.
- If your secretary provides a sample form which must be retyped, type or write out a draft copy first.
- Complete as much of the form as you can following your secretary of state's form and specific instructions. If you get stuck with a particular article or provision, refer to our instructions below.
- To locate a particular incorporation requirement in your state (for example, the number of directors to be named in your articles) see your State Sheet in Appendix B and browse your state's nonprofit corporation statute.

Sample Article Provisions

Below we provide sample language and explanations of the provisions you are likely to find in the articles of incorporation provided by your secretary of state (or in the article of incorporation provisions of your state's nonprofit corporation law). An article number and heading identifies the subject matter of the provision or clause and explanatory text follows each sample article. Blanks indicate information that needs to be inserted in the text of the provision or clause.

Heading and Format of Articles

Articles of Incorporation

of

a Non-Profit Corporation

Article 1.   ....

Article 2.   ....

Article 3.   ....

State law does not normally specify any format for the heading or body of the articles. Typically, the name of the corporation is shown in the heading of the articles and each provision is numbered sequentially. Your secretary of state's office may provide guidelines for retyping articles.

Statement of Statutory Authority

The undersigned incorporator(s), in order to form a corporation under the *(name of state's nonprofit corporation law)*, adopt the following Articles of Incorporation:

Although not required in many states, a statement of statutory authority is included at the beginning of the articles stating the name or section numbers of the state's nonprofit corporation act under which the corporation is being formed.

In some states, it is customary to recite that the incorporators or the corporation meet specific statutory requirements (for example, that the incorporators are of legal age or that the corporation is not formed for pecuniary profit).

Here are examples of statutory authority clauses taken from the official forms of several states:

California

This corporation is a nonprofit public benefit corporation and it is not organized for the private gain of any person. It is organized under the Nonprofit Public Benefit Corporation Law for _____ purposes.

Specific forms and instructions for forming a California nonprofit are contained in *How to Form a Nonprofit Corporation in California*, by Anthony Mancuso (Nolo). Use this more specialized book if you are incorporating in California. (Nolo will give you a discount for the California book.)

Florida

The undersigned, acting as incorporator(s) of a Corporation pursuant to Chapter 617, Florida Statutes, adopt(s) the following Articles of Incorporation of such corporation:

Illinois

Pursuant to the provisions of "The General Not For Profit Corporation Act of 1986," the undersigned incorporator(s) hereby adopt the following Articles of Incorporation.

Article 1. Name of Corporation

The name of this CORPORATION is _____

_____.

The heading to the articles and the first article of incorporation normally specify the name of the corporation. See Section B above to select a name for your corporation. If you have reserved a corporate name, make sure to use the exact spelling of the reserved name in your articles.

Article 2. Registered Agent and Office

The name and address of the registered agent of this corporation are: _____

_____.

Most states require that articles include the name and address of the corporation's initial registered agent (or agent for service of process). The agent is the person authorized to receive legal papers on behalf of the corporation; the agent's office is also known as the registered office of the corporation. Generally, the agent must be a resident of the state and at least 18 years of age. Although the registered office may be different from the principal office of the corporation in many states, most nonprofits keep things simple and appoint one of the directors as the initial agent, showing the principal address of the corporation as the registered office of the corporation.

You must usually use a street address, not a post office box, as your agent's address. Also, some states require the filing of a separate Designation of Registered Agent form with the articles.

The State Sheets in Appendix B list any special requirements for registered agents

and indicate whether a separate registered agent form must be filed with the articles.

Article 3. Statement of Purpose

The purposes for which this corporation is organized are: _____

_____.

A statement of purpose clause is a standard feature in nonprofit articles of incorporation. Your statement of purpose should be used to satisfy state corporate law and federal 501(c)(3) tax exemption requirements. Let's look at the federal requirements first.

Federal 501(c)(3) Tax Exempt Purpose Clause

In the purpose clause in your articles of incorporation, you must include language stating that your corporation is organized for 501(c)(3) tax exempt purposes. We refer to this language in later discussions as your *statement of tax exempt purposes*.

Here is the standard IRS-approved language for this statement of tax exempt purposes:

> Article 3. The purposes for which this corporation is organized are:
> This corporation is organized exclusively for one or more of the purposes as specified in Section 501(c)(3) of the Internal Revenue Code, including, for such purposes, the making of distributions to organizations that qualify as exempt organizations under Section 501(c)(3) of the Internal Revenue Code, or corresponding section of any future federal tax code.

This statement authorizes the corporation to engage in one or more 501(c)(3) tax-exempt purposes, including making distributions to other 501(c)(3) organizations.

The official form of articles promulgated by your secretary of state may already contain this statement of tax-exempt purposes (or a slight variation on the clause shown above). Some official forms include this clause in a statement of purposes article; others include it under a space set aside on the form for "additional provisions." In all cases, if this (or similar) tax-exempt purpose language does not appear in your articles, make sure to include it somewhere on the form. You'll need it to get your federal income tax exemption.

Your secretary of state form may include other tax exemption provisions. See Article 8 below for a discussion of additional federal tax exemption language that is required, or may be included, in your articles.

If You Get Stuck on Your Statement of Nonprofit Purposes

We provide instructions for dealing with the types of purpose clauses required in the majority of states. However, if you encounter special language or special format requirements not covered in our discussion, here are two suggestions:

- Rely primarily on the instructions to the sample and printed forms on your secretary of state's website—these will usually show you how to cope with any special state statutory requirements.
- For further assistance, check your state's articles statute (use the link shown in your State Sheet in Appendix B) for the special statutory language you must include or special requirements you must follow to complete your purpose clause.

Additional Statements of Purpose Required Under State Law

In many states, a statement of 501(c)(3) tax-exempt purposes will be all you need to satisfy the requirements for completing the purpose clause in your articles. Some states, however, have their own unique requirements for purpose clause wording in the articles. Below we look at the most common types of statements required under state statutes.

These special statements of purpose satisfy state law requirements. To satisfy the federal 501(c)(3) tax requirements, make sure to also include a statement of your federal tax-exempt purposes somewhere in your articles (see above).

Statement of Lawful Purpose

Some states require that the articles contain specific statutory wording indicating that the corporation is formed for a lawful purpose under the laws of the state (we call this a *statement of lawful purposes*).

A typical statement of lawful purposes, taken from the Delaware form for articles, reads as follows:

> The purpose of the corporation is to engage in any lawful act or activity for which corporations may be organized under the General Corporation Law of Delaware.

Statement of Specific Purposes

Some states also require a brief, one- or two-sentence description of the purposes and activities of your corporation in the purpose clause of the articles (we call this *a statement of specific purposes*). If you can't determine whether your state requires a statement of specific purpose by reading your secretary of state materials, we suggest you include one just to be safe.

Tips on Preparing a Statement of Specific Purposes

Make sure to keep your specific purpose statement brief—one or two short sentences is best (for example, to set up a child care center, home for the aged, AIDS hotline, dance or musical troupe; to provide scholarships to needy students, establish a book fair, and so on). The secretary of state usually doesn't want much detail or narrative here. You will provide a fuller description of your nonprofit purposes and activities in your bylaws and on your federal tax exemption application.

If possible, describe the kinds of activities you pursue in language that will clearly identify them as ones that the IRS considers to be tax-exempt.

For example, if your specific purpose is to set up a hospital, indicate that you are forming a charitable hospital; if establishing a child care center, state that *it is open to the general public and will allow parents to be gainfully employed*; if setting up a scientific organization, that *scientific research will be carried on in the public interest*.

Avoid using keywords, terms, or phrases associated with organizations exempt from taxation under other (non-501(c)(3)) sections of the Internal Revenue Code, such as *social, fraternal, recreational, political*, and so on.

The following examples should give you an idea of how to draft a specific purpose statement.

Environmental Education: Here is a sample statement of specific purposes for an environmental group:

Article 3. The purposes for which this corporation is organized are:
to publish a newsletter providing information to the public on preserving tropical rain forests.

Publishing and Lectures: Here is a sample specific purpose clause for a group that wishes to publish books and give public lectures:

Article 3. The purposes for which this corporation is organized are:
to develop an institution to teach and disseminate educational material to the public, including, but not limited to, material relating to   *(the areas of instruction are mentioned here)* , through publications, lectures, or otherwise.

Dance Group: The following sample clause is for a group that wishes to set up studios where it can teach dance and hold performances. The educational purposes of the group are clearly identified in the specific purpose clause and the general public is identified as the recipient of these services. For future flexibility, the group leaves itself the option of teaching and promoting other art forms.

Article 3. The purposes for which this corporation is organized are:
to educate the general public in dance and other art forms. The means of providing such education includes, but is not limited to, maintaining facilities for instruction and public performances of dance and other art forms.

Housing Improvement: Here is a sample clause for a group planning to get grants and tax exemptions to improve housing conditions for low- and moderate-income people by organizing a housing information and research exchange. Note that the following example simply and succinctly states the group's specific purposes, characterizing them as charitable and educational purposes in the interests of the general public—no further embellishment or narrative in the specific purpose clause is needed here.

Article 3. The purposes for which this corporation is organized are:
to provide education and charitable assistance to the general public by organizing a housing information and research exchange.

Medical Clinic: This sample clause is for a community health care clinic for low-income individuals.

Article 3. The purposes for which this corporation is organized are:
to establish and maintain a comprehensive system of family-oriented health care aimed primarily at the medically underserved areas of   *(city and county)* .

Religious Teachings and Publishing: Here is a statement that is appropriate for a religious group devoted to the teachings and works of a particular religious leader or religious order:

Article 3. The purposes for which this corporation is organized are:
to establish a religious organization to promote the teachings of, and publish materials of and concerning, *(name of spiritual leader or religious order)*.

Scientific Research: Sometimes, the most general description of the tax-exempt purposes of the group will suffice, as follows:

Article 3. The purposes for which this corporation is organized are:
to engage in scientific research in the public interest.

Article 4. Number, Names, and Addresses of Initial Directors

The number of initial directors of this corporations is _____.
Their names and address are as follows:

Many states require you to include the number of persons who will serve on the first board of directors, followed by their names and addresses. In some states, this information is not (or is only optionally) included in the articles sent out by the secretary of state.

Each State Sheet in Appendix B indicates the minimum number of directors required in your state and any residency, age, or other qualifications for directors imposed under state law.

To fill in this article, type the number of directors of your corporation, then list the names and addresses (street, not P.O. box) of the persons appointed to your initial board. Initial board members serve until the first meeting held to reelect directors—the date of this meeting will be specified in your bylaws.

Article 5. Names and Addresses of Incorporators

The names and addresses of the incorporators of this corporation are: _____

_____.

The incorporator is the person who forms the corporation by signing and filing articles of incorporation. Although more than one incorporator may be used, most nonprofits, if allowed, designate one person to assume this responsibility. Most articles of incorporation require the name and address of the incorporator of the corporation either in the body of the articles or at the end of the document after the incorporator's signature line.

Although the incorporator is usually one of the initial directors of the corporation, usually any person may be designated the incorporator and prepare, sign, and file articles on behalf of your corporation.

Your State Sheet in Appendix B indicates whether more than one incorporator is required in your state and lists any special incorporator requirements.

Article 6. Duration of Corporation

The period of duration of this corporation is:

_____.

.

In many states, the articles include a provision specifying the duration of the corporation. Almost all nonprofit corporations wish to continue into the indefinite future and will insert the word "perpetual" in this provision. In the extremely rare circumstance that you wish to limit the duration of your corporation's existence, insert a specific period or date in this clause.

Article 7. Membership Provisions

The classes, rights, privileges, qualifications, and obligations of members of this corporation are as follows: _____

_____.

In a number of states, the articles of incorporation include a membership clause similar to the sample shown above.

As explained in Chapter 2, most smaller nonprofit corporations will not wish to set up a formal membership structure and will indicate "No Members" if this clause appears in their articles. If you do decide to adopt a formal membership structure, it's usually best to indicate here that "The membership provisions of this corporation shall be stated in the bylaws of this corporation." This approach gives you the most flexibility—bylaw provisions may be repealed, changed, and added with relative ease, while amendments to articles must be filed with the secretary of state.

Finally, if you wish to adopt membership provisions and your state requires you to summarize these provisions in your articles, here is some standard language you may wish to use that provides for one class of dues-paying membership in the corporation:

This corporation shall have one class of membership. Any person shall be qualified to become a member upon payment of the initial dues and shall continue as a member upon paying the annual dues. The amount, method, and time of payment of dues shall be determined, and may be changed, from time to time, by the board of directors. Additional provisions specifying the rights and obligations of members shall be contained in the bylaws of this corporation pursuant to, and in accordance with, the laws of this state.

For further information and suggested language to set up a formal membership structure in your bylaws, see Chapter 7.

Article 8. Additional Provisions

Insert additional provisions for operating the corporation in the space provided below: _[Insert required and optional 501(c)(3) tax exemption provisions, special language from state statutes for the operation of the corporation, and so on]._

In many states, a blank article for additional provisions is included in the standard articles form. In some states, this blank article begins with wording similar to the language shown above (with suggestions for the types of optional clauses that may be inserted given in parentheses).

Below, we discuss some required and optional federal and state language you should include in this portion of your articles if it is not already included on your state's form.

Additional Federal Tax Exemption Language

To be eligible for your 501(c)(3) tax exemption, your articles must dedicate the assets of the corporation to exempt purposes. Technically, this dedication clause is not required in a few states (including Arkansas, California, Louisiana, Massachusetts, Minnesota, Missouri, Ohio, and Oklahoma)—nonetheless, we recommend all incorporators make sure a dedication of assets clause appears in their articles. This will help you to minimize delay in the processing of your federal tax exemption and avoid problems if your state laws change in the future. Here is a standard dedication of assets clause you can include in the Additional Provisions article:

> Article 8. Additional Provisions
> Upon the dissolution of this corporation, its assets remaining after payment, or provision for payment, of all debts and liabilities of this corporation shall be distributed for one or more exempt purposes within the meaning of Section 501(c)(3) of the Internal Revenue Code or shall be distributed to the federal government, or to a state or local government, for a public purpose.

⚠ Always include a dedication statement. Make sure to include this dedication of assets statement in your articles if one does not already appear on your form.

Alternative Wording for Dedication: The sample dedication language above (from IRS publications) dedicates the assets of the nonprofit corporation to one or more allowable 501(c)(3) tax-exempt purposes. The sample or printed language found in some state's articles, however, may provide blanks for dedicating assets of the nonprofit corporation to a specific 501(c)(3) tax-exempt purpose. Here is an example of a dedication clause of this type:

> The property of this corporation is irrevocably dedicated to_____ purposes and no part of the net income or assets of this corporation shall ever inure to the benefit of any director, officer, or member thereof or to the benefit of any private person. Upon the dissolution or winding up of the corporation, its assets remaining after payment, or provision for payment, of all debts and liabilities of this corporation shall be distributed to a nonprofit fund, foundation, or corporation which is organized and operated exclusively for _____
> _____ purposes and which has established its tax-exempt status under Section 501(c)(3) of the Internal Revenue Code.

To fill in this dedication clause, insert the 501(c)(3) tax-exempt purpose of your group in each blank (specify *charitable, educational, literary, religious,* or *scientific*).

Optional 501(c)(3) Tax Exemption Language

Now let's look at optional federal tax exemption language which is commonly included in nonprofit articles. If there is space, we suggest you include these provisions in your articles (if these federal tax exemption provisions are not already included on your secretary's sample or printed form). Note that many secretaries allow you to expand the portion of the articles set aside for additional provisions by attaching a typewritten page to your form.

Limitation on Political Activities: The following clause shows that your nonprofit group will comply with the 501(c)(3) limitation on political activities as discussed in Chapter 3, Section C3:

> No substantial part of the activities of this corporation shall consist of carrying on propaganda, or otherwise attempting to influence legislation (except as otherwise provided by Section 501(h) of the Internal Revenue Code), and this corporation shall not participate in, or intervene in (including the publishing or distribution of statements), any political campaign on behalf of, or in opposition to, any candidate for public office.

Limitation on Private Inurement (Private Benefits): Below is standard IRS-approved language prohibiting private inurement—private or personal benefits to individuals associated with the nonprofit corporation, such as directors, officers, employees, and so on, as discussed Chapter 3. The last portion of this clause indicates that reasonable compensation for services rendered is allowed under federal tax law.

> No part of the net earnings of this corporation shall inure to the benefit of, or be distributable to, its members, directors, officers, or other private persons, except that this corporation shall be authorized and empowered to pay reasonable compensation for services rendered and to make payments and distributions in furtherance of the purposes set forth in these articles.

General Limitation on Nonprofit Activities: The statement below limits the activities of the corporation to those permitted to 501(c)(3) organizations and those allowed to corporations to which contributions are deductible under Section 170(c)(2) of the Internal Revenue Code:

> Notwithstanding any other provision of these articles, this corporation shall not carry on any other activities not permitted to be carried on (1) by a corporation exempt from federal income tax under Section 501(c)(3) of the Internal Revenue Code or (2) by a corporation contributions to which are deductible under Section 170(c)(2) of the Internal Revenue Code.

For a discussion of the deductibility of charitable contributions made to 501(c)(3) organizations, see Chapter 4.

Private Foundation Restrictions: The following language relates to technical aspects of the 501(c)(3) tax exemption and states that the corporation will comply with all the operating restrictions that apply to private foundations if the corporation is classified as a private foundation by the IRS. Because you will want your nonprofit to be classified as a 501(c)(3) public charity rather than a private foundation, you do not need to include this language in your articles. We mention it only because it may appear in the official form promulgated by your secretary of state (it is required only for private foundations formed in Arizona and New Mexico).

In any taxable year in which this corporation is a private foundation as described in Section 509(a) of the Internal Revenue Code, the corporation (1) shall distribute its income for said period at such time and manner as not to subject it to tax under Section 4942 of the Internal Revenue Code; (2) shall not engage in any act of self-dealing as defined in Section 4941(d) of the Internal Revenue Code; (3) shall not retain any excess business holdings as defined in Section 4943(c) of the Internal Revenue Code; (4) shall not make any investments in such manner as to subject the corporation to tax under Section 4944 of the Internal Revenue Code; and (5) shall not make any taxable expenditures as defined in Section 4945(d) of the Internal Revenue Code.

 For a discussion of private foundation and public charity tax status, see Chapter 4.

3. Sample Completed Articles

We've covered a lot of ground in the individual sample articles of incorporation and explanations above. To help you tie all this information together, we include a sample completed articles below together with our comments (which appear in italicized type).

The Forms CD-ROM includes a copy of the articles of incorporation form. A copy has also been included in Appendix D.

Articles of Incorporation

of

The Bluegrass Music Society of the Appalachians, Inc.

A Nonprofit Corporation

Pursuant to the provision of the Nonprofit Corporation Act of this state, the undersigned incorporators hereby adopt the following Articles of Incorporation:

Article 1

The name of this corporation is: The Bluegrass Music Society of the Appalachians, Inc.

Article 2

The name and address of the registered agent and registered office of this corporation is:
[Name of one of the initial directors, address of corporation.]

Article 3

The purposes for which this corporation is organized are: To establish a musical society open to the general public to foster an appreciation of American bluegrass music, through lectures, seminars, study groups, public and classroom performances, exhibits, and any and all other appropriate means. *[This is a statement of specific purposes requested by the secretary of state.]*

    This corporation is organized exclusively for one or more of the purposes as specified in Section 501(c)(3) of the Internal Revenue Code, including, for such purposes, the making of distributions to organizations that qualify as exempt organizations under Section 501(c)(3) of the Internal Revenue Code, or corresponding section of any future federal tax code. *[This is a statement of tax-exempt purposes required under IRC Section 501(c)(3).]*

Article 4

The number of initial directors of this corporation shall be ___three___ and the names and addresses of the initial directors are as follows:
[Names and addresses of three initial directors]

Article 5

The name and address of the incorporators of this corporation are:

[Name and address of one of the initial directors listed above]

Article 6

The period of the duration of this corporation is: _perpetual._

Article 7

The classes, rights, privileges, qualifications, and obligations of members of this corporation are as follows:

As stated in the bylaws of this corporation.

Article 8

Additional provisions (attach separate page if necessary):

Upon the dissolution of this corporation, its assets remaining after payment, or provision for payment, of all debts and liabilities of this corporation shall be distributed for one or more exempt purposes within the meaning of Section 501(c)(3) of the Internal Revenue Code or shall be distributed to the federal government, or to a state or local government, for a public purpose. *[This is the dedication of assets statement required under IRC Section 501(c)(3).]*

No substantial part of the activities of this corporation shall consist of carrying on propaganda, or otherwise attempting to influence legislation (except as otherwise provided by Section 501(h) of the Internal Revenue Code), and this corporation shall not participate in, or intervene in (including the publishing or distribution of statements), any political campaign on behalf of, or in opposition to, any candidate for public office. *[This is the optional limitation on political activities statement under IRC Section 501(c)(3).]*

No part of the net earnings of this corporation shall inure to the benefit of, or be distributable to, its members, directors, officers, or other private persons, except that this corporation shall be authorized and empowered to pay reasonable compensation for services rendered and to make payments and distributions in furtherance of the purposes set forth in these articles. *[This is the optional limitation on private inurement statement under IRC Section 501(c)(3).]*

Notwithstanding any other provision of these articles, this corporation shall not carry on any other activities not permitted to be carried on (1) by a corporation exempt from federal income tax under Section 501(c)(3) of the Internal Revenue Code or (2) by a corporation contributions to which are deductible under Section 170(c)(2) of the Internal Revenue Code. *[This is the optional general limitation on activities statement under IRC Section 501(c)(3).]*

The undersigned incorporators hereby declare under penalty of perjury that the statements made in the foregoing Articles of Incorporation are true.

Dated: _____

(signature of incorporator) _____

Name and Address of Incorporator: _____

_____

_____

[Normally, the incorporator(s) must sign the articles. Some states require initial directors, if named in articles, to sign instead. If notarization is required, the signature(s) must be given in the presence of a notary.]

Customizing Your Articles

Although the standard articles discussed in this chapter and included in your secretary of state form will be sufficient for most incorporators, some may wish to adopt special operating rules or provisions. Although it is preferable to include these special rules in the bylaws (which can be adopted and changed with relative ease), some special provisions must, under state law, be included in the articles to be effective. For example, the following types of provisions, if adopted by the corporation, must often be included in the articles:

- establishing different classes of membership (such as voting and non-voting members)
- allowing specific members of the board to be designated by individuals rather than elected by the board or voting membership
- requiring a supermajority vote (such as 2/3 or 3/4) of directors or members for the approval of certain matters, and
- providing for special indemnification or immunity for directors and officers.

Your state website instructions may list the special provisions you have to include in your articles.

I. File Your Articles of Incorporation

File your articles with your secretary of state following the instructions on your secretary of state's website. Most corporations file by mail, although many offices will accept articles in person. A few states allow you to fill in and file your articles online (see your State Sheet for information).

The Forms CD-ROM disk includes a copy of the Articles Filing Letter and there is a blank tear-out copy in Appendix D. You may wish to use (or modify) it to submit your articles of incorporation to the secretary of state. Complete it as indicated on the following sample and special instructions below.

Articles Filing Letter

(Name and address of Incorporator) ❶ _____

_____

_____

_____

Date:_____

(Name and address of secretary of state office from your

State Sheet in Appendix B) _____

_____

_____

Re: Articles of Incorporation Filing

I enclose an original and *(number)* ❷ copies of the proposed Articles of Incorporation of

(name of corporation) _____.

Please file the Articles of Incorporation and return a Certificate of Incorporation (or file-stamped copy of the original Articles) to me at the above address.

A check/money order in the amount of $_____❸_____, made payable to your office, for total filing and processing fees is enclosed.

The above corporate name was reserved for my use pursuant to reservation # _____❹_____ issued on _____.

Sincerely,

(signature of incorporator) ❶ _____

(typed name) _____, Incorporator

Special Instructions

❶ A person who signs your articles should prepare and sign this cover letter.

Note: If you have reserved a corporate name, the person who reserved the corporate name should prepare and sign this letter—the corporate name will be reserved for this person's use only.

❷ In some states, you need only submit an original of the articles—the secretary will file the original and send you a certificate of incorporation as proof of filing. In other states, you need to submit the original and one or more copies. The secretary will file the original and file-stamp and return one or more copies to you. In some states, an additional fee is charged for submitting more than one copy of your articles for file-stamping. One copy should be sufficient—you can make copies of this file-stamped copy to send to financial institutions, grant agencies, and others when necessary as proof of your incorporation.

❸ Include a check for the total fees, made payable to the "Secretary of State" or other official title of the office that files articles in your state. Check your secretary of state instructions carefully to make sure your total fee payment is correct—otherwise, your articles may be returned to you, unfiled.

❹ If you have reserved your corporate name, fill in the blanks here to show the certificate number and/or date your reservation was issued. In some states, the secretary simply sends you a file-stamped copy of your reservation letter—if so, just show the file-stamped date on the letter in the second blank.

Your next step is to wait. The secretary of state will make sure your corporate name is available for use and that your articles conform to law. If there are no problems, the secretary of state will mail you a certificate of incorporation (or file-stamped copy of your articles). If there are any problems with your articles, the secretary of state will usually return your articles, indicating the items that need correction. Often the problem is technical, not substantive, and easy to fix. If the problem is more complicated (such as an improper or insufficient corporate purpose clause), you may be able to solve the problem by rereading our examples and suggestions for completing the articles. If you get stuck, you will need to do a little research or obtain further help from a nonprofit lawyer with experience in drafting and filing nonprofit articles (see Chapter 11).

Sign Documents on Behalf of the Corporation

Congratulations! Once your articles are filed, your organization is a legally recognized nonprofit corporation. But before you rush out to pursue your nonprofit objectives, remember that your corporation is the one who is now doing business, not you as an individual. This means that signatures on any document, such as an agreement with a vendor, application for a grant, lease, or other financial or legal form must clearly show that you're acting on behalf of the corporation (and not for yourself). Your signature should be a block of information (plus a signature), which looks like this:

Parents for a Better Society, Inc.
By: _____(your signature)_____
     (your corporate title, such as
      director, president, secretary)

If you fail to sign documents on behalf of the corporation and in your capacity as a corporate director, officer, or employee, you are leaving yourself open to possible personal liability for corporate obligations. From now on, it is extremely important for you to maintain the distinction between the corporation that you've organized and yourself. As we've said, the corporation is a separate legal "person" and you want to make sure that other organizations, businesses, the IRS, and the courts respect this distinction.

It's also very important to realize that until you obtain your state and federal tax exemptions, your corporation is liable for the payment of state and federal income taxes. Furthermore, until you obtain your federal 501(c)(3) tax exemption and public charity status, your corporation will be unable to receive most public and private grant funds, and will be unable to assure donors that contributions made to the corporation are tax deductible. Therefore, make sure to follow through with the procedures contained in the succeeding chapters—doing so is vital to the success of your new corporation. ■

Chapter 7

Prepare Your Bylaws

*Y*our next step is to prepare your bylaws. This document is, for all practical purposes, your corporation's internal affairs manual. It sets forth the rules and procedures for holding meetings, electing directors and officers, and taking care of other essential corporate formalities. Specifically, the bylaws:

- ∞ Contain information central to the organization and operation of your particular corporation (for example, dates of meetings, quorum requirements).
- ∞ Restate the most significant legal and tax provisions applicable to tax-exempt nonprofit corporations. This is useful for your own reference and necessary to assure the IRS and the state that you are eligible for these tax exemptions.
- ∞ Provide a practical, yet formal, set of rules for the orderly operation of your corporation: to resolve disputes, provide certainty regarding procedures, and manage corporate operations.

Preparing bylaws for a nonprofit corporation is not difficult. It simply involves filling in blanks. Before you begin work on your bylaws, you'll need to decide whether your nonprofit will have members. Section A will guide you through that issue.

⚠ Don't think of your bylaws as meaningless fine print. On the contrary, because the bylaws are so important to the functioning of your organization, be sure to read through the bylaws carefully, making sure you understand the purpose and effect of the different provisions included.

A. Choose a Membership or Nonmembership Structure

Your first step in preparing bylaws is to decide whether you want your nonprofit corporation to be a membership or nonmembership corporation. There are significant differences between the two structures and significant legal consequences that will result from your decision.

📖 See Chapter 2, Section E, for a discussion of the two different types of structures and the legal consequences of setting up a membership versus a nonmembership structure.

Most smaller groups will probably want to form a nonmembership corporation. Why? Because a nonmembership corporation is simpler to establish and operate. Nonmembership corporations are run by a board of directors, as opposed to membership corporations where members have the right to vote on major corporate decisions. And you don't lose any significant advantages by not having members—most people who want to support your group aren't interested in having the technical legal rights given to members.

Some groups, however, will decide that the nature of their activities requires a membership structure. This is a reasonable decision in circumstances where membership participation in the affairs of the nonprofit corporation is essential or desirable (for example, to increase member involvement in the nonprofit's mission and program). Members of a nonprofit corporation are given specific legal rights under state law to participate in corporate affairs. Such membership rights typically include the right to:

- vote for the election of the board of directors
- approve changes to the articles or bylaws of the corporation
- vote for a dissolution of the corporation, and
- approve a sale of substantially all of the corporation's assets.

Some nonprofits may even decide to combine a legal, voting membership structure with a larger group of dues-paying supporters.

EXAMPLE: A large botanical society may have one class of formal members who elect the board of directors and an informal group of dues-paying supporters who receive the society's magazine and attend special events sponsored by the society.

If you do decide to adopt a formal membership structure for your nonprofit corporation, we show you how to add basic membership provisions to your bylaws in Section D below.

Why Not Having Members Makes Sense

Here are some reasons why most nonprofit incorporators prefer not to have members:

- Setting up a formal membership with voting rights dilutes directorship control over corporate operations.
- It isn't always easy to expel a member. State law may require that members only be expelled for good cause following a formal hearing.
- Nonmembership groups can still receive support from subscribers, sponsors, patrons, friends, benefactors, and so on. You can offer discounts or other benefits to outsiders who participate in the activities and programs of the corporation without giving them a legal right to participate in the management and other affairs of the corporation.

In some states, you may even call these outside supporters "members" of the corporation without running the risk of entitling these persons to voting and other legal membership rights in the corporation. Nonetheless, to be safe and to avoid confusion and controversy later on, we suggest you use another term for persons who will not be legal members of your corporation but who will otherwise contribute to, or participate in, corporate affairs and activities.

B. Purpose and Scope of Our Bylaws

Appendix D contains a tear-out bylaws form that is suitable for all types of 501(c)(3) nonprofits—nonmembership and membership groups alike. This form is also included on the CD-ROM. The provisions contained in this document were drafted to serve the following purposes:

- they contain information central to the organization and operation of your corporation (time, place, date, call, notice, and quorum requirements for meetings)
- they restate the most significant provisions applicable to tax-exempt nonprofit corporations, useful for your own reference and necessary to assure the IRS that your corporation is eligible for its tax exemptions, and
- they provide a practical, yet formal, set of rules for the orderly operation of your corporation—to resolve disputes, to provide certainty regarding legal procedures, and to ensure at least minimum control over corporate operations.

How We Deal With State Law Differences

As you know, nonprofit corporation laws vary slightly from state to state. The provisions contained in our general-purpose bylaws will conform to the statutory requirements of most states. In areas where state legal rules do diverge somewhat, our bylaw provisions simply refer to the laws of your state. For example, the indemnification provisions in the bylaws state that your directors and officers are entitled to indemnification *to the fullest extent permissible under the law of this state.*

If a specific area of nonprofit law or procedure is particularly important to you or your legal advisor, you can easily replace the general-purpose provisions in the bylaws with the exact provisions contained in your state's nonprofit corporation code. For a discussion about looking up the law yourself, see Chapter 11.

Should You Consult a Nonprofit Professional?

The primary practical reason to adopt the rules contained in the bylaws is to allow the incorporators to arrive at a good, workable consensus regarding the ground rules of the corporation. However, these may not meet all your needs or you may have questions about one or more of them. If so, check the provisions in our form against your state's nonprofit statutes or have them reviewed and customized by a lawyer with nonprofit experience.

C. Prepare Your Bylaws

Tear-out bylaws are contained in Appendix D; the CD-ROM also contains a bylaws form. Make a photocopy of this form and fill in the blanks on the form as you follow the instructions below. Or fill in the blanks on the CD-ROM version of the form. Instructions are provided for bylaws containing blanks or for special bylaw provisions that warrant a further explanation.

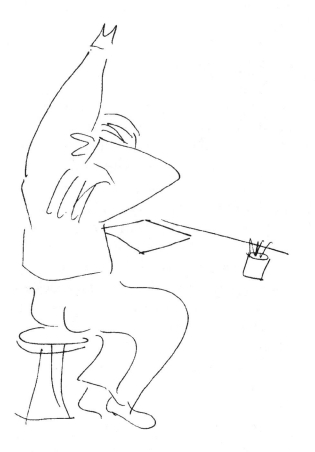

Making Modifications to the Bylaws

In the text, we discussed various reasons why some groups may wish to insert specific statutory rules from their state's nonprofit corporation law in the tear-out bylaws. There are many good reasons why groups may wish to customize their bylaws to add special language or provisions.

For example, if your nonprofit corporation plans to receive federal or other public grants or monies, some funding agencies may require that you include special provisions in your bylaws which state that no member of the board, officer, or other person exercising supervisory power in the corporation or any of their close relatives can individually benefit from the receipt of grant funds. Generally, provisions of this sort are meant to prohibit board members, officers (president, vice president, secretary, treasurer) and their families from being paid from, or directly benefited by, grant monies given to the organization.

Or, if your state follows the disinterested directors rule (see Chapter 2), your corporation will have to follow it whether you include this language in your bylaws or not. However, you may want to include the appropriate disinterested director language anyway, as a reminder to the group.

> ### Don't Worry About References to Members in the Bylaws
>
> There are certain provisions in the bylaws that refer to "the members, if any," of the corporation or use other language making certain provisions applicable to the corporation only if the corporation has members. These provisions have no effect for non-membership corporations using these bylaws—they simply allow membership corporations to add membership provisions to the bylaws as explained in Section D below.

Below we go over the sample bylaw provisions. An article number and heading identifies the subject matter of each provision and explanatory text with examples or blanks, if applicable, follow.

Heading

Type the name of your corporation.

Article I, Section 1. Principal Office

Type the name of the county and state where the corporation's principal office is located—this is the corporate office where you will keep a copy of your bylaws, records of meetings, and other formal corporate records mentioned in various bylaw provisions. Customarily, the principal office designated here will be the same as the legal office of the corporation (the address specified in the articles as the registered office of the corporation where legal papers must be served on the corporation).

⚠ Don't fill in the blanks for change of address at the end of Section 2. Use these blanks later, if necessary, to change the principal office of the corporation to another location within the same county, by showing the new address and date of the address change.

Article 2, Section 1. IRC Section 501(c)(3) Purposes

This section contains a standard statement of 501(c)(3) tax-exempt purposes (similar to the tax-exempt purpose clause discussed earlier for the articles of incorporation). We include this statement in the bylaws to remind the IRS that your corporation is organized exclusively for a bona fide 501(c)(3) purpose.

Article 2, Section 2. Specific Objectives and Purposes

Use the space provided here to state the specific tax-exempt objectives and purposes of your nonprofit corporation. If you included a statement of specific purposes in your articles of incorporation, it should have been brief. Here you can go into as much detail as you want in describing the specific purposes and activities of your corporation. We suggest you list your major purposes and activities, showing your nonprofit goals and the means by which you plan to achieve them. This will be useful not only as an exercise to help define and clarify your nonprofit objectives, but also as a way to give the IRS additional information regarding the tax-exempt purposes and activities of your corporation.

Dance Group. Here's an example of an expanded list of objectives and purposes that might be used by an educational-purpose, nonprofit dance group. It is illustrative of the large number of 501(c)(3) nonprofit corporations that will derive tax-exempt revenue primarily from the performance of services related to their exempt purposes, rather than from grants and contributions:

Section 2. Specific Objectives and Purposes
The specific objectives and purposes of this corporation shall be:

(a) to provide instruction in dance forms such as jazz, ballet, tap, and modern dance;

(b) to provide instruction in body movement and relaxation art forms such as tumbling, tai-chi, and yoga;

(c) to give public performances in dance forms and creative dramatics;

(d) to sponsor special events involving the public performance of any or all of the above art forms as well as other performing arts by the corporation's performing troupe as well as by other community performing arts groups; and

(e) to directly engage in and to provide facilities for others to engage in the promotion of the arts, generally.

Nonprofit Book Festival. Here's a completed statement of specific objectives and purposes for a nonprofit educational-purpose group that sponsors a book fair and promotes book reading and publishing in the local community:

Section 2. Specific Objectives and Purposes
The specific objectives and purposes of this corporation shall be:

(a) to sponsor an annual book fair with an emphasis on exhibiting books created and published in our community;

(b) to sponsor other informational events open to the public which focus on books;

(c) to educate the public concerning our community's contributions to book creation, publication, and distribution;

(d) generally, through educative and other efforts, to help make books and reading as inviting and accessible to as broad an audience as possible; and

(e) to engage in other activities related to educating the public about book writing, publishing, and distribution in our community.

Women's Health Information Resource Center. Here's a completed statement for a women's health group:

Section 2. Specific Objectives and Purposes
The specific objectives and purposes of this corporation shall be:

(a) to maintain a women's health library open to the public containing books, articles, and other material related to women's health issues;

(b) to maintain a physicians referral listing containing patient evaluations of physicians practicing in the community;

(c) to sponsor seminars and workshops open to the general public where ideas, opinions, and writings relating to women's health issues and health concerns may be expressed and shared with others;

(d) to publish a monthly newsletter containing articles informative of women's health issues; and

(e) to engage in other activities related to educating the public concerning women's health issues and health concerns.

Environmental Conservation and Protection Organization. Here's a sample for an environmental group:

Section 2. Specific Objectives and Purposes
The specific objectives and purposes of this corporation shall be:

(a) to educate the public concerning the necessity of preserving the nation's wetlands;

(b) to publish a newsletter which focuses on information related to wetlands preservation efforts and developments;

(c) to sponsor seminars and other educational events where community and environmental leaders, governmental and organizational representatives, and other concerned members of the public and government may meet to exchange ideas, suggest solutions, and implement strategies to protect the nation's wetlands;

(d) to meet with governmental representatives; report to governmental committees, agencies, and boards; and generally to attempt to help local, state, and federal lawmakers establish enforceable legislation to help protect wetland areas; and

(e) to expand and redefine our educational and environmental program from time to time as necessary to meet the continuing challenge of protecting the nation's wetland resources.

Private College. Here's a completed statement for a private school:

Section 2. Specific Objectives and Purposes
The specific objectives and purposes of this corporation shall be:

(a) to establish a private university, licensed by the state and accredited by a recognized regional accreditation organization;

(b) to maintain a regularly enrolled student body, an established curriculum, and a full-time faculty;

(c) to participate in federal and state student loan and other student educational and financial incentive programs; and

(d) to have the normal functions, operations, programs, and pursuits incidental to a fully recognized and operational nonprofit center of learning and higher education.

Be sure to authorize related activities. The last item in each of the above examples contains a clause that authorizes the corporation to engage in activities necessary or incidental to its main purposes and pursuits. We suggest you use similar language to allow your corporation to engage in activities related to its specific objectives and purposes.

Article 3, Section 1. Number of Directors

Insert the total number of directors who will serve on your board. Make sure the number of directors you specify here is equal to or greater than the minimum number required in your state as shown under the Director Qualifications heading in the Articles of Incorporation section on your State Sheet. Also, consider how many directors you will need to efficiently run your nonprofit corporation. We discuss this point further in Chapter 2.

Often, the number shown here will be the same as the number of initial directors specified in your articles (if initial directors are listed in the articles). However, you may state a greater number at this time if you wish to allow additional directors to be elected to your board.

Article 3, Section 2. Qualifications for Directors

Our bylaws provide that directors must be of the age of majority in your state. Although not a legal requirement in every state, we think this is a sensible provision to avoid legal problems that can occur if minors conduct or manage business.

Check the State Sheets for additional director requirements. If the director qualifications information on your State Sheet indicates that any additional requirement applies to directors, such as a state residency requirement, insert the requirement in the space provided in this bylaw.

Unless required in your state, we suggest that you not add additional qualifications to limit the makeup of your board to a particular group of individuals (for example, to educators or enrolled students of a school or to parents of children who attend a nonprofit day care center). The IRS likes to see various segments of the community represented on the board of a 501(c)(3) tax-exempt group, not just a select group with a singular nonprofit perspective or interest.

Instead of imposing a blanket qualification requirement on all board positions, it often makes sense to allocate a certain number of director positions to specific groups of individuals. This type of "selective diversity" is, in fact, encouraged by the IRS.

EXAMPLE: A nonprofit hospital wishes to set aside three board positions for physicians, three for health care administrators, and three for community representatives. This section of the bylaws is completed as follows:

Section 2. Qualifications
Directors shall be of the age of majority in this state. Other qualifications for directors of this corporation shall be as follows: Three board positions shall be filled by licensed physicians in private practice in

Jefferson County; three board positions shall be filled by health care administrators of nonprofit hospitals in Jefferson County; three board positions shall be filled by representatives of the Jefferson County community who are not health care professionals.

Article 3, Section 5. Term of Office of Directors

Indicate the length of the term of office for directors in this blank.

Check the State Sheets for your state's requirements for directors' terms. Many states require a one-year term for directors. A number of states allow longer terms. Others require an annual meeting for the election of directors only if you don't specify a longer term of office in the corporation's articles or bylaws.

Although it is common for nonprofit bylaws to provide for a one-year term of office for directors, you may wish (if permitted by your state statutes) to lengthen this period. By doing so, you increase the chances of assembling a seasoned board with practical experience in dealing effectively with corporate affairs. The first year or so for most nonprofit directors is an acclimation or initiation period. While this first year provides insight into nonprofit programs, problems, and the decision-making process generally, the later years of nonprofit service are usually the most productive ones for any board member. Note also that while a single term may be limited to one year, a director may serve many consecutive one-year terms. Here are sample bylaws for appointing directors for one year and three years:

Each director shall hold office for a period of <u>one year</u> and until his or her successor is elected and qualifies.

Each director shall hold office for a period of <u>three years</u> and until his or her successor is elected and qualifies.

Customizing Director Provisions. Some nonprofits with larger boards or other special requirements may wish to draft their own term of office or board election provisions. For example, some may wish to provide for a staggered board, in which only a portion of the full board is elected each term to guarantee that there will always be a majority of experienced members. Or some may want to allow certain members of the board to be appointed by specified individuals or organizations (such as a city council, board of directors of a hospital, or a committee of an environmental organization). There are other possibilities as well. For example, you may wish to provide that a director can only serve two or three consecutive terms so as to bring in new directors periodically.

Check before you use alternative bylaw provisions. In all cases, we suggest that you check your nonprofit corporation law to determine whether the alternate provisions are permitted by your state's statutes.

Staggered Board Provision. Here's an example of a substitute bylaw that provides for the election of a staggered board. A corporation with a 12-person board, for instance, could use this provision to elect four directors each year:

Each year, one-third [*or some other percentage or number*] of the authorized number of directors shall be elected to serve on the board of directors. Each director shall hold office until his or her successor is elected and qualifies.

The above provision can be used to elect a portion of the board each term. Of course, more complicated schemes are possible with different classes of directors serving for different lengths of time.

Are Staggered Boards Allowed in Your State?

The nonprofit laws of some states specifically allow staggered boards. Staggered boards are also allowed in a number of states whose nonprofit statutes are silent on this issue (for example, in states whose statutes only specify particular terms of office for directors). However, if your state law doesn't address this issue but requires that all directors must be elected at an annual (or other periodic) meeting for the election of directors, staggered boards may not be valid—the statutes can be read to require that all board members be elected at one time. Check with a nonprofit lawyer if you wish to authorize a staggered board and have a question regarding your state's statute on directors' terms of office.

By the way, how do you tell which members of the initial board should first be selected to serve staggered terms? Here's one idea (simply a fancy way of saying that the corporate secretary can draw straws to make this selection):

If, at a meeting for the election of directors, more than one group of initial board members is elected to serve for a first staggered term of office, then the secretary of the corporation shall assign each director to a numbered group and shall make a chance selection between or among the numbered groups (by selecting among numbered lots or by some other chance selection procedure). The group corresponding to the number so chosen shall be subject to election to a staggered term at the meeting.

Article 3, Section 6. Director Compensation

As we've said, nonprofit directors customarily serve without compensation because the IRS will probably view substantial payments to directors for performing director duties as instances of prohibited private inurement. This is the wise approach. This bylaw section, however, does allow the corporation to pay directors a reasonable fee for attending meetings as well as reasonable advancement or reimbursement for expenses incurred in performing director duties. In practice, many nonprofits do not pay directors even these lesser amounts except to reimburse directors who must travel a long distance to attend board meetings. However, some nonprofits may authorize minimal payments as incentives to individuals for serving on the board.

Article 3, Section 8. Regular Board Meetings

In the blanks in the first paragraph, specify the date(s) and time(s) when regular meetings of the board will be held. Many nonprofits with active agendas hold regular board meetings on a monthly or more frequent basis. Smaller or less active organizations may schedule a regular board meeting less frequently (quarterly, semiannually, or even annually) and call special meetings during the year to take care of specific items of business.

We recommend that you use this bylaw provision to schedule regular board meetings on at least a monthly basis. The majority of nonprofit corporations, whether large, midsized, or small, should keep their boards busy managing corporate projects and programs; setting up, supervising, and hearing back from a number of corporate committees; and just generally taking care of business on an ongoing basis. And remember, to help avoid personal liability for management decisions, each board member should be able to show that she is as fully informed of, and actively involved in, corporate business as possible. Corporate records showing director attendance at, and participation in, regular meetings of the board are an excellent way to show that your directors meet this standard of corporate conduct. Here is a sample bylaw calling for regular board meetings:

> Regular meetings of Directors shall be held on the second Tuesday of each month at 7:30 P.M.

In the second paragraph of this section, nonmembership nonprofits should fill in the blank to indicate which one of the regular board meetings will be specified for election (or reelection) of corporate directors.

Membership Note: The provisions in the second paragraph of this section only take effect for nonmembership corporations— membership corporations can leave this item blank since they will add provisions to their bylaws which specify that the members, not the directors, elect directors of the corporation.

In a nonmembership corporation, the directors vote for their own reelection or replacement. The frequency of this regular meeting to elect directors depends upon their term of office. If the term is one year, then one regular meeting per year will be designated for election of the board. Likewise, if you have specified a three-year term for directors, then one regular meeting every third year will be designated as the meeting to elect directors. Under the terms of this bylaw, each director casts one vote for each candidate (up to the number of candidates to be elected) and the candidates receiving the highest number of votes are elected.

Directors Elected Annually. Here's an example of a bylaw for a nonmember corporation where the directors are to be elected annually:

> If this corporation makes no provision for members, then, at the regular meeting of directors held on <u>January 1st of each year</u>, directors shall be elected by the board of directors. Voting for the election of directors shall be by written ballot. Each director shall cast one vote per candidate, and may vote for as many candidates as the number

of candidates to be elected to the board. The candidates receiving the highest number of votes up to the number of directors to be elected shall be elected to serve on the board.

Directors Elected Every Three Years. Here's an example of a bylaw for a nonmember corporation where the directors' term is three years:

If this corporation makes no provision for members, then, at the regular meeting of directors held on the first Friday of July every third year, directors shall be elected by the board of directors....

EXAMPLE: Your nonprofit board consists of 15 members. The names of 20 candidates to the board are placed in nomination at the beginning of the regular meeting for election of the board. Pursuant to this bylaw provision, each director casts one vote for 15 (of the 20) candidates. The 15 candidates receiving the highest number of votes are elected to the board. Smaller nonmembership nonprofits commonly hold uncontested elections in which each director simply places himself in nomination and the board votes itself in for another term.

If you wish to add special nomination, balloting or other director election procedures to your bylaws in place of this standard provision, check your nonprofit statutes before doing so (look for a section heading entitled "Election of Directors").

Article 3, Section 10. Notice of Board Meetings

Section (a) of this bylaw dispenses with notice of all regular meetings of directors (this includes the regular meeting for the election of directors). This is a standard provision codified in the nonprofit statutes of most states. It is assumed that directors will keep track of, and attend, regular meetings, once they have been given the schedule. As a practical matter, you may wish to call and remind less active directors of all upcoming meetings of the board.

Section (b) requires that the date, time, place, and purpose of special director meetings be communicated to each director at least one week in advance. Our bylaw specifies that notice may be given in person, or by mail, telephone, or fax machine. Since fax messages may go unnoticed or unread (or occasionally be eaten by the machine), they must be acknowledged by a return fax or telephone call within 24 hours.

Section (c) allows the corporation to obtain a written consent from a director prior to or after a meeting. Written consents and waivers of this sort are specifically authorized under the nonprofit statutes of many states and are a good way to ensure that a director is informed of the meeting. Also, this avoids having to worry about complying with any special statutory rules that may exist for calling, noticing, or holding the meeting. If a director consents in writing to the meeting, she cannot protest later that the corporation failed to comply with a formality contained in your nonprofit corporation code.

You may want to customize your notice provisions. We think these are reasonable notification provisions, which keep all directors informed of special business while eliminating premeeting preliminaries and delays for all regular meetings. You may wish to adopt provisions that match exactly any special requirements in your state or you may wish to customize these provisions to suit your own needs or circumstances. For example, you may wish to mail written notice and agendas of all regular and special board meetings to each director one week prior to the meeting date.

Article 3, Section 11. Quorum for Board Meetings

Indicate the percentage of the full board (or the number of directors) who must be present at a directors' meeting to constitute a quorum so that business can be conducted. The percentage or number shown here must be at least equal to any minimum quorum rule for directors established in your state. State director quorum requirements are listed on the State Sheets.

Quorum Specified as Percentage of Full Board. Here is a sample bylaw, which defines a quorum as a percentage of the board:

> A quorum shall consist of <u>a majority</u> of the members of the board of directors.

Quorum Specified as Number of Directors. Here is a sample bylaw which qualifies a quorum as a specific number of members of the board:

> A quorum shall consist of <u>three</u> of the members of the board of directors.

Most corporations specify a majority of the board as the director quorum requirement, even if state law allows a smaller percentage or number of directors to be specified. Of course, you can set a larger quorum requirement if you wish. Whatever you decide, you should realize that this section of the bylaws concerns a quorum, not a vote requirement. Under the provisions of the next section in the bylaws, normal board action can be taken by a majority of directors at a meeting at which a quorum is present.

> **EXAMPLE:** If a six-director corporation requires a majority quorum and a meeting is held at which a minimum quorum (four) is present, action can be taken by the vote of three directors, a majority of those present at the meeting.

Article 3, Section 13. Conduct of Board Meetings

Use this blank to specify the rules of order which will be used at directors' meetings. Some larger nonprofits use Robert's Rules of Order (major editions change every ten years or so), but you may indicate any set of procedures for proposing, approving, and tabling motions that you wish. If you will have a small informal board, you may wish to leave this line blank if you see no need to specify formal procedures for introducing and discussing items of business at board meetings, or you may wish to specify "such procedures as may be approved from time to time by the board of directors" to allow your board to develop its own set of procedures for conducting meetings.

Article 4, Section 1. Designation of Officers

This section provides for the four standard officer positions of president, vice president, secretary, and treasurer and allows the board to designate and fill other corporate officer positions as needed. In most nonprofits, directors are appointed to serve as the unpaid officers of the corporation. The officers, in turn, oversee the salaried staff. For a list of the formal duties and responsibilities associated with each officer position, see Sections 6 through 9 of this article in the form.

In most states, one or more corporate officer positions cannot be filled by the same person. Commonly, the same person cannot serve as both the corporate president and corporate secretary. The State Sheets include the rules for filling officer positions in your state.

Even if you set up a small nonprofit run by just a few individuals, it is customary to fill these four primary officer slots. You will elect officers when you hold your first meeting of directors. Under this bylaw provision, your board may designate and fill other officer titles and positions whenever it wishes to do so.

Article 5, Section 1. Executive Committee of the Board

This section allows the board to appoint an executive committee of directors to make management decisions for the corporation. If you wish to use this provision, insert the number of directors who will serve on this committee. Note that this provision requires

that the designation of an executive committee be approved by a majority of directors.

The State Sheets list the number of directors required on an executive committee. They also list the major corporate actions which cannot be taken by the executive committee, typically the amendment of articles or bylaws or the approval of director compensation. Full board approval (and, when appropriate, membership approval) must be obtained for these larger corporate decisions.

While we do not necessarily recommend that board authority be delegated, establishing an executive committee of directors may be advisable in certain nonprofits where action must routinely be taken in between formal board meetings or where distance, time, or other constraints sometimes make it difficult to achieve a quorum for board meetings. In all cases, the executive committee should keep minutes of its meetings and document all formal action. Regular and timely reports of executive committee actions should be presented to the full board.

Directors can be personally liable for board action. Under state law and court decisions, less active board members (those who sit on the full board and approve actions taken by the more active executive committee members) can be held personally accountable (and, in extreme cases, personally liable) for executive committee decisions. Mostly, such personal liability occurs if members of the full board are willfully or grossly negligent in carrying out their duties, which includes reasonably monitoring executive committee action.

Article 7, Sections 3 and 4. Director and Member Inspection Rights

These provisions give directors and members broad rights to inspect the corporation's properties and financial and corporate records. State law may impose additional inspection rights and obligations (or may allow you to restrict these rights). For the details of any additional inspection provisions which may apply in your state, see your nonprofit corporation law.

Article 7, Section 6. Periodic Report Requirements

In most states, nonprofit corporations must file an annual or other periodic report form with the secretary of state, the attorney general's office, or some other state office or agency, showing the names and addresses of the corporation's directors and officers and other information. Standard corporate financial statements and reports of charitable solicitation programs and finances may also be required.

The bylaws section of the State Sheets lists the basic corporate report requirements in your state. Your secretary of state website should provide—or show you how to order—a copy of your state's corporate report form.

Special Membership Reports

Your nonprofit corporation act may also require you to furnish annual corporate financial statements to members. In addition, it may require you to make an annual written report to members detailing specific transactions, such as the making of loans or guarantees to directors or officers. Your state nonprofit law will contain any special membership reporting requirements that apply in your state.

Article 8. 501(c)(3) Tax Provisions

The various sections in this article contain language that will help show the IRS and, if applicable, your state revenue or tax department, that you qualify for tax-exempt status:

- Section 1 contains specific and general limitations on your nonprofit activities. The first paragraph indicates that you will comply with the specific 501(c)(3) prohibitions against substantial lobbying activities and involvement with political campaigns for public candidates (the reference to IRC Section 501(h) is a reminder that you may elect to fall under the alternative political expenditures test available to 501(c)(3) public charities—see Chapter 3, Section C3). The second paragraph limits the activities of the corporation, generally, to those permitted to 501(c)(3) organizations and to organizations that qualify for tax deductible charitable contributions (under IRC § 170(c)(2)).

- Section 2 restates the 501(c)(3) prohibition against private inurement (benefiting individuals associated with the nonprofit organization). Payments made to individuals as reasonable compensation for services rendered and to further the tax-exempt purposes of the group are specifically authorized.

- Section 3 irrevocably dedicates the assets of the organization to another 501(c)(3) group or to a governmental office or agency for a public purpose. The last sentence is a reminder that such assets must be distributed in accordance with state law.

- Section 4 contains technical language restating the requirements applicable to 501(c)(3) organizations classified as private foundations. These provisions state that for any year the corporation is classified as a 501(c)(3) private foundation, it will operate in such a way as to avoid all private foundation excise taxes imposed under various sections of the Internal Revenue Code. As you will not want to be classified as a private foundation (but, rather, as a public charity), why include these provisions in the bylaws? Simply to show the IRS that you mean business (in a nonprofit sense of course) and will comply with any and all 501(c)(3) restrictions— whether your organization is classified as a public charity or as a private foundation.

Adoption of Bylaws

Use the Adoption of Bylaws page as the last page of your completed bylaws. In the blank, specify the number of preceding pages in your bylaws. Fill in the date and have each of the persons named as an initial director in your articles sign on a blank line below the first paragraph. If directors were not named in your articles, have each of your incorporators (the person or persons who signed your articles) sign here.

After you adopt your bylaws, make sure to keep a copy with your corporate records (so the organization can refer to them as needed in the future). You will also need to make a copy of your bylaws to attach to your federal tax exemption application, as explained in the next chapter.

D. Prepare Membership Provisions

This section shows how to add membership provisions to the bylaws prepared in the preceding section.

➡ If you have decided to form a nonmembership corporation (as most nonprofits will), this section does not apply to you and you should skip ahead to Chapter 8.

To add membership provisions to your bylaws, fill in the blanks in the tear-out membership provisions in Appendix D or in the bylaws form on the CD-ROM, following the instructions below.

Customizing Your Membership Provisions

There are significant state law differences with respect to membership rules and procedures. In drafting the membership provisions, we have specified general membership rules that avoid significant state differences and provide a skeletal membership structure for your corporation to help you complete your bylaws and continue with your incorporation process (apply for your tax exemptions, and so on).

You may need to customize your membership rules—for example to provide for different classes of membership, proxy voting, special director nomination or selection procedures, additional grounds and procedures for terminating memberships, and so on. Drafting extra membership provisions that comply with your state's rules will require legal research or a consultation with a nonprofit lawyer.

Heading

Type the name of your corporation in this blank.

Article 11. Membership Provisions

The membership provisions start with Article 11. You will include these membership provision pages at the end of the basic bylaw pages as explained below.

Article 11, Section 2. Qualifications of Members

Use this blank to indicate any special qualifications required of members in your corporation. We suggest you do not limit or qualify membership in your corporation unless the qualification is of obvious utility (members must be of the age of majority) or is clearly related to the tax-exempt purposes or activities of your organization.

> **EXAMPLE:** A nonprofit private college decides to limit membership to alumni because the founders wish to confer legal membership power only on those who have attended and completed the educational program. Because any person may enroll in the school, the IRS should have no objection.

> **EXAMPLE:** A specialized philanthropic and fundraising newsletter only admits as members persons who can show a few years' prior experience working with or for nonprofit organizations. This selection criterion is intended to generate a membership that is involved in the organization's areas of interest and should be acceptable to the IRS.

No Specified Membership Qualification. If you do not wish to limit or qualify membership in your corporation, complete this blank as follows:

> The qualifications for membership in this corporation are as follows: Any person <u>is qualified to become a member of this corporation.</u>

⚠ **Dues and fees go in Section 4, below.** Do not use this blank to limit your membership to those who pay membership fees or dues—you will specify any initial and ongoing payments required of members in separate membership provisions as explained below.

Article 11, Section 3. Admission of Members

Most smaller nonprofit corporations do not require formal application for membership in the corporation. A few, however, may do this to determine if prospective members meet the qualification requirements set forth in Article 11, Section 2, as discussed above. Others will use this bylaw to indicate that members must pay an admission fee and/or annual dues prior to acceptance as a member in the corporation.

Specified Membership Qualification. Here is a sample bylaw which provides for membership qualification, an application fee, and annual dues:

> Applicants shall be admitted to membership on making <u>application therefor in writing</u> <u>and upon approval of the application by the</u> <u>membership committee of this corporation</u> <u>[and/or] upon payment of the application</u> <u>fee and first annual dues, as specified in the</u> <u>following sections of this bylaw.</u>

The actual amounts paid by members will be specified in the following sections of this bylaw.

Article 11, Section 4. Membership Fees and Dues

Use these blanks to authorize or specify any application fee or annual dues charged to members:

> (a) The following fee shall be charged for making application for membership in the corporation: [*state specific admission fee or leave to discretion of board, for example, "in such amount as may be specified from time to time by resolution of the Board of Directors charged for, and payable with, the application for membership," or, if no fee, type "None".*]
>
> (b) The annual dues payable to the corporation by members shall be [*state amount of annual dues, or leave to discretion of board, for example, "in such amount as may be determined from time to time by resolution of the Board of Directors" or type "None"*].

Article 11, Section 9. Termination of Membership

The termination of membership provisions here are basic ones. Membership can be terminated voluntarily by a member or by the corporation if the member fails to pay dues. The corporation may also terminate a member for cause if the member is provided written notice and an opportunity to be heard.

🏛 **The statutes and court decisions of your state may contain specific substantive and procedural rules for terminating membership in a nonprofit corporation.** If you do need to expel a member, we suggest you do so only after checking the latest annotated nonprofit statutes in your state (look under Membership Provisions in your state's nonprofit corporation act).

Article 12, Section 2. Regular Meetings of Members

In the blanks in the first paragraph of this section, indicate the date and time of the regular meeting of members held to elect the board of directors. Many membership nonprofits will specify an annual meeting to elect the board here. The frequency of this meeting will, of course, depend on the length of the term of office for your directors (see the instructions for Article 3, Section 5, above).

Directors Elected Annually. Here is a sample bylaw for electing directors annually:

A regular meeting of members shall be held on January 2nd of each year, at 1 PM, for the purpose of electing directors and transacting other business as may come before the meeting...

Directors Elected Every Three Years. Here is a sample bylaw for electing directors every three years:

A regular meeting of members shall be held on the first Friday of July every third year, at 9 AM, for the purpose of electing directors and transacting other business as may come before the meeting...

In the second paragraph, type the date and time of any *additional* regular meetings

of members you wish to schedule. Although we encourage frequent membership meetings, some smaller membership nonprofits may not wish to provide for regular meetings (other than the regular meeting to elect directors as specified in the preceding paragraph of the bylaws) and will leave these items blank. Others with a more active membership will use these blanks to specify frequent or occasional (for example, monthly or semiannual) regular meetings of members.

Remember special meetings. Your nonprofit membership corporation can also call and hold special meetings of members during the year—see the discussion below.

Article 12, Section 3. Special Meetings of Members

This provision allows the chairperson of the board or the president of the corporation to call special meetings of members—this represents standard practice (and the standard state rule) for most nonprofits. Your nonprofit corporation law may allow other special meetings to be called by a specified percentage of the membership of the corporation—see your nonprofit corporation law if you wish to allow members to call special meetings (look under "Special Meetings of Members").

Article 12, Section 4. Notice of Members' Meetings

Our notice provisions for members' meetings are, for the most part, standard provisions found in state nonprofit statutes, requiring personal or mailed notice for regular and special membership meetings. If you wish to extend or shorten the notice period (ten to 50 days), dispense with notice for regular meetings, or make other changes, check that your language conforms to your state's nonprofit law before making your changes.

As with the director notice provisions, members can waive notice of a meeting in writing—this procedure can come in handy if you don't have time to give formal notice of a meeting to members.

You can use telephone and fax machine notice. Our bylaw permits personal notification by telephone or fax machine. Again, a fax notice must be personally acknowledged by a return fax message or telephone call within 24 hours.

Article 12, Section 5. Quorum for Members' Meetings

Most smaller nonprofits indicate a majority quorum rule here (a majority of the members must be present to hold a members' meeting). The nonprofit corporation laws of a number of states are flexible on this point and allow the corporation to set its own member meeting quorum requirement. In the absence of a specific provision in the articles or bylaws, many states set this quorum requirement at one-tenth of the membership. This is reasonable for larger membership nonprofits whose members are spread over a large geographical area.

See your State Sheet in Appendix B for the specific membership quorum rules in your state.

Specifying a Quorum as a Majority of Voting Members:

A quorum shall consist of <u>a majority</u> of the voting members of the corporation.

For membership approval at a meeting, the vote of a majority of those present is required. (See Article 12, Section 6, of the membership provisions.) For example, in a corporation with 50 members and a majority-quorum rule for membership meetings, a quorum for meetings consists of 26 members. If 26 members attend a meeting, action can be approved at the meeting by 14 members, a majority of those present.

Article 12, Section 8. Action by Written Ballot

To make membership provisions more applicable and realistic, we have included this written ballot procedure to allow members to elect directors and transact other membership business by mail. These are standard, workable provisions—but they may not cover all the technical requirements found in your state's nonprofit statutes. To be certain, check our provisions against the membership written consent or written ballot procedures in your nonprofit statute or check with a lawyer.

Many states authorize membership action by written consent but require notice to any nonconsenting members. If you follow our provisions and mail a written ballot to each member, you should satisfy this notice requirement.

Article 12, Section 9. Conduct of Members' Meetings

Indicate, if you wish, the set of rules that will govern the proposing and taking of action at your membership meetings. Robert's Rules of Order is the standard, of course, but you may specify another set of procedures if you wish or leave this item blank if you see no reason to adopt formal rules for conducting membership meetings.

Completion of Membership Bylaws

Assemble your membership bylaws by adding the completed membership provision pages to the end of your completed bylaw pages. Then use the Adoption of bylaws page as the last page of your bylaws—this page is included as the last page of the tear-out bylaws in Appendix D and the bylaws form on the CD-ROM. Fill in this page according to the Adoption of Bylaws instructions given earlier. ■

Chapter 8

Apply for Your Federal 501(c)(3) Tax Exemption

*n*ow that you've filed your articles and prepared your bylaws, it's time to prepare your federal exemption application (IRS Form 1023). Obtaining your federal exemption is a critical step in forming your nonprofit organization because most of the real benefits of being a nonprofit flow from 501(c)(3) tax-exempt status. You can submit your federal tax exemption application after or at the same time as you apply for your state tax exemption. Your 1023 application must be postmarked within 27 months after the end of the month in which your articles of incorporation were filed.

This is not an easy form to complete, particularly for nonprofit corporations that are eight months old or more—these groups will have to answer a lot of technical questions and pay close attention to the fine print in the instructions. For what it's worth, the IRS estimates that it takes the average person a little over four hours to learn about the form and about eight hours to prepare and send it to the IRS. Hopefully, by reading and following our line-by-line instructions below, you will accomplish this task in substantially less time.

So, let us make a suggestion: If you get stuck on a difficult question or run low on energy, take a break and return to this task when you feel better able to follow and absorb this material. The time and effort you devote to this task will be well worth it.

⚠️ **Special purpose nonprofits use a different IRS form.** If yours is a special purpose nonprofit group (formed for other than religious, educational, charitable, scientific, or literary purposes), you're likely to be exempt under sub-sections of Section 501(c) other than Subsection (3). To apply for your federal tax exemption, you'll need IRS Form 1024 instead of IRS Form 1023. Certain cooperative hospital service organizations and cooperative educational service organizations *can* use Form 1023—see the General Instructions to Form 1023, "Other Organizations."

A. Getting Started

Before diving into the task at hand, take a moment to read this section, which sets out the various tax forms and other IRS publications you'll encounter. We'll also give you tips on how to fill out the forms and deal with the additional information you may need to supply. Think of this portion of the chapter as your orientation.

1. Forms and Publications

You'll encounter several IRS forms as you make your way towards federal exempt status. You'll find tear-out versions of the following federal forms in Appendix D and on the CD-ROM at the back of this book:

- Package 1023. *Application for Recognition of Exemption* with official instructions (September 1998).
- Form 8718. *User Fee for Exempt Organization Determination Letter Request* (November 2003).
- Form SS-4. *Application for Employer Identification Number* (December 2001).
- Form SS-4. *Instructions* (December 2003). The CD-ROM instructions are contained in a separate file.

- Form 5768. *Election/Revocation of Election by an Eligible Section 501(c)(3) Organization To Make Expenditures To Influence Legislation* (December 1996).

⚠ **Check that your IRS 1023 form is current.** If you are using the IRS 1023 form included with this book (whether in Appendix D or on the CD-ROM), check to see that the form is current. Go to the IRS website (www.irs.gov) and access the form online following the instructions in the third bullet in Subsection 2. The heading on the form will tell you the revision date for the most current 1023 booklet. If the date of the online booklet is more recent than the version included with this book (September 1998), then use the newer online version—you probably will want to use the fill-in version to avoid having to print the form and fill in the blanks manually.

If you do prepare an IRS 1023 form that is newer than the one we provide with this book, the instructions below should still work since changes to the form usually consist of reorganization and format changes. If a newer form contains questions not covered in this chapter, call the IRS (800-TAX-1040) and ask a tax-exempt organization specialist for help with the new material. Or check Nolo's website for instructions for the new form (look for updates to this book). If the changes are minor or insignificant, Nolo won't provide any updates.

We have also included some federal tax publications on the CD-ROM. These publications are surprisingly readable and give you lots of practical information. You can get copies or updated versions by calling your local IRS forms request telephone number (or the national IRS forms and publications request

number, 800-TAX-FORM), by going online to www.irs.gov/formspubs/lists/0,,id=97817,00.html, or by stopping by your local IRS office in person.

- Publication 557, *Tax-Exempt Status for Your Organization* (May 2003)
- Publication 578, *Tax Information for Private Foundations and Foundation Managers* (January 1989).

💡 **You can find everything in one place at the IRS Exempt Organization Information page www.irs.gov/charities/index.html.** It links you to the most important IRS forms, publications, regulations, and other information that applies to 501(c)(3) tax-exempt corporations.

2. Ways to Complete the Exemption Application

There are three ways to complete the federal tax exemption application:

- Use the tear-out form and fill it in by hand or typewriter.
- Open the IRS package 1023 on the CD-ROM file. This booklet contains two copies of the federal IRS 1023 form, plus official instructions to the form. The booklet has a version of the IRS 1023 form that you can fill in on your computer, then print out and mail in to the IRS. The IRS booklet file is provided in PDF format. To view, fill in, and print this file, you must have Adobe® Reader installed on your computer. This free program is provided on the CD-ROM, and also is available from the Adobe website at www.adobe.com.

You cannot save the IRS 1023 form with data you supply in the blanks unless you have purchased the Adobe Acrobat® program. The free Adobe Reader program only lets you save a blank version of the form—any data you supply in the blanks will not be saved. For additional information on installing and using PDF files, see Appendix A.

- Go to the IRS website and access a fill-in version of Form 1023 online. To do this, go to www.irs.gov. In the upper left box labeled Search Forms and Publications for: type "1023." Then click Go to open a page that lists the IRS publications that reference Form 1023. The second publication listed should be the fill-in version of Form 1023. The IRS booklet file is provided in PDF format. To view, fill in, and print this file, you must have Adobe Reader installed on your computer. For more information on how to install and use Adobe Reader, see the CD-ROM instructions above and in Appendix A.

3. Preliminary Reading

Before starting your federal tax exemption application, read the General and Specific Instructions to Package 1023 (the federal 501(c)(3) tax exemption application package). Also read through the information in IRS Publication 557.

If you find this reading a bit technical, don't let it bog you down. The information in this book about the requirements for federal tax-exempt status and how to achieve public charity status, together with our line-by-line

instructions for the forms, should be enough to get you through. If you need to, you can always refer back to the IRS publications and instructions when answering questions or filling out schedules.

4. Form 1023 Schedules, Attachments, and Exhibits

Form 1023 contains several schedules that only certain nonprofits (such as schools, churches, and hospitals) need to complete. Don't worry about these schedules—we will tell you if your group needs to complete a schedule and how to do it.

Some questions on the form ask you to prepare an attachment page or pages. Use letter-sized paper (8-1/2" x 11") and make sure each attachment page contains the following information in the heading, as shown on the sample below:

- a description of the information on the attachment (specify Form 1023 and identify the part and line number)
- the name, address, and EIN (Employer Identification Number) of your corporation, and
- the page number if you include more than one attachment page to your application (most groups will have multiple attachment pages).

You do not need to have a separate attachment page for each response—just list your responses one after the other on your attachment pages (as shown on the sample below). The federal form has space under each question for your response, but often this space is insufficient. You can use attachment pages to continue any responses you start on the form. As we explain later in this chapter, you also can use attachments to indicate you are including additional information as exhibits.

You will need to attach documents, such as articles and bylaws, and other materials, such as copies of solicitations for financial support, to your application. Mark each attachment as an exhibit and label them in alphabetical order. You can write the exhibit letter at the top of the document, or you can staple a page or note to the first page of the document and write the exhibit reference (for example "Exhibit A") on the attached cover page or note. We recommend that you use a separate cover page or note for your certified copy of your articles of incorporation since the articles you include as an exhibit should exactly match the articles you filed with the secretary of state. Make sure each document has a heading that identifies its content and the name of your nonprofit. The copies of your legal documents should have headings printed on the first page already, such as "Articles of [name of your corporation]" or "Bylaws of [name of your corporation]." Put similar identifying headings on all financial statements and other exhibits you prepare yourself and number each page if the document has multiple pages.

Sample Attachment Page

GoodWorks, Inc.
1220 Buena Vista Avenue
Phoeniz, Arizona 85007
EIN # XXXXXXXX

Attachment to Form 1023, Page 1

Part II, Line 1 (continuation): The nonprofit organization also will engage in the following activities: …

Part II, Line 2 (continuation): The nonprofit organization also expects to receive financial support from the following sources: …

5. Public Inspection Rights

As you begin entering information on the federal form, you might want to keep in mind that your readership may at some point be members of the public, not just some unknown bureaucrat at the IRS. Your federal 1023 tax exemption application, any papers submitted with the application, and your tax exemption determination letter from the IRS must be made available for public inspection during regular business hours at your organization's principal office. Any information that has been approved as confidential need not be disclosed (see "How to Keep Form 1023 Information Confidential," below), and you do not have to disclose the names and addresses of contributors.

If your organization regularly maintains one or more regional or district offices having three or more employees, copies of the documents must be available for public inspection at each of these offices. Copies of your organization's three most recent annual information returns must also be available for public inspection at your principal office (and, if applicable, your regional or district office).

Members of the public can also make a written request for copies of your organization's tax exemption application and its tax returns for the last three years. You must comply within 30 days and are allowed to charge only reasonable copying and postage costs. The public also can obtain copies of these documents at a local IRS Disclosure Office for a small fee, or by sending a written request to IRS, Chief FOIA Branch, c/o Ben Franklin Station, P.O. Box 795, Washington,

DC 20044. These public inspection requirements apply to 501(c)(3) public charities, not to 501(c)(3) private foundations—again, we expect most incorporators to qualify as public charities.

It's important to comply with inspection requests. If you don't permit public inspection, you could face a $20-per-day penalty. The IRS will impose an automatic $5,000 additional penalty if your failure to comply is willful. These penalties are not imposed on the organization—they are applied against "the person failing to meet (these) requirements." See IRS Publication 557 and IRC §§ 6104(e), 5562(c)(1)(C) and (D), and 6685 for further information on these rules.

 For additional information about IRS regulations on required disclosures by 501(c)(3) nonprofits, see the CD-ROM file:

Update: The Final Regulations on the Disclosure Requirements for Annual Information Returns and Applications for Exemption.

How to Keep Form 1023 Information Confidential

Any information submitted with your 1023 is open to public inspection. However, if an attachment or response to your application contains information regarding trade secrets, patents, or other information that would adversely affect your organization if released to the public, you can clearly state "NOT SUBJECT TO PUBLIC INSPECTION" next to the material and include your reasons for requesting secrecy. If the IRS agrees, the information will not be open to public inspection.

(IRS Regulation § 301.6104(a)-5 says that the IRS will agree if you convince them that "the disclosure of such information would adversely affect the organization.")

See the CD-ROM file, *Disclosure, FOIA and The Privacy Act*, for additional information on the restrictions applicable to the IRS and its employees regarding disclosures of information submitted to the IRS.

6. The Consequences of Filing Late

You must file your 1023 within 27 months after the end of the month in which you filed your articles of incorporation. In our experience, the most common problem faced by nonprofits is failing to file their Form 1023 on time. What happens if you file late?

First, if you file on time and the IRS grants your exemption, the exemption takes effect on the date on which you filed your articles.

The same is true if you can show "reasonable cause" for your delay (this means you have convinced the IRS that your tardiness was understandable and excusable). If you file late and don't have reasonable cause (or the IRS doesn't buy your story), your tax-exempt status will begin as of the postmark date on your form. For more information, see Section C3, Part III, below.

If your nonprofit has been organized for several years and you're just now getting around to filing your Form 1023, don't despair—you've got plenty of good company. The important point here is to persevere, complete your application, and mail it to the IRS as soon as possible.

B. Do You Need to File Form 1023?

Almost all nonprofit groups that want 501(c)(3) tax-exempt status will file Form 1023. Form 1023 serves two important purposes:

- It is used by nonprofit organizations to apply for 501(c)(3) tax-exempt status, and
- It serves as your notice to the IRS that your organization is a public charity, not a private foundation. Remember, as discussed earlier, the IRS will presume that 501(c)(3) nonprofit groups are private foundations unless you notify the IRS that you qualify for public charity status.

This said, there are a few groups that are not required to file a Form 1023. You aren't required to file if you are:

- a group that qualifies for public charity status and normally has gross receipts of not more than $5,000 in each tax year (the IRS uses a special formula to determine whether a group "normally" has annual gross receipts of not more than $5,000—for specifics, see IRS Publication 557, "Gross Receipts Test")
- a church, interchurch organization, local unit of a church, convention, or association of churches, or an integrated auxiliary of a church, or
- a subordinate organization covered by a group exemption letter (but only if the parent organization timely submits a notice to the IRS covering the subordinate organization—see the group exemption letter requirements in IRS Publication 557).

Even if one of the above exceptions applies to you, we recommend that you file a Form 1023 anyway. Why? First, it's risky to second-guess the IRS. If you're wrong and the IRS denies your claim to 501(c)(3) tax status several years from now, your organization may have to pay substantial back taxes and penalties. Second, the only way, on a practical and legal level, to assure others that you are a bona fide 501(c)(3) group is to apply for an exemption. If the IRS agrees and grants your tax exemption, then, and only then, can you assure contributors, grant agencies, and others that you are a qualified 501(c)(3) tax-exempt, tax-deductible organization listed with the IRS.

C. Prepare Your Tax Exemption Application

Now it's time to go through Form 1023, line by line and fill it in. The form is divided into four parts, which we track with our instructions. Here we go.

1. Part I: Identification of Applicant

Lines 1a-e: Write the name of your corporation exactly as it appears in your articles of incorporation. If you have operated (or plan to operate) your corporation under a fictitious corporate name (one different from the name shown in your articles), include this name in parentheses after your formal name in Line 1(a).

Provide the address of the corporation in blanks 1(c)-(d). The IRS wants you to include the full nine-digit zip code in your address. Include it, if you know it (zip code information can be obtained online at the U.S. Postal Service Zip Code lookup page at www.usps.com/zip4). If you have designated one person to receive tax information and forms from the IRS (usually your corporate treasurer or CFO), list this person's name as the "c/o name" in Line 1(b). On Line 1c, insert the URL for your organization's website, if you have one.

Line 2: All nonprofit corporations (whether or not they have employees) must obtain a federal Employer Identification Number (EIN)—you will use this identification number on all your federal tax returns and reports. Even if your organization held an EIN prior to incorporation, you must obtain a new one for the corporate entity. Most new groups will not have obtained their EIN yet and should do so now.

The easiest and quickest way to get an EIN is to apply online from the IRS website. Go to www.irs.gov and type "EIN" in the top Site Search box. (Don't use the second search box labeled Forms and Publications—it will lead you to the paper version of the SS-4 form.) Then click Go to open a page with a link to the Online Application. You can fill in an online version of the SS-4 form and click Submit to submit the application and receive your EIN immediately. All EINs obtained online start with the number "20." You also can apply by phone. To do this, fill in the SS-4 form, *Application for Employer Identification Number* included as a tear-out and on the CD-ROM. Then call the IRS Tele-TIN number for your state listed in the SS-4 instructions (be sure to complete the form before making the phone call). Remember: the CD-ROM version has two SS-4 files—a fill-in version of the form and separate IRS instructions. Follow the instructions, below, when completing the SS-4 form or answering the online SS-4 application questions:

- **Type of entity.** Check "church" if you are forming one; if not, check "other nonprofit organization" and specify its 501(c)(3) purpose (educational, charitable, etc.).
- **GEN number.** Most groups will ignore this—it applies only to a group exemption application request. Members of an affiliated group of nonprofits can specify a previously assigned Group Exemption Number.

- **Reason for applying.** Check "started new business," then specify "formed nonprofit corporation" in the blank.
- **Date.** The date you started your business is the date your articles were filed with the state filing office. Use the file-stamped date on the copy of your articles returned by the state office.
- **Date you'll pay wages.** You can state that the date you will pay wages is "unknown."
- **Signature.** Have an incorporator or initial director sign the form, indicating his or her title as incorporator or director.

If you apply for an EIN online or by phone, you will be assigned an EIN number. Type this number in Line 2 of your 1023 form, then mail or fax a copy of your completed SS-4 form to the IRS as explained in the SS-4 instructions.

You can also get an EIN the slow way by mailing your SS-4 form to the IRS without calling. Expect to wait at least four weeks. If you apply by mail, type the following in Line 2: "Applied for: *[insert date of mailing of SS-4 form]* ."

Line 3: State the name and telephone number of a director or other person whom the IRS can contact regarding your application, and the phone number where this person can be reached during business hours. We suggest you list the name and telephone number of the person who is preparing the tax exemption. Nevertheless, don't expect the IRS to call to ask questions (or just to say "Hi"). If the IRS has questions about your application, it will usually contact you by mail.

Line 4: Specify the month your accounting period will end. The accounting period must be the same as your corporation's tax year. Most nonprofits use a calendar year as their accounting period and tax year—if you choose to do the same, specify December here.

If you anticipate special seasonal cycles for your activities or noncalendar year record keeping or grant accountability procedures, you may wish to select a noncalendar accounting period for your corporation. For example, a federally funded school may wish to specify June in this blank, which reflects an accounting period of July 1 to June 30.

If you have any questions regarding the best accounting period and tax year for your group, check with your (probable) funding sources and consult your accountant or bookkeeper for further guidance.

Line 5: Insert the date your articles were filed by the secretary of state.

Line 6: The boxes that appear here will not apply to most incorporators and should be ignored by most groups:

- 501(e) applies to organizations that perform cooperative services for hospitals.
- 501(f) applies to groups that perform collective investment services for educational organizations.
- 501(k) applies to child care organizations. Certain child care groups will be treated as 501(c)(3) educational organizations if they meet special requirements contained in this IRC section—see Chapter 3, Section B5, and IRS Publication 557, page 13, "Child Care Organizations."

- 501(n) applies to charitable risk pools set up to insure risks of 501(c)(3) nonprofits. See "Charitable Risk Pools" in Publication 557.

Line 7: Naturally, we assume this is your first application for your federal tax exemption and that you will check "no" here. If your organization has previously applied for its federal tax exemption (perhaps because it incorrectly applied under another section of the code), check "yes" and include a statement on an attachment page explaining the status or determination of the previous application. You could start the statement on your attachment page as follows: "Line 7: Organization previously applied for an exemption as follows: [*state the IRC section under which you applied and what happened—did you fail to follow up and let the application lapse? Was the exemption denied? If so, why?*]"

Line 8: Some nonprofits using this box will be exempt from filing IRS Form 990, the annual information return for nonprofits or the shorter 990-EZ form for smaller groups—see Chapter 10, Section B. If you expect to be exempt—for example, if you are forming a church or plan to have gross receipts of less than $25,000 per year—mark "no" and state the reason why you are exempt. All other nonprofits using this book should mark "yes" here. Only 501(c)(3) private foundations can check the not applicable ("N/A") box—as explained in Chapter 4, we're sure most incorporators will not want to form a private foundation.

For more information on the exemptions from the annual information return filing requirements, see Publication 557, "Annual Information Returns," and the instructions to the 990 form (call 800-TAX-FORM or go to www .irs.gov for a copy of this and the 990-EZ tax form).

Line 9: If your corporation has previously filed regular income tax returns or tax-exempt information returns, check "yes" and provide the information requested. Most groups should be able to answer "no" to this question. If you answer "yes" to either of these questions, you're probably converting a profit corporation to a nonprofit corporation or are late in submitting your exemption application. If you do answer "yes," be sure to specify the form number of each return filed, the year covered by the return, and the IRS office where it was filed.

If the deadline for filing the annual information return for a tax-exempt organization (IRS Form 990 and Form 990 Schedule A) falls when your federal exemption is pending, you still have to file the return. You also must file a 990-T Business Income Tax Return if your corporation makes $1,000 or more of unrelated business income in a tax year while your 1023 is pending. (See Chapter 10, Section B4, for more on unrelated business income.) Indicate that your 1023 is pending on any returns you must file.

Line 10: Check box (a) to indicate that your group is a corporation and attach copies of your articles and completed bylaws to your application. Use a *conformed* copy of the original articles (a copy received from the state filing office with the file-date stamped on the first page, which proves that it's an exact copy of the original). Make sure you have filled in all the blanks in your printed bylaws.

Although not required, you can have the person who will be designated to serve as corporate secretary sign and date the certificate section at the end of the bylaws. Since you are enclosing your bylaws, do not check the box at the right of the last line of this item on the application.

2. Part II: Activities and Operational Information

You should be thoroughly familiar with the material in Chapter 3 concerning the basic requirements for obtaining a 501(c)(3) tax exemption in order to answer the questions in this part of the form. We will refer to earlier explanations as we go along, but you may want to look over Chapter 3 now before you proceed.

Line 1: Describe *all* of your organization's activities—past, present, and future—in their order of importance (that is, in order of the amount of time and resources devoted to each activity). For each activity, explain in detail:

- the activity itself, how it furthers an exempt purpose(s) of your organization, and the percentage of time your group will devote to it
- when it was begun (or, if it hasn't yet begun, when it will begin), and
- where and by whom it will be conducted.

Many new groups will be describing proposed activities that are not yet operational, but you must still provide very thorough information.

If you plan to conduct any unrelated business (business that doesn't directly further your nonprofit goals), describe it here. Most nonprofits will not have planned unrelated business activities at this point. If you have, you will not want to stress the importance or scope of these incidental unrelated activities (for an explanation of the tricky issues surrounding unrelated business activities, see Chapter 3, Section C1).

Tempting though it might be, resist copying the language that already appears in the purpose clause in your articles—the IRS wants a narrative, not an abbreviated, legal description of your proposed activities. You may include a reference to, or repeat the language of, the longer statement of specific objectives and purposes included in Article 2, Section 2, of your bylaws. However, unless your bylaw language includes a detailed narrative of both your activities and purposes, we suggest you use it only as a starting point for a fuller response here. Generally, we recommend starting over with a fresh, straightforward statement of your group's nonprofit activities.

EXAMPLE 1: A response by an environmental organization might read in part as follows:
The organization's purpose is to educate the public on environmental issues with an emphasis on energy conservation. Since January 2003, the organization has published brochures promoting solar energy heating systems as an alternative to traditional energy sources. The price for the brochures is slightly above cost—see copies of educational material enclosed, Attachments A-D. The brochures are published in-house at [address of principal office]. Both paid and volunteer staff con-

tribute to the research, writing, editing, and production process. This work constitutes approximately 80% of the group's activities. In addition to publishing, the organization's other activities include the following [list in order of importance other current, past, or planned activities and percentage of time devoted to each]...

EXAMPLE 2: A nonprofit organization plans to sponsor activities for the purpose of supporting other nonprofit charities. It should describe both the activities in which it will engage to obtain revenue at special events and the manner in which this money will be spent to support other groups. Percentages of time and resources devoted to each should be given.

If you are forming an organization that automatically qualifies for public charity status (a church, school, hospital, or medical research organization) or has special tax exemption requirements, you will want to show that your organization meets the criteria that apply to your type of organization. See Chapter 4, Section B1, for a discussion of each of these special types of nonprofits. In the 1023 package, you'll find schedules and instructions that apply to each type of special group (for example, Schedule A for churches, Schedule B for schools, and Schedule C for hospitals—see the table below). If you are forming one of these special types of nonprofits, read through this material first so that you have a better understanding of what the IRS is looking for in your statement about your nonprofit activities.

SCHEDULES FOR SPECIAL GROUPS

Type of Organization	See Schedule
Church	A
School, College, or University	B
Hospital and Medical Research Organization	C
Home for the Aged or Handicapped	F
Child Care Organization	G
Student Aid or Scholarship Benefit Organization	H

Line 2: Briefly indicate your organization's anticipated sources of financial support in the order of their magnitude (most money to least money). Here are a few additional tips to help you respond to this item:

- Your sources of support should be related to your exempt purposes—particularly if you plan to be classified as a public charity under the support test described in Chapter 4, Section B4, where the group's primary support is derived from the performance of tax-exempt activities.
- If you plan to qualify as a publicly supported public charity described in Chapter 4, Section B2, your responses here should show significant support from various governmental grants, private agency funding, or individual contributions.
- If you expect your principal sources of support to fluctuate substantially, attach a statement describing and explaining

anticipated changes—see the specific instructions to Part II, Line 2, in the 1023 package.

There is not much room here to list your anticipated sources of financial support. Although your response should be as brief as possible, continue it on an attachment page if it won't fit in the allotted space.

Line 3: This question asks how your corporation will obtain revenue from the sources of expected support that you have just listed in your answer to the preceding question. If you provided the details of your fundraising activities in the previous response, simply state, "Fundraising activities are described in Part II, Line 2, above."

Otherwise, indicate how you will raise funds. For example, if you will give classes, state how you will recruit instructors and attract students. If you will rely on grants, state how you'll solicit grant funds and the particular or general categories of grant agencies you plan to approach. The question also asks you to explain whether you've begun fundraising. For newly incorporated groups, most fundraising activities will not yet be operative and you should say so, perhaps including a general description of what set-up work and initial operations you will undertake to implement your fundraising program during your first year.

Include as exhibits any literature you plan to distribute to solicit support and indicate that this material is attached in your response to this item.

Fundraising activities include unrelated business activities that will bring cash into your nonprofit (as explained under Line 2, above). If you have concrete plans to engage in unrelated activities (which, of course, you will clearly characterize as an insubstantial part of your overall activities), include the details here. At this point, most nonprofits will not have formulated specific plans for unrelated business activities.

Lines 4(a) and 4(b): Provide the names and addresses of the initial directors named in your articles. List the residence or business address of each director, not the address of the corporation. Because directors will not be paid a salary, you may wish to reply: "Pursuant to Article 3, Section 5, of the corporation's bylaws, directors will not be paid a salary. They may be paid a reasonable fee for attending meetings of the board and may be allowed reasonable reimbursement or advancement for expenses incurred in the performance of their duties."

Since you will formally elect officers (president, vice president, secretary, and treasurer) and provide for any officer salaries later at your first board meeting, you may wish to insert the following in your response to this item: "The persons who will serve as officers, and the compensation they will receive, if any, have not yet been determined by the board of directors. Any such compensation will be reasonable and will be paid in return for the performance of services related to the tax-exempt purposes of the corporation."

Alternatively, if you have decided who will be elected to serve as officers (and the amounts of any salaries to be paid), you can give the details of these officer arrangements.

Line 4(c): Check "yes" or "no." The IRS likes to see public officials (or people appointed by public officials) on your board when they consider whether you have a rep-

resentative governing body, particularly if you are seeking public charity status as a publicly supported organization (as discussed in Chapter 4, Section B2). These officials or appointees are not a prerequisite to getting your exemption, however. If you check "yes," give the information requested.

Line 4(d): This question will give the IRS information about your directors and whether or not they wear several hats in your nonprofit. "Who Are Disqualified Persons?" below, explains how to tell whether a director is disqualified, and the IRS's instruction for this line also explains it. For purposes of answering this question, you can ignore the fact that a director is disqualified simply because he is a director (under the disqualified persons rules, a director is a foundation manager and is disqualified as such). Here the IRS wants to know if the director is disqualified for another reason—that is if the director also is an officer, a substantial contributor, or related to another disqualified person. The question also asks if any director also has either a business or a family relationship with a disqualified person.

Of course, the IRS would like to see people on the board who are not disqualified persons (other than as directors)—they are likely to have less personal and self-interested motives for carrying out the public purposes of the organization. Don't worry, though—it's quite common, particularly in small nonprofits, for directors or officers to be disqualified in a tax sense either because they also serve as corporate officers or are members of the family of a disqualified person (for example, directors related to each other or to officers) or for some other reason.

Who Are Disqualified Persons?

People who are "disqualified" in the eyes of the IRS are not necessarily prohibited from participating in the operation of the 501(c)(3) nonprofit corporation. Instead, their contributions to the nonprofit may not count when figuring the public support received by groups classed as public charities. If the corporation is classified as a 501(c)(3) private foundation (we assume yours won't be), the corporation and the disqualified individual can be held liable for certain private foundation excise taxes. Disqualified persons include:

1. Substantial contributors. These are donors who give more than $5,000, if the amount they contributed is more than 2% of the total contributions and bequests received by the organization. For example, suppose Ms. X makes a gift of $20,000 to your nonprofit corporation. If this gift exceeds 2% of all contributions and bequests made to your organization from the time it was created until the end of the corporate tax year in which Ms. X made the contribution, Ms. X is a substantial contributor.

For purposes of determining whether a substantial donor is a disqualified person, gifts and bequests made by that individual include all contributions and bequests made by the individual's spouse. Once a person is classified as a substantial contributor, he generally remains classified as one (regardless of future contributions made, or not made, by the individual or future support received by the organization). However, if other conditions are met, a person will lose his status as a substantial contributor if he makes no contribution to the organization for ten years.

2. All foundation managers. Directors, trustees, and officers (or people with similar powers or responsibilities), or any employee with final authority or responsibility to act on the matter in question, are disqualified as "foundation managers"—this is a buzzword that means the bigwigs in a nonprofit who exercise executive control. Officers include persons specifically designated as "officers" in the articles, bylaws, or minutes, and persons who regularly make administrative and policy decisions. Officers do not include independent contractors such as accountants, lawyers, financial and investment advisors, and managers. Generally, any person who simply makes recommendations for action but cannot implement these recommendations will not qualify as an officer.

3. Owners and substantial players in entities that contribute. An owner of more than 35% of the total combined voting power of a corporation, the profits of a partnership, or the beneficial interest of a trust or unincorporated enterprise are all disqualified, if any of these entities is a substantial contributor.

4. Family members. A member of the family—including ancestors, spouse, and lineal descendants, such as children and grandchildren but not brothers and sisters—of any of the individuals described in 1, 2, or 3 above, is disqualified.

5. Other business entities. Corporations, partnerships, trusts, and so on in which the persons described in 1–4 above have at least a 35% ownership interest.

For further information on disqualified persons, see Chapter V of IRS Publication 578 (included on the CD-ROM). For information on how the definition of disqualified persons is tied to the information some groups must provide on the federal exemption application, see Part II, item 4(d), and Part III, items 13(a) and (b), in Section C of this chapter.

Line 5: There are two main questions on this line. The first asks about your organization's independence. The IRS instructions to this line define "control." Basically, it means that 50% or more of your directors, officers, or key employees are involved with another nonprofit, are appointed by another organization, or appoint 50% or more of the people running another organization. Answer "yes" or "no" as appropriate. If you answer "yes" because your nonprofit controls, or is controlled by, another organization, your operations are somewhat complex and you should consult a lawyer before applying for your federal exemption.

The second question has two parts—the first asks if you have incorporated a preexisting organization (such as an unincorporated association). A short explanation will suffice if the answer is yes, such as, "'The Better Living Center, Inc.,' is an outgrowth of, and successor to, the operations of an unincorporated association, 'The Better Living Association.'"

The second part of the second question asks whether you share directors, officers, employees, or office space (or other special relationships) with another group. If you check "yes," the IRS will want additional information on the purposes and activities of the other group. Again, consult a lawyer for help with this complex incorporation scheme.

Line 6: If your nonprofit plans to conduct financial transactions with one or more non-501(c)(3) nonprofits—such as receiving or distributing cash or assets with a 501(c)(4) political nonprofit or another nonprofit that is not tax exempt under 501(c)(3)—check "yes"

and provide the details. We expect most 501(c)(3)s will check "no." Normally, only unique groups, such as those that will set up, share facilities with, or support a politically active organization or another non-501(c)(3) nonprofit, will answer "yes" here. A "yes" response means that you should be applying for your tax exemption with the help of an experienced nonprofit professional.

Line 7: You should be able to answer "no" to this question, unless you are financially accountable to another organization (that is, you must report income and expenses to another tax-exempt, or taxable, organization). If so, you will need to provide the information requested—and check with a tax advisor or lawyer to make sure you will qualify for your 501(c)(3) tax exemption.

Line 8: Indicate any assets you have obtained since your incorporation, or at the time of your incorporation from a preexisting unincorporated organization (such as land, buildings, equipment, and publications—don't include cash and income-producing property). Indicate if your assets are not fully operational, as would be the case if a building is under construction.

Most newly formed nonprofit corporations will have few, if any, operational assets unless they have incorporated an existing organization. Some may have made arrangements for acquiring assets or putting them into use. If so, you should provide this information.

If you have not acquired assets or made arrangements for the acquisition of assets, indicate "N/A" as your response.

EXAMPLE: Brand Name Computer System, Inc., answered the question on Line 8, Part II, as follows: "Brand Name Computer has the following operational assets: one file server and four workstations. Once the main system hub is connected to the four workstations in approximately one month, the system will be fully operational and will be used to maintain organizational mailing lists, keep corporate books, generate organizational invoices and purchase orders, make and record payroll transactions, and pay ongoing bills."

Line 9: This question asks whether your organization will receive tax-exempt bond financing in the next two years. Frankly, we're not sure why the IRS is asking this question, but most groups will check "no" here anyway. If you answer "yes," the IRS may have a few extra questions about this item when it responds to your tax exemption application.

Line 10(a): Indicate whether any of your facilities will be managed by another organization or individual under the terms of a contract, explaining the relationship of the parties involved. The IRS is trying to figure out whether this type of managerial contract will unduly benefit some person or organization closely associated with your nonprofit corporation. If, for instance, a day care center plans to hire a director, officer, or other person who is closely associated with the corporation to manage the center, the IRS will want to make sure that the corporation is not paying more than fair value for these services. (Of course, it helps if the director or officer volunteers some portion of these services. If

you have reduced the terms of this type of management agreement to writing, include a copy of the contract as an attachment.)

Line 10(b): If your nonprofit corporation leases property (as the landlord or tenant), check "yes" here, attach a copy of the lease or rental agreement, and explain the relationship of the parties to the lease in your response. (For a discussion of leases together with a sample assignment of lease, see Chapter 9, Section L.)

The IRS is generally looking for lopsided or special-interest rental agreements, as would be the case if a director leases space in his home to the nonprofit for an excessive rent payment. Of course, the director can charge a fair market value rent—she is not required to let the nonprofit occupy the space rent free. Conversely, if the director or officer donates the use of a portion of the space or rents the premises to the nonprofit at a substantial discount, it will help make clear to the IRS that no self-dealing is involved as well as cast the director/nonprofit relationship in its most favorable light.

Line 11: Indicate whether you are a membership organization. If you have included membership provisions in your bylaws or you have used the tear-out or CD-ROM membership provisions as explained in Chapter 7, you should check "yes" and answer questions in Lines 11(a), (b), and (c). If you have not formed a formal membership organization, check "no" and go on to Line 12.

Line 11(a): Indicate any membership qualifications you will require and attach a schedule of fees and dues members will pay. If you haven't determined fee amounts yet, say so and state that "the amounts shall be reasonable and as specified from time to time by resolution of the board of directors."

Line 11(b): The IRS likes to see you actively solicit the general public to become members of the corporation. With that in mind, describe your present and proposed efforts to attract members. If you have final or draft copies of literature for soliciting members, mention that they are enclosed and include them as attachments. If you haven't prepared (but plan to distribute) such literature, explain that "promotional literature to attract members of the general public to become members of the corporation is not yet prepared, but will be prepared and distributed to members of the general public" (or to "members of the community served by the corporation").

Line 11(c): Certain membership groups give members exclusive rights to participate in the activities and events of the corporation in exchange for payment of dues. This is acceptable in most cases, as long as you allow members of the general public, or a broad cross section of the community, to become members and actively solicit public or community membership in your corporation.

If corporate programs, activities, and benefits are available to members and nonmembers alike, say so in your response. If members are given special discounts or preferences, list them in your answer. Use an attachment page to continue your response if you run out of room on the application form.

Line 12(a): It's a common (and completely permissible) practice to charge members of the public for services related to your exempt functions. (Of course it helps overall with your tax exemption application if you charge less than a commercial enterprise would for

goods or services, but this is not a tax requirement.) Many groups will derive income primarily from these services. This might be the case for a performing arts group, a dance studio, a health clinic, or a nonprofit school. If your group is in this category, answer "yes" and state, if appropriate, that benefits, services, and products will be available to the "general public." A "yes" response requires you to list the services for which you will charge and the amount of such charges. At this point, most groups have not fully determined what they will charge for services. If this is the case, first list the services and benefits that will be provided to the public and explain how the fees for them will be determined. Indicate that "charges for the above benefits, products, or services, although at present undetermined, will be reasonable and related to the cost of the service to be provided." If you already know what the charges are, attach a copy of your fee schedule as requested.

Line 12(b): Most groups will answer "no" to this question because the IRS frowns on groups that limit benefits or services to a specific class of individuals. However, if the class of people benefited by the corporation is broad (not limited to specific individuals) and related to the exempt purposes of the nonprofit group, the IRS should have no objection.

EXAMPLE: A nonprofit musical heritage organization plans to provide programs and benefits to needy musicians residing in the community. If the overall tax-exempt purpose of the organization is allowed, the IRS will permit this limitation of benefits.

Line 13: This question concerns your group's plans, if any, to affect legislation. Most groups will answer "no" to this question. If you plan to engage in efforts to influence legislation, check "yes" and read the discussion in Chapter 3, Section C3. You should state in your response that you will attempt to influence legislation either "to an insubstantial degree" or, if you plan to elect to fall under the political expenditures test, "within the limits allowed under Section 501(h) of the Internal Revenue Code." Be sure to give an estimate of the percentage of your organization's time and funds that will go into activities to influence legislation. Keep in mind that if the IRS considers the percentages "substantial," you risk putting your 501(c)(3) status in jeopardy (again, see Chapter 3, Section C3).

Line 14: A 501(c)(3) nonprofit organization may not participate in political campaigns. The IRS may deny or revoke your tax-exempt status if you participate in or donate to a campaign. Most groups should answer "no" here.

If you must answer "yes" to this question, your activities should be strictly limited to nonpartisan voter education work and statements. See Chapter 3, Section C3, and check with a nonprofit lawyer or tax consultant to make sure you are on safe ground before proceeding with your exemption application.

3. Part III. Technical Requirements

You should be familiar with the material in Chapter 4 in order to answer the questions in this part of the form. This is where terms such as "public charity" and "private foundation" start to become important. We will refer to earlier explanations as we go along, but you may want to look over Chapter 4 now before you proceed.

Line 1: Most new groups will be able to answer "yes" to indicate that they are mailing their exemption application within 15 months after the end of the first month in which their articles of incorporation were filed. If you answer "yes," skip Lines 2-6 and go on to Line 7.

Lines 2 (a)-(c): If you are filing your application late (that is, you answered "no" to Line 1), you may qualify for one of the three exceptions to the 15-month filing deadline listed here (other extensions to the normal filing deadline are covered in later lines of this part). These three groups are not required to file Form 1023: churches; public charities that normally have gross receipts of not more than $5,000 in each year; and subordinate organizations exempt under a group exemption letter. If you are mailing your exemption application late (more than 15 months after the end of the month of incorporation) and feel that you fall within one of these exceptions, check the box that applies to you and go on to line 7. (If you are filing within 27 months of your incorporation date, you may prefer to ask for the automatic late-filing extension available under Line 3 instead—see below.) If the IRS agrees that you qualify under one of the three special tests listed here, your federal exemption will be effective retroactively from the date of your incorporation.

The 2(b) exception is often applicable to new nonprofits. Your group qualifies if: (a) it is a public charity rather than a private foundation (because one of the purposes of completing your 1023 application is to establish that you are eligible for public charity status, we assume that you meet this requirement); and (b) it "normally" has gross receipts of not more than $5,000 in each tax year. Groups that have been in existence for two tax years qualify if they have gross receipts of $12,000 or less during the first two years (we assume you are into your second tax year at this point because you missed the 15-month filing deadline). Many new groups without outside sources of support can meet this gross receipts test during their beginning tax years. For more information on the gross receipts exception, see IRS Publication 557, Chapter 3, "Gross Receipts Test."

There's a safer way to qualify for an exception to the normal 15-month filing deadline. Ask for the automatic extension available under Line 3 of this part. If you submit your application within 27 months after the end of the month of your incorporation, you will qualify for late filing without having to take your organization's gross receipts or activities into account.

Line 3: If you will not mail Form 1023 within the 15-month limit and you are unable—or don't wish—to qualify under the exceptions discussed in Lines 2 (a)-(c) above, you will still automatically qualify for an extension of time to file as long as you submit a completed 1023 application to the IRS within 12 months after the end of the normal 15-month period—in other words, before the end of the 27th month following the date of your incorporation. This is a handy extension and allows you to apply within two years

plus from your date of incorporation—ample time for most groups (just don't miss this extended 27-month deadline—finish your application and mail it to the IRS, pronto). This means your tax exemption, if granted, will apply retroactively to the date of your incorporation. If you are filing your application late and qualify for this extension, check "yes" and go on to Line 7. If you don't qualify for this automatic extension, check "no" and go on to Line 4.

Line 4: Here is where you end up if your group is filing the 1023 application more than 27 months from the date of your incorporation and you don't meet one of the three exceptions listed in Line 2 of this part.

To qualify for late filing under these circumstances, check "yes" and attach a statement giving the reasons why you failed to complete the 1023 application process within 27 months of your incorporation. Federal rules, contained in Treasury Regulations 301.9100-1 and 301.9100-3, include a list of the reasons that are normally acceptable to the IRS, as well as those that aren't. For example, you relied on the advice of a lawyer, accountant, or an IRS employee, and received inaccurate information or were not informed of the deadline. These rules are summarized in the 1023 instructions for this line. After attaching your statement, perhaps with the help of your tax advisor, go on to Line 7.

If you don't think you can qualify for an extension under this Revenue Ruling (or if you decide not to bother—see "If You End Up on Line 4, Should You Ask for Relief?" below), check "no" and go on to Line 5.

If You End Up on Line 4, Should You Ask for Relief?

Most groups will not end up on Line 4 in Part III—they will submit their 1023 application within 27 months of their incorporation. If your group does end up here, you may decide not to bother seeking an extension and simply check "no" on Line 4. This means that your 501(c)(3) exemption, if granted, will be effective only from the date the IRS receives it, not from the date of your incorporation. Is this so terrible? Often, it isn't. Here's why: many nonprofits will not have any taxable income or contributions from donors during these early start-up months (the 27-plus months of operation prior to filing their 1023 application). Consequently, obtaining a tax exemption for these early months will not provide a tax benefit. However, if your group is facing tax liability for early operations, the need to provide donors with tax deductions for gifts contributed during the first 27-plus months, or the need to obtain 501(c)(3) tax-exempt status from the date of its creation for some other pressing reason, then it makes sense to prepare a special statement under Line 4 as explained in the text. If you are unsure, check with your tax advisor.

Line 5: If you checked "no" on Line 4 (you don't want to qualify for an extension under the special Line 4 rules), you should check "yes" here, then go on to Line 6. This means that you agree that your 501(c)(3) exemption can be recognized only from the date of its

receipt by the IRS, not retroactively to the date of your incorporation. By the way, we don't know what happens if you check "no" here—literally, this response means that you are not asking for an extension to file your application late, but don't agree that it should be treated as late. Such stubbornness is to be commended, but the IRS probably will not be impressed and will likely hold up the processing of your application until you give in and answer "yes" to this question in later correspondence with them (or may even deny your exemption outright). A "no" response here simply makes you ineligible to ask for 501(c)(4) tax status during your late-filing period (see Line 6). Not such a terrible fate, really, but we've speculated enough on these technical niceties—let's get back to more important questions.

Line 6: If you end up here (which means that your application for 501(c)(3) status will be considered only from the date of its receipt by the IRS), you may wish to check the box. If you do, you are asking the IRS to grant your group tax-exempt status as a 501(c)(4) organization—a social welfare group or a civic league—during your late filing period (the 27-month-plus period from the date your articles were filed up to the date your 1023 application is received by the IRS). What does this do for you? If your request for 501(c)(4) status is approved, your organization will be exempt from paying federal corporate income taxes (as a 501(c)(4) organization) from the date of its formation until the date of approval of your 501(c)(3) tax-exempt status. For most newly formed groups without taxable income during this initial period, obtaining this extra tax exemption will not be necessary and you can ignore this box.

However, if you or your tax advisor determine that your organization is subject to tax liability for this initial period, check this box and call 800-TAX-FORM to order IRS Publication 1024 (or go to www.irs.gov). Fill in the first page of Form 1024 and submit it with your exemption application. If you qualify as a 501(c)(4) social welfare group (as many 501(c)(3)s do—see "501(c)(4) Organizations," below), your 501(c)(3) tax determination letter will indicate that you qualify as a 501(c)(4) organization during your initial late filing (your pre-501(c)(3)) period.

501(c)(4) Organizations

IRC Section 501(c)(4) provides a federal corporate income tax exemption for nonprofit social welfare groups and civic leagues (see "Special Nonprofit Tax-Exempt Organizations," in Appendix D). Since the promotion of public welfare is defined as "promoting the common good and general welfare of the people of the community," many 501(c)(3) nonprofits also qualify as 501(c)(4) social welfare organizations. Although 501(c)(4) nonprofits are exempt from federal corporate income taxation, they are not eligible to receive tax-deductible contributions from donors. They also do not enjoy many of the other advantages associated with 501(c)(3) tax-exempt status, such as eligibility to receive public and private grant funds, participate in local, state, and federal nonprofit programs, obtain county real and personal property tax exemptions, and other benefits.

But 501(c)(4) organizations do enjoy one advantage not available to 501(c)(3) groups: They may engage in substantial legislative activities and may support or oppose candidates to public office. For further information on 501(c)(4) tax-exempt status, see IRS Publication 557.

Line 7: Lines 7 though 14 relate to whether you are seeking to be classified as a 501(c)(3) public charity or as a 501(c)(3) private foundation. In Chapter 4, we discussed the distinction between these two classifications and the reasons that you should try to meet one of the three primary tests for being classified as a public charity.

The 1023 instructions for Line 7 briefly explain the differences between public charity and private foundation status and the types of organizations that qualify as public charities. The table below shows how the organizations listed under the IRS instructions to Line 7 fit in with our organizational scheme in Chapter 4:

IRS Line 7 Instructions Covered in Chapter 4	
Groups listed in Line 7 instructions (1), (2), (3), (6), and (7)	Section B1
Groups listed in (4)	Section B2
Groups listed in (5)	Section B4

Check "yes" or "no" on Line 7 to indicate whether you are a private foundation. Hopefully, you will expect to qualify as a public charity and will mark "no" to this question. If your response is "no," go on to Line 9. If you are forming a 501(c)(3) private foundation, check "yes" and go on to Line 8.

Line 8: If you've checked "yes" on Line 7 indicating that you are a private foundation and you believe you can obtain the benefits of being a private operating foundation as explained in Chapter 4, Section C4 (also see the heading "Private Operating Foundations" in IRS Publication 557 and IRS Publication 578), check this box and complete Schedule E of the application. To understand the technical requirements of this special classification, you will need to refer to various subsections of Federal Income Tax Regulation § 53.4942 and

will probably wish to consult a tax advisor for help in preparing this schedule.

If you are forming a 501(c)(3) private foundation but do not seek to be classified as a private operating foundation, check "no" here.

All private foundations go on to Part III, Line 14.

Line 9: Check the box (letters [a]-[j]) that corresponds to the basis of your claim to public charity status. First, absorb what you can of the technical material given in the 1023 Line 9 instructions. Then reread Chapter 4, Section B—this section provides the names of these public charity organizations, the requirements they must meet, and the Internal Revenue Code sections that apply to them. Note that letter (j) is a special case that allows certain groups to have the IRS determine which public charity support test best suits their activities and sources of revenue. We cover this special choice in more detail in Box (j), below.

After checking the appropriate public charity classification box for your organization under Line 9, make sure to go on to the next question on the 1023 that applies to your organization (see the boldface instruction under the 1023 Line 9 Table of Organizations).

The following chart shows how the different types of groups listed in this part of the application fit within the three different categories of public charity status discussed in Section B of Chapter 4. If you concentrate on our basic division of these different groups into the three public charity categories, rather than focusing on the individual Internal Revenue Code sections, this part will go more smoothly.

IRS Line 9 Public Charities Covered in Chapter 4	
Line 9 (a)	Chapter 4, Section B1
Line 9 (b)	Chapter 4, Section B1
Line 9 (c)	Chapter 4, Section B1
Line 9 (d)	Chapter 4, Section B1
Line 9 (e)	Chapter 4, Section B1
Line 9 (f)	Chapter 4, Section B1
Line 9 (g)	Chapter 4, Section B1
Line 9 (h)	Chapter 4, Section B2
Line 9 (i)	Chapter 4, Section B4
Line 9 (j)	Chapter 4, Sections B2 and B4

Let's look a little more closely at each of the lettered boxes in Line 9:

Box (a): If you seek to qualify automatically for public charity status as a church, also see the instructions to Schedule A in the 1023 package and our discussion of this schedule in the Line 14 instructions below. Go on to Part III, Line 14.

Box (b): Groups seeking to qualify as private schools should refer to the IRS instructions to Schedule B and see our discussion of this schedule under the Line 14 instructions below. Go on to Part III, Line 14.

Boxes (c)-(g): Few groups will choose one of these boxes—each applies to a special type of organization such as a hospital, public safety organization, or government agency.

Box (c) hospitals and medical research groups will need to complete Schedule C—you should refer to the 1023 instructions for this schedule before checking this box.

Box (e) organizations operated solely for the benefit of, or in connection with, any of the other public charity organizations (except one testing for public safety) must complete Schedule D. This information helps the IRS determine whether this type of organization supports other qualified public charities. For further information, refer to the 1023 instructions and Publication 557, "Section 509(a)(3) Organizations."

Groups checking boxes (c) through (f), go on to Part III, Line 14. Governmental organizations checking box (g), go on to Part III, answer questions 11 and 12, skip 13, then answer Line 14.

When to get outside help. If you check one of the (c)-(g) boxes, the lawyer, accountant, or other advisor who is helping you organize one of these special corporations should help you with your application.

Box (h): This box is for organizations that receive a substantial part of their support from government agencies or from the general public. These are the publicly supported groups discussed in Chapter 4, Section B2. If you believe this is the public charity best suited to your organization's sources of support, check the box on this line. If you are unsure whether this is the best support test to use for your group (that is, if you think that the public charity support test listed in Box (i) also may apply to your organization), you may wish to let the IRS make this decision for you as explained in the Box (j) instructions below.

As discussed in Chapter 4, Section B2, many groups will not want to fall under this public charity test, because it does not allow you to include receipts from the performance of services related to the corporation's exempt purposes to be included as "qualified public support."

Groups checking Box (h) go on to Part III, Line 10.

Box (i): This box is for organizations that normally receive 1/3 of their support from contributions, membership fees, and gross receipts from activities related to the exempt functions of the organization (subject to certain exceptions) but not more than 1/3 from unrelated trades and businesses or gross investment income. This support test is discussed in Chapter 4, Section B4—this is the most common and often the easiest way to qualify a new nonprofit organization as a public charity. So reread the requirements of this test and the definition of terms associated with it in Chapter 4. If you believe this public charity test best suits your expected sources of support, check this box. If you are unsure, see the instructions to Box (j) just below.

Groups checking Box (i), go on to Part III, Line 10.

Box (j): If you feel that your group may qualify as a public charity either under Box (h) or Box (i) but aren't sure which to choose, you can check this box. The IRS will decide which of these two public charity classifications best suits your organization based upon the financial data and other financial support information included in your 1023 application. For many new groups, Box (j) is the best way to go. Rather than working through the math and technical definitions necessary to approximate whether you will qualify as a public charity under Box (h) or

Box (i), checking this box lets the IRS do the work for you.

Groups checking Box (j), go on to Part III, Line 10.

Sample Responses to Line 9

Here are some examples of how groups might answer Line 9:

The First Fellowship Church, a religious organization that plans to maintain a space to provide weekly religious services to its congregation, checks Box (a) to request automatic public charity status as a church.

The Workshop for Social Change, an educational group that plans to receive support from public and private grant funds and from individual and corporate contributions, checks Box (h) to request public charity status as a publicly supported organization.

Everybody's Dance Studio and Dinner Theater—a group that expects to derive most of its operating revenue from student tuitions, special workshops, and ticket sales (as well as from other exempt purpose activities)—selects Box (i) to be classified as a group that meets the public charity public support test discussed in Chapter 4, Section B4.

The School for Alternative Social Studies—an accredited private post-graduate school with a formal curriculum, full-time faculty, and regularly enrolled student body—checks Box (b) to request automatic public charity status as a formal private school.

The Elder Citizens' Collective and Information Exchange, which plans to derive support from contributions and grants as well as subscriptions to its weekly newsletter (and other exempt-purpose services and products made available to members and the public at large), checks Box (j) to have the IRS decide whether Box (h) or Box (i) is the appropriate public charity classification.

Line 10: This question deals with "advance" and "definitive" rulings on whether you qualify as a public charity. (See Chapter 4, Sections B2 and B4, for an explanation of these rulings, and "What's Better—An Advance or a Definitive Ruling?" below.) Groups that checked Line 9 Boxes (h), (i), or (j) must answer this question (we refer to these groups as "Line 10 groups"). These are groups that believe they qualify as public charities because of their support—either because of public support (covered in Chapter 4, Sections B2 and B3) or support from exempt purpose activities (covered in Chapter 4, Section B4). These groups have either chosen the method by which they'll qualify by checking Line 9 (h) or (i), or they've asked the IRS to choose it for them by checking Line 9 (j). Remember: Groups that check Line 9, Boxes (a) through (f), skip this and the next several questions and go directly to Line 14. Groups that check Line 9, Box (g), answer questions 11 and 12, and then go to Line 14.

Line 10 groups are first asked whether they've completed a tax year consisting of at least eight months. You'll check the "yes" box or the "no" box.

How to Figure Your First Tax Year: The language of the tax form requires you to have completed at least one tax year, which must consist of eight months or more. This is different from saying that your nonprofit has been in existence for at least eight months. Even if your nonprofit has been in existence for more than eight months, if it has not completed its first tax year, it should answer "no" here.

To figure out whether to say "yes" or "no" here, realize the following:

Most tax years of a nonprofit (or any other entity or person) are 12 months long, but the first and last tax years may be "short" tax years consisting of less than 12 months.

The start of your first tax year is the date when your articles were filed.

The end of your first tax year is the last date of the month of the nonprofit's fiscal year (also called "tax year" or "accounting period") specified in its bylaws. The bylaws date is a "soft" date—it simply reflects the nonprofit's best expectation as to when the first tax year will end. In reality, a nonprofit's first tax year is determined according to when the nonprofit files its first information tax return (you state on the return when your tax year really ends). This is how the tax year is determined for all tax entities that can choose their tax year.

EXAMPLE 1: If a nonprofit files articles on February 10, and its tax year will end on December 31, it should respond "no" to this question if it is preparing its exemption application in November of its first year. Even though it's been in operation for more than eight months, it has not filed an informational return for and completed its first tax year. Its first tax year will end on December 31, and it will file its first informational tax return (IRS Form 990) within 4-1/2 months of December 31 (by May 15 of the following year).

EXAMPLE 2: Let's assume that the same group prepares its exemption application in January of the next year after it was formed. It will respond "yes" to this question because it has completed its first tax year, and this tax year consisted of at least eight months (the first tax year included the full months of March through December—ten full months).

EXAMPLE 3: If the same group incorporated on May 15 and it applied for the exemption in January of the next year after it incorporated, it would answer "no." In this case, it has completed one full tax year—its first short tax year from May 15 to December 31, but this tax year only included 7-1/2 months.

Yes. (Line 10.) Those that answer "yes" have the option of requesting either an advance or a definitive ruling. If you request a definitive ruling, you have to answer additional questions (11 through 14) in Part III. If you request an advance ruling, you'll have to answer additional questions (11 and 14—skip questions 12 and 13) in Part III, and fill out two copies of IRS Form 872-C (instructions for this form are below). See "What's Better— An Advance or a Definitive Ruling?" below, for guidance on which type of ruling to request.

No. (Line 10.) If your answer is "no," you have no choice. As you'll see when looking at the "no" box, the IRS insists that you request an advance ruling (you can't request a definitive ruling unless you can show that you've completed a tax year with at least eight months in it). You will need to complete two copies of Form 872-C and attach them to your application. Although there are no explicit directions to do so, skip questions 11 to 13 and go on to question 14—our experience has shown that this is the proper course.

Your responses in Line 10 will indicate whether your group is requesting an advance or definitive IRS ruling as to its public charity status and whether you must go on to answer additional questions 11 through 14 in Part III.

EXAMPLE: The Nonprofit Center, Inc., filed its articles with the secretary of state on September 1 and closed its first tax year on December 31 (it specified December as the ending month of its accounting period in Part I, Line 4, of the 1023 application). The corporation is a Line 10 group and is preparing its 1023 tax exemption application during October of the following year. The group must check the "no" box here and request an advance-ruling period because it has completed only one tax year consisting of less than eight months. Its first and only completed tax year was a "short year" running from September 1 to December 31 of the previous calendar year. For further tax year examples, see the back of IRS Form 872-C.

What's Better—An Advance or a Definitive Ruling?

Broadly speaking, an advance ruling on your public charity status is tentative; a definitive ruling is for keeps. The IRS automatically makes a definitive ruling as to the public charity status of groups that are not required to fill in Line 10. Line 10 groups—those that are seeking public charity status because of the nature of their support—can only ask for a definitive ruling if they have completed a tax year of at least eight months. If they haven't, Line 10 groups must ask for an advance ruling. Even though an advance ruling is tentative and does not become final until the end of a five-year advance ruling period, it does have a few advantages over a definitive ruling. Specifically, an advance ruling is likely to come sooner, and you risk less by asking for it. Here's why.

For a definitive ruling, the IRS will look at the actual support received to date by your group. If this support is not sufficient to qualify your group under the applicable public charity category, your public charity status will be denied (or, if you're lucky, the IRS will issue an advance, not a definitive, public charity ruling and wait to make a final determination on your qualification for public charity status at the end of the advance ruling period). Further, requesting a definitive ruling may take extra time and could require you to respond to additional IRS questions before your tax exemption is approved.

Obtaining an advance public charity ruling is easier. The IRS will issue an advance ruling if it appears from the financial statements and other information you submit with the 1023 application that the group's anticipated sources of support will qualify the organization for public charity status. At the end of a

five-year advance-ruling period, the IRS will look at the annual information returns of the organization. If actual support meets the requirements of the selected public charity category, the group will then receive final approval of its 501(c)(3) public charity status. If the group does not qualify for public charity status at the end of this period, it will be classified as a 501(c)(3) private foundation during succeeding tax years.

You probably know by now that classification as a private foundation at the end of your advance ruling period would not be a good turn of events. Your foundation and its managers will be subject to private foundation excise taxes. The group will not, however, be retroactively liable for most of the private foundation excise taxes during its advance-ruling period (see "Private foundation taxes" in Section H, below). And even if the IRS denies you public charity status at the end of the advance-ruling period, contributions made during the advance-ruling period by individual donors will still be treated as having been made to a valid public charity.

In our opinion, it usually makes the most sense for Line 10 groups to request an advance-ruling period for their public charity status, even if they have completed one tax year of at least eight months at the time of their application (and can, therefore, request a definitive ruling if they want to). Generally, obtaining an advance ruling is quicker and easier, and it lets your actual sources of support during a five-year period speak for themselves. Of course, if your group is the exception and you can reasonably predict that its past support qualifies it for public charity status, go ahead and request a definitive ruling.

If your Line 10 group has completed one tax year consisting of at least eight months, remember to check the second or third box in Line 10 to specify the type of public charity ruling you are requesting. Check the second box to request a definitive ruling (and go on to answer lines 11 through 14). To request an advance ruling, check the third box, then go on to answer questions 11 and 14 (skip questions 12 and 13), and make sure to attach two completed 872-C forms to your application.

EXAMPLE: Remember the Workshop for Social Change from the earlier example? This is a group that plans to qualify for public charity status as a Line 9 Box (h) publicly supported organization. If the group has not completed one tax year of at least eight months, it must request an advance ruling by checking the Line 10 "no" box and going on to Line 14.

Everybody's Dance Studio and Dinner Theater is seeking public charity status as a Line 9 Box (i) group. It has completed its first tax year consisting of 11 months and checks the first Line 10 "yes" box. It decides to check the third Line 10 box to request an advance ruling of its public charity status and goes on to Line 11.

Now, Take a Break!

Completing the Technical Requirements section can be tricky. If you're feeling lost, overwhelmed, or just plain disgusted, take a break. When you come back and read our instructions to this part once or twice more, most of you will be able to successfully tackle this material and move on to the next (and last!) part of this federal form.

If you get stuck when choosing the proper public charity classification or responding to questions that apply to your group, ask a board member, friend, or a friend of a friend with some legal or tax background to give you a hand. A little help will usually get you over this incorporation hurdle.

Line 11: This line applies only to Line 10 groups that have checked the first Line 10 box (the "yes" box) indicating that they have completed a tax year consisting of at least eight months. Government groups that have checked the Line 9 Box (g) must also complete Line 11. Few readers will be applying on behalf of this special sort of group.

To answer this question, you must skip ahead and complete the statement of revenue and expenses, which is the first page of the two-page Financial Data information in Part IV of the 1023 form (follow our instructions to Part IV(a), below, to complete the Statement of Revenue and Expenses). After filling in the Statement, if you have listed any unusual grants on Line 12 of the Statement of Revenue and Expenses in any of the columns, list them here along with the donor's name, date, and amount and the nature of the grant (what the grant was for, whether it was restricted to a specific use, and other terms of the grant).

Unusual Grants

Unusual grants are contributions, bequests, or grants that your organization receives because it is publicly supported but which are so large that they could jeopardize your ability to meet your public support test The benefit of having a large grant qualify as an unusual grant is that it does not jeopardize the group's public charity status (as do other large sums received from a single source). It is unlikely that your beginning nonprofit has received sums that should be classified as unusual grants. For further information on this technical area, see the 1023 instructions to Line 11 of Part IV-A, the discussion and examples of unusual grants in Chapter 4, Section B, and the specific rules on unusual grants contained in IRS Publication 557.

Line 12: Check the box on this line only if:

- your group checked Line 9, Box (g), (h), or (j), and
- you checked the first and second Line 10 boxes indicating that your organization has completed a tax year consisting of at least eight months and you wish to obtain a definitive ruling as to its public charity status. If both of these

statements don't apply to you, skip this line and go on to Line 13.

Those who check the box in Line 12 will need to answer sections 12(a) and 12(b) (following the instructions below). Like Line 11, Lines 12(a) and (b) should only be completed after you have completed Part IV-A (statement of revenue and expenses) of the exemption application.

Line 9 Box (j) Groups Do More Work Here: Line 9 Box (j) groups—those who are asking the IRS to do the math to determine whether they meet the public charity support requirements test under Line 9(h) or Line 9(i)—must complete both Line 12 and Line 13 if they are requesting a definitive ruling. If an organization simply checks Line 9(h) and requests a definitive ruling, it only fills in Line 12 (not Line 13). Conversely, if a group checks Line 9(i) and requests a definitive ruling, it only fills in Line 13 (not Line 12). In other words, what the IRS giveth with one hand, it taketh away with the other: Line 9(j) groups end up doing a little more work here because they got off the hook by not checking either Line 9, Box (h) or (i).

Line 12(a): Enter 2% of the amount shown in Part IV-A, Line 8, column (e)—this is 2% of your organization's total public support received over the tax years shown in Part IV.

Line 12(b): If any individual or organization—other than a government unit or another 501(c)(3) public charity described in Line 9, Boxes (h) or (i)—has contributed more than the amount shown in Line 12(a) during the tax years covered in Part IV-A of your application, supply the name(s) of the contributor(s) and the amount(s) contributed on an attachment page. Why does the IRS want this information? For Line 9(h) public charities, the IRS generally does not count amounts that exceed 2% of the group's total support as qualified public support (see Chapter 4, Section B, and IRS Publication 557, "Support From the General Public").

Line 13: These questions require you to disclose sources of support that the IRS does not consider qualified public support for groups in this public charity category (the groups covered in Chapter 4, Section B4, that rely on support received primarily from their exempt-purpose activities). We're talking about contributions from disqualified persons or gross receipts from other individuals that exceed $5,000 in any tax year. Fill out this line only if both of the following are true:

- Your group checked Line 9, Box (i) or (j), and
- You checked the first and second Line 10 boxes indicating that your organization has completed a tax year consisting of at least eight months and wishes to obtain a definitive ruling as to its public charity status.

Those who check the box in Line 13 will also answer Sections 13(a) and 13(b) (following the instructions below) after consulting their completed Part IV-A (statement of revenue and expenses) of the exemption application.

Line 13(a): For a definition of disqualified persons, see "Who Are Disqualified Persons?" in Section C2. If a disqualified person provided gifts, grants or contributions, membership fees, or payments for admissions or other exempt-purpose services or products (these are the categories listed in Lines 1, 2, and 9 of Part IV-A) during any tax year

shown in Part IV-A, list the disqualified persons and amounts contributed or paid on an attachment page.

Line 13(b): If any person (other than a disqualified person) has paid more than $5,000 to your organization for admissions or other exempt-purpose services or products (these payments are reported in Part IV-A, Line 9) during any tax year shown in Part IV-A, provide the information requested on an attachment page. You must also disclose payments by government agencies and other public charities described in Line 9, Boxes (a)-(d) and (g).

Line 14: All groups seeking 501(c)(3) public charity status should answer "yes" or "no" to each question listed here. (All groups classified as private foundations [Line 8 groups] also must complete this line.) If you answer "yes" to any question, fill out the schedule indicated. For the most part, the IRS uses these schedules to make sure that particular types of organizations are "charitable" in nature, meet special 501(c)(3) exemption requirements applicable to their activities, or meet special requirements associated with the Part III, Line 9, public charity classification they are seeking. For further help in following this material, see the 1023 instructions to Line 14 and any instructions included on the schedules.

The following information will help you determine whether you need to fill out a particular schedule and how to do it.

a. Churches

We've discussed requirements for churches in Chapter 3, Section B2. If you checked Line 9,

Box (a), to seek automatic public charity status as a church or an association of churches, check this "yes" box and complete Schedule A.

Questions 1 through 15 on Schedule A seek to determine whether your organization possesses conventional, institutional church attributes. Questions 16 through 19 relate to whether your organization unduly benefits, or was created to serve the personal needs of, your pastor, or the pastor's family and relatives.

b. Schools

A school is defined as an educational organization that has the primary function of presenting formal instruction, normally maintains a regular faculty and curriculum, normally has a regularly enrolled body of students, and has a place where its educational activities are carried on (for example, private primary or secondary schools and colleges). Check the "yes" box and fill in Schedule B if you checked Line 9, Box (b), to seek automatic public charity classification as a formal private school. Make sure to check "no" to Line 2 on Schedule B—only state schools answer "yes" to this question.

Your responses to this schedule should show that your operations are nondiscriminatory and in accordance with a nondiscrimination statement included in your bylaws and published in the community that you serve (you must attach this bylaw resolution to Schedule B). For information on drafting and publishing this statement of nondiscrimination, see IRS Publication 557, "Private Schools."

c. Hospitals and Medical Research Institutions

If you will operate a hospital or medical research organization (and you checked Line 9, Box (c), check the "yes" box and complete Schedule C. Make sure to check the appropriate boxes at the top of the schedule and fill out the appropriate section of the form. Generally this schedule seeks to determine two things: (1) whether the hospital is charitable in nature and qualifies for 501(c)(3) tax-exempt status and (2) whether the hospital or medical research organization qualifies for automatic public charity status (see the Schedule C instructions and IRS Publication 557, "Hospitals and Medical Research Organizations").

If you are submitting your 1023 on behalf of a cooperative hospital service organization under IRC Section 501(e)—that is, you checked the 501(e) box in Part I, Line 6a—do not complete Schedule C. Your tax advisor can help you obtain an exemption for this special type of organization.

A 501(c)(3) charitable hospital normally has many of the following characteristics:

- staff doctors are selected from the community at large
- the hospital has a community-oriented board of directors (directors come from the community served by the hospital)
- emergency room facilities are open to the public
- at least some patients are admitted without charge (on a charity basis)
- the hospital does not discriminate with respect to its admissions (doesn't pick and choose its patient population) and

particularly does not discriminate against Medicare or Medicaid patients, and

- the hospital has a medical training and research program that benefits the community.

Hospitals need to be careful when it comes to renting space to physicians who are members of the board—and carrying out a private practice that's unrelated to the community service programs of the hospital. The IRS will be particularly suspicious if such physicians are prior tenants and their rent is below fair market value. Question 6 of Schedule C addresses this issue.

For additional information on tax issues related to health care organizations and for a sample community board and conflicts of interest policy promulgated by the IRS, see the file, *Tax-Exempt Health Care Organizations Community Board and Conflicts of Interest Policy*, on the CD-ROM included at the back of this book.

d. Supporting Organizations

A supporting organization is a special type of nonprofit set up to support other public charities. If you checked Line 9, Box (e), complete Schedule D. This is a complicated schedule—you must meet a number of tests. Refer to the 1023 instructions and Publication 557, "Section 509(a)(3) Organizations." Your nonprofit legal or tax advisor can help you qualify for this special type of 501(c)(3) public charity classification.

e. Private Operating Foundations

Few groups using this book will fall within this classification—we expect your organization to qualify as a 501(c)(3) public charity, not as this special type of 501(c)(3) private foundation. Still, if you are applying for a tax exemption for a private foundation that qualifies as a "private operating foundation," see our instructions to Part III, Line 8, and complete Schedule E.

f. Homes for the Aged or Handicapped

If you are forming a 501(c)(3) charitable organization that is a home for the aged or handicapped, check "yes" and fill in Schedule F. This schedule attempts to determine whether the home is charitable in nature, including whether the facilities are available to members of the public or the particular community at reasonable rates, whether provision is made for indigent residents, whether health care is adequate, and whether facilities are adequate to house a sufficient number of residents. For further information on IRS Guidelines, see Chapter 3, Section B1, and IRS Publication 557, "Home for the Aged."

g. Child Care Organizations

If you are forming a child care organization—you have checked the 501(k) box under Part I, Line 6c—check "yes" and complete Schedule G. The IRS uses this schedule to see if you qualify as a 501(c)(3) educational organization providing child care under IRC § 501(k). If your child care center also may qualify under 501(c)(3) as a private school, complete Schedule B—see our instructions for schools above.

h. Scholarship Benefit Organizations

Whether you are a formal "school" or not, if you provide or administer scholarship benefits, student aid, and so on, check "yes" to this question and fill out Schedule H. Of course, it's unlikely that you will be able to administer any private or public student aid funds unless you have set up a school with institutional attributes. The basic intent of Schedule H is to ensure that you administer or provide financial aid on a nondiscriminatory basis. For further information on IRS guidelines, see IRS Publication 557, "Charitable Organization Supporting Education" and "Organization Providing Loans."

Lines 1(b)-(c) allow your 501(c)(3) organization to apply for approval of your grant procedures if your organization is classified as a private foundation (in the event that your request for public charity classification under Part III, Line 9, is denied). If you wish to plan for this contingency, consult your tax advisor to help you select the appropriate IRC section on Line 1(c).

i. Successors to Profit-Making Organizations

If you have incorporated a preexisting profit organization (for instance, one that has been doing business and filed tax returns for prior tax years), check the "yes" box and fill in Schedule I. If you have incorporated an unincorporated association or similar nonprofit organization in which no person was allowed

a proprietary (monetary or property) interest, this question does not apply to you. A proprietary interest includes stock ownership, a right to profits, or a right to assets of the organization when the organization dissolves.

The IRS requests Schedule I to see if the activities, principals, or policies of the preexisting group and the newly formed nonprofit corporation are the same or different. The IRS wants to know whether the former profit-making enterprise that served the needs of a few individuals is now truly directed by, and serving the interests of, the community or general public. Yes, you may engage in the same activities as those of the preexisting organization and still obtain your tax exemption (if the activities qualify for tax-exempt status), but the more differences, the better. You should not, of course, still be serving the interests of, or providing special benefits to, the major figures of the former for-profit business.

You'll notice that Question 4(a) on the schedule asks that you attach a copy of an agreement of sale or other contract relating to the transfer of the assets of the predecessor organization to the new nonprofit corporation. If you have prepared this formal paperwork (it is not legally necessary), attach it to your application. If you haven't (this is normally the case for a small nonprofit), state that no agreement has been formalized, including, if applicable, the general nature of the terms of the agreement you will prepare later for the sale of the assets of the predecessor organization to the nonprofit corporation.

Question 4(b) of this schedule requests that you have an independent qualified expert attach an appraisal of the facilities or property interest sold, showing the fair market value at the time of sale. Have an accountant or tax advisor prepare this statement. The advisor can help you prepare an agreement of sale at this time, if you wish, or provide you with a boilerplate form for you to fill in and attach to your exemption application.

If your nonprofit corporation will lease property or equipment used by the predecessor organization, include an explanation and copies of any leases as required by Question 5. The IRS will scrutinize a lease to ensure that it does not require excessive rent payments to the principals of the former business. It's usually best, if possible, simply to assign such leases to the nonprofit corporation without payment and have the corporation deal with the landlord directly (or have the corporation renegotiate the lease with the landlord), rather than have the former business owners retain the lease and require rent payments from the nonprofit corporation. For an example of an assignment of lease form, see Chapter 9, Section L).

4. Part IV: Financial Data

All groups should complete the financial data sheets (Statement of Revenue and Expenses and the Balance Sheet) contained in Sections A and B in this part. As mentioned in our instructions for Lines 11 and 12, some groups will do this part before finishing Part III, Technical Requirements.

a. Statement of Revenue and Expenses

The financial data listed here includes your group's past and current receipts and expenses (many groups will need to show proposed receipts and expenses as explained below). The IRS will use this financial data to make sure that:

- your group's actual and/or proposed receipts and expenses correspond to the exempt-purpose activities and operational information you've supplied in Part II of the application
- you do not plan to engage substantially in unrelated business activities, and
- you do or most likely will meet the appropriate public charity support test if you checked Part III, Line 9, Box (h), (i), or (j).

The number of columns you use in Section A will depend on how long your group has been in existence. Use column (a) to show revenues and expenses for the current tax year. The ending date for this period cannot be more than 60 days before you mail the application.

Groups with prior tax years. If your nonprofit has been in existence in prior tax years (remember—a nonprofit corporation begins its existence on the date its articles of incorporation are filed with the secretary of state), use the remaining (b)-(d) columns to show revenues and expenditures for the corporation's previous tax years. For example, go back three tax years if your corporation has been in existence that long.

Groups without prior tax years. If your nonprofit has not been in existence for any prior tax year, use columns (b) and (c) to show proposed revenues and expenditures for your next two years (indicate the future year to which each column applies in the blank at the top of each column).

For example, if you are a new nonprofit applying for your tax exemption during the corporation's first tax year, the beginning date of the period shown at the top of column (a) is the date when your articles were filed. The ending date for this period must be within 60 days of the date you expect to mail your application to the IRS. Use columns (b) and (c) to show projected figures for your next two tax years. Many new groups will repeat much of the information from their first tax year for the next two proposed tax years, unless they anticipate a major change in operations or sources of support.

New groups should read the 1023 instructions describing the items on the Section A statement. Don't expect to fill in all the items. The IRS knows you've just commenced operations and expects to see a few blank lines. In fact, the bulk of the revenues and expenses shown by many new groups for their first tax year and the two proposed tax years do not neatly fit the categories shown in Section A. Rather, they often attach this information as schedules in response to Revenue Item 7 (other income) and Expense Item 22 (other expenses). If you attach these schedules of other income and expenses, make sure to break down the amounts as much as possible—the IRS does not like to see large lump-sum amounts.

b. Balance Sheet

Prepare the Balance Sheet to show assets and liabilities of your corporation as of the last date of the tax year period covered by column (a) of your Statement of Revenue and Expenses in Part IV-A.

EXAMPLE: You have organized a new nonprofit corporation, formed on April 1. You are preparing your 1023 application in November of the same year. The current tax year period covered by column (a) of your Statement of Revenue and Expenses is April 1 to October 31. Your Balance Sheet ending date will be October 31. This date should appear in the blank at the top right of the Balance Sheet page.

It's not uncommon for a small starting nonprofit without liabilities and accounts receivable to simply show a little cash as its only reportable Balance Sheet item. Other common items reported are Line 8 depreciable assets—equipment owned by the corporation and used to conduct its exempt activities.

If you have difficulty preparing the financial information under this part, get the help of a tax or legal advisor.

D. Form 872-C

If you request an advance ruling of your public charity status (by checking the first and third—or just the fourth—box of Part III, Line 10), you must complete and file two copies of Form 872-C with your 1023 application. One copy is in the 1023 file on the CD-ROM. It is also provided as a tear-out form in Appendix D. If you have ordered a 1023 package from the IRS, it contains three copies of this form.

By completing and filing this form, you allow the IRS to assess an additional year of excise taxes on investment income if your group is not granted public charity status at the end of its advance-ruling period. By signing this form, you're not signing your life away. You are letting the IRS collect one excise tax from you for a limited, but longer than usual, period of time—only if the IRS determines that you are not a public charity at the end of the extended advance-ruling period and only if you are then liable for this particular excise tax because of your operations during the extended advance-ruling period. The IRS can assess this tax for any of the five years in the advance-ruling period at any time up to eight years, four months, and 15 days after the end of the first tax year in the advance-ruling period.

If this form applies to you, complete it by typing the name of the corporation and the address of its principal office in the spaces at the top of the form. Show the ending date of your first tax year in the last paragraph (the month when your accounting period and tax year ends is given in Part I, Line 4, of Form 1023). Finally, fill in the bottom portion of the form. Type in the name of the corporation and the name of one of your directors, indicating this person's title as director. Have the director sign and date the form. This person should sign your exemption application and User Fee Form (Form 8718) as well. Do not fill in the items under "For IRS use only" at the bottom of the form.

E. User Fee Form 8718

You must complete and submit Form 8718, User Fee for Exempt Organization Determina-tion Letter Request, with your federal tax exemption application. You use this form to compute and pay the fees due for applying for your tax exemption. Before you fill in this form, make sure the Form 8718 included with this book is the most current (if there is a newer form, it may show that the user fees have changed). Go to the IRS site at www.irs.gov and type "8718" in the search box at the upper right of the page labeled Search Forms and Publications for. A link to the latest Form 8718 should appear at the top of the page that opens. If the revision date shown in the link is more recent than the revision date of the form included with this book (November 2003), use the newer form on the IRS site—and make sure to follow its directions for paying your user fee since the fees may have changed.

Fill in the tear-out or CD-ROM 8718 form included with this book by following these instructions:

Item 1: Type the name of your corporation.

Item 2: Insert your Federal Employer ID Number or, if you haven't received it yet, state "Applied for [*date of mailing IRS SS-4 form*]." See Section C1, Part I, Line 2, instructions above.

Item 3: Groups that qualify for a reduced user fee of $150 check Box "a." Your organization qualifies for this reduced fee if it is submitting its initial exemption application and:

- it is a new organization (in operation for less than four years) that anticipates annual gross receipts averaging not more than $10,000 during its first four tax years, or

• it has been in operation for four tax years or more and has had annual gross receipts averaging not more than $10,000 during the preceding four years.

If you check Box "a" to qualify for the lower $150 fee, complete the Certification section in the middle of Item 3. Type the name of your corporation in the blank and have the person who signs your exemption application sign on the line below the Certification, showing this person's title in the blank to the right.

You may be concerned about what will happen if you estimate that your gross receipts will average no more than $10,000 during your first four tax years, but your actual gross receipts exceed this amount in one or more years. We don't know for sure, but if you make more than this threshold amount, it seems reasonable to assume that the IRS would monitor your annual information returns and ask you to pay the remaining balance on the full Form 8718. Of course, if the financial information you submit with your 1023 exemption application shows that your group has, or expects to have, average gross receipts exceeding $10,000 for its first four years and you check the wrong box here, expect the IRS to return your exemption application due to insufficient payment.

Other nonprofit groups (except those seeking a group exemption letter) should check Box "b"—the user fee in this case is $500 (don't complete the Certification section if you check this box).

Box "c" applies only to special organizations seeking an exemption for a group of nonprofits, such as an association of churches. You can't use Form 1023 if you fall into this category; see Publication 557 and check with a nonprofit advisor for more help.

Write a check payable to the United States Treasury for the amount of the user fee and staple your check to the 8718 form (place the check in the box at the bottom of the form). The check does not have to be an organizational check. The person preparing the application or any other incorporator may write a personal check.

Whew! You're just about done. Follow the instructions in Section F, below, for assembling your entire federal exemption package.

F. Sign and Mail Your Application to the IRS

You've accomplished the most difficult part of your paperwork. The only task left is to gather up your application forms and papers and send them off to the IRS. Follow these steps:

• **Sign Form 1023.** Have a director sign and date the application at the bottom of the first page. Show the person's title as director in the blank provided.

• **Organize your federal tax exemption materials.** These will include your original Form 1023 application papers and any necessary attachments (such as copies of your articles and bylaws). All groups should submit pages 1 through 9 of the form. Include any schedules (A through I) you may have prepared under Part III, Line 14, of the application. Don't include blank schedules that do not apply to your organization. Don't staple any pages together yet.

- **Include Form 872 Consent form, if applicable.** For those who have requested an advance public charity ruling, place two completed Form 872-C Consent forms beneath your stack of Form 1023 papers. Don't staple any pages together yet.

- **Include an 8718 User Fee form.** Make sure to include a completed 8718 User Fee form. (You'll staple the check after you've made copies of the packet for your files.) Place the form on top of your 1023 form.

- **Make copies.** Make at least one photocopy of all pages and attachments to your application and file them in your corporate records book.

- **Attach check and staple 1023.** Now, staple your check to the space provided at the bottom of the completed User Fee form. Then, staple the pages of your completed, original 1023 application together.

- **Check your sequence.** Your stack of papers should look like this: first, the User Fee form (with check stapled as directed), then the 1023 form with attachment pages stapled together (if you prefer, a big paper clip will work just as well), then two copies of Form 872-C (for those who have requested an advance ruling).

- **Address your exemption application papers.** Send your package to the IRS District office listed on the User Fee Form. At this writing, the address is:

Internal Revenue Service
P.O. Box 192
Covington, KY 41012-0192

- **Consider using express mail.** To speed things up, use an express mail service. If you do so, send it to:

Internal Revenue Service
210 West Rivercenter Blvd.
Attn: Extracting Stop 312
Covington, KY 41011

Your next step is to wait. Although the IRS turnaround time is usually about two months, you may have to wait three to six months for a response to your exemption application.

⚠ **You must file annual federal and state information returns for your organization while your federal tax exemption application is pending (see Chapter 10).** Indicate on your annual returns that your federal 1023 application is pending approval by the IRS.

G. What to Expect From the IRS

After reviewing your application, the IRS will do one of three things:

- grant your federal tax exemption
- request further information, or
- issue a proposed adverse determination (a denial of tax exemption that becomes effective 30 days from the date of issuance).

If the IRS asks for more information and you are not sure what they want from you—or you just feel that you are in over your head—consult a nonprofit attorney or tax advisor. If you receive a proposed denial and you wish to appeal, see a lawyer immediately. For further information on appeal procedures, see the general instructions to the 1023 package and IRS Publication 892, *Exempt Organization Appeal Procedures for Unagreed Issues*—the IRS should mail this publication to you with the denial letter.

H. The Federal Determination Letter

The fortunate among you—and we trust it will be most of you—will get good news from the IRS. It will come in the form of a favorable determination letter, telling you that you are exempt from federal corporate income taxes under Section 501(c)(3) of the Internal Revenue Code, as a public charity. Unless you filed your application late and were not entitled to an extension, your tax exemption and public charity status will be effective retroactively to the date when your articles were filed with the secretary of state.

⚠ **If your determination letter tells you that you are exempt as a private foundation,** see a tax or legal advisor immediately.

Resist the natural temptation to file the letter without reading past the first sentences. In fact, the letter contains important information regarding the basis for your exemption and the requirements for maintaining it. Here's what to look for:

• **Are you properly classified?** Check to make sure that the public charity section listed by the IRS corresponds to the kind of public charity status you asked for. (You will find the various public charity code sections listed in Part III, Line 9, of your copy of the 1023 form.) Some groups will have checked Part III, Line 9(j), to let the IRS determine the proper public charity category support test for the organization.

• **Must you file a federal tax return?** The determination letter will tell you whether you must file a federal annual information return, IRS Form 990. Most 501(c)(3) groups must file this form (it's explained in Chapter 10).

• **Are you liable for excise taxes?** The determination letter also should state that you are not liable for excise taxes under Chapter 42 of the Internal Revenue Code. These are the taxes applicable to private foundations. With the exceptions noted below (for groups that have requested an advance public charity ruling), these excise taxes do not apply to you. The letter will also refer to other excise taxes for which you may be liable. These are the regular excise taxes applicable to all businesses that engage in certain activities, such as the sale of liquor, the manufacturing of certain products, and so on. For further information, see IRS Publication 510, *Excise Taxes*.

• **Information on deductions for donors.** Your letter will include information on the deductibility of charitable contributions made to your organization, and will refer to Internal Revenue Code sections that cover the deductibility of such donations.

- **Must you pay FUTA taxes?** Most groups will be told in their letter that they are exempt from federal unemployment (FUTA) taxes. You are, however, subject to filing nonprofit unrelated business income tax returns (Form 990-T). Nonprofits and their employees, however, are subject to Social Security (FICA) taxes—see Chapter 10, Section D.

- **Advance ruling information.** If you requested an advance-ruling period for determining your public charity status, the letter will indicate that a final determination of your status will be made 90 days after the end of your advance-ruling period. Check to make sure that the IRS has the correct ending date of your annual accounting period. At the end of this period, the IRS will review your past annual information returns and determine whether you have, in fact, met the public charity support requirements during the advance-ruling period.

- **Submitting more information for the advance ruling.** Although the determination letter indicates that you must submit information to the IRS, this is not usually necessary. You can submit additional information if you want to, and you must if you are asked to do so later to help the IRS determine that you have qualified as a public charity during the advance-ruling period.

- **Private foundation taxes.** The determination letter also may refer to IRC §§ 507(d) and 4940—these sections will apply to you if you are found to be a private foundation, not a public charity, at the end of your advance-ruling period. We have already mentioned the Section 4940 tax on investment income that may apply to you in such a case (see Chapter IV, "Tax on Net Investment Income," in IRS Publication 578 (included on the CD-ROM)). Section 570(d) refers to an extra tax imposed on private foundations if they repeatedly engage in activities that give rise to the private foundation excise taxes discussed in Chapter 4.

If the IRS determines that you are a private foundation rather than a public charity, your current and previous corporate activities will be scrutinized at the end of your advance-ruling period and you may be subject to private foundation excise taxes. Don't be too alarmed by this. These taxes usually don't apply to newly formed nonprofits. Again, your organization should be able to meet the support requirements of its public charity category during the advance-ruling period.

Congratulations! You've just finished the most complicated, and indeed most crucial, part of your nonprofit incorporation process. The remaining formal incorporation steps are explained in the next chapter. ■

Chapter 9

Final Steps in Organizing Your Nonprofit Corporation

*M*ost of the hard work is over, but there are still a few important details to attend to. Don't be overwhelmed by the number of steps that follow—many will not apply to your nonprofit corporation and others are very simple.

To chart your way through the tasks that follow, we recommend you use the Incorporation Checklist included in Appendix D and on the CD-ROM.

A. Obtain State Corporate Income Tax Exemption

Most states impose an annual corporate income, franchise, or other tax based on the net earnings of the corporation. In these states, your corporation must obtain an exemption from payment of these corporate taxes. In many cases, obtaining this state tax exemption is a formality—you will generally receive it once you file nonprofit articles in your state and obtain a federal 501(c)(3) tax exemption.

Your State Sheet indicates whether your state imposes a corporate income or other type of tax and, if so, the name and website address of the state agency from which your state corporate tax exemption must be obtained. We also show the general requirements and procedures for obtaining this exemption (whether the state tax exemption is based upon filing articles of incorporation or obtaining a federal 501(c)(3) exemption or separate state tax exemption application). We suggest you browse your state corporate tax agency website now and request all information and forms necessary for you to apply for your state exemption from corporate taxes.

The state tax exemption application process will be simple and self-explanatory in most cases. In the few instances where you must answer detailed questions or submit separate financial data, the responses and attachments to your federal 1023 package should serve as sufficient responses on the state form.

Make sure to take care of your state tax exemption in a timely fashion (usually by the end of your first tax year). As with the federal form, if you reach the deadline date for your annual state tax return and your state tax exemption is pending, make sure to file your required annual state return, indicating that the state tax exemption application is pending. Remember, like the IRS, state tax departments can impose severe fines and penalties for failing to file required tax returns, whether or not your corporation is subject to, or liable for, any corporate taxes.

B. Set Up a Corporate Records Book

Now take a few minutes to set up or order a corporate records book—this is an important part of your incorporation process.

1. Corporate Records Book

You will need a corporate records book to keep all your papers in an orderly fashion. These documents include articles of incorporation, bylaws, minutes of your first board meeting and ongoing director and shareholder meetings, tax exemption applications and determination letters, membership certificates (for those nonprofits with formal members), and any other related documents. You should keep your corporate records book at the principal office of your corporation at all times to make sure you always know where to find it.

To set up a corporate records book, you can simply place all your incorporation documents in a three-ring binder. If you prefer, however, you can order a custom-designed corporate records book through Nolo, as described below.

2. Corporate Kits

If you wish to order a nonprofit corporate kit through Nolo, complete the order form at the back of this book. These nonprofit corporate kits include:

- a corporate records book with minute paper and index dividers for charter (articles of incorporation), bylaws, minutes, and membership certificates
- a metal corporate seal (a circular stamp with the name of your corporation, the state's name, and year of incorporation), which you can use on important corporate documents (see Section 3, below, for more on corporate seals)
- 20 membership certificates, printed with the name of your corporation.

The corporate kits come in three styles:

The Legacy Kit: The basic kit with everything described above.

The Corporate Traveler Kit: Includes everything described above and is specially designed for easy portability.

The Attache Kit: Includes everything in the Legacy and the Corporate Traveler and also has a hardcase attaché.

3. Corporate Seals

Placing a corporate seal on a document is a formal way of showing that the document is the authorized act of the corporation. Nonprofits don't normally use a seal on everyday business papers (such as invoices and purchase orders), but they do use them for more formal documents, such as leases, membership certificates, deeds of trust, and certifications of board resolutions. A corporation is not legally required to have or use a corporate seal, but many find it convenient to do so.

As explained above, a good quality, reasonably priced metal seal is available as part of the corporate kits you can purchase through Nolo. For $25 to $50, you can order a customized seal from a legal stationery store.

4. Corporate Membership Certificates

If you have decided to adopt a formal membership structure with members entitled to vote for the board of directors, you may want to use membership certificates. Unlike stock certificates used in profit corporations, membership certificates in nonprofit 501(c)(3) corporations do not represent an ownership interest in the assets of the corporation. They serve only as a formal reminder of membership status.

Each certificate that you issue should be numbered sequentially. Type the certificate number at the top of the form. Type the name of the corporation in the heading and the name of the member in the blank in the first paragraph. Have the certificate signed by your president and secretary, then place an impression of the seal of the corporation at the bottom. You should also record the name and address of the member and the number of the issued membership certificate in the membership list in your corporate records. (If you want, you can order membership certificates printed with the name of your corporation from Nolo, as explained in Section 2, above.)

C. Prepare the Minutes of Your First Board of Directors Meeting

Your next step is to prepare minutes of your first board of directors meeting. The initial board of directors named in your articles of incorporation attends this meeting. If you did not name an initial board in your articles, see "If You Have Not Named Initial Directors in Your Articles," below, for instructions on having your incorporator(s) appoint the initial board. The purpose of this meeting is to transact the initial business of the corporation (elect officers, fix the legal address of the corporation, and so on) and to authorize the newly elected officers to take actions necessary to get your nonprofit corporation going (set up bank accounts, admit members if appropriate, and so on). Your directors should also discuss any other steps necessary at this point to get your nonprofit activities and operations started.

Prepare the minutes by filling in the blanks on the tear-out Minutes of the First Meeting of Board of Directors included in Appendix D, or on the Minutes form on the CD-ROM, following the instructions below.

We have flagged optional resolutions in the special instructions below. If an optional resolution does not apply to you, do not include the optional resolution page in your final minutes.

Here are some instructions to help you prepare your minutes.

Waiver of Notice form. You can find this Waiver of Notice form preceding the tear-out minutes in Appendix D; a copy is also included on the CD-ROM. The purpose of this form is to obtain the prior written consent of each initial director to hold your first board meeting. Under the statutes of many states, if the directors consent in writing the corporation may dispense with special notice procedures that would otherwise apply to this first unscheduled meeting of the board. Even if this written consent procedure does not apply in your state, you can use this form to notify each of your directors of the upcoming first meeting of the board.

Fill in this form showing the name and address of your corporation and the date, time, and place of the meeting. Date the form and have each initial director sign.

Preamble to Minutes. The first page of the minutes contains several standard paragraphs reciting facts necessary to hold a meeting of directors. Type the name of your corporation, the date and time of the meeting and the address of the corporation, in the first few blanks. Next, list the names of the initial directors present at and, if applicable, absent from, the meeting. Remember, a quorum of the board, as specified in the bylaws, must be in attendance to carry out corporate business. Name one of the directors as chairperson and another as secretary of the meeting. You will elect permanent officers later in the meeting.

Articles of Incorporation. Indicate the name of the state corporate filings office (usually the secretary of state) where the articles were filed and the date of this filing.

Bylaws. This resolution shows that your directors accept the contents of the bylaws.

Corporate Tax Exemptions. This resolution shows that your organization has obtained a favorable IRS determination of its 501(c)(3) tax-exempt status and is exempt from any applicable state corporate income taxes as well. Put the date of your federal determination letter in the blank in the first paragraph.

Election of Officers. Type the names of the persons that the directors elect as officers of your corporation. Most nonprofits will wish to fill each of the four officer positions listed in this resolution. In many cases, particularly in larger nonprofits, officers are selected from among the board of directors.

Your State Sheet indicates which officer positions must be filled in your state and any special requirements for filling these positions. Often, the same person may not be elected to serve as president and secretary.

If You Have Not Named Initial Directors in Your Articles

In some states, initial directors need not be named in the articles. If this is the case, then the incorporators (the person or persons who signed the articles) must appoint the initial board of directors. To do this, type the following form, fill in the name of the persons appointed to the board, and have each incorporator sign the form. Then prepare the minutes of your first board meeting as explained in the text. Make sure to place a copy of this form in your corporate minutes.

Meeting of Incorporators

On _____, 20___, at _____o'clock, a meeting of the incorporator(s) of (name of corporation) was held to elect the initial members of the board of directors. After nomination and discussion, the following persons were unanimously voted to serve on the board of directors of this corporation, and until their successors shall be elected and qualified:

_____
_____
_____
_____

There being no further business, the meeting was adjourned.

Dated: _____

[signature(s) of incorporator(s)]

Principal Office. Article 1, Section 1, of the bylaws indicates the county of the principal office of your corporation. Here you should provide the street address and city of this office. You should not list a post office box.

Bank Account. You must keep corporate funds separate from any personal funds by depositing corporate funds into, and writing corporate checks out of, at least one corporate checking account. Indicate the bank and branch office where you will maintain corporate accounts in the first blank. In the second blank, indicate the number of persons (one or more) who must cosign corporate checks. In the remaining blanks, list the names of individuals allowed to cosign checks. Many corporations list the president and treasurer, among others.

Optional Compensation of Officers. Indicate any salaries to be paid to the officers in the blanks in this resolution. Type a zero to show unpaid officers' resolutions. Most nonprofits do not compensate officers, or do so only minimally. If you do provide for real officer salaries, make sure they are reasonable and are related to what people in the nonprofit sector make for providing similar services.

Optional Corporate Seal. If you've ordered a corporate seal, impress the seal in the space to the right of this resolution.

Optional Corporate Certificates. This is an optional resolution. Include this page in your final minutes if you have ordered director, sponsor, membership, or other certificates for your corporation and attach a sample of each certificate to your completed minutes. Director, sponsor, and membership certificates may be ordered as part of the corporate kits you order through Nolo.

Secretary Certification Page. Your secretary should date and sign the blanks on the last page of the minutes.

D. Place Minutes and Attachments in Corporate Records Book

You are now through preparing your minutes. Place your minutes and all attachments in your corporate records book. Your attachments may include the following forms or documents:

- Waiver of Notice and Consent to Holding of the First Meeting
- Copy of your articles, or certificate of incorporation, file-stamped or certified by the secretary of state
- Copy of your bylaws
- Federal 501(c)(3) tax exemption determination letter
- Copy of state tax exemption application determination letter, or other correspondence, and
- Sample director, sponsor, or membership certificates.

Remember, you should continue to place an original or copy of all formal corporate documents in your corporate records book (including minutes of director, committee, and membership meetings) and keep this book at your principal office.

E. Issue Membership Certificates

If you have set up a membership corporation and have membership certificates, you will want to issue them to members after they have applied for membership in the corporation and paid any fees required by the membership provisions in your bylaws. The corporate president and secretary should sign each certificate before giving it to the member.

If you have ordered membership materials as part of a corporate kit available from Nolo, record each member's name and address, together with the number of the certificate, in the membership register in your corporate records book. When you prepare your membership certificates, complete each certificate by typing the number of the certificate, the name of the corporation, and the name of the member on the certificate. Then execute the certificate by filling in the date and having the president and secretary sign at the bottom (if you have a seal, impress it at the bottom of each certificate). Give the certificate to the member, then record the member's name, address, certificate number, and date of issuance on a separate page in your corporate records book. The information on these pages, kept in the corporate records book, constitutes the "membership book" of the corporation.

F. File Fictitious or Assumed Business Name Statement

If your nonprofit corporation will engage in activities (raise funds, apply for grants, advertise, sell goods or services, and so on) under a name other than the exact corporate name given in your articles of incorporation, you will need to file an assumed or fictitious business name statement with your secretary of state and/or county clerk's office.

> **EXAMPLE:** If the name stated in your articles is "THE ART WORKS, INC.," and the corporation plans to continue using the name of the preexisting organization which was incorporated as "THE ART STUDIO," (or chooses another name different from the one set out in the articles), you should file an assumed corporate name statement.

Your secretary of state website should contain information on assumed corporate name statements. If not, call or email your secretary of state or other corporate filings office and ask if this filing is made at the state or county level (or both). Order the form from the appropriate office and prepare and file the statement. In most cases, a small fee is charged for this filing. Also, the statement may need to be published locally in a legal newspaper and a proof of publication filed with your county clerk. Check the instructions to the form for the requirements in your state.

Filing an assumed or fictitious business name statement does not authorize you to use a name that another business is already using as a trademark, tradename, or service mark. Before you settle on a fictitious name, make sure the name is not already in use (just as you did with your corporate name—see Chapter 6, Section B, for details).

G. Apply for a Federal Nonprofit Mailing Permit

Most 501(c)(3) tax-exempt nonprofit corporations will qualify for and want to obtain a third-class nonprofit mailing permit from the U.S. Post Office. This permit entitles you to lower rates on mailings, an important advantage for many groups since the nonprofit rate is considerably lower than the regular third-class rate.

To obtain your permit, bring to your local or main post office branch:

- a file-stamped or certified copy of your articles
- a copy of your bylaws
- a copy of your federal and state tax-exemption determination letters, and
- copies of program literature, newsletters, bulletins, and any other promotional materials.

The post office clerk will ask you to fill out a short application and take your papers. If your local post office branch doesn't handle this, the clerk will send you to a classifications office at the main post office. You'll pay a onetime fee and an annual permit fee. The clerk will forward your papers to the classification office at the regional post office for a determination. In a week or so, you will receive notice of the post office's determination.

Once you have your permit, you can mail letters and parcels at the reduced rate by affixing stamps to your mail; taking the mail to your post office and filling out a special mailing form; or by using the simpler methods of either stamping your mail with an imprint stamp (made by a stampmaker) or leasing a mail stamping machine that shows your imprint information. Ask the classifications clerk for further information.

H. Apply for Property Tax Exemptions

We've already discussed state tax exemptions for real and personal property taxes in Chapter 5. Now is the time to apply for any property tax exemptions available to your group. Remember:

- Apply for an exemption from local personal property taxes if real property is owned or leased by the corporation.
- If you establish an exemption on leased premises, your landlord should give you a corresponding reduction in rent payments.
- Even if your federal tax exemption is pending, you may want to submit your application for a property tax exemption as soon as possible. When you get your federal tax exemption, forward a copy to the taxing agency. This way, you may be able to obtain at least a partial exemption for the current property tax year.

The procedure for applying for an exemption from local personal and real property taxes varies. Often you will need to submit a completed application form, copies of your articles and bylaws, and current and projected financial statements. You can copy the initial financial statements from, or base them on, the financial statement information you submitted with your federal 1023 form.

Call your county tax assessor or collector to find out what property tax exemptions are available for your tax-exempt 501(c)(3) nonprofit corporation and the procedures for applying. In some cases, you must apply to an office in the state capital; in others, the county office will process the papers locally. There may be multiple exemption categories to choose from. For example, a religious group may qualify for a church property tax exemption and for a separate property exemption available to 501(c)(3) nonprofit organizations. The county office should be able to advise you as to the most appropriate property exemption available to your group.

I. File an Initial Corporate Report Form

In most states you must file a periodic nonprofit corporate report form or statement with the secretary of state's office. Most states require you to file this form annually.

Your State Sheet lists the corporate report requirements in your state. Your secretary of state website should contain further information on any periodic corporate report requirements and provide a downloadable form you can use.

While the nature and extent of the information required in each state varies, most states require certain basic organizational information, such as the address of your principal office, the names and addresses of your directors and officers, your registered agent and office, and so on. In some cases, you

must also submit financial information, such as directors' and officers' salaries, officer and supervisory staff compensation, fundraising receipts, and so on. Usually, the secretary of state makes this information available to the public.

Because failing to file a periodic report may lead to a fine or, for repeated failures, a suspension or forfeiture of corporate powers, make sure to file your corporate reports on time.

J. Register With the Attorney General

In some states, nonprofit corporations must register and report to the state attorney general's office. The attorney general scrutinizes nonprofit activities to make sure that the assets of the 501(c)(3) organization are being used for valid charitable or public purposes, not for private purposes.

The information sought on attorney general reporting forms varies. Most commonly, the financial reporting requirements seek to determine whether funds solicited from the public are being used for their stated purpose and whether any of the principals of the nonprofit (directors, officers, staff) are benefiting unduly from nonprofit funds or programs.

In some states, you must file an initial registration form, with a periodic report required each succeeding year or so. We suggest you check with the attorney general's office by calling the main office in your state capital (the website of your state filing office may provide a link to the state attorney general's office). Ask if your 501(c)(3) tax-exempt nonprofit corporation must register or report to this office. In many states, this reporting function is handled by the charitable trusts division or department. Ask if your state has a similar division or department in the attorney general's office.

Check Local Ordinances

If you plan to solicit contributions locally (for example, as part of a door-to-door fundraising drive), make sure to comply with all local solicitation ordinances and regulations. Some counties and cities enforce local registration and reporting requirements. Other localities require you to furnish specific statements and disclose information to persons solicited by the nonprofit corporation.

K. Comply With Political Reporting Requirements

If your nonprofit corporation plans to lobby for legislation, hire a lobbyist, or otherwise be politically active (for example, by supporting or opposing state, county, or city measures to be voted on by the public), we suggest you check to see if your state imposes political registration or reporting requirements. (See Chapter 3, Section C3, for more on political activities and 501(c)(3) nonprofits.) Often, a

Fair Political Practices Commission or similar body in the state capitol oversees and administers these requirements. Another politically active nonprofit organization in your community should have experience with these requirements and should be able to direct you to the proper state office.

If you are active in campaigns for candidates to federal political office, also check whether you are subject to the registration and reporting rules under the Federal Election Campaign Act. For information on FECA and the rules and regulations administered under this act by the Federal Election Commission, go to www.fec.gov.

The final three steps of this chapter apply only to groups that have incorporated a preexisting organization.

L. Prepare Assignments of Leases and Deeds

If you have transferred a prior business or organization to your corporation, the prior owners or nonprofit organization may want to prepare assignments of leases or deeds if they are transferring real property interests to the corporation. Under an assignment, you step into the shoes of the old tenant—the terms and conditions of the lease don't change.

Here is a basic Assignment of Lease form you can use, or modify for use.

Sample Assignment of Lease

(Name of original lessee, for example, the unincorporated nonprofit organization), Lessee of those premises commonly known as _(address of leased property)_ , hereby assigns the attached Lease relating to the above premises, executed _(date original lease was signed)_ , and all rights, liabilities, and obligations thereunder to a proposed corporation, _(name of corporation)_ .

Dated: _____

(name of Lessee)
By: _(signature of Lessee representative)_
(typed name of representative)

The undersigned Lessor of the above premises hereby assents to this Assignment of Lease.

Dated: _____

By: _(signature of Lessor)_
(typed name of Lessor) , Lessor

💡 **Renegotiate rental agreements or leases.** Of course, assignments can be dispensed with if rental agreements or leases are simply renegotiated between the landlord and the new corporation. Even if you do prepare an assignment, the terms of the lease itself will normally require you to get the landlord's consent (the sample assignment of lease form above includes a clause showing the lessor's consent to the assignment). It is particularly important to communicate with the landlord if the nonprofit cor-

poration expects to obtain an exemption from local real property taxes on the leased premises (see Section H, above). Nonprofit groups in this situation will want to insert a clause in their new lease allowing them a credit against rent payments for the amount of the decrease in the landlord's property tax bill as a result of obtaining their real property tax exemption.

A real estate broker or agent can help you obtain and prepare new leases and deeds. If a mortgage or deed of trust is involved, you may need the permission of the lender.

M. File Final Papers for Prior Organization

If you have incorporated a preexisting group, you may need to file final sales tax, employment tax, and other returns for the prior organization. You will also want to cancel any permits or licenses issued to the prior organization or its principals, obtaining new licenses in the name of the nonprofit corporation.

N. Notify Others of Your Incorporation

If a preexisting group has been incorporated, notify creditors and other interested parties, in writing, of the termination and dissolution of the prior organization and of its transfer to the new corporation. This is advisable as a legal precaution and as a courtesy to those who have dealt with the prior organization.

To notify past creditors, suppliers, organizations, and businesses of your incorporation, send a friendly letter that shows the date of your incorporation, your corporate name, and its principal office address. Retain a copy of each letter for inclusion in your corporate records book.

If the prior group was organized as a partnership (not a common situation), some states require the publication of a Notice of Dissolution of Partnership in the county or judicial district where the partnership office or property was located. To do this, call a local legal newspaper and ask if this notice form is published by the paper. If so, the newspaper will charge a small fee to publish the statement the required number of times and send you a proof of publication form for your files. If required, the newspaper should also file the proof of publication with the county clerk, the county recorder, or other appropriate county office. ■

Chapter 10

After Your Corporation Is Organized

*Y*ou have now incorporated your nonprofit and have handled many initial organizational details. But before you close this book, read just a little more. After incorporating, you need to become familiar with the formalities of corporate life, such as filing tax returns, paying employment taxes, and preparing minutes of formal corporate meetings. In this chapter, we look at some tax and other routine filings required by federal, state, and local governmental agencies. At the end, we give you an overview of what's involved in dissolving a nonprofit corporation.

The information presented here won't tell you everything you will need to know about these subjects, but will provide some of the basics and indicate some of the major areas that you (or your tax advisor) will need to go over in more detail.

A. Piercing the Corporate Veil— If You Want to Be Treated Like a Corporation, It's Best to Act Like One

After you've set up a corporation of any kind, your organization should act like one. Although filing your articles of incorporation with the secretary of state brings the corporation into existence as a legal entity, this is not enough to ensure that a court or the IRS will treat your organization as a corporation. What we are referring to here is not simply maintaining your various tax exemptions or even your nonprofit status with the state—we are talking about being treated as a valid corporate entity in court and for tax purposes. Remember, it is your legal corporate status that allows your organization to be treated as an entity apart from its directors, officers, and employees and allows it to be taxed (or not taxed), sue, or be sued, on its own. It is the corporate entity that insulates the people behind the corporation from taxes and lawsuits.

Courts and the IRS do, on occasion, scrutinize the organization and operation of a corporation, particularly if it is directed and operated by a small number of people who wear more than one hat (such as those who fill both director and officer positions). If you don't take care to treat your corporation as a separate legal entity, a court may decide to disregard the corporation and hold the principals (directors and officers) personally liable for corporate debts. This might happen if the corporation doesn't have adequate money to start with, making it likely that creditors or people who have claims against the corporation won't be able to be paid; if corporate and personal funds are commingled; if the corporation doesn't keep adequate corporate records (such as minutes of meetings); or generally doesn't pay much attention to the theory and practice of corporate life. Also, the IRS may assess taxes and penalties personally against those connected with managing the affairs of the corporation if it concludes that the corporation is not a valid legal or tax entity. In legal jargon, holding individuals responsible for corporate deeds or misdeeds is called "piercing the corporate veil."

To avoid problems of this type, be careful to operate your corporation as a separate legal entity. Hold regular and special meetings of your board and membership as required by your bylaws and as necessary to take formal corporate action. It is critical that you document formal corporate meetings with neat and thorough minutes. Also, it is wise to have enough money in your corporate account to pay foreseeable debts and liabilities that may arise in the course of carrying out your activities—even nonprofits should start with a small cash reserve. Above all, keep corporate funds separate from the personal funds of the individuals who manage or work for the corporation.

B. Federal Corporate Tax Returns

In this section, we list and briefly discuss the main IRS tax paperwork you can expect to face as a 501(c)(3) nonprofit corporation.

Make sure your tax forms are current. IRS forms, instructions, fees, and penalties are subject to constant change. Be sure to get the most current information (on return deadlines, tax rates, penalties, and so on) when you file. You can download the federal tax forms discussed in this section from the IRS website at www.irs.gov.

1. Public Charities: Annual Exempt Organization Return

Nonprofit corporations exempt from federal corporate income tax under Section 501(c)(3) and qualified (under an advance or definitive ruling) as public charities must file IRS Form 990, *Annual Return of Organization Exempt From Income Tax* (together with Form 990, Schedule A). The filing deadline is on or before the 15th day of the fifth month (within four and a half months) following the close of their accounting period (tax year). You should file this even if your 1023 federal application for exemption is still pending.

Some groups may be eligible to file IRS Form 990-EZ instead of Form 990. This is a short form annual return that can be used by small tax-exempt public charities—those with gross receipts of less than $100,000 and total assets of less than $250,000.

Watch out for short deadlines. Your first 990 return deadline may come up on you sooner than you expect if your first tax year is a "short year"—a tax year of less than 12 months.

EXAMPLE: If your accounting period as specified in your bylaws runs from January 1 to December 31 and your articles were filed on December 1, your first tax year consists of one month, from December 1 to December 31. In this situation, your first Form 990 would have to be filed within four and a half months of December 31 (by May 15 of the following year), only five and a half months after your articles were filed. It is likely that your federal tax exemption application would still be pending at this time.

2. Groups Exempt from Filing Form 990

The Internal Revenue Code exempts certain public charities from filing Form 990, including certain churches, schools, mission societies, religious activity groups, state institutions, corporations organized under an Act of Congress, tax-exempt private foundations, certain trusts, religious and apostolic organizations, and public charities. In general, these groups cannot normally have more than $25,000 in gross receipts in each taxable year. See the official instructions to IRS Form 990 for the details of these exemptions.

Your federal exemption determination letter should state whether you must file Form 990. Most public charities will be publicly supported organizations or receive a majority of their support from exempt-purpose revenue (see Chapter 4, Sections B2 and B4). Because these groups are not institutional public charities falling under one of the automatic exemptions to filing listed above, they will have to file Form 990 unless they meet the normally not more than $25,000 gross receipts exemption. To rely on this exemption, fill in the top portion of the 990 form and check the box indicating that you are eligible for this exemption.

If your nonprofit corporation makes the political expenditures election by filing Federal Election Form 5768 (discussed in Chapter 3, Section C3), indicate on Form 990, Schedule A, that you made this election and fill in the appropriate part of the schedule showing your actual lobbying expenditures during the year.

3. Private Foundations: Annual Exempt Organization Return

Very few 501(c)(3) nonprofits will be classified as private foundations. If you are one, however, you must file a *Federal Annual Return of Private Foundation Exempt From Income Tax*, Form 990-PF, within four and one-half months of the close of your tax year. You file this Form 990-PF instead of Form 990 discussed above. You'll provide information on receipts and expenditures, assets and liabilities, and other information that will help the IRS determine whether you are liable for private foundation excise taxes. You should receive the form and separate instructions for completing it close to the end of your accounting period. Again, watch out for a short first year and an early deadline for filing your Form 990-PF.

The foundation manager(s) must publish a notice telling the public that they may see the annual report. Do so in a local county newspaper before the filing deadline for the 990-PF. The notice must state that the annual report is available for public inspection, at the principal office of the corporation, within 180 days after the publication of the inspection notice. A copy of the published notice must be attached to the 990-PF.

4. Unrelated Business Income: Annual Exempt Organization Tax Return

With a few minor exceptions, Section 501(c)(3) federal tax-exempt corporations that have gross incomes of $1,000 or more during the year from an unrelated trade or business must file an *Exempt Organization Business Income Tax Return* (Form 990-T). The form is due within two and a half months after the close of their tax year. For a definition and discussion of unrelated trades and businesses, see Chapter 5, Section C, and obtain Federal Publication 598, *Tax on Business Income of Exempt Organizations*. Use booklet 598 and the separate instructions to Form 990-T to prepare this form.

The taxes imposed on unrelated business income are the same rates applied to normal federal corporate income. Remember that too much unrelated business income may indicate to the IRS that you are engaging in non-exempt activities to a "substantial" degree and may jeopardize your tax exemption.

More Information on Taxes

We suggest all nonprofits obtain IRS Publication 509, *Tax Calendars*, prior to the beginning of each year. This pamphlet contains tax calendars showing the dates for corporate and employer filings during the year.

Information on withholding, depositing, reporting, and paying federal employment taxes can be found in IRS Publication 15, Circular E, *Employer's Tax Guide*, and the Publication 15-A Supplement

Other helpful IRS publications are Publication 542, *Tax Information on Corporations*, and Publication 334, *Tax Guide for Small Business*.

Helpful information on accounting methods and bookkeeping procedures is contained in IRS Publication 538, *Accounting Period and Methods*, and Publication 583, *Starting a Business and Keeping Records*.

You can get IRS publications online at www.irs.gov. You can also pick them up at your local IRS office (or order them by phone—call your local IRS office or try the toll-free IRS forms and publications request telephone number, 800-TAX-FORM).

File Your Returns on Time

The IRS and states are notoriously efficient in assessing and collecting late filing and other penalties. So, while it's generally true that your nonprofit corporation does not have to worry about paying taxes, you should worry a bit about filing your annual information returns on time (including your employment tax returns and payments). Too many nonprofit corporations have had to liquidate when forced to pay late filing penalties for a few years' worth of simple informational returns that they inadvertently forgot to file.

Another important aspect of late filing penalties and delinquent employment taxes is that the IRS (and state) can, and often do, try to collect these often substantial amounts from individuals associated with the corporation if the corporation doesn't have sufficient cash to pay them. Remember, one of the exceptions to the concept of limited liability is liability for unpaid taxes and tax penalties. The IRS and state can go after the person (or persons) associated with the corporation who are responsible for reporting and/or paying taxes.

C. State Corporate Tax Returns and Reports

Make sure to file your state corporate tax returns on time. In many states, the state forms are based on or follow the federal nonprofit corporate tax returns discussed above and are due on the same date. You can obtain state tax corporate forms online at your state tax office website (see your State Sheet for this link). Or you can make a call to your state department of taxation and revenue (or similar state tax agency or department) to order annual nonprofit corporation tax forms, schedules, and instructions.

D. Federal and State Corporate Employment Taxes

You must withhold and pay federal and state employment (payroll) taxes on behalf of the people who work for your nonprofit corporation. Directors, with certain exceptions, are not considered employees if they are paid only for attending board meetings. However, if they are paid for other services or as salaried employees of the corporation, the IRS will consider them employees whose wages are subject to employment taxes. Check with the IRS and your local state employment tax office for further information.

501(c)(3)s are exempt from paying federal unemployment insurance (FUTA) taxes but must collect, withhold, report, and pay federal Social Security (FICA) and individual income taxes on employees' salaries. Your tax-exempt nonprofit may be exempt from having to pay some state employment taxes as well.

For information and help in computing your federal withholding and employer contribution payments, obtain the IRS publications listed in "More Information on Taxes," in Section B, above. To register as an employer in your state and for information on meeting state payroll tax requirements, call the state employment tax office in your vicinity (or go to the employer registration office online—your state tax office website may provide a link).

Generally, independent contractors, such as consultants, who are not subject to the control of the corporation—both as to what shall be done and how the work is to be performed—are not considered employees. Wages paid to these people are not subject to payroll tax withholding or payment by the nonprofit corporation.

⚠ **Be careful when classifying people as "independent contractors."** The law in this area is fuzzy, and the IRS (as well as the state employment tax office) is obstinate about trying to prove that outsiders really work for the corporation (and must be covered by payroll taxes). For more information, see IRS Publication 937. An excellent legal guide to the ins and outs of independent contractor status is *Working for Yourself: Law & Taxes for Independent Contractors, Freelancers & Consultants*, by Stephen Fishman (Nolo).

E. Employee Income Tax Returns

Corporate staff and other compensated corporate personnel must report and pay taxes on employment compensation on their individual annual federal income tax returns (IRS Form 1040). If your state imposes a personal income tax, state income taxes are computed and paid with the employee's state personal income tax return.

F. Sales Tax Forms and Exemption From Sales Tax

Your corporation may be required to charge and collect state, county, and city sales, use, transit, excise, and other state taxes from customers or clients. In some cases, nonprofit exemptions from one or more of these state taxes may be available to your 501(c)(3) nonprofit corporation. Contact your state department of revenue, taxation, or similar state agency to register your corporation for sales tax and obtain any exemptions to which you may be entitled.

G. Licenses and Permits

Many businesses, whether operating as profit or nonprofit corporations, partnerships or sole proprietorships, are required to obtain state licenses and permits before commencing business. So, while you may not be subject to the usual kind of red tape applicable to strictly profit-making enterprises (such as contractors, real estate brokers, or engineers), you should check with your state department of consumer affairs (or similar state licensing agency or department) for information concerning any state licensing requirements for your activities or type of organization. Many nonprofit institutions, such as schools or hospitals, will need to comply with a number of registration and reporting requirements administered by the state and, possibly, county government. A local business license or permit may also be required for your activities—check with your city business license department.

H. Workers' Compensation

Workers' compensation insurance coverage compensates workers for losses caused by work-related injuries and protects the corporation from lawsuits brought to recover these amounts. In some states, this coverage is mandatory; in others it is optional. Specific exemptions from coverage may be available to directors and officers in some instances. Make sure to check with your insurance agent or broker, or call your state compensation insurance commission, for names of carriers, rates, and extent of required coverage.

I. Private Insurance Coverage

Nonprofit corporations, like other organizations, should carry the usual types of commercial insurance to prevent undue loss in the event of an accident, fire, theft, and so on. Although the corporate form may insulate directors, officers, and members from personal loss, it won't prevent corporate assets from being jeopardized by such eventualities. Examine coverage for general liability, product liability, and fire and theft. You should also consider liability insurance for directors and officers, particularly if your nonprofit corporation wants to reassure any passive directors on the board that they will be protected from personal liability in the event of a lawsuit.

J. Dissolving a Nonprofit Corporation

A corporation may be dissolved either voluntarily or involuntarily. Voluntary dissolution occurs when a corporation decides to wind up its affairs by a vote of the board of directors, or a vote of the board in conjunction with the formal membership. The corporation might decide to dissolve because it runs out of program or administrative funds, because of an internal dispute within the nonprofit, or simply because the nonprofit program has accomplished its purposes or done as much as is reasonably possible in its area of endeavor.

A corporation dissolves voluntarily by filing articles of dissolution (or a similar document) with the secretary of state and, in some cases, obtaining a tax clearance from the state department of taxation or revenue. (The materials you receive or download from the secretary of state's office should contain information on obtaining the forms and instructions necessary to dissolve a nonprofit corporation in your state.)

Involuntary dissolution may occur if the corporation has failed to file its required annual financial report or pay state taxes for which it is liable for a given number of years. In such instances, the secretary of state or the attorney general will initiate the dissolution, depending on which department has jurisdiction over the misfeasance. The nonprofit corporation itself may petition the court to involuntarily dissolve it if its board is deadlocked, if it has been inactive for a number of years, or for other reasons specified under state statutes.

After a board decision to dissolve, the corporation must cease transacting business except to the extent necessary to wind up its affairs. All corporate debts and liabilities, to the extent of the corporation's remaining assets, must be paid or provided for. If any corporate assets are left after paying corporate debts, a 501(c)(3) tax-exempt nonprofit corporation must distribute them to another 501(c)(3) group. ■

Chapter 11

Lawyers and Accountants

While we believe you can take care of the bulk of the work required to organize and operate your nonprofit corporation, you may need to consult a lawyer or accountant on complicated or special issues. It also makes sense to have a lawyer or accountant experienced in forming nonprofits and preparing tax exemption applications look over your papers. Reviewing your incorporation papers with an attorney or accountant is a sensible way to ensure that all of your papers are up to date and meet your needs. Besides, making contact with a legal and tax person early in your corporate life is often a sensible step. As your group grows and its programs expand, you'll be able to consult these professionals for help with ongoing legal and tax questions.

The professionals you contact should have experience in nonprofit incorporations and tax exemption applications. They should also be prepared to help you help yourself—to answer your questions and review, not rewrite, the forms you have prepared.

The next sections provide a few general suggestions on how to find the right lawyer or tax advisor and, if you wish to do your own legal research, how to find the law.

A. Lawyers

Finding the right lawyer is not always easy. Obviously, the best lawyer to choose is someone you personally know and trust, who has lots of experience advising smaller nonprofits. Of course, this may be a tall order. The next best is a nonprofit advisor whom a friend, another nonprofit incorporator, or someone in your nonprofit network recommends. A local nonprofit resource center, for example, may be able to steer you to one or more lawyers who maintain active nonprofit practices. With patience and persistence (and enough phone calls), this second word-of-mouth approach almost always brings positive results.

Another approach is to locate a local nonprofit legal referral panel. Local bar associations or another nonprofit organization typically run panels of this sort. A referral panel in your area may be able to give you the names of lawyers who are experienced in nonprofit law and practice and who offer a discount or free consultation as part of the referral panel program. Ask about (and try to avoid) referral services that are operated on a strict rotating basis. With this system, you'll get the name of the next lawyer on the list, not necessarily one with nonprofit experience. Also watch out for private (and highly suspect) commercial referral services that often refer you to their own lawyers—you'll want to avoid these.

When you call a prospective lawyer, speak with the lawyer personally, not just the reception desk. You can probably get a good idea of how the person operates by paying close attention to the way your call is handled. Is the lawyer available, or is your call returned promptly? Is the lawyer willing to spend at least a few minutes talking to you to determine if she is really the best person for the job? Does the lawyer seem sympathetic to, and compatible with, the nonprofit goals of your group? Do you get a good personal feeling from your conversation? Oh, and one more thing: Be sure to get the hourly rate the lawyer will charge set in advance. If you are using this book, you will probably want to eliminate lawyers who charge $200 per hour to support an office on top of the tallest building in town.

What About Low-Cost Law Clinics?

Law clinics advertise their services regularly on TV and radio. Can they help you form a nonprofit organization? Perhaps, but usually at a rate well above their initial low consultation rate. Because the lawyer turnover rate at these clinics is high and the degree of familiarity with nonprofit legal and tax issues is usually low, we recommend you spend your money more wisely by finding a reasonably priced nonprofit lawyer elsewhere.

B. Legal Research

Many incorporators may want to research legal information on their own. You can browse most state nonprofit laws online (see the link to your state statute in your State Sheet). And in most states, county law libraries are open to the public (you need not be a lawyer to use them) and are not difficult to use once you understand how the information is categorized and stored. They are an invaluable source of corporate and general business forms, federal and state corporate tax procedures, and other information. Research librarians will usually go out of their way to help you find the right statute, form,

or background reading on any corporate or tax issue.

Whether you are leafing through your own copy of your state's nonprofit corporation law or browsing corporate statutes online or at your local county law library, finding a particular corporate provision is usually a straightforward process. First define and, if necessary, narrow down the subject matter of your search to essential key words associated with your area of interest. For example, if one of the directors on your board resigns and you want to determine whether your state has any statutory rules for filling vacancies on the board, you will define and restrict your

search to the key areas of "directors" and "vacancies." Look for these headings in your state's nonprofit corporation law.

At the beginning of your corporation law, a main table of contents will show headings for the major topics covered in the corporation law. One of these major topics will probably be labeled "Directors," followed by a range of code sections devoted to this subject area. Just before the first of these code sections in the corporation code, a subsidiary table of contents should be included showing individual headings for each code section in this range. In this mini table of contents for the "Directors" code sections, one heading may be listed for a code section devoted to "Vacancies."

Another search strategy is to simply start at the beginning of the corporation law and leaf through all the major and minor headings. Eventually—usually after just a few minutes or so—you will hit upon your area of interest or will satisfy yourself that the area in question is not covered by your corporate statutes. By the way, after going through your nonprofit law this way once or twice, you should become acquainted with most of its major headings. This will help you locate specific nonprofit subject areas and statutes quickly when searching this material in the future.

Legal Shorthand and Definitions

A number of the rules contained in the corporate statutes are often given in legal shorthand—in short legal catchwords and phrases that are defined elsewhere in the code. For example, a common requirement contained in corporate statutes is that a matter or transaction be "approved by the board" or "approved by a majority of the board." Each of these phrases is defined in separate sections of the corporations code. (By the way, the first phrase usually means approval by a majority of directors present at a meeting at which a quorum of directors is present; the second usually means approval by a majority of the full board.) Special definitions of this sort are usually listed at the beginning of the state's nonprofit corporation law—read this starting definition section first to understand any special rules and legal shorthand used throughout your nonprofit corporation statutes.

When you look up a nonprofit statute, whether online or in a book, you might want to use an "annotated" version of the codes. Annotated codes include not only the text of the statutes themselves, but also brief summaries of court cases that discuss each statute. After you find a relevant statute, you may want to scan these case summaries—and perhaps even read some of the cases—to get an idea of how courts have interpreted the language of the statute.

If you are interested in doing your own legal research, an excellent source of information is *Legal Research: How to Find & Understand the Law*, by Stephen Elias and Susan Levinkind (Nolo).

C. Accountants and Tax Advice

As you already know, organizing and operating a nonprofit corporation involves a significant amount of financial and tax work. While much of it is easy, some of it requires a nitpicking attention to definitions, cross-references, formulas, and other elusive or downright boring details, particularly when preparing your federal 1023 tax exemption application. As we often suggest in the book, you may find it sensible to seek advice or help from an accountant or other tax advisor when organizing your nonprofit corporation.

For example, you may need help preparing the income statements, balance sheets, and other financial and tax information submitted with your IRS tax exemption application. Also, if your organization will handle any significant amount of money, you will need an accountant or bookkeeper to set up your double-entry accounting books (cash receipts and disbursement journals, general ledger, and so on). Double-entry accounting techniques are particularly important to nonprofits that receive federal or private grant or program funds—accounting for these "restricted funds" usually requires the assistance of a professional.

Nonprofit corporation account books should be designed to allow for easy transfer of financial data to state and federal nonprofit corporate tax returns and disclosure statements. It should be easy to use the books to determine, at any time, whether receipts and expenditures fall into the categories proper for maintaining your 501(c)(3) tax exemption, public charity status, and grant or program eligibility. You will also want to know whether your operations are likely to subject you to an unrelated business income tax under federal and state rules.

Once your corporation is organized and your books are set up, corporate personnel with experience in bookkeeping and nonprofit tax matters can do the ongoing work of keeping the books and filing tax forms. Whatever your arrangement, make sure to at least obtain the tax publications listed in "More Information on Taxes" in Chapter 10, Section B. These pamphlets contain essential information on preparing and filing IRS corporation and employment tax returns.

When you select an accountant or bookkeeper, the same considerations apply as when selecting a lawyer. Choose someone you know or whom a friend or nonprofit contact recommends. Be as specific as you can regarding the services you want performed. Make sure the advisor has had experience with nonprofit taxation and tax exemption applications, as well as regular payroll, tax, and accounting procedures. Many nonprofit bookkeepers work part-time for several nonprofit organizations. Again, calling people in your nonprofit network is often the best way to find this type of person. ∎

How to Use the CD-ROM

The tear-out forms in Appendix D, as well as numerous forms and publications discussed in this book, are included on a CD-ROM in the back of the book. This CD-ROM, which can be used with Windows computers, installs files that can be opened, printed, and edited using a word processor or other software. It is *not* a stand-alone software program. Please read this appendix and the README.TXT file included on the CD-ROM for instructions on using the Forms CD.

Note to Mac Users: This CD-ROM and its files should also work on Macintosh computers. Please note, however, that Nolo cannot provide technical support for non-Windows users.

How to View the README File

If you do not know how to view the file README.TXT, insert the Forms CD-ROM into your computer's CD-ROM drive and follow these instructions:

• Windows 9x, 2000, Me, and XP: On your PC's desktop, double click the My Computer icon; (2) double click the icon for the CD-ROM drive into which the Forms CD-ROM was inserted; (3) double click the file README.TXT.

• Macintosh: (1) On your Mac desktop, double click the icon for the CD-ROM that you inserted; (2) double click on the file README.TXT.

While the README file is open, print it out by using the Print command in the File menu.

Two different kinds of forms are contained on the CD-ROM:

• Word processing (RTF) forms that you can open, complete, print, and save with your word processing program (see Section B, below), and

• Forms from the IRS (PDF) that can be viewed only with Adobe Acrobat Reader 4.0 or higher. You can install Acrobat Reader from the Forms CD (see Section C below). Some of these forms have "fill-in" text fields, and can be completed using your computer. You will not, however, be able to save the completed forms with the filled-in data. PDF forms without fill-in text fields must be printed out and filled in by hand or with a typewriter.

• Publications from government agencies in both RTF and PDF format. These publications have been included on the Forms CD for your reference.

See Appendix C for a list of forms, their file names, and file formats.

A. Installing the Form Files Onto Your Computer

Before you can do anything with the files on the CD-ROM, you need to install them onto your hard disk. In accordance with U.S. copyright laws, remember that copies of the CD-ROM and its files are for your personal use only.

Insert the Forms CD and do the following:

1. Windows 9x, 2000, Me, and XP Users

Follow the instructions that appear on the screen. (If nothing happens when you insert the Forms CD-ROM, then (1) double click the My Computer icon; (2) double click the icon for the CD-ROM drive into which the Forms CD-ROM was inserted; and (3) double click the file WELCOME.EXE.)

By default, all the files are installed to the \Nonprofit Forms folder in the \Program Files folder of your computer. A folder called "Nonprofit Forms" is added to the "Programs" folder of the Start menu.

2. Macintosh Users

Step 1: If the "Nonprofit Forms CD" window is not open, open it by double clicking the "Nonprofit Forms CD" icon.

Step 2: Select the "Nonprofit Forms" folder icon.

Step 3: Drag and drop the folder icon onto the icon of your hard disk.

B. Using the Word Processing Files to Create Documents

This section concerns the files for forms that can be opened and edited with your word processing program.

All word processing forms come in rich text format. These files have the extension ".RTF." For example, the form for the Request for Nonprofit Corporation Information discussed in Chapter 6 is on the file CONTACT .RTF. All forms, their file names, and file formats are listed in Appendix C.

RTF files can be read by most recent word processing programs including all versions of MS Word for Windows and Macintosh, WordPad for Windows, and recent versions of WordPerfect for Windows and Macintosh.

To use a form from the CD to create your documents you must: (1) open a file in your word processor or text editor; (2) edit the form by filling in the required information; (3) print it out; (4) rename and save your revised file.

The following are general instructions on how to do this. However, each word processor uses different commands to open, format, save, and print documents. Please read your word processor's manual for specific instructions on performing these tasks.

Do not call Nolo's technical support if you have questions on how to use your word processor.

Step 1: Opening a File

There are three ways to open the word processing files included on the CD-ROM after you have installed them onto your computer.

- Windows users can open a file by selecting its "shortcut" as follows: (1) Click the Windows "Start" button; (2) open the "Programs" folder; (3) open the "Nonprofit Forms" subfolder; (4) open the "RTF" subfolder; and (5) click on the shortcut to the form you want to work with.

- Both Windows and Macintosh users can open a file directly by double clicking on it. Use My Computer or Windows Explorer (Windows 9x, 2000, Me, or XP) or the Finder (Macintosh) to go to the folder you installed or copied the

CD-ROM's files to. Then, double click on the specific file you want to open.

- You can also open a file from within your word processor. To do this, you must first start your word processor. Then, go to the File menu and choose the Open command. This opens a dialog box where you will tell the program (1) the type of file you want to open (*.RTF); and (2) the location and name of the file (you will need to navigate through the directory tree to get to the folder on your hard disk where the CD's files have been installed). If these directions are unclear you will need to look through the manual for your word processing program—Nolo's technical support department will *not* be able to help you with the use of your word processing program.

the book. Underlines are used to indicate where you need to enter your information, frequently followed by instructions in brackets. *Be sure to delete the underlines and instructions from your edited document*. If you do not know how to use your word processor to edit a document, you will need to look through the manual for your word processing program—Nolo's technical support department will *not* be able to help you with the use of your word processing program.

Where Are the Files Installed?

Windows Users
- RTF files are installed by default to a folder named \Nonprofit Forms\RTF in the \Program Files folder of your computer.

Macintosh Users
- RTF files are located in the "RTF" folder within the "Nonprofit Forms" folder.

Step 2: Editing Your Document

Fill in the appropriate information according to the instructions and sample agreements in

---

Editing Forms That Have Optional or Alternative Text

Some of the forms have optional or alternate text:

- With optional text, you choose whether to include or exclude the given text.
- With alternative text, you select one alternative to include and exclude the other alternatives.

When editing these forms, we suggest you do the following:

Optional text

If you *don't want* to include optional text, just delete it from your document.

If you *do want* to include optional text, just leave it in your document.

In either case, delete the italicized instructions.

Alternative text

First delete all the alternatives that you do not want to include, then delete the italicized instructions.

Step 3: Printing Out the Document

Use your word processor's or text editor's "Print" command to print out your document. If you do not know how to use your word processor to print a document, you will need to look through the manual for your word processing program—Nolo's technical support department will *not* be able to help you with the use of your word processing program.

Step 4: Saving Your Document

After filling in the form, use the "Save As" command to save and rename the file. Because all the files are "read-only," you will not be able to use the "Save" command. This is for your protection. *If you save the file without renaming it, the underlines that indicate where you need to enter your information will be lost and you will not be able to create a new document with this file without recopying the original file from the CD-ROM.*

If you do not know how to use your word processor to save a document, you will need to look through the manual for your word processing program—Nolo's technical support department will *not* be able to help you with the use of your word processing program.

C. Using IRS Forms

Electronic copies of useful forms from the IRS are included on the CD-ROM in Adobe Acrobat PDF format. You must have the Adobe Acrobat Reader installed on your computer (see below) to use these forms. All forms, their file names, and file formats are listed in Appendix C. These form files were created by the IRS, not by Nolo.

Some of these forms have fill-in text fields. To create your document using these files, you must: (1) open a file; (2) fill in the text fields using either your mouse or the tab key on your keyboard to navigate from field to field; and (3) print it out.

Note: While you can print out your completed form, you will NOT be able to save your completed form to disk.

Forms without fill-in text fields cannot be filled out using your computer. To create your document using these files, you must: (1) open the file; (2) print it out; and (3) complete it by hand or typewriter.

Installing Acrobat Reader

To install the Adobe Acrobat Reader, insert the CD into your computer's CD-ROM drive and follow these instructions:

- Windows 9x, 2000, Me, and XP: Follow the instructions that appear on screen. (If nothing happens when you insert the Forms CD-ROM, then (1) double click the My Computer icon; (2) double click the icon for the CD-ROM drive into which the Forms CD-ROM was inserted; and (3) double click the file WELCOME.EXE.)
- Macintosh: (1) If the "Nonprofit Forms CD" window is not open, open it by double clicking the "Nonprofit Forms CD" icon; and (2) double click on the "Acrobat Reader Installer" icon.

If you do not know how to use Adobe Acrobat to view and print the files, you will need to consult the online documentation that comes with the Acrobat Reader program.

Do *not* call Nolo technical support if you have questions on how to use Acrobat Reader.

Step 1: Opening PDF Files

PDF files, like the word processing files, can be opened one of three ways.

- Windows users can open a file by selecting its "shortcut" as follows: (1) Click the Windows "Start" button; (2) open the "Programs" folder; (3) open the "Nonprofit Forms" subfolder; (4) open the "PDF" folder; and (5) click on the shortcut to the form you want to work with.

- Both Windows and Macintosh users can open a file directly by double clicking on it. Use My Computer or Windows Explorer (Windows 9x, 2000, Me, or XP), or the Finder (Macintosh) to go to the folder you created and copied the CD-ROM's files to. Then, double click on the specific file you want to open.

- You can also open a PDF file from within Acrobat Reader. To do this, you must first start Reader. Then, go to the File menu and choose the Open command. This opens a dialog box where you will tell the program the location and name of the file (you will need to navigate through the directory tree to get to the folder on your hard disk where the CD's files have been installed). If these directions are unclear you will need to look through Acrobat Reader's help—Nolo's technical support department will *not* be able to help you with the use of Acrobat Reader.

Step 2: Filling in PDF Files

Use your mouse or the Tab key on your keyboard to navigate from field to field within these forms. Be sure to have all the information you will need to complete a form on hand, because you will not be able to save a copy of the filled-in form to disk. You can, however, print out a completed version.

NOTE: This step is only applicable to forms that have been created with fill-in text fields. Forms without fill-in fields must be completed by hand or typewriter after you have printed them out.

Where Are the PDF Files Installed?

- **Windows Users:** PDF files are installed by default to a folder named \Nonprofit Forms\PDF in the \Program Files folder of your computer.
- **Macintosh Users:** PDF files are located in the "PDF" folder within the "Nonprofit Forms" folder.

Step 3: Printing PDF Files

Choose Print from the Acrobat Reader File menu. This will open the Print dialogue box. In the "Print Range" section of the Print dialog box, select the appropriate print range, then click OK. ■

State Sheets

How to Use the State Sheets

The State Sheets that follow provide users of this book in all states with the essential, state-specific information necessary to prepare articles of incorporation, bylaws, and other state incorporation forms. Locate the State Sheet pages for the state in which you plan to incorporate, then tear out and refer to these pages as you follow your incorporation steps (starting with Chapter 6, Section B, "Choose a Corporate Name").

⚠ **This information changes frequently and may not always be current on all points in every state.** For this reason—and so you can obtain forms and other online assistance—we've included the website URL and physical addresses and phone numbers (also subject to change) of the corporate filing and tax agencies that deal with nonprofit corporations. The state corporate filing office website is the first and best place to go to get current nonprofit articles and formation instructions for your state. We also provide the website link so you can browse your state's Nonprofit Corporation Act. Statutes on the Internet are the most current source of your state's latest nonprofit corporation law.

Each State Sheet is divided into five main sections:

- secretary of state information (with website URL and link to state statutes)
- corporate name requirements
- articles of incorporation (with online forms availability)
- bylaws, and

- state corporate tax exemption (with state tax agency link).

Secretary of State Information

This section shows you where to go for incorporation information and forms. The state website is the first place to look. In most states, you'll find a downloadable articles form with instructions to form your nonprofit corporation. You'll also see links to your state tax agency where you can check for state forms for applying for and obtaining a state income tax exemption. If the state website is sparse, you can call or write to your state filing office for nonprofit forms and information (see the State Corporate Tax Exemption subsection, below). We list the name and address of the secretary of state or other corporate filing office, along with a phone number for the corporate filing office or for general corporate information. Next, we indicate whether your secretary of state provides a sample or ready-to-use articles of incorporation form or publishes guidelines for preparing this form. In the few states where neither forms nor published guidelines are available, you should consult your state law to determine the specific requirements for preparing articles in your state. We list the location and Internet link (if available) to your state's nonprofit corporation act. For more on obtaining secretary of state materials, see Chapter 6, Section A.

💡 **Internet links are subject to change.** Although the links we provide are current at the time this book went to press, they can get out of date in fairly short order. If you find that the link for your state's nonprofit corporation act no longer works, follow these tips:

- Try a shorter version of the same link. Delete the last part of the URL and see whether that leads you to your state's legislative materials. If you still reach a dead end, delete another section of the address. By using this method, you can usually get to a state site (or to the site of the company that publishes your state's laws).
- If shorter versions of the URL still don't work, go to your state government's website.

Once you reach a site, look for a tab or link to your state's legislative materials. If you are starting from a state website, the link might be called "statutes," "acts," legislation," or "laws." If you reach a publishing company's website, look for a link to your state's statutes. From that point, you should be able to use the instructions we provide to get to your state's nonprofit statute.

Corporate Name Requirements

We indicate whether you are required to include a corporate designator, such as "Corporation," "Incorporated," "Corp.," "Inc.," and so on, in your corporate name.For further information on selecting a corporate name, see Chapter 6, Section B.

Articles of Incorporation

Chapter 6, Section H, explains how to fill in standard nonprofit articles of incorporation. The State Sheets provide additional information you'll need to complete the articles in your state.

Articles of Incorporation Statute: If your state does not provide an articles form, we provide the citation for the section of your state's nonprofit corporation law that spells out what you need to put in your articles of incorporation—we call this section your state's "articles statute." As we've said, in most cases your secretary of state provides either a standard form for filling in the information required in the articles or guidelines for creating your own articles. If not, you'll be able to look up your state's requirements for preparing articles of incorporation by referring to this section of the law in your state's Nonprofit Corporation Act (use the link to your state's Nonprofit Corporation Act to find this section of law, and see Chapter 11 for information on doing your own research).

We also cover this additional information that you may have to include in your articles:

- **Director Qualifications:** We show the number of directors required in your state and other applicable qualifications, such as age and residency.
- **Incorporator Qualifications:** If your state requires more than one incorporator, the number necessary will be indicated here. We also tell you whether there are age, residency, or other requirements for incorporators.
- **Special Requirements:** This section, if applicable, is included to point out important special publication or other requirements associated with filing articles in your state.

Bylaws

This section contains state-specific information necessary to prepare your bylaws (and, if appropriate, membership provisions), found in Appendix D. For detailed directions on creating bylaws, see Chapter 7. This information includes:

- **Quorum Requirements for Directors' and Members' Meetings:** We give the state rule on how many directors or members must be present to hold a valid meeting under state law. In many instances, the state quorum rules only go into effect if the corporation does not specify its own quorum rules in its bylaws.
- **Directors' Term of Office:** We give the state rule for how long a director may serve on the board.
- **Officer Requirements:** We indicate the officer positions that must be filled in each state and any special officer qualifications or other requirements under state law.

State Corporate Tax Exemption

Finally, each State Sheet includes information on obtaining a state exemption from corporate income tax. The information presented here includes:

- whether your state has a corporate income or franchise tax
- the website URL you can use to obtain your state's nonprofit tax exemption forms and annual corporate reporting returns (the state tax office website listed here is your first and best source of state nonprofit tax exemption information and forms)
- online state tax office links: For an online listing of state tax office links, go to the Federation of Tax Administrators website at www.taxadmin.org/fta/link/forms .html.
- the name and city location of the state agency concerned with corporate income tax, and

- what you have to do to be exempt from your state corporate tax (if any).

There are four common scenarios here, labeled in the State Sheets as follows:

- **Automatic upon filing articles:** You are automatically eligible for the state exemption upon filing nonprofit articles of incorporation with your secretary of state.
- **Automatic with federal 501(c)(3) exemption:** You are automatically eligible for a state exemption when you receive your federal 501(c)(3) exemption—no separate state notification or registration is required.
- **Separate state notification required but determination follows federal:** You are eligible for the state exemption once you notify the state of your federal 501(c)(3) tax exemption. You may have to submit copies of your articles and bylaws, as well as financial and program information, to the state tax department.
- **Separate state determination:** You must apply and qualify for a separate state corporate tax exemption.

Any additional state tax information is listed at the end of this State Sheet section. Keep in mind that we are mostly interested in state corporate or franchise tax requirements and exemptions. As discussed in Chapter 5, Section E, there may be other state and local taxes you'll either be eligible to apply for exemption from, or liable to pay, including sales and use taxes, property tax, excise tax, and hotel and meal taxes. You may also be subject to state and local license fees. Check with your state and local tax agencies to find out about these additional nonprofit taxes and exemptions.

Alabama

Secretary of State Information

Secretary of State
Corporations Division
P.O. Box 5616
Montgomery, AL 36103
www.sos.state.al.us/business/corporations.cfm

Phone Number of Corporations Division:
334-242-5324

Provides Articles of Incorporation: yes

Internet Forms: Nonprofit Articles of Incorporation and other statutory forms can be downloaded from the state website

Online Statutes: The Alabama Nonprofit Act is contained in Title 10, Chapter 3A, of the Alabama statutes, and is browsable from the following website page (Select "Title 10," then "Chapter 3A"):
www.legislature.state.al.us/CodeofAlabama/1975/coatoc.htm

Corporate Name Requirements

Corporate Designator: not required

Articles of Incorporation

Director Qualifications:
Number: 3 or more [Section 10-3A-35]
Residency: no
Age: no

Incorporator Qualifications:
Residency: no
Age: no

Special Requirements: Articles (plus two copies) must be filed with the probate judge in the county of incorporation; within ten days of filing, the probate judge must send a copy of the certificate of incorporation and the articles to the secretary of state

Bylaws

Directors' Quorum: majority of the directors in office unless a percentage is specified in the articles or bylaws, which may not be less than 1/3 of the number in office [Section 10-3A-37]

Members' Quorum: as stated in bylaws, or else 10% of the number of voting members, in person or represented by proxy [Section 10-3A-32]

Directors' Term of Office: as specified in bylaws; if not specified, then one year [Section 10-3A-35]

Officer Requirements: must designate president, one or more vice presidents, secretary, and treasurer. One person may hold any two offices except president and secretary. Officers' terms may not exceed three years. [Section 10-3A-41]

State Corporate Tax Exemption

Corporate Income or Franchise Tax: yes

State Tax Office: Department of Revenue, Montgomery
www.ador.state.al.us

State Tax Exemption Requirements:

- Separate state notification required but determination follows federal
- Send a copy of your federal determination letter to the Department of Revenue to receive your state corporate income tax exemption
- In addition to corporate income tax, there is a corporate permit fee. The permit fee ranges from $10 to $100, and only religious, benevolent, and educational corporations are exempt; other types of nonprofits must file Form FT2-1N in their first year of existence and Form FT2-1 thereafter. Exempt organizations must report unrelated business income on Form 20C together with a copy of Federal Form 990T

Alaska

Secretary of State Information

Department of Commerce & Economic Development
Division of Banking, Securities, and Corporations
P.O. Box 110808
Juneau, AK 99811-0808
www.dced.state.ak.us/bsc/corps.htm
Phone number of Corporations Section:
 907-465-2530

Provides Articles of Incorporation: yes

Internet Forms: Fill-in-able Alaska Nonprofit Articles
and other statutory forms can be downloaded from
the state website

The Alaska Nonprofit Corporation Act is contained
in Title 10, Chapter 10.20, of the Alaska statutes
(starting at Section 10.20.005) and can be browsed
online. Go to the Web page listed below (the
corporations section home page), select the link to
"Alaska Statutes and Regulations," then select "The
Current Alaska Statutes," expand the Title 10 heading and select "Chapter 10.20" to view the Nonprofit Corporation Act

 www.dced.state.ak.us/bsc/corps.htm

Corporate Name Requirements

Corporate Designator: not required

Articles of Incorporation

Director Qualifications:
 Number: 3 or more [10.20.086]
 Residency: no
 Age: no

Incorporator Qualifications:
 Number: 3 or more [10.20.146]
 Residency: no
 Age: 19 or older

Special Requirements: Two copies of articles must be
submitted to the Dept. of Commerce and Economic
Development.

Bylaws

Directors' Quorum: majority of directors in office, or
else a greater percentage as stated in articles or
bylaws [10.20.106]

Members' Quorum: as stated in bylaws, but no lower
than 10% of voting membership, or else 10% of the
voting membership [10.20.076]

Directors' Term of Office: as specified in the blaws
[10.20.096]

Officer Requirements: must designate president, one or
more vice presidents, secretary, and treasurer. Any
offices may be held simultaneously by the same person, except president and secretary [10.20 .121]

State Corporate Tax Exemption

Corporate Income or Franchise Tax: yes

State Agency to Contact:
 State Tax Office
 Department of Revenue, Juneau
 www.revenue.state.ak.us

State Tax Exemption Requirements:

- Automatic with federal 501(c)(3) exemption
- Alaska adopts by reference those portions of the
 IRC that concern nonprofit corporations (including exemption requirements, unrelated business
 income tax filings, and so on)
- If a federal unrelated business income tax is imposed, complete Form 04-611 or 04-611SF reporting the taxable income and calculating the
 tax. Attach a signed copy of federal form 990-T

Arizona

Secretary of State Information

Arizona Corporation Commission
Corporation Filing Section
1300 West Washington
Phoenix, AZ 85007
www.cc.state.az.us/corp/index.htm
Phone number of corporate filing section:
 800-345-5819 (in AZ only) or 602-542-3135
Corporate filings and phone calls are also handled
 by Tucson office: 520-628-6560

Provides Articles of Incorporation: yes

Internet Forms: The latest Arizona nonprofit articles
of incorporation with instructions, Certificate of
Disclosure for Nonprofit Corporations, plus other
Arizona statutory forms can be downloaded from
the state filing office website. General instructions
for forming a nonprofit corporation also are available for downloading.

   The Arizona Nonprofit Corporation Act is contained in Title 10, Chapter 24, of the Arizona Statutes, starting at Section 10.3101, and is browsable
from the following website page (click "Arizona
Revised Statutes" in the left pane, then click "Title
10," then scroll down to "Chapter 24"):
www.azleg.state.az.us

Corporate Name Requirements

Corporate Designator: not required

Articles of Incorporation

Director Qualifications:
 Number: yes; 1 or more [10-3803]
 Residency: no
 Age: no
Incorporator Qualifications:
 Residency: no
 Age: no
Special Requirements:
 • Certificate of Disclosure for Non-Profit Corporations (available online) must be submitted with
   the articles; this contains information about
   officers, directors, incorporators: whether any
   felony convictions for securities violations,
   consumer fraud, antitrust, theft, restraint of trade
   during seven previous years; whether subject to
   any federal injunction, judgment during the same
   period. [10-3202]
 • Publication of articles is required within 60 days
   of filing, in three consecutive issues in newspaper of general circulation in the county of incorporation; affidavit of proof of publication must
   be filed with the Arizona Corporations Commission within 90 days of filing articles

Bylaws

Directors' Quorum: majority of the directors in office
unless a percentage is specified in bylaws or
articles, which may not be less than 1/3 of the number in office [10-3824]

Members' Quorum: as stated in bylaws, or else 10%
of voting members represented in person or by
proxy [10-372]

Directors' Term of Office: as specified in bylaws; if
not specified, then one year [10-3805]

Officer Requirements: corporation may have the offices specified in the articles of incorporation or
bylaws. One person may hold one or more offices.
[10-3480]

State Corporate Tax Exemption

Corporate Income or Franchise Tax: yes
State Agency to Contact:
State Tax Office: Department of Revenue, Phoenix
www.revenue.state.az.us
State Tax Exemption Requirements:
 Automatic with federal 501(c)(3)

Arkansas

Secretary of State Information

Secretary of State
Corporations Division
Arkansas State Capitol
Little Rock, AR 72201-1094
www.sosweb.state.ar.us/corp_ucc_business.html
Phone number of corporations section:
  888-233-0325

Provides Articles of Incorporation: yes

Internet Forms: The latest nonprofit articles of incorporation plus other Arkansas statutory forms can be downloaded from the state filing office website. For $5 less than the paper-filing fee, articles can be filled out and filed online.

The 1993 Arkansas Nonprofit Corporation Act is located in Title 4 (Business and Commercial Law), Subtitle 3 (Corporations and Associations), Chapter 33, starting with Section 4-33-101, and is browsable from the following website page (first click "Arkansas Code," then select "Title 4," then "Subtitle 3," then "Chapter 33"):
  www.arkleg.state.ar.us/Siteindex.asp?

Corporate Name Requirements

Corporate Designator: none

Articles of Incorporation

Director Qualifications:
Number: 3 or more [4-33-803]
Residency: no
Age: no
Other: Directors must be individuals [4-33-802]

Incorporator Qualifications:
Residency: no
Age: no

Special Requirements: Articles must specify whether the corporation being formed is a public benefit, mutual benefit, or religious corporation. Most 501(c)(3) tax exempt nonprofit corporations are organized as public benefit corporations (or religious corporations if their 501(c)(3) purposes are religious).

Bylaws

Directors' Quorum: a majority of the directors in office, or a different percentage specified in articles or bylaws [4-33-824]

Members' Quorum: unless the articles or bylaws provide for a higher or lower quorum, ten percent (10%) of the votes entitled to be cast on a matter must be represented at a meeting of members to constitute a quorum on that matter; unless one-third (1/3) or more of the voting power is present in person or by proxy, the only matters that may be voted upon at an annual or regular meeting of members are those matters that are described in the meeting notice [4-33-722]

Directors' Term of Office: as specified in articles, but it may not be more than six years. If not specified, each director has a one-year term. [4-33-805]

Officer Requirements: unless otherwise stated in the articles or bylaws, must designate a president, secretary, and treasurer. One person may hold more than one office. [4-33-840]

State Corporate Tax Exemption

Corporate Income or Franchise Tax: yes

State Agency to Contact: Department of Finance & Administration, Revenue Division, Little Rock
www.ark.org/dfa

State Tax Exemption Requirements:

- Separate state notification required but determination follows federal
- To apply for state exemption, submit copies of the federal determination letter and federal Form 1023 or 1024 to the Income Tax director
- Exempt organizations must report unrelated business income on Form 1100CT
- If you do not have a federal tax exemption, but wish to separately apply for a state corporate income tax exemption, use Form AR-1023CT, available on the tax office website (with separate downloadable instructions)

California

Secretary of State Information
Office of the Secretary of State
Corporations Unit
1500 11th St
Sacramento, CA 95814
www.ss.ca.gov/business/business.htm
Phone number of corporate filing section:
 916-657-5448
Corporate filings and phone calls are also handled
 by Fresno, Los Angeles, San Diego, and San Francisco branch offices of the secretary of state

Provides Articles of Incorporation: yes

Internet Forms: Sample California nonprofit articles of
incorporation with instructions, plus other California corporate statutory forms (Reservation of Corporate Name and others) can be downloaded from the
secretary of state's website

The California Nonprofit Corporation Act is broken into three parts, with a separate part for public
benefit, religious, and mutual benefit nonprofit corporations. The Nonprofit Public Benefit law starts at
Section 5110 of the Corporations Code; the Nonprofit Religious Corporation Law starts at Section
9110, and the Nonprofit Mutual Benefit Law starts at
Section 7110 (see the Note, below, to determine the
part of the law that applies to your nonprofit). To
browse the law, go to the following website page
(check the "Corporations Code" box, then click the
search button at the bottom of the page; then scroll
down to the section you wish to view):
www.leginfo.ca.gov/calaw.html

Note: the following information applies to
California public benefit corporations (nonprofit
corporations formed for public or charitable purposes)—most corporations applying for a 501(c)(3)
tax exemption will be classified as California public
benefit corporations. Requirements for religious
corporations are the same in most cases, but religious corporations have more flexibility in tailoring
certain provisions. Requirements for mutual benefit
corporations also differ slightly (generally, mutual
benefit corporations do not qualify for a federal
501(c)(3) tax exemption)

Corporate Name Requirements
Corporate Designator: not required

Articles of Incorporation
Director Qualifications:
 Number: 1 or more [5151]
 Residency: no
 Age: no

Incorporator Qualifications:
 Residency: no
 Age: no

Special Requirements:
- Articles require a statement specifying whether
 the corporation being formed is a public benefit,
 mutual benefit, or religious corporation, using
 specific terms that can be found in the statute
 (Sec. 5130)
- File the articles with the secretary of state, then
 apply for your state and federal income tax
 exemptions

Bylaws
Directors' Quorum: majority of the number of directors in office, or else the percentage stated in the
 articles or bylaws, which may not be less than 1/5
 of the number in office. A quorum may not be less
 than two directors, unless there is only one director
 [5211(a)(7)]

Members' Quorum: As determined by the bylaws, but
 if not specified, one-third of the voting power, represented in person or by proxy, constitutes a quorum at a meeting of members. If the bylaws set
 quorum at less than one-third of the membership
 voting power, the only matters that can be voted
 upon at a regular meeting attended, in person or by
 proxy, by less than one-third of the voting power
 are matters that were specified in the notice for the
 meeting. [5512]

Directors' Term of Office: as specified in articles or
 bylaws; if not specified, then one year. The maximum term for a director of a membership corporation is three years; of a nonmembership corporation, six years [5220]

Special Director Requirements: A majority of the directors of a public benefit corporation cannot be
 paid in a nondirector capacity (for example, as a
 paid officer, employee, or consultant) nor related
 (the term "related" is defined to included only
 specified relationships) to another person paid in a
 nondirector capacity. [5227]

Officer Requirements: must designate president or
 chairman of the board, secretary, and chief financial
 officer. One person may hold any two positions,
 except that neither the secretary nor the chief financial officer may serve concurrently as the president
 or chairman of the board [5213]

If the articles or bylaws provide for the election
 of an officer by the members, the term of the
 elected officer is one year if not otherwise specified
 in the articles or bylaws, and, in any case, may not
 be more than three years.

State Corporate Tax Exemption

Corporate Income or Franchise Tax: yes

State Agency to Contact:

Franchise Tax Board, Sacramento

www.ftb.ca.gov

State Tax Exemption Requirements:

- Separate state determination
- The California franchise tax exemption application (Form FTB 3500) requires the following:
  1. Current financial statements itemized to show income and expenses, or a proposed budget for a new organization
  2. Articles of incorporation and bylaws
  3. Supporting documents including a detailed description of activities

For complete forms and instructions on how to form a California nonprofit corporation, which includes line-by-line instructions to prepare the California tax exemption application, see *How to Form a Nonprofit Corporation in California,* by Anthony Mancuso (Nolo). Nolo offers the California book at a discount to purchasers of *How to Form a Nonprofit Corporation.*

Colorado

Secretary of State Information

Secretary of State
Corporations Office
1560 Broadway, Suite 200
Denver, CO 80202
www.sos.state.co.us/pubs/business/main.htm
Phone number of corporate filing section:
303-894-2200

Provides Articles of Incorporation: yes

Internet Forms: The latest nonprofit articles of incorporation, plus other Colorado statutory forms (Reservation of Corporate Name and others) can be downloaded from the state filing office website. Forms are provided in WordPerfect and Adobe Acrobat format

The Colorado Revised Nonprofit Corporation Act is contained in Title 7, Articles 121 through 137 of the Colorado Statutes, starting with Section 7-121-101, and is browsable from the following website page (select "Colorado Statutes" (ignore the first "Corporations" heading), then "Nonprofit corporations," then select from the list of headings to browse sections of the BCA):

http://198.187.128.12/colorado/
lpext.dll?f=templates&fn=fs-main.htm&2.0

Corporate Name Requirements

Corporate Designator: not required

Articles of Incorporation

Director Qualifications:
Number: one or more [7-128-103]
Residency: not required
Age: individual 18 years of age or older [7-128-102]

Incorporator Qualifications:
Residency: no
Age: 18 or older [7-122-101]

Bylaws

Directors' Quorum: majority of the number in office, unless a percentage is specified in the articles or bylaws, which may not be less than 1/3 of the number in office [7-128-205]

Members' Quorum: generally, 25%— twenty-five percent of the votes entitled to be cast on the matter by the voting group constitutes a quorum of that voting group for action on that matter [7-127-205]

Directors' Term of Office: as specified in the articles or bylaws; if not specified, then one year [7-128-105]

Officer Requirements: unless otherwise stated in bylaws, corporation must have president, secretary, and treasurer. One person may hold more than one office at a time. Officers must be 18 years of age or over [7-128-301]

State Corporate Tax Exemption

Corporate Income or Franchise Tax: yes

State Agency to Contact:
Revenue Department, Denver
www.revenue.state.co.us/main/home.asp

State Tax Exemption Requirements:
Automatic with federal 501(c)(3) exemption, but may owe Colorado corporate income tax on unrelated business income earned within the state

Connecticut

Secretary of State Information

Connecticut Secretary of State
30 Trinity Street
Hartford, CT 06106
www.sots.state.ct.us
Phone number of Secretary of State's Office:
860-509-6001

Provides Articles of Incorporation: yes

Internet Forms: The latest Nonprofit Certificate of
Incorporation with instructions, plus other
Connecticut statutory forms (Reservation of Corporate Name and others) can be downloaded from the
state filing office website

The Connecticut Revised Nonstock Corporation
Act is contained in Title 33, Chapter 602, of the
Connecticut Statutes, starting with Section 33-1000,
and is browsable from the following website page
(click "Connecticut General Statutes," then click
"Browse One Chapter at a Time," then click "Title
33," then click "Chapter 602"):
www.cgastate.ct.us/lco

Corporate Name Requirements

Corporate Designator: name must contain "corporation,"
"company," "incorporated," or an abbreviation
[Sec. 33-1045]

Articles (Certificate) of Incorporation

Director Qualifications:
Number: 3 or more
Residency: no
Age: no

Incorporator Qualifications:
Residency: no
Age: no

Special Requirements:
- Special provisions, both general and by denomination, concern the formation and operation of
  religious corporations. If you are planning to
  form a religious nonprofit corporation, check
  Conn. General Statutes Section 33-264a-281
- A person or organization planning to grant
  college credit or call itself a college or university
  must comply with Section 10a-34 of Conn. General Statutes

Bylaws

Directors' Quorum: majority of number of directors
in office, unless a different percentage is specified
in the certificate of incorporation or the bylaws,
which may not be less than 1/3 of the directors in
office or at least two directors [Sec. 33-1100]

Members' Quorum: unless otherwise stated in bylaws, the number of members present at a meeting
who are entitled to vote, represented in person or
by proxy, constitutes a quorum [Sec. 33-1074]

Directors' Term of Office: until next annual meeting
unless terms are staggered [Sec. 33-1085]

Officer Requirements: corporation may have officers
specified in articles or bylaws. One person may
hold more than one [Sec. 33-1109]

State Corporate Tax Exemption

Corporate Income or Franchise Tax: yes

State Agency to Contact:
Department of Revenue Services, Hartford
www.ct.gov/drs/site/default.asp

State Tax Exemption Requirements:
Automatic with federal 501(c)(3) exemption

Delaware

Secretary of State Information

State of Delaware
Division of Corporations
P.O. Box 898
Dover, DE 19903
www.state.de.us/corp
Phone number for general information:
302-739-3073

Provides Articles of Incorporation: yes

Internet Forms: The latest Certificate of Incorporation, plus other statutory forms (Reservation of Name and others) can be downloaded from the state filing office website

The Delaware General Corporation Law (nonprofit statutes are interspersed with regular for-profit corporation statutes) is contained in Title 8 (Corporations), Chapter 1, of the Delaware Statutes, starting with Section 101, and is browsable from the following website page (click "Delaware Laws Online" under Services, then click the "General Corporation Law" under Title 8, Chapter 1):

www.state.de.us/corp

Corporate Name Requirements

Corporate Designator: name must include one of following: "Association," "Company," "Corporation," "Club," "Foundation," "Fund," "Incorporated," "Institute," "Society," "Union," "Syndicate," "Limited"; or "Co.," "Corp.," "Inc.," "Ltd." [102]

Articles (Certificate) of Incorporation

Director Qualifications:
Number: one or more individuals [141]
Residency: no
Age: no

Incorporator Qualifications:
Residency: no
Age: no

Bylaws

Directors' Quorum: majority or greater of the directors in office, unless a percentage is specified in the bylaws, which may not be less than 1/3 of the number in office. If a one-director board is authorized, then one director constitutes a quorum. However, under Section 141(j), the certificate of incorporation of a nonstock corporation may provide for a quorum of less than 1/3 of the board [141]

Members' Quorum: if not specified in the certificate of incorporation or bylaws, 1/3 of the voting members constitute a quorum [215]

Directors' Term of Office: as specified in the articles or bylaws [141]

Officer Requirements: corporation may have officers as specified in bylaws or by resolution of board, so long as there are as many as are needed to sign legal documents. One person can hold any number of offices [142]

State Corporate Tax Exemption

Corporate Income or Franchise Tax: yes

State Agency to Contact:
Department of Finance, Division of Revenue, Dover
www.state.de.us/revenue

State Tax Exemption Requirements:

- Automatic with federal 501(c)(3) exemption
- Tax-exempt 501(c) nonprofits—including 501(c)(3) groups and others—are exempt from obtaining a business license and paying the accompanying gross receipts tax on the sales of most goods and services. Some services such as leasing tangible personal property or providing accommodations are taxable regardless of the entity providing such services.
- Registration with the Division of Revenue is required and nonprofits must withhold Delaware state income taxes on employees performing services within Delaware
- Registration with the Department of Labor is required
- If the nonprofit activities are conducted in Delaware, a copy of Federal Form 990 PF must be filed with the State of Delaware, Attorney General

District of Columbia

Secretary of State Information

Dept. of Consumer and Regulatory Affairs
Corporations Division
941 North Capitol Street, NE
Washington, DC 20002
http://dcra.dc.gov/services/busresource/index.shtm
Phone number for general information:
   202-442-4432

Provides Articles of Incorporation: yes; provides
sample form (called guidelines)

Internet Forms: Sample nonprofit corporation articles
are available for downloading online

   The DC Nonprofit Corporation Act is contained in
Title 29 (Corporations), Chapter 3, of the DC Code,
starting with Section 29-301.01, and is browsable
from the following website page (select "District of
Columbia," "District of Columbia Code," then "Division 5," then "Title 29," then "Chapter 3"):
   http://www.michie.com

Corporate Name Requirements

Corporate Designator: not required

Articles of Incorporation

Director Qualifications:
Number: 3 or more [29-301.19]
Residency: no
Age: no

Incorporator Qualifications:
Number: 3 or more
Residency: no
Age: 18 or older

Special Requirements: submit two originally signed
sets of articles

Bylaws

Directors' Quorum: majority of directors in office,
unless a percentage is specified in bylaws, but not
less than 1/3 of the number in office [29-301.21]

Members' Quorum: as specified in bylaws or else
10% of voting membership [29-301.17]

Directors' Term of Office: as specified in bylaws, but
not to exceed 3 years; if not specified, then one
year [29-301.19]

Officer Requirements: must designate president, secretary, and treasurer. Each officer elected for terms
not exceeding three years as specified in the articles
of incorporation or the bylaws. In the absence of
such a provision, all officers must be elected or appointed annually by the board of directors. One
person may hold two offices simultaneously, except
offices of president and secretary [29-301.24]

State Corporate Tax Exemption

Corporate Income or Franchise Tax: yes

State Agency to Contact:
Office of Tax and Revenue
http://cfo.dc.gov/otr/site/default.asp

State Tax Exemption Requirements:
DC has single exemption application (Application
For Exemption, Form FR-164) for income and franchise tax, sales and use tax, and personal property
tax, which must be filed with the following:

1. Copy of federal tax determination letter
2. Statement of activities engaged in during the past
   year, or planned to be engaged in during the
   coming year
3. Copy of articles and bylaws
4. Complete statement of assets and liabilities, receipts and expenditures, at the end of the most
   recent accounting period
5. Sample copies of organization's publications and
   literature, if any

Florida

Secretary of State Information

Department of State
Division of Corporations
Corporate Filings
P.O. Box 6327
Tallahassee, FL 32314
www.dos.state.fl.us/doc/index.html
Phone number of Division of Corporations:
  850-245-6052

Provides Articles of Incorporation: yes;

Internet Forms: Nonprofit articles of incorporation and other statutory forms are available for downloading from the Division of Corporations' website. Articles can be prepared and filed online from the state filing office website

The Florida Not For Profit Corporation Act is contained in Title XXXVI (Business Organizations), Chapter 617, of the Florida Statutes, starting with Section 617.01011, and is browsable from the following website page (click the "Statutes and Constitution" tab, then "Florida Statutes," then select "Title XXXVI," then "Chapter 617" from the index): www.leg.state.fl.us/Welcome/index.cfm

Corporate Name Requirements

Corporate Designator: name must contain one of the following: "corporation," "incorporated," or their abbreviations. It may not contain the word "company" or its abbreviation [617.0401]

Articles of Incorporation

Director Qualifications:
Number: three or more [617.0803]
Residency: no
Age: 18 or older [617.0802]

Incorporator Qualifications:
Number: one or more
Residency: no
Age: no

Bylaws

Directors' Quorum: majority of the directors in office, or else as specified in the articles or bylaws, but no fewer than 1/3 of the number in office [617.0824]

Members' Quorum: as stated in the articles or bylaws

Directors' Term of Office: as specified in articles or bylaws [617.0803]

Officer Requirements: may have officers as specified in articles or bylaws. If not specified in articles or bylaws, officers are appointed or elected by the board for one-year terms of office. One person may hold more than one office simultaneously. [617.0840]

State Corporate Tax Exemption

Corporate Income or Franchise Tax: yes

State Agency to Contact:
Dept. of Revenue, Tallahassee
http://sun6.dms.state.fl.us/dor

State Tax Exemption Requirements:

- Separate state notification required but determination follows federal
- For state income tax exemption, federal determination letter, attached to Form FL1120 (Florida Corporation Income Tax), must be filed with Florida Dept. of Revenue. No further state filings necessary, except to report and pay any unrelated business income taxes owed
- Florida law requires all entities, except federal agencies, desiring to qualify for sales tax exemptions to complete a Consumer's Certificate of Exemption available from the Florida Department of Revenue. Exemption certificates expire 5 years after the date of issuance and are subject to review and reissuance procedures
- Chapter 496, F.S., requires charitable organizations or sponsors intending to solicit contributions from the public in the state of Florida to register annually with the Division of Consumer Services (call the Division at 850-488-2221 or 800-435-7352 for more information)

Georgia

Secretary of State Information

Secretary of State
Corporations Division
Suite 315, West Tower
2 Martin Luther King Jr. Dr.
Atlanta, GA 30334
www.sos.state.ga.us/corporations
Phone number of corporate filing section:
 404-656-2817

Provides Articles of Incorporation: not a form, but provides "Filing Procedures for Profit and Nonprofit Corporations," which includes sample articles.

Internet Forms: provides sample articles online as part of "Filing Procedures for Profit and Nonprofit Corporations," plus downloadable Transmittal of Articles form (BR231), which must be filed with articles

The Georgia Nonprofit Corporation Code starts with Section 14-3-101 of the Georgia Code, and is browsable from the following website page (select "GA Code" in the left panel. Select Title "14" in the top Titles grid, then select Chapter "14-3" in the Chapters column, then select sections in the right Sections column to browse the BCA):
 www.legis.state.ga.us
 www.legis.state.ga.us/legis/GaCode/index.htm

Corporate Name Requirements

Corporate Designator: name shall contain "corporation," "company," "incorporation," "limited," or an abbreviation [14-3-401]

Articles of Incorporation

Director Qualifications:

Number: 1 or more [14-3-803]
Residency: no
Age: 18 or older [14-3-802]

Incorporator Qualifications:

Residency: no
Age: no

Special Requirements: Publication is required (once a week for two consecutive weeks) of notice of filing of articles in newspaper in the county of principal place of business. The notice should be published no later than one business day after filing articles—it's best to start the publication of notice before mailing articles to the state filing office. A sample notice form is included in the "Filing Procedures for Profit and Nonprofit Corporations," provided online

Bylaws

Directors' Quorum: majority of the directors in office, unless a percentage is specified in the articles or bylaws, which may not be less than 1/3 of the directors in office

Members' Quorum: as specified in bylaws, or else 10% of the voting members; unless 20% or more of the voting power is present in person or by proxy, the only matters that may be voted upon at an annual or regular meeting of members are those matters that are described in the meeting notice [14-3-722]

Directors' Term of Office: as specified in the articles or bylaws; if not specified, then one year [14-3-805]

Officer Requirements: may have as specified in the articles or bylaws. One person may hold more than one office simultaneously [14-3-840]

State Corporate Tax Exemption

Corporate Income or Franchise Tax: yes

State Agency to Contact:

Georgia Dept. of Revenue, Atlanta
www2.state.ga.us/departments/dor

State Tax Exemption Requirements:

- Apply for state corporate income tax exemption application with Form 3605. Form 3605 asks principally for copies of articles, bylaws, federal tax-exemption determination letter, certificate of Georgia corporate registration, and description of organization's activities. Exempt organizations that file federal Form 990-T must also file Georgia Form 660-T to report unrelated business income.

- Nonprofit corporations that will be soliciting or accepting contributions in Georgia should call the Charitable Organizations section of the Office of Secretary of State (404-656-4910) to determine if additional registration is required by law.

Hawaii

Secretary of State Information

Dept. of Commerce and Consumer Affairs
Business Registration Division
335 Merchant Street
Honolulu, HI 96813
www.businessregistrations.com
Phone: 808-586-2744

Provides Articles of Incorporation: yes

Internet Forms: Nonprofit forms, including articles with instructions, are available for downloading from the state filing office website. Nonprofit articles can be completed and filed online from the state corporate filing office website.

The Hawaii Nonprofit Corporation Act is contained in Chapter 414D of the Hawaii Statutes, and is browsable from the following website page (enter the site; select "Legal Info" at the side of the page; click "Statutes"; then select "Hawaii Nonprofit Corporation Act"):

    www.businessregistrations.com

Corporate Name Requirements

Corporate Designator: not required

Articles of Incorporation

Director Qualifications:
Number: 3 or more [414D-133]
Residency: no
Age: no

Incorporator Qualifications:
Residency: no
Age: no

Bylaws

Directors' Quorum: majority of the directors in office, or else as specified in the articles or bylaws. A quorum must consist of at least one-third of the total number of directors, or two directors, whichever is greater [414D-147]

Members' Quorum: 10% of the votes entitled to be cast on a matter, unless otherwise stated in the articles or bylaws. Unless one-third or more of the voting power is present in person or by proxy at a members' meeting, the only matters that may be voted upon at an annual or regular meeting of members are those matters that are described in the meeting notice [414D-111]

Directors' Term of Office: as specified in the articles or bylaws; if not specified, then one year. Maximum term, except for designated or appointed directors, is five years [414D-135]

Officer Requirements: may have officers as specified in articles or bylaws; one person may hold any two or more offices simultaneously [414D-153]

State Corporate Tax Exemption

Corporate Income or Franchise Tax: yes

State Agency to Contact:
Hawaii Tax Department, Honolulu
www.state.hi.us/tax/tax.html

State Tax Exemption Requirements:

- State corporate income tax exemption is automatic with federal 501(c)(3) exemption
- To apply for state general excise tax exemption, complete Form G-6, "Application for Exemption From General Excise Taxes," and submit the application, copies of the articles of organization, bylaws, and IRS determination letter, and $20 registration fee to the Technical Section of the Department of Taxation's Taxpayer Services Branch.

Idaho

Secretary of State Information

Secretary of State
Corporations Division
700 W. Jefferson St.
P.O. Box 83720
Boise, ID 83720-0080
www.idsos.state.id.us/corp/corindex.htm
Phone number of Secretary of State's office:
  208-334-2300

Provides Articles of Incorporation: yes

Internet Forms: Nonprofit forms, including articles and other statutory forms, are available for downloading from the state filing office website

The Idaho Nonprofit Corporation Act is contained in Title 30, Chapter 3 of the Idaho Statutes, starting with Section 30-3-1, and is browsable from the following website page (click "Title 30," then "Chapter 3" to start browsing the Act).
  www3.state.id.us/idstat/TOC/idstTOC.html

Corporate Name Requirements

Corporate Designator: name shall contain "Corporation," "Company," "Incorporated," "Limited," or an abbreviation; "Company" shall not be preceded immediately by "and" [30-3-27]

Articles of Incorporation

Director Qualifications:

Number: 3 or more; for a religious corporation, 1 or more [30-3-65]

Residency: no

Age: no

Other: If the corporation is a cooperative, all directors must be members of the corporation, except, that unless otherwise provided in the bylaws, a person who has the right to vote on behalf of an entity which is a member of the cooperative corporation may serve as a director. [30-3-64]

Incorporator Qualifications:

Residency: no

Age: no

Bylaws

Directors' Quorum: majority of the number of directors unless specified in the bylaws or articles, but no fewer than 1/3 of the number in office (but if there are fewer than 6 directors, no fewer than 2 directors for quorum)

Members' Quorum: as specified in bylaws, or else 10% of the voting members present or represented by proxy. Unless one-third (1/3) or more of the voting power is present in person, by proxy, by mailed written ballot, or by absentee ballot, the only matters that may be voted upon at an annual or regular meeting of members are those matters that are described in the meeting notice [30-3-56]

Directors' Term of Office: as specified in the articles or bylaws, but not to exceed 5 years; if not specified, then one year [30-3-67]

Officer Requirements: must designate president, secretary, and treasurer. One person may hold more than one office simultaneously, except offices of president and secretary. Religious corporations are not required to have officers. [30-3-83]

State Corporate Tax Exemption

Corporate Income or Franchise Tax: yes

State Agency to Contact:

State Tax Commission, Boise
www2.state.id.us/tax/home.htm

State Tax Exemption Requirements: Automatic with federal exemption

Illinois

Secretary of State Information
Secretary of State
Department of Business Services
Corporations Division
Michael J. Howlett Bldg.
501 S. 2nd St., Rm. 328
Springfield, IL 62756
www.cyberdriveillinois.com/departments/
  business_services/home.html
Phone number for corporate information:
  800-252-8980
Corporate filings and phone calls are also handled
  by the Chicago Department of Business Services,
  Corporations Division Office, 312-793-3380.
Provides articles of incorporation: yes
Internet Forms: The latest Illinois nonprofit articles of
organization, plus other Illinois statutory forms
(Reservation of Corporate Name and others), can be
downloaded from the state office website. Also provides "A Guide For Organizing Not-For-Profit Corporations," online.

    The Illinois General Not For Profit Corporation
Act is contained in Chapter 805 (Business Organizations), starting with Section 180/105, and is
browsable from the following website page (click
"Chapter 805," then click "805 ILCS 105" to browse
the Act):
    www.legis.state.il.us/legislation/ilcs/ilcs.asp

Corporate Name Requirements
Corporate Designator: although not required, corporate name may contain "corporation," "incorporated," "company," "limited," or an abbreviation.
Name must end with the letters "NFP" if the corporate name contains any word or phrase that indicates or implies that the corporation is organized
for any purpose other than a purpose for which
corporations may be organized under the Illinois
General Not For Profit Corporation Act [104.05]

Articles of Incorporation
Director Qualifications:
Number: 3 or more [108.10]
Residency: no
Age: no
Incorporator Qualifications:
Residency: no
Age: individual 18 or older. Incorporator also may
be corporation [102.05]
Special Requirements: within 15 days of the secretary
of state filing your articles and returning other
documents to you, they must be filed with the Re-
corder of Deeds in the county in which the
corporation's registered office is located

Bylaws
Directors' Quorum: majority of the directors in office,
unless a percentage is specified in the articles or
bylaws, which may not be less than 1/3 of the directors in office
Members' Quorum: as specified in bylaws, or else
10% of the voting membership, in person or
represented by proxy [107.60]
Directors' Term of Office: until next meeting for
election of directors, unless terms are staggered
[108.05]
Officer Requirements: may have officers as specified
in bylaws. If allowed in the bylaws, one person
may hold any two or more offices [108.50]

State Corporate Tax Exemption
Corporate Income or Franchise Tax: yes
State Agency to Contact:
Illinois Dept. of Revenue, Springfield and Chicago
www.revenue.state.il.us
State Tax Exemption Requirements:
- Automatic with federal 501(c)(3) exemption
- To find out if you qualify for a state sales tax
  exemption, write a letter of request to the Illinois
  Department of Revenue, Sales Tax Division, and
  enclose photocopies of your articles of incorpo-
  ration, bylaws, constitution, IRS exemption letter,
  or any other document that may help in determining your status. The Department of Business
  Services will notify you of your status as soon as
  practicable.

Indiana

Secretary of State Information

Secretary of State
Corporations Division
302 W. Washington St., Rm. E018
Indianapolis, IN 46204
www.in.gov/sos/business/index.html
Phone number of Corporations Division:
  317-232-6576
Provides Articles of Incorporation: yes
Internet Forms: articles and other statutory forms are provided online

The Indiana Not For Profit Corporation Act is contained in Title 23 (Business and Other Associations), Article 17, of the Indiana Code, starting with Section 23-17-1-1, and is browsable from the following website page (select "Title 23," then "Article 17"):

  www.in.gov/legislative/ic/code

Corporate Name Requirements

Corporate Designator: name must include "corporation," "incorporated," "limited," "company," or an abbreviation [17-5-1]

Articles of Incorporation

Director Qualifications:
  Number: 3 or more [23-17-12-3]
  Residency: no
  Age: no
Incorporator Qualifications:
  Residency: no
  Age: no
Special Requirements: articles must specify whether the corporation being formed is a public benefit, mutual benefit, or religious corporation. Most 501(c)(3) tax-exempt nonprofit corporations are organized as public benefit corporations (or religious corporations if their 501(c)(3) purposes are religious).

Bylaws

Directors' Quorum: majority of the directors in office, or else the percentage specified in the articles or bylaws, which may not be less than 1/3 of the number in office or 2 directors, whichever is smaller [23-17-15-5]
Members' Quorum: as specified in bylaws, or 10% of members qualified to vote. Unless at least one-third (1/3) of the voting power is present in person or by proxy, the only matters that may be voted upon at an annual or a regular meeting of members are those matters that are described in the meeting notice [23-17-11-4]
Directors' Term of Office: as specified in the articles or bylaws but not more than five years. In the absence of a provision in the articles or bylaws, the term for directors is one year [23-17-12-5]
Officer Requirements: unless otherwise provided in articles of incorporation or bylaws, a corporation must have a president, a secretary, and a treasurer. One person may hold more than one office [23-17-14-1]

State Corporate Tax Exemption

Corporate Income or Franchise Tax: yes
State Agency to Contact:
  Dept. of Revenue, Indianapolis.
  www.state.in.us/dor
State Tax Exemption Requirements:
* state corporate income tax exemption follows federal
* provide notification of tax-exempt status to state and apply for a state sales tax exemption by completing and submitting Form NP-20A along with a copy of articles and bylaws and a copy of the federal determination letter. Exempt organizations must file an annual state informational report (Form NP-20) and report unrelated business income (on Form IT-20NP).

Iowa

Secretary of State Information

Secretary of State
Corporations Division
Lucas Building, 1st Floor
321 East 12th Street
Des Moines, IA 50319
www.sos.state.ia.us/business
Phone number of Corporations Division:
  515-281-5204

Provides Articles of Incorporation: no, but provides the articles statute that contains the required contents of articles

Internet Forms: Article statute (Section 504A.29 of the Nonprofit Corporation Act), which contains the required contents of articles, can be viewed online from the state filing office website. Site also provides a guide to nonprofit corporation requirements with links to the relevant sections of the Nonprofit Corporations Act. Also provides a link to the Iowa Nonprofit Resource Center (http://nonprofit.law.uiowa.edu)

The Iowa Nonprofit Corporation Act is contained in Title XII (Business Entities), Chapter 504A, of the Iowa Code, starting with Section 504A.1, and is browsable from the following website page:
  www.legis.state.ia.us/IACODE/1999
SUPPLEMENT/504A

Corporate Name Requirements

Corporate Designator: not required

Articles of Incorporation

Articles Statute: Iowa Code Annotated, Nonprofit Corporations, 504A.29

Director Qualifications:
  Number: 1 or more [504A.17]
  Residency: not required
  Age: no

Incorporator Qualifications:
  Residency: no
  Age: capacity to contract (of legal age) [504A28]

Bylaws

Directors' Quorum: majority of the directors in office, or else the percentage specified in the bylaws, which may not be less than 1/3 of the number in office [504A.20]

Members' Quorum: as stated in bylaws If not specified in bylaws, members holding one-tenth of the votes entitled to be cast on the matter to be voted upon, represented in person or by proxy at a meeting, constitute a quorum [504A.16]

Directors' Term of Office: as specified in the articles or bylaws; if not specified, then one year [504A.18]

Officer Requirements: must designate president, vice president, secretary, treasurer. One person may hold any two or more offices simultaneously [504A.23]

State Corporate Tax Exemption

Corporate Income or Franchise Tax: yes

State Agency to Contact:

Iowa Dept. of Revenue & Finance, Des Moines
www.state.ia.us/government/drf/index.html

State Tax Exemption Requirements:
- Automatic with federal 501(c)(3) exemption
- Exempt organizations report unrelated business income on state Form IA 1120. Note that exempt organizations may also be subject to the Iowa alternative minimum tax (see Form IA 4626).

Kansas

Secretary of State Information
Secretary of State
Corporation Division
First Floor, Memorial Hall
120 SW 10th Ave
Topeka, KS 66612
www.kssos.org/main.html
Phone number of Corporation Division:
 785-296-4564

Provides Articles of Incorporation: yes

Internet Forms: Kansas nonprofit corporation articles (Form CN) plus other forms can be downloaded from the state filing office website. Nonprofit articles can be prepared and filed online from the Business Center Business Center at www.accesskansas.org/businesscenter/index.html

The Kansas corporate statutes are contained in Chapter 17 of the Kansas statutes, beginning with Article 60 (the profit and nonprofit statutes are consolidated together). In the box at the bottom of the page titled "Statute Table of Contents," select "Chapter 17" (use the arrow keys to navigate through the list), then click "Get Articles in Chapter." Select Article 60 to browse the corporate statutes:

www.kslegislature.org/cgi-bin/statutes/index.cgi

Corporate Name Requirements
Corporate Designator: name must include "incorporated," "association," "church," "college," "club," "company," "corporation," "foundation," "fund," "institute," "limited," "society," "syndicate," "union," or an abbreviation such as "co.," "corp.," "inc.," "ltd." The name must be written in roman characters or letters [17-6002]

Articles of Incorporation
Director Qualifications:
Number: 1 or more [17-6301]
Residency: no
Age: no
Incorporator Qualifications:
Residency: no
Age: no

Bylaws
Directors' Quorum: unless otherwise specified, a majority of the directors in office, but the articles may specify a quorum less than 1/3 of the number of directors [17-6301(j)]

Members' Quorum: as specified in the articles or bylaws, or 1/3 of members if not specified [17-6505]

Directors' Term of Office: as specified in bylaws

Officer Requirements: the bylaws or a resolution of the board of directors may specify offices to be filled. One person may hold more than one office unless articles or bylaws provide otherwise [17-6302]

State Corporate Tax Exemption
Corporate Income or Franchise Tax: yes
State Agency to Contact:
Kansas Dept. of Revenue, Topeka
www.ksrevenue.org
State Tax Exemption Requirements:
- Automatic with federal 501(c)(3) exemption
- Kansas law requires charitable organizations to register with the Secretary of State's office prior to soliciting contributions, and solicitors working for the charitable organization also must register (go to www.kscharitycheck.org to register your 501(c)(3) tax-exempt nonprofit)

Kentucky

Secretary of State Information

Secretary of State
P.O. Box 718
Frankfort, KY 40602
www.sos.state.ky.us
Phone number of corporate filing section:
 502-564-3490

Provides Articles of Incorporation: yes

Internet Forms: Kentucky nonprofit corporation
articles plus other statutory forms can be downloaded from the state office website

 The Kentucky nonprofit statutes are contained in
Title XXIII (Private Corporations and Associations),
Chapter 273, of the Kentucky Statutes, starting with
Section 273.161, and are browsable from the
following website page (select "Title XXIII, Chapter
273," then scroll to "Section .161" to begin browsing
the nonprofit corporation statutes):
 www.lrc.state.ky.us/krs/titles.htm

Corporate Name Requirements

Corporate Designator: name shall include "corporation," "incorporated," "company," "inc.," or "co.";
but if "company" or "co." is used, it may not be immediately preceded by "and" or "&" [273.177]

Articles of Incorporation

Director Qualifications:

Number: 3 or more [273.211]
Residency: no
Age: no

Incorporator Qualifications:

Residency: no
Age: no

Special Requirements: file-stamped copy of articles
filed with secretary of state must also be filed with
county clerk of the county where the registered office is located

Bylaws

Directors' Quorum: majority of the directors in office,
or else as stated in articles or bylaws

Members' Quorum: as specified in the bylaws, or else
10% of the voting membership present or represented by proxy [273.203]

Directors' Term of Office: as specified in the articles
or bylaws; if not specified, then one year [273.211]

Officer Requirements: may have officers as specified
in the bylaws. One person may hold more than one
office at a time. Officers' term as specified in articles or bylaws, but not more than three years. In
the absence of a provision, officers elected or appointed annually by board of directors [273.227

State Corporate Tax Exemption

Corporate Income or Franchise Tax: yes

State Agency to Contact:

Kentucky Revenue Cabinet, Frankfort
http://revenue.state.ky.us

State Tax Exemption Requirements:

Automatic with federal 501(c)(3) exemption

Louisiana

Secretary of State Information

Secretary of State
Corporations Division
P.O. Box 94125
Baton Rouge, LA 70804
www.sos.louisiana.gov/comm/corp/corp-index.htm
Phone number of corporate filing section:
225-925-4704

Provides Articles of Incorporation: yes

Internet Forms: provides articles online plus other statutory forms, such as a Reservation of Name

The Louisiana Nonprofit Corporation Law is contained in Title XII Corporations and Associations, Chapter 2, of the Louisiana Revised Statutes, starting with Section 12:201. To start browsing the Act, click the "Louisiana Laws" link on the website page whose URL is shown in the next paragraph. Use the topmost "Search by Specific Law Body" section of the page. Type "12" in the Title box, and "201" in the Section box.

www.legis.state.la.us

Corporate Name Requirements

Corporate Designator: not required. It cannot contain the words "bank," "banking," "banker," "savings," "trust," "deposit," "insurance," "mutual," "assurance," "indemnity," "casualty," "fiduciary," "homestead," "building and loan," "surety," "security," "guarantee," "cooperative," "state," "parish," "redevelopment corporation," "electric cooperative," or "credit union" [204] Also, except as allowed in Section 201.4, the corporate name of a nonprofit corporation or organization shall not contain the name of any public park, playground, or other public facility together with the word "benefit," "benevolent," "endowment," "philanthropic," "foundation," or "fund" [204.1]

Articles of Incorporation

Director Qualifications:
Number: 3 or more; in a membership corporation, if there are less than 3 members, then the same number of directors as there are members [224]
Residency: no
Age: no

Incorporator Qualifications:
Residency: no
Age: capable of contracting (legal age) [202]

Special Requirements: File a transmittal form with articles, which is included at the beginning with the online articles form. If the articles of incorporation are filed within five (5) working days (exclusive of legal holidays) after the date of notarization of the registered agent's acknowledgement at the end of the articles, the corporate existence shall begin as of the time of such acknowledgement.

Two original copies or one certified copy of the articles, along with a copy of the certificate of incorporation, must be filed with recorder of mortgages of the parish in which the registered office of the corporation is located, within 30 days of filing

Bylaws

Directors' Quorum: majority of the directors in office [224]

Members' Quorum: except as specified in articles or bylaws, majority of voting members, in person or represented by proxy at a meeting [231]

Directors' Term of Office: as specified in the articles or bylaws, but may not exceed five years; if not specified, then one year [224] But see Section 229 which requires annual meeting of members for the election of directors in a membership nonprofit.

Officer Requirements: must designate president, secretary, and treasurer. One person may hold two offices; but if 2 signatures required on form, must be 2 persons [225]

State Corporate Tax Exemption

Corporate Income or Franchise Tax: yes

State Agency to Contact:
Dept. of Revenue and Taxation, Baton Rouge
www.rev.state.la.us

State Tax Exemption Requirements:
- Separate state notification required but determination follows federal
- To obtain the state corporate income tax exemption, submit a copy of your federal determination letter to the Department of Revenue and Taxation

Maine

Secretary of State Information

Secretary of State
Bureau of Corporations, Elections and Commissions
101 State House Station
Augusta, ME 04333-0101
www.state.me.us/sos/cec/cec.htm
Phone number of Bureau of Corporations:
  207-624-7740

Provides articles of incorporation: yes

Internet Forms: The latest fill-in-able Maine nonprofit articles of organization, plus other Maine statutory forms (Reservation of Corporate Name and others), can be downloaded from the state's website. Most 501(c)(3) nonprofits use Form MNPCA-6 (not the other special-purpose nonprofit articles provided on the website)

The Maine Nonprofit Corporation Act is contained in Title 13B of the Maine Statutes, starting with Section 101, and is browsable from the following website page (select Title 13B):
  http://janus.state.me.us/legis/statutes

Corporate Name Requirements

Corporate Designator: not required

Articles of Incorporation

Director Qualifications:

Number: 3 or more [702] Maine requires that no more than 49% of the individuals on the board of directors may be "financially interested persons." An individual who has received or is entitled to receive compensation for personal services rendered to the corporation by that individual within the previous 12 months is a financially interested person. The spouse, brother, sister, parent, or child of the board member is also considered in determining financial interest [713-A] For more information, see the Attorney General's Guide for Board Members of Charitable Corporations, which is linked to the state corporate filing office website.
Residency: no
Age: no

Incorporator Qualifications:

Residency: no
Age: no

Special Requirements: articles must specify whether the corporation being formed is a public benefit, or mutual benefit corporation. (Unlike other states that classify nonprofit corporations as public and mutual benefit corporations, a separate religious corporation category is not included under the Maine Act.) Apparently, all 501(c)(3) tax exempt nonprofit corporations, including religious corporations, are considered public benefit corporations, for purposes of the Maine Act [see 1406].

Bylaws

Directors' Quorum: majority of directors in office, unless a percentage is specified in the articles or bylaws, which may not be less than 1/5 of the number in office [706]

Members' Quorum: as specified in bylaws or else 10% of the voting membership, represented in person or by proxy [605]

Directors' Term of Office: as specified in the bylaws; if not specified, then one year [702]

Officer Requirements: must designate president, secretary, or clerk and treasurer. One person may hold two or more offices [710]

State Corporate Tax Exemption

Corporate Income or Franchise Tax: yes

State Agency to Contact:

Bureau of Taxation, Augusta
www.state.me.us/revenue

State Tax Exemption Requirements:

- Separate state notification required but determination follows federal
- To provide this notification, mail a copy of the federal determination letter to the Bureau of Taxation

Maryland

Secretary of State Information

Maryland Department of Assessments & Taxation
Charter Unit
Room 809
301 West Preston Street, Room 801
Baltimore, MD 21201
www.dat.state.md.us/sdatweb/charter.html
Phone number for corporate inquiries: 410-767-1184
  Toll-free: 888-246-5941

Provides Articles of Incorporation: yes

Internet Forms: nonprofit articles of incorporation,
plus other statutory forms can be downloaded from
the state's website

  The Maryland General Corporation Law, Titles 1
through 3 of the Corporations and Associations
Code of Maryland, covers both profit and nonprofit
corporations unless a special provision of Title 5,
Subtitle 2, of the Corporations and Associations
Code provides otherwise. To browse Titles 1
through 3, and Title 5, Subtitle 2, go to the following website page (select Maryland, then click the
Maryland Code folder, then the Corporations and
Associations Code, then browse Titles 1 through 3
and Title 5, Subtitle 2. Also see Title 5, Subtitle 3,
for special provisions that can apply to religious
nonprofit corporations formed by churches):
www.michie.com

Corporate Name Requirements

Corporate Designator: name must include "corporation," "limited," "incorporated," or an abbreviation,
or "Company" or its abbreviation if it is not preceded by the word "and" or a symbol for the word
"and" [1-502]

Articles (Charter) of Incorporation

Director Qualifications:
  Number: 1 or more [2-402]
  Residency: no
  Age: no
Incorporator Qualifications:
  Age: adult (18 or older) [2-102]

Bylaws

Directors' Quorum: majority of the directors in office,
unless otherwise specified in the bylaws, but not
less than 1/3 of the board (but if 2 or 3 directors, at
least 2 directors for quorum) [2-408]
Members' Quorum: majority of the voting members
represented in person or by proxy, or else as
specified in the charter or bylaws [2-506]

Directors' Term of Office: as specified in the bylaws,
but term must be at least for one year [5-202]
Officer Requirements: must designate president, secretary, and treasurer [2-412]; one person may hold
any two offices except president and vice president
(if there is one); also, if 2 signatures required on
form, must be 2 persons [2-415]

State Corporate Tax Exemption

Corporate Income or Franchise Tax: yes
State Agency to Contact:
Comptroller, Baltimore
www.comp.state.md.us/default.asp
State Tax Exemption Requirements:
- Separate state notification required but determination follows federal
- To obtain state income tax exemption, nonprofits
  must register with the Maryland Revenue Administration Division. To register, an authorized official of the nonprofit must submit a letter of request accompanied by a copy of the Internal
  Revenue Service determination of tax-exempt
  status
- There is a single Combined Registration Application that can be used to claim exemption from
  all state taxes other than income tax (the application can be completed and filed online from the
  Comptroller's website)

Massachusetts

Secretary of State Information

Secretary of the Commonwealth
Corporations Division
One Ashburton Place, 17th Floor
Boston, MA 02108
www.state.ma.us/sec/cor
Phone number of corporate filing section:
617-727-9640

Provides articles of incorporation: yes

Internet Forms: Articles of organization as well as statutory forms are available from the state's website. The articles can be filled out and filed online from the state website.

The Massachusetts Nonprofit Corporation Act is contained in Chapter 180 of the Massachusetts General Laws, and is browsable from the following website page (select "General Laws," then select "Link to a Specific Chapter or Section," then type "180" in the Chapter No. box, leave the section number field empty, and click "get Link"; then click on "Chapter 180 Table of Contents" and browse specific section from the table of contents). Nonprofit corporations also are subject to general provisions of the Business Corporation Law contained in Chapter 156B of the Laws):

www.state.ma.us/legis/legis.htm

Corporate Name Requirements

Corporate Designator: name must include "Limited," "Incorporated," "Corporation," or an abbreviation [Chapter 156B, Section 11]

Articles of Incorporation (Organization)

Director Qualifications:

Number as provided in bylaws (one or more) [6A]
Residency: no
Age: no

Incorporator Qualifications:

Residency: no
Age: 18 or older [Chapter 180: Section 3]

Bylaws

Directors' Quorum: as provided in the bylaws [6A]
Members' Quorum: as provided in bylaws [6A]
Director's Term: as provided in bylaws [6A]
Officer Requirements: president, treasurer, and clerk (or one or more officers whose duties are those normally associated with those of a president, treasurer, and clerk). The clerk shall be a resident of the commonwealth unless the corporation shall have a duly appointed resident agent [6A]

State Corporate Tax Exemption

Corporate Income or Franchise Tax: yes
State Agency to Contact:

Department of Revenue, Boston
www.dor.state.ma.us/Dorpg.htm

State Tax Exemption Requirements:

- Separate state notification required but determination follows federal
- To obtain state income tax exemption, send a photocopy of the IRS exemption letter to the Corporate Exemptions Division of the Department of Revenue
- To apply for exemptions on local property taxes fill out Form 3ABC supplied by your local assessor or obtained from the Planning and Research division of the Department of Revenue. Submit this form to your local assessor with a copy of the IRS exemption letter. Some local assessors grant exemptions if the IRS does; others may not do so without further investigation
- If the IRS grants a federal tax exemption, the corporation is also eligible for an exemption on state sales tax. In order to obtain this exemption fill out Form TA1 and submit it, with a copy of the IRS exemption letter, to the Bureau of Sales Excise of the Department of Revenue.

Michigan

Secretary of State Information

Commercial Services & Corporations
Corporation Division
P.O. Box 30053
Lansing, MI 48909
www.michigan.gov/cis
Phone number of Corporation Division:
517-241-6470

Provides articles of incorporation: yes

Internet Forms: Fill-in-able Michigan nonprofit corporation articles are available for downloading from the state filing office website. Articles can be filed electronically after filling out an application (by telephone at 517-214-6400 or online) for a filer number.

The Michigan Bureau of Commercial Services, Corporation Division, offers a seminar for nonprofit officers, directors, and members. The seminars are offered monthly from March to October and cover a variety of topics including director and officers' duties and responsibilities, indemnification, charitable solicitations, financing, tax issues, filing requirements, and record keeping. Call the state corporate filing office for more information.

The Michigan Nonprofit Corporation Act is contained in Chapter 450 (Corporations) of the Michigan Compiled laws, starting with Section 450.2101, and is browsable from the following website page (select "Chapter Index" under " Laws" in the left pane, then select "Chapter 450," then scroll down and select "Act 162 of 1982—Nonprofit Corporation Act" at the bottom of the page):
www.michiganlegislature.org

Corporate Name Requirements

Corporate Designator: not required

Articles of Incorporation

Director Qualifications:

Number: one or more

Residency: no

Age: 501(c)(3) tax-exempt nonprofit may include 1 or more directors on its board who are 16 or 17 years of age as long as that number does not exceed 1/2 the total number of directors required for a quorum for the transaction of business. In this case, the articles of incorporation must state the number of directors who may be 16 or 17 years of age [450.2501a]

Incorporator Qualifications: [450.2201]

Residency: no

Age: 18 or older

Special Requirements:

- For most nonprofits, only one incorporator is required
- If there are three or more incorporators they may, by resolution, designate one to sign the articles; if so, a certified copy of that resolution must be filed along with the articles
- Typically, tax-exempt nonprofits are formed on a nonstock basis. A nonstock corporation's articles must include the value of its assets, classified as personal and real property, along with the general financing terms of the corporation
- Under Sections 178 through 185 of Act 327, P.A. of 1931, three or more persons can form a church corporation for the purpose of teaching and spreading of religious beliefs and principles. To form this special type of nonprofit, prepare and file BCS/CD-503, articles of incorporation for use by Ecclesiastical Corporations, available on the state corporate filing office website

Bylaws

Directors' Quorum: majority of the directors in office, or else a greater percentage specified in the bylaws or articles (if there are more than 7 directors, the articles or bylaws may specify a percentage less than a majority, but not less than 1/3 of the number in office) [450.2523]

Members' Quorum: as specified in articles or bylaws, or else a majority of the voting members [450.2415]

Directors' Term of Office: as specified in the articles or bylaws; if not specified for membership nonprofits, one year. [450.2505]

Officer Requirements: must designate president, secretary, and treasurer. One person may hold more than one office at a time, but alone may not execute a document required to be signed by two people [450.2531]

State Corporate Tax Exemption

Corporate Income or Franchise Tax: yes

State Agency to Contact:

Dept. of Treasury, Lansing
www.michigan.gov/treasury

State Tax Exemption Requirements:

- Automatic with federal 501(c)(3) exemption [MCL 208.35(1)(c)]
- Michigan has a single business tax, which is a modified value-added tax (VAT) replacing corporate income and various franchise taxes. Although not required, we suggest you notify the Dept. of Treasury of your federal 501(c)(3) tax-exempt status with Form C8030, "Single Business Tax Notice of No SBT Return Required," or by letter to the Single Business Tax Administration The exemption from SBT does not extend to un-related business income earned by the nonprofit

Minnesota

Secretary of State Information

Secretary of State
Business Services Division
180 State Office Building
100 Rev. Dr. Martin Luther King Jr. Blvd.
St. Paul, MN 55155-1299
www.sos.state.mn.us/business/index.html
Phone number for corporate information:
  877-551-6SOS (6767)

Provides Articles of Incorporation: yes

Internet Forms: articles and other statutory forms are available for downloading from the state filing office website. Nonprofit and business corporations use the same articles form

  The Minnesota Nonprofit Corporation Act is contained in Chapter 317A of the Minnesota Statutes, starting with Section 317A.001, and is browsable from the following website page (select "Chapter 300 through 319B," then select "Chapter 317A"):
  www.revisor.leg.state.mn.us/stats

Corporate Name Requirements

Corporate Designator: not required

Articles of Incorporation

Director Qualifications:
  Number: 3 or more [317A.203]
  Residency: no
  Age: must be natural persons and a majority of the directors must be adults [317A.205]

Incorporator Qualifications:
  Residency: no
  Age: one or more adult persons [317A.105]

Special Requirements:

- Religious corporations authorized by Ch. 315 of MN statutes may be organized under that Chapter or Chapter 317A
- Religious corporations may benefit members as follows: support and payment of ministers, teachers, employees, and payment of benefits to their survivors; may create, maintain, and disburse an endowment that funds a "Church Plan" as defined in IRC Sec. 414(e). Property of religious corporations is exempt from taxation. The board of directors may appoint its own peace officers to keep order on its own grounds

Bylaws

Directors' Quorum: majority of the directors in office, unless a percentage is specified in the articles or bylaws, which may not be less than 1/3 of the number in office [317A.235]

Members' Quorum: as specified in the bylaws or else 10% of the voting membership present or represented by proxy [317A.451]

Directors' Term of Office: as specified in bylaws, but not to exceed 10 years; if not specified, then one year [317A.207]

Officer Requirements: must designate president and treasurer [317A.301] One person may hold any two or more offices simultaneously. If a document must be signed by persons holding different offices or functions and a person holds or exercises more than one of those offices or functions, that person may sign the document in more than one capacity, but only if the document indicates each capacity in which the person signs [317A.315]

State Corporate Tax Exemption

Corporate Income or Franchise Tax: yes

State Agency to Contact:
  Minnesota Dept. of Revenue, St. Paul
  www.taxes.state.mn.us

State Tax Exemption Requirements:

- Automatic with federal 501(c)(3) exemption
- File Form M4NP if your nonprofit earns unrelated business income in the state

Mississippi

Secretary of State Information
Secretary of State
Corporate Division
P.O. Box 136
Jackson, MS 39205
www.sos.state.ms.us
Phone number of Corporate Division: 601-359-1350
(toll fee: 800-256-3494)

Internet Forms: The latest version of the Mississippi certificate of formation (Form F0001, used for nonprofit and profit corporations) can be downloaded from the state filing office website)

The Mississippi Nonprofit Corporation Act is contained in the Title 79 (Corporations, Associations and Partnerships) of the Mississippi Code, Chapter 11, starting with Section 79-11-101, and is browsable from the following website page (select "Mississippi," open the "Mississippi Code" folder, then the "Title 79" folder, then the "Chapter 11" folder, then the "Mississippi Nonprofit Corporation Act" folder):
www.michie.com

Corporate Name Requirements
Corporate Designator: none required, but secretary of state prefers that the name include "corporation," "incorporated," "company," or "limited"

Articles of Incorporation
Number: as fixed by articles or bylaws [79-11-235]
Residency: no
Age: no
Incorporator Qualifications:
Residency: no
Age: no
Special Requirements: Some of the nonprofit corporation requirements do not apply to religious corporations (see 79-11-403)

Bylaws
Directors' Quorum: majority of the directors in office, unless a percentage is specified in the articles or bylaws [79-11-263]
Members' Quorum: 10% of the voting membership or else as specified in the articles or bylaws. If less than one-third of the voting members attend a meeting, only matters contained in the notice for the meeting may be approved [79-11-217]
Directors' Term of Office: as specified in the articles or bylaws but not more than five years (except for religious corporations); if not specified, then one year [79-11-239]

Officer Requirements: may have officers as specified in the bylaws. One person may hold more than one office at a time. An officer must be delegated the responsibility for preparing minutes of corporate meetings [79-11-271]

State Corporate Tax Exemption
Corporate Income or Franchise Tax: yes
State Agency to Contact:
Miss. State Tax Commission, Jackson
www.mstc.state.ms.us
State Tax Exemption Requirements:
- Automatic with federal 501(c)(3) exemption
- Prior to soliciting contributions in the state, the organization must register with the sectary of state and make annual registration filings (see Forms URS and FS available on the Charities Forms page on the state corporate filing office website)

Missouri

Secretary of State Information

Secretary of State
Corporation Division
P.O. Box 778
Jefferson City, MO 65102
www.sos.mo.gov
Phone number for general corporate information:
573-751-4153; toll free: 866-223-6535

Provides Articles of Incorporation: yes

Internet Forms: Missouri nonprofit articles of incorporation form, plus other statutory forms, are available for downloading from the state filing office website

The Missouri Nonprofit Corporation Act is contained in the Title XXIII (Corporations, Associations and Partnerships) of the Missouri Statutes, Chapter 355, starting with Section 355.001, and is browsable from the following website page:

www.moga.state.mo.us/STATUTES/C355.HTM

Corporate Name Requirements

Corporate Designator: not required

Articles of Incorporation

Director Qualifications:

Number: 3 or more [355.321]
Residency: no
Age: no

Incorporator Qualifications:

Residency: no
Age: none in statutes (although secretary of state says must be 18 years of age)

Special Requirements: articles must specify whether the corporation being formed is a public benefit or mutual benefit corporation; 501(c)(3) tax-exempt nonprofit corporations are classified and organized as public benefit corporations

Bylaws

Directors' Quorum: majority of the directors in office unless a percentage is specified in the articles or bylaws, which may not be less than 1/3 of the number in office and in no case less than two directors [355.401]

Members' Quorum: as specified in the bylaws or else 10% of the voting membership present or represented by proxy. If less than one-third of the voting members are present at a meeting, the only matters that may be approved are those stated in the notice for the meeting [355.281]

Directors' Term of Office: as specified in the articles or bylaws, but not to exceed six years; if not specified, then one year [355.331]

Officer Requirements: must designate president, secretary, and treasurer. One person may hold more than one office; officer must be delegated with the responsibility for preparing minutes of meetings [355.431]

State Corporate Tax Exemption

Corporate Income or Franchise Tax: yes

State Agency to Contact:

Missouri Dept. of Revenue, Jefferson City
http://dor.state.mo.us/tax

State Tax Exemption Requirements:

- Automatic with federal 501(c)(3) exemption (any corporation filing a Federal Form 990, 990EZ, or 990PF is not required to file a Missouri corporation income tax return)

- Exempt organizations file Form MO-1120 to report and pay tax on unrelated business income earned in the state

Montana

Secretary of State Information

Secretary of State
Corporation Bureau
P.O. Box 202801
Helena, MT 59620
http://sos.state.mt.us/css/index.asp
Phone number of Business Services Bureau:
  406-444-3665

Provides Articles of Incorporation: yes

Internet Forms: The latest version of the Montana nonprofit articles of incorporation, plus other statutory forms, can be downloaded from the state filing office website

The Montana Nonprofit Corporation Act is contained in the Title 35 (Corporations, Partnerships and Associations) of the Montana Code, Chapter 2, starting with Section 35-2-113, and is browsable from the following website page (select "Title 35," then "Chapter 2," then "Part 1," then scroll down to start browsing at "Section 113"):

  http://data.opi.state.mt.us/bills/mca_toc/index.htm

Corporate Name Requirements

Corporate Designator: not required

Articles of Incorporation

Director Qualifications:
Number: 3 or more [35-2-415]
Residency: no
Age: no

Incorporator Qualifications:
Residency: no
Age: no

Special Requirements: articles must specify whether the corporation being formed is a public benefit, mutual benefit, or religious corporation. Most 501(c)(3) tax exempt nonprofit corporations are organized as public benefit corporations (except religious-purpose 501(c)(3)s, which organize as religious corporations). Section 35-2-128 of the Montana Nonprofit Corporation Acts says "If the religious doctrine governing the affairs of a religious corporation is inconsistent with the provisions of this chapter on the same subject, the religious doctrine controls to the extent required by the United States or the Montana constitution."

Bylaws

Directors' Quorum: majority of the directors in office, unless a percentage is specified in the articles or bylaws, which may not be less than 1/3 of the number in office and in any case may not be less than two [35-2-431]

Members' Quorum: as specified in the bylaws or else 10% of the voting members represented in person or by proxy. If less than one-third of the voting members attend a meeting, only matters specified in the notice of meeting may be approved [35-2-537]

Directors' Term of Office: as specified in bylaws, but not to exceed 5 years except for designated or appointed directors; if not specified, then one year [35-2-419]

Officer Requirements: unless otherwise provided in articles or bylaws, must designate president, secretary, and treasurer. One person may hold more than one office at the same time [35-2-439]

State Corporate Tax Exemption

Corporate Income or Franchise Tax: yes

State Agency to Contact:
State Dept. of Revenue, Helena
www.state.mt.us/revenue/css/default.asp

State Tax Exemption Requirements:
- Separate state determination
- After filing articles with the secretary of state, you should receive a welcome letter, which will include a form for the state income tax exemption. To apply for state tax exemption, you must send the following information to the Dept. of Revenue:
1. Character of the organization, the purpose for which it was organized, and its actual activities
2. Sources and disposition of its income and whether or not the income may inure to the benefit of any private shareholder or individual
3. In addition the applicant must supply a copy of the corporate articles and bylaws; and the latest financial statement showing assets, liabilities, receipts, and disbursements
4. A copy of the federal exemption letter
5. Copies of articles and bylaws

Nebraska

Secretary of State Information
Secretary of State
Corporate Division
P.O. Box 94608
Lincoln, NE 68509
www.sos.state.ne.us//corps/corpform.htm
Phone number of Corporate Office: 402-471-4079

Provides Articles of Incorporation: no. See Articles Statute, below, for the required contents of nonprofit corporation articles

Internet Forms: does not provide downloadable articles, but other statutory forms, such as Reservation of Name, provided online

The Nebraska Nonprofit Corporation Act is contained in Chapter 21 (Corporations and Other Companies) of the Nebraska Statutes, starting with Section 21-1901, and is browsable from the website page listed below (click on "Laws of Nebraska," "Statutes & Constitution," open the Chapter 21 folder, then click the "View Chapter" link under the search box and scroll down to Section 21-1901 to begin browsing the Nonprofit Corporation Act):
www.unicam.state.ne.us/index.htm

Corporate Name Requirements
Corporate Designator: not required

Articles of Incorporation
Articles Statute: RSN, Ch. 21-1921
Director Qualifications:
Number: 3 or more [21-1970]
Residency: no
Age: no
Incorporator Qualifications:
Residency: no
Age: no
Special Requirements: A duplicate copy of the filed articles must be recorded in the office of the clerk of the county where the registered office is located. Articles must specify whether the corporation being formed is a public benefit, mutual benefit, or religious corporation. Most 501(c)(3) tax-exempt nonprofit corporations are organized as public benefit corporations (or religious corporations if their 501(c)(3) purposes are religious). For religious nonprofits, Section 21-1919 of the Nonprofit Act provides: "If religious doctrine governing the affairs of a religious corporation is inconsistent with the provisions of the Nebraska Nonprofit Corporation Act on the same subject, the religious doctrine shall control to the extent required by the Constitution of the United States or the Constitution of the State of Nebraska or both."

Bylaws
Directors' Quorum: majority of the directors in office, unless a percentage is specified in the articles or bylaws, which may not be less than 1/3 of the directors in office or in any case less than two directors [21-1972]

Members' Quorum: as specified in the articles or bylaws or else 10% of the voting membership. Unless at least one-third of voting members attend an annual or regular meeting, only matters contained in the notice of meeting may be approved at the meeting [21-1961]

Directors' Term of Office: as specified in bylaws, but not to exceed 5 years except for designated or appointed directors; if not specified, then one year [21-1972]

Officer Requirements: must designate president, vice president, secretary, and treasurer. One person may hold more than one office at a time, but may not simultaneously be both president and secretary or president and vice president

State Corporate Tax Exemption
Corporate Income or Franchise Tax: yes
State Agency to Contact:
Nebraska Dept. of Revenue, Lincoln
www.revenue.state.ne.us/index.html
State Tax Exemption Requirements:
Automatic with federal 501(c)(3) exemption

Nevada

Secretary of State Information
Office of the Secretary of State
New Filings Section
202 N. Carson Street
Carson City, NV 89701
http://sos.state.nv.us/comm_rec/index.htm
Phone number of Secretary of State's office:
775-684-5708; Las Vegas office: 702-486-2880
Provides Articles of Incorporation: yes
Internet Forms: provides articles of incorporation and
other nonprofit corporation forms online at the
state filing office website. Also provides Customer
Order Instructions Form, which should be com-
pleted and mailed with articles.

The Nevada Nonprofit Corporation Act is contained in Title 7 (Business Associations; Securities;
Commodities), Chapter 82, of the Nevada Statutes,
starting with Section 82.006. You can browse it
from the following website page (select the "Table
of Contents to the Nevada Revised Statutes" from
the submenu that appears from the "Law Library"
item in the left panel, then select "Title 7, Chapter
82"):
www.leg.state.nv.us

Corporate Name Requirements
Corporate Designator: not required; unless a natural
person's name is used (for example, Paul Peterson's
Nonprofit). Then must add "incorporated," "corporations," "limited," "company," or an abbreviation.
[82.086]

Articles of Incorporation
Director (or Trustee) Qualifications: [82.196]
Number: 1 or more
Residency: no
Age: 18 or older
Incorporator Qualifications:
Residency: no
Age: no
Special Requirements: 501(c)(3) tax-exempt nonprofit
corporations are classified by the Nonprofit Act as
"corporations for public benefit" that are subject to
regulation and enforcement proceedings by the
state attorney general's office [82.021 & 82.536]

Bylaws
Directors' Quorum: a majority of the directors or else
as specified in articles or bylaws [82.271]
Members' Quorum: as specified in the articles or bylaws, or else 10% of the voting membership [82.291]

Directors (Trustees) Term of Office: in a membership nonprofit, directors elected annually for one-
year terms [82.286]
Officer Requirements: must designate president or
chairman of the board, secretary, treasurer. Officers
who are natural persons may hold two or more offices [82.211]

State Corporate Tax Exemption
Corporate Income or Franchise Tax: no state corporate income tax or franchise tax
**State Agency to Contact (for information about other
taxes):**
Dept. of Taxation, Carson City
http://tax.state.nv.us
State Tax Exemption Requirements: none (no state
personal or corporate income tax, and 501(c) tax-
exempt nonprofits are exempt from the state's business license and business tax requirements)

New Hampshire

Secretary of State Information
Secretary of State
Corporation Division
Department of State
107 North Main Street, Room 204
Concord, NH 03301
www.state.nh.us/sos/corporate/index.htm
Phone number for general corporate information:
  603-271-3244
Provides Articles of Incorporation: yes
Internet Forms: The state filing office website provides downloadable articles (of agreement) to form a nonprofit corporation (Form NP 1), plus other nonprofit corporation forms

The New Hampshire nonprofit corporation laws are contained in Title XXVII (Voluntary Corporations and Associations), Chapter 292, of the New Hampshire Statutes, starting with Section 292:1, and is browsable from the website page listed below (select "Form & Laws" in the left pane, then select "Non Profits," then select "State of New Hampshire Revised Statutes Online*Voluntary Corporations & Associations (Chapter 292*)"):
  www.sos.nh.gov/corporate

Corporate Name Requirements
Corporate Designator: not required

Articles of Incorporation (Articles of Agreement):
Director Qualifications:
  Number: charitable nonprofit corporations (does not include religious nonprofits) shall have at least 5 voting members, who are not of the same immediate family or related by blood or marriage. Can apply for waiver from this requirement from director of charitable trusts [292:6-a]
  Residency: no
  Age: no
Incorporator Qualifications: [292:1]
  Number: 5 or more
  Residency: no
  Age: lawful age (capable of contracting)
Special Requirements:
- Articles of agreement must be recorded in the office of the clerk of the town in which the principal office of the corporation is located, *prior* to filing with secretary of state
- Orthodox Church articles: in its statement of purpose in the articles, an Orthodox Church corporation must declare that its purpose is to maintain, propagate, practice, and forever perpetuate

religious worship, services, sacraments, and teachings in accordance with the doctrine, law, and traditions of the Orthodox Church [292:17]

Bylaws
Directors' Quorum: not specified in Chapter 292 (Section 292:6 provides: "The bylaws may contain any provisions for the regulation and management of the affairs of the corporation not inconsistent with the laws of the state or the articles of agreement, including provisions for issuance and reacquisition of membership certificates")
Members' Quorum: not specified in Chapter 292 (see language from Section 292:6, above)
Directors' Term of Office: not specified in Chapter 292 (see language from Section 292:6, above)
Officer Requirements: No requirement for specific officer positions in Chapter 292. However, Section 292:6-a provides: "No employee of a charitable nonprofit corporation shall hold the position of chairperson or presiding officer of the board" (requirement waivable by approval of director of charitable trusts)

State Corporate Tax Exemption
Corporate Income or Franchise Tax: no
State Agency to Contact (for information about other taxes):
Dept. of Revenue Administration, Concord
http://webster.state.nh.us/revenue/index.htm
State Tax Exemption Requirements:
- New Hampshire has no corporate income tax (nor sales tax)
- Federally tax-exempt organizations are also exempt from the New Hampshire Business Profits Tax and Business Enterprise Tax (but are subject to these taxes on unrelated business income earned in the state)
- For information on financial reporting requirements for charitable corporations, contact the Charitable Trusts Division of the Attorney General's Office (www.doj.nh.gov/charitable)

New Jersey

Secretary of State Information

Department of State
Division of Revenue/Corporate Filing Unit
P.O. Box 308
Trenton, NJ 08625
www.state.nj.us/njbgs/index.html
Phone number for general corporate information:
609-292-9292

Provides Articles of Incorporation: no (Nonprofit corporation formation can be accomplished by filing business registration form provided by state as explained below)

Internet Forms: New Jersey provides an online corporate formation and business registration service (scroll through the list of Online Services and select "Form or register a Business," then select "File a Certificate of Incorporation"). If you do not have an Internet connection or prefer to file paperwork to form your corporation, complete the Public Records Filing for New Business Entity portion of the New Jersey Business Registration Package (Form NJ-REG provided online or by telephone). This is a two-page section that can be used to form a nonprofit corporation. Nonprofits that submit a Form Reg-1E exemption form should not need to complete the other sections of the standard "NJ"-Reg package (see "State Tax Exemption Requirements," below).

The New Jersey Nonprofit Corporation Act is contained in Title 15A of the New Jersey Statutes, starting with Section 15A: 1-1, and is browsable from the following website page (select "Statutes," then select "Browse by Table of Contents," then select Title 15A):

www.njleg.state.nj.us

Corporate Name Requirements

Corporate Designator: the name shall contain "a New Jersey nonprofit corporation," "incorporated," "corporation," "corp.," or "inc." unless it is a religious corporation [15A:2-2]

Articles (Certificate) of Incorporation

Director (Trustee) Qualifications:
Number: 3 or more [15A:6-2]
Residency: no
Age: 18 or older [15A:6-1]
Incorporator Qualifications:
Residency: no
Age: 18 or older [15A:2-7]
Special Requirements: Religious societies and congregations also may incorporate under Title 16 of the New Jersey Statutes

Bylaws

Directors' (Trustees') Quorum: majority of the directors, or else as specified in Certificate of Incorporation or bylaws, but no less than 1/3 of the number in office or two directors, whichever is greater [15A:6-7]

Members' Quorum: a majority of voting members, or else as specified in articles or bylaws [15A:5-9]

Directors' (Trustees') Term of Office: one or two years as specified in certificate of incorporation or bylaws. If not specified, term is one year for nonmembership nonprofit (where the board itself votes to elect or reelect the board) [15A:6-3]

Officer Requirements: must designate president, secretary, and treasurer (alternate titles are allowed, but the bylaws must specify which of the alternate officer positions are associated with the duties of president, secretary, and treasurer). One person may hold any two or more offices at the same time; but if 2 signatures required on form, must be 2 persons [15A:6-15]

State Corporate Tax Exemption

Corporate Income or Franchise Tax: yes
State Agency to Contact:
Dept. of Treasury, Division of Taxation, Trenton
www.state.nj.us/treasury/taxation
State Tax Exemption Requirements:
- Automatic with federal 501(c)(3) exemption
- To apply for sales and use tax exemption and obtain exemption from New Jersey business registration, complete and submit Form Reg-1E, "Application for ST-5 Exempt Organization Certificate" (call 609-292-5995 to obtain the form)
- File Form CIT-1 to report and pay taxes on any unrelated business income earned in the state

New Mexico

Secretary of State Information

Public Regulation Commission
Corporations Bureau
Chartered Documents Bureau
P.O. Box 1269
Santa Fe, NM 87504
www.nmprc.state.nm.us/corporations/
corpshome.htm
Phone number of Corporation Commission:
800-947-4722

Provides Articles of Incorporation: yes

Internet Forms: New Mexico nonprofit articles of incorporation, plus other statutory forms, are
available for downloading from the state filing
office website

The New Mexico Nonprofit Corporation Act is
contained in Chapter 53 (Corporations), Article 8, of
the New Mexico Statutes, starting with Section
53-8-1, and is browsable from the following website
page (first select "Statutes" in the left panel, then
click the HTML tab at the top of the page; in the
left panel select "New Mexico Statutes," then the
folder titled "Statutory Chapters in New Mexico Statutes Annotated 1978," then scroll down in the left
panel and open the Chapter 53 folder, then open
the Article 8 folder and select sections of the Act to
browse):
http://legis.state.nm.us

Corporate Name Requirements

Corporate Designator: not required

Articles of Incorporation

Director Qualifications:
Number: 3 or more [53-8-18]
Residency: no
Age: no

Incorporator Qualifications:
Residency: no
Age: no

Bylaws

Directors' Quorum: majority of the number of directors set in the bylaws or articles, unless a quorum
percentage is specified in the articles or bylaws,
which may not be less than 1/3 of the fixed number
of directors [53-8-20]

Members' Quorum: as specified in bylaws, or else
10% of the voting membership [53-8-16]

Directors' Term of Office: as specified in the articles
or bylaws, or else one year [53-8-18]

Officer Requirements: may have officers as stated in
bylaws or by board resolution. If not provided, officers elected or appointed annually. One person
may hold two offices at the same time if allowed in
the bylaws. One of the officers must be given the
duty to record the proceedings of the meetings of
the members and directors in the corporate records
book [53-8-23]

State Corporate Tax Exemption

Corporate Income or Franchise Tax: yes

State Agency to Contact:
NM Taxation and Revenue Dept., Santa Fe
www.state.nm.us/tax

State Tax Exemption Requirements:
* Automatic with federal 501(c)(3) exemption
* Federally exempt nonprofits are exempt from
state corporate income tax as well as the annual
corporate franchise tax
* File Form CIT-1 to report and pay corporate income tax and the state franchise tax for unrelated business income earned in the state

New York

Secretary of State Information

Department of State
Division of Corporations
41 State Street
Albany, NY 12231
www.dos.state.ny.us/corp/corpspub.html
Phone number of Corporations Division:
518-473-2492

Provides Articles of Incorporation: yes

Internet Forms: Nonprofit certificate of incorporation, plus other statutory forms, provided online. 501(c)(3) tax-exempt nonprofit corporations use Form DOS-1511. As explained in the instructions to Form 1511 online, most nonprofit corporations with 501(c)(3) tax-exempt purposes are formed as Type B corporations under New York law.

The New York Not For Profit Corporation Law is contained in Chapter 35 of the New York Consolidated Laws, starting with Section 101, and is browsable from the following website page (click "New York State Laws," then "New York State Consolidated Laws," then "Not For Profit Corporation" then select article headings to view each part of the law):

http://assembly.state.ny.us/leg

Corporate Name Requirements

Corporate Designator: unless the corporation is formed for charitable or religious purposes, name shall contain "corporation," "incorporated," "limited," or an abbreviation. Corporate name may not contain any words prohibited by New York statutes, including the following: "acceptance," "annuity," "assurance," "bank," "bond," "casualty," "doctor," "endowment," "fidelity," "finance," "guaranty," "indemnity," "insurance," "investment," "lawyer," "loan," "mortgage," "savings," "state police," "state trooper," "surety," "title," "trust," "underwriter" [301]

Articles (Certificate) of Incorporation

Director Qualifications:

Number: 3 or more [702]

Residency: no

Age: Generally, 18 or older [see 701 for exceptions for youth groups and the like]

Incorporator Qualifications:

Residency: no

Age: 18 or older [401]

Special Requirements:

- There are four types of not-for-profit corporations in New York; 501(c)(3) nonprofits formed for charitable, educational, religious, scientific, or literary purposes are classified as Type B nonprofit corporations under New York law. Your articles must state that you are forming a Type B corporation (see the instructions to Form 1511 available online from the state filing office website)

- Additional approvals by various departments, agencies, and functionaries of state government are needed for nonprofit corporations that will engage in certain activities (for example, you must get approval from the SPCA to incorporate an animal shelter) or approval of Education Dept. for a school; check Sec. 404 of the New York Not-For-Profit Corporation Law to see if your group's purposes will require further approval

- Special forms and rules for forming a church: Corporations formed for the purpose of operating a church are generally filed pursuant to the Religious Corporations Law, rather than the Not-for-Profit Corporation Law. Corporations with religious purposes, other than the formation of a church, can be filed pursuant to the Not-for-Profit Corporation Law as described in the remainder of this state sheet. Corporations formed pursuant to the Religious Corporations Law are generally created by filing a Certificate of Incorporation with the office of the county clerk (See Religious Corporations Law, Sec. 2.). Corporations that do not have a principal office or place of worship are filed with the New York State Department of State. Certificates of Incorporation for all other religious corporations (churches) are filed directly with the office of the county clerk in which the principal office or place of worship is located. The form for filing under the Religious Corporations Law must be drafted by the filer by following the requirements of the Religious Corporations Law. We recommend you get the help of an experienced New York nonprofit lawyer to help you with the procedures and forms for forming a church. The Religious Corporations law can be browsed at http://public.leginfo.state.ny.us/menuf.cgi (click "Laws of New York," then click "RCO Religious Corporations").

Bylaws

Directors' Quorum: majority of the directors in office, or else the percentage stated in the certificate of incorporation or a bylaw adopted by the members, but in the case of a board with fifteen or fewer members, no less than 1/3 of directors. If there are more than 15 members, the quorum must be at least 5, plus one additional person for every 10 members (or fraction thereof) in excess of 15 [707]

Members' Quorum: majority of voting members, or else as specified in bylaws, but in no case less than 10% of the voting members, or 100 votes, whichever is less [608]

Directors' Term of Office: as specified in bylaws, but not more than five years; if not specified, then one year [703]

Officer Requirements: may have officers as specified in bylaws or as determined by the board of directors. One person may hold two offices simultaneously, except for offices of president and secretary, or similar offices; unless otherwise stated in articles or bylaws, an officer's term shall be one year [713]

State Corporate Tax Exemption

Corporate Income or Franchise Tax: yes

State Agency to Contact:

NY State Dept. of Taxation and Finance, Albany
www.tax.state.ny.us

State Tax Exemption Requirements:

- Apply for separate state corporate franchise tax exemption by preparing and filing Form CT-247, Application for Exemption from Corporation Franchise Taxes By a Not-for-Profit Organization. You must include a copy of your federal tax-exemption determination to qualify for the state exemption
- Unrelated business income earned in New York is reported on state Form CT-13

North Carolina

Secretary of State Information

Department of the Secretary of State
Corporations Division
P.O. Box 29622
Raleigh, NC 27626-0622
www.secretary.state.nc.us/corporations
Phone number of Corporations Division:
919-807-2225 (toll free 888-246-7636)

Provides Articles of Incorporation: yes

Internet Forms: North Carolina nonprofit corporation articles with instructions, plus other statutory forms and a Nonprofit Corporation Guide, are available for viewing and downloading from the state filing office website. The North Carolina Nonprofit Corporation Act is contained in Chapter 55A of the North Carolina Statutes, starting with Section 55A-1-01, and can be browsed at the website page shown below (click "NC General Statutes" at the bottom of the page, then click "Browse Table of Contents" in the right pane, then select "Chapter 55A, North Carolina Nonprofit Corporation Act"; also note that name and registered agent requirements for all types of corporations are contained in Chapter 55D of the NC General Statutes):
www.secstate.state.nc.us

Corporate Name Requirements

Corporate Designator: The name of a corporation must contain the word "corporation," "incorporated," "company," or "limited," or the abbreviation "corp.," "inc.," "co.," or "ltd." [55D-20]

Articles of Incorporation

Director Qualifications:
Number: 1 or more [55A-8-03]
Residency: no
Age: no

Incorporator Qualifications:
Residency: no
Age: no

Special Requirements: 501(c)(3) tax-exempt nonprofit corporations are classified under North Carolina Nonprofit Law as "charitable or religious" corporations, and their articles must include a statement that the corporation is a "charitable or religious" corporation

Bylaws

Directors' Quorum: majority of directors in office just prior to the meeting, but if the articles or bylaws specify another percentage, it may not be less than 1/3 of the directors in office [55A-8-24]

Members' Quorum: as specified in bylaws or else 10% of the voting membership. If one-third or less of the voting members are not present at a meeting, only matters contained in the notice of the meeting may be approved [55A-7-22]

Directors' Term of Office: as specified in articles or bylaws; if not specified, then one year [55A-8-05]

Officer Requirements: may have such officers as specified in bylaws. One person may hold two or more offices, but if 2 signatures required on form or action is required to be taken by two officers, must be by two persons [55A-8-40]

State Corporate Tax Exemption

Corporate Income or Franchise Tax: yes

State Agency to Contact:
NC Dept. of Revenue, Raleigh
www.dor.state.nc.us

State Tax Exemption Requirements:

- Separate state determination
- After the corporation is incorporated, the Department of Revenue will send you a questionnaire (Form CD-345), which it uses to determine if you qualify for its state corporate tax exemption. The corporation should submit, along with the questionnaire, a copy of its articles of incorporation, bylaws, and a copy of its federal 501(c)(3) tax-exemption determination letter. The Department of Revenue will evaluate the documents and notify the corporation by mail as to whether it will be exempt from state franchise and income taxes
- After obtaining your state corporate tax exemptions, file Form CD-404 to report and pay taxes on any unrelated business income earned in the state

North Dakota

Secretary of State Information

Secretary of State
Corporations Division
Main Capitol Bldg.
600 East Boulevard Ave.
Bismarck, ND 58505-0500
www.state.nd.us/sec/Business/
businessinforegmnu.htm
Phone number of Corporations Division:
800-352-0867 ext. 84284

Provides Articles of Incorporation: yes

Internet Forms: Corporate forms currently not available for downloading from the secretary of state's website

The North Dakota Nonprofit Corporation Act is contained in Title 10-33 of the North Dakota Century Code, starting with Section 10-33-01, and is browsable from the website page listed below (select "State Laws" in the top pane, then click "ND Century Code" in the left pane, then click "10 Corporations," then select the "Chapter 10-33" to browse sections of the Nonprofit Corporation Act): www.state.nd.us/lr

Corporate Name Requirements

Corporate Designator: not required

Articles of Incorporation

Director Qualifications:

Number: 3 or more (or at least the number of voting members if there are fewer than three voting members) [10-33-28]

Residency: no

Age: no

Other: A majority of the board must be unpaid (in a capacity other than as a director) and unrelated to unpaid directors. See 10-33-27 for more information.

Incorporator Qualifications:

Residency: no

Age: 18 years or older 10-33-05

Bylaws

Directors: Quorum—a majority, or a larger or smaller proportion or number as provided in the articles or bylaws, of the directors currently holding office [10-33-41]

Members' Quorum: as specified in the bylaws, or else 10% of the voting membership [10-33-76].

Directors' Term of Office: Directors are elected or appointed and hold office for fixed terms provided for in the articles or bylaws. A fixed term of a director, other than an ex officio director, may not exceed ten years. If the articles or bylaws do not provide for a fixed term, the term is one year. An ex officio director serves as long as the director holds the office or position designated in the articles or bylaws [10-33-30]

Officer Requirements: The officers of a corporation must be 18 years of age or more and must include a president and secretary. One person may hold two or more offices. If a officer signs a document in more than one capacity, each capacity must be stated on the document [10-33-51]

State Corporate Tax Exemption

Corporate Income or Franchise Tax: yes

State Agency to Contact:

ND State Tax Commissioner, Bismarck
www.state.nd.us/taxdpt

State Tax Exemption Requirements:

- Automatic with federal 501(c)(3) exemption
- Exempt organizations must file Form 99 (Information from Organization Exempt from Income Tax) annually with the Office of State Tax Commissioner, along with a copy of federal Form 990 (Return of Organization Exempt from Income Tax). Form 99 simply identifies a nonprofit's claim of exemption according to its IRC Section 501 classification. Exempt organizations report unrelated business income on Form 40 (regular income tax return)
- See "How to Begin and Maintain a Nonprofit Corporation in The State of North Dakota," available online at the state corporate filing office website. It contains information on state requirements for registering a 501(c)(3) as a charitable nonprofit and making annual reports to the state, state fundraising and lobbying requirements, plus additional information helpful to North Dakota nonprofits

Ohio

Secretary of State Information

Secretary of State
Business Services Division
P.O. Box 670
Columbus, OH 43216
www.state.oh.us/sos/
  business_services_information.htm
Phone number of corporate filing section:
  877-SOS-FILE (877-767-3453)
Corporate filings and phone calls are also handled
  by the Cleveland office, 216-622-3260

Provides Articles of Incorporation: yes

Internet forms: Downloadable nonprofit corporation articles (the form can be used for nonprofit, profit, and professional corporations) and other statutory forms are provided online at the state filing office website. The site also provides fill-in-able articles, which you can fill in and print (to use the Microsoft Excel® version, you must have Microsoft Excel installed on your computer)

The Ohio Nonprofit Corporation Law is contained in Title XVII (Corporations-Partnerships), Chapter 1702, of the Ohio Statutes, starting with Section 1702.01, and is browsable from the following website page (click "Revised Code," select "Title 17" in the left pane, click "Chapter 1702," then select each section of the law you wish to view):
http://onlinedocs.andersonpublishing.com

Corporate Name Requirements

Corporate Designator: not required

Articles of Incorporation

Director (Trustee) Qualifications:
Number: 3 or more; if fewer than 3 members, then the number of directors can be equal to the number of members [1702.27]
Residency: no
Age: no

Incorporator Qualifications:
Residency: no
Age: no

Bylaws (Regulations)

Directors' (Trustees') Quorum: a majority of the authorized number, or else as specified in articles or bylaws [1702.32]

Members' Quorum: the number of voting members present at a meeting constitutes a quorum, but articles or regulations may require a higher percentage to be present for certain actions [1702.22]

Directors' Term of Office: Unless otherwise provided in the articles or regulations (bylaws), annually until next election of directors at voting members' annual meeting [1702.28]

Officer Requirements: must designate president, secretary, and treasurer. One person may hold any number of offices simultaneously [1702.34.]. All officers elected annually unless otherwise stated in the articles or bylaws

State Corporate Tax Exemption

Corporate Income or Franchise Tax: yes

State Agency to Contact:
Department of Taxation, Columbus
http://tax.ohio.gov

State Tax Exemption Requirements:
- Automatic upon filing articles
- See the "Legal Guide for Nonprofit Organizations," available from the state corporate filing office website, which provides information on state nonprofit corporate income, sales, and property tax exemptions

Oklahoma

Secretary of State Information

Secretary of State
2300 N. Lincoln Blvd., Rm. 101
State Capitol Building
Oklahoma City, OK 73105
www.sos.state.ok.us/business/business_filing.htm
Phone number of secretary of state's office:
  405-521-3912

Provides Articles of Incorporation: yes

Internet Forms: Nonprofit certificate of incorporation plus other statutory forms are available for downloading from the state filing office website. Also view the procedures for forming a nonprofit available online, which contains instructions for completing the certificate form

The Oklahoma nonprofit corporation statutes are consolidated with the profit corporation statutes in the Oklahoma General Corporation Act contained in Title 18 of Oklahoma Statutes, starting with Section 18-1001. The GCA is browsable from the website page listed below. Select "Link to Statutes" in the left panel, then click "Expand" for Title 18, then scroll down to Section 1001 to the start of the General Corporation Act.

  www.sos.state.ok.us/exec_legis/
exec_leg_home.htm

Corporate Name Requirements

Corporate Designator: name must contain one of following: "association," "company," "corporation," "club," "foundation," "fund," "incorporated," "institute," "society," "union," "syndicate," or "limited," or one of the abbreviations "co.," "corp.," "inc.," "ltd.," or words or abbreviations of like import in other languages so long as they are written in roman characters or letters [1006]

Articles (Certificate) of Incorporation

Director (Trustee) Qualifications:
  Number: 1 or more [1027]
  Residency:
  Age: no

Incorporator Qualifications:
  Residency: no
  Age: no
  Number: 3 [1005]

Special Requirements: If the corporation is a church, the certificate of incorporation must state the street address of the location of the church [1006]

Bylaws

Directors' Quorum: majority of the total number of directors, unless the certificate or bylaws require a greater percentage. A nonstock corporation may provide that less than one-third (1/3) of the directors may constitute a quorum and may otherwise provide that the business and affairs of the corporation shall be managed in a manner different from that provided under Section 1027 of the Act [1027(G)]

Members' Quorum: for nonstock corporations, as specified in the certificate or bylaws, or else one-third of the members [1060]

Directors' Term of Office: as specified in the articles or bylaws [1027]

Officer Requirements: may have officers as specified in the bylaws or by resolution of the board and as necessary to sign corporate documents and keep records of corporate meetings. One person may hold two or more offices simultaneously without restrictions [1028]

State Corporate Tax Exemption

Corporate Income or Franchise Tax: yes

State Agency to Contact:
  Oklahoma Tax Commission, Oklahoma City
  www.oktax.state.ok.us

State Tax Exemption Requirements:
- Automatic with federal 501(c)(3) exemption
- Exempt organizations must file Form 512-E, "Return of Organization Exempt from Income Tax," annually with Oklahoma Tax Commission
- Most 501(c)(3) nonprofits that solicit contributions in the state must register and report annually to the secretary of state by submitting and initial and annual renewal "Registration Statement of Charitable Organization," available from the state corporate filing office website (click the link for "Charitable Organization Packet" on the Charitable Organizations section of the Business Forms page)

Oregon

Secretary of State Information

Secretary of State
Corporation Division
255 Capitol St. NE, Suite 151
Salem, OR 97310-1327
www.sos.state.or.us/corporation
Phone number of Corporation Division:
  503-986-2200

Provides Articles of Incorporation: yes

Internet Forms: Fill-in-able Oregon nonprofit corporation articles, which can be filled in and printed with your browser, plus separate instructions, as well as other statutory forms, are available on the state filing office website. TACS (Technical Assistance for Community Services) is launching a new service for Oregon nonprofits—a monthly clinic for new groups seeking 501c(3) tax exempt status (go to www.tacs.org for more information)

The Oregon Nonprofit Corporation Act is contained in Chapter 65 of the Oregon Statutes, starting with Section 65.001, and is browsable from the following website page:
  www.leg.state.or.us/ors/065.html

Corporate Name Requirements

Corporate Designator: Not required. Name cannot contain the word "cooperative" [65.094]

Articles of Incorporation

Director Qualifications:
  Number: 1 or more for a religious corporation; 3 or more for a public benefit corporation [65.307]
  Residency: no
  Age: no

Incorporator Qualifications:
  Residency: no
  Age: 18 or older [65.044]

Special Requirements: Articles must specify whether the corporation being formed is a public benefit, mutual benefit, or religious corporation. Most 501(c)(3)s are formed either as public benefit or religious corporations. Section 65.042 provides: "If religious doctrine or practice governing the affairs of a religious corporation is inconsistent with the provisions of this chapter on the same subject, the religious doctrine or practice shall control to the extent required by the Constitution of the United States or the Constitution of this state, or both. Religious corporations also can be formed with one person as a founder under special rules as a "corporation sole"—see Section 65.067

Bylaws

Directors' Quorum: majority of the fixed number of directors, unless a percentage is specified in the articles or bylaws, which may not be less than 1/3 of the fixed number of directors [65.351]

Members' Quorum: the voting members actually present or represented by proxy, or else a greater number specified in the articles or bylaws [65.241]

Directors' Term of Office: as specified in bylaws; except for designated or appointed directors, term must not exceed 5 years; if not specified, then one year [65.314]

Officer Requirements: must designate president and secretary (or other titles with the duties of president and secretary). One person may hold two or more offices [65.371]

State Corporate Tax Exemption

Corporate Income or Franchise Tax: yes

State Agency to Contact:
Oregon Dept. of Revenue, Salem
www.dor.state.or.us

State Tax Exemption Requirements:

- Automatic with federal 501(c)(3) exemption
- Special state tax rules apply to nonprofit homes for the elderly; contact the Department of Revenue for more information
- File OR Form 20 and a copy of federal Form 990-T for unrelated business income earned in the state
- For further state tax information and special rules that apply to certain nonprofit organizations, see "Information for Tax-Exempt Organizations" at the Depart of Revenue's website at www.dor.state.or.us/InfoC/102-617.html

Pennsylvania

Secretary of State Information

Department of State
Corporation Bureau
P.O. Box 8722
Harrisburg, PA 17105-8722
www.dos.state.pa.us/corps/site/default.asp
Phone number for general corporate information:
717-787-1057

Provides Articles of Incorporation: yes

Internet Forms: Pennsylvania fill-in-able nonprofit articles with instructions, plus the New Entity Docketing Statement (which must be filed with the articles) and other statutory forms are available for downloading from the state filing office website

The Pennsylvania Nonprofit Corporation Law of 1988 is contained in Title 15 of the Pennsylvania Statutes, starting with Section 5101. While state rules (contained in a state code) are provided on the link shown below, the statutes are not provided online at this time

www.pacode.com/secure/data/019/019toc.html

Corporate Name Requirements

Corporate Designator: None required. The name cannot include the word "college," "university," or "seminary" if it is used to imply that it is an educational institution conforming to the standards and qualifications prescribed by the State Board of Education, unless there is submitted a certificate from the Department of Education certifying that the corporation or proposed corporation is entitled to use that designation. The word "cooperative" or an abbreviation cannot be used unless the corporation is a cooperative corporation organized under special provisions of Pennsylvania law [5303]

Articles of Incorporation

Director Qualifications:
Number: 1 or more [5723]
Residency: no
Age: "of full age" (18 years or older) [5722]

Incorporator Qualifications:
Residency: no
Age: "of full age" (18 years or older) [5302]

Special Requirements:
- Publication of either the intent to file or the filing of articles of incorporation must be made in two newspapers of general circulation, one a legal journal, if possible. A county by county list of legal publications may be viewed on the state

corporate filing office website. Proofs of publication of the advertising should not be submitted to the Corporation Bureau, but should be placed in the corporate records [5307]
- An educational nonprofit that wishes to confer degrees must have the following information in its articles: 1) amount of assets incorporators have for establishing the institution; 2) minimum number of regular faculty; 3) brief statement of admissions requirements and courses. The clerk of the Court of Common Pleas in the county where the registered office of the corporation is located must send the articles to the Superintendent of Public Instruction for approval

Bylaws

Directors' Quorum: majority of the directors in office, unless otherwise provided in bylaws [5727] The board can make a special election under Section 5547(c) to be governed by special provisions having to do with meeting their responsibilities as fiduciaries for the investment of corporate funds. This election involves the adoption of a written investment policy by the board that seeks a specified return from invested assets, which is specified annually by the board. Ask your lawyer or investment advisor for further information

Members' Quorum: Unless otherwise provided in a bylaw adopted by the members, a majority of members present at meeting who are entitled to vote on the matters presented [5756]

Directors' Term of Office: Except for directors chosen because of their office held in the corporation or in another corporation, as stated in bylaws; if not specified, one-year [5724]

Officer Requirements: must designate president, secretary, and treasurer (or similar officers by different titles). One person may hold all offices. President and secretary must be of full age (18 years or older); treasurer may be a corporation or a person of full age. Unless otherwise provided in bylaws, each officer shall hold office for a term of one year and until his successor has been selected and qualified or until his earlier death, resignation, or removal [5732]

State Corporate Tax Exemption

Corporate Income or Franchise Tax: yes

State Agency to Contact:
Dept. of Revenue, Harrisburg
www.revenue.state.pa.us

State Tax Exemption Requirements:

Generally, Pennsylvania nonprofit corporations without authority to issue capital stock are exempt from state corporate income and capital stock-franchise taxes [72 P.S. § 7401 (1) and § 7601]

- Exempt organizations must file Form RCT-101 to report any unrelated business income earned in the state
- Nonprofits that solicit funds from Pennsylvania citizens must register with:

  Department of State
  Bureau of Charitable Organizations
  207 North Office Building
  Harrisburg, PA 17120
  717-783-1720 or
  800-732-0999 within Pennsylvania

Rhode Island

Secretary of State Information

Secretary of State
Corporations Division
100 North Main Street, First Floor
Providence, RI 02903
http://155.212.254.78/corporations.htm
Phone number of Corporations Division:
  401-222-3040
Provides Articles of Incorporation: yes
Internet Forms: Fill-in-able nonprofit corporation articles plus other statutory forms are available from the state filing office website

  The Rhode Island Nonprofit Corporation Act is contained in Title 7 (Corporations, Associations and Partnerships), Chapter 7-6, of the Rhode Island General Laws, starting with Section 7-6-1, and is browsable from the following website page (select Chapter 7-6 from the Index):
  www.rilin.state.ri.us/Statutes/TITLE7/INDEX.HTM

Corporate Name Requirements
Corporate Designator: not required

Articles of Incorporation
Director Qualifications: none
  Number: no less than 3 [7-6-23]
  Residency: no
  Age: no
Incorporator Qualifications:
  Residency: no
  Age: no

Bylaws
Directors' Quorum: majority of the authorized number, unless a percentage is specified in the articles or bylaws, which may not be less than 1/4 of the authorized number [7-6-25]
Members' Quorum: as specified in bylaws, or else 10% of voting members represented in person or by proxy [7-6-21]
Directors' Term of Office: as specified in the articles or bylaws; if not specified, then one year [7-6-23]
Officer Requirements: must designate president, vice president (if specified in bylaws), secretary, and treasurer. One person may hold any two offices simultaneously, except for the offices of president and secretary. An officer's term may not exceed three years, and if not specified in the articles or bylaws, it shall be one year [7-6-28]

State Corporate Tax Exemption
Corporate Income or Franchise Tax: yes
State Agency to Contact:
  Division of Taxation, Providence
  www.tax.state.ri.us
State Tax Exemption Requirements:
  Automatic with federal 501(c)(3) exemption

South Carolina

Secretary of State Information

Secretary of State
Corporations Dept.
P.O. Box 11350
Columbia, SC 29211
www.scsos.com/Corporations.htm
Phone number of Corporation Department:
  803-734-2158

Provides Articles of Incorporation: yes

Internet Forms: Fill-in-able nonprofit corporation articles, which can be filled in and printed from your browser, and other statutory forms available for downloading from the state filing office website. Also see *Guidelines for South Carolina Nonprofit Organizations,* available on the website.

The South Carolina Nonprofit Corporation Act is contained in Title 33 (Corporations, Partnerships and Associations), Chapter 31, of the South Carolina Code, starting with Section 33-31-101, and is browsable from the website page listed below (select Title 33, then scroll down and select "SOUTH CAROLINA NONPROFIT CORPORATION ACT (t33c031)"):

www.scstatehouse.net/code/statmast.htm

Corporate Name Requirements

Corporate Designator: not required

Articles of Incorporation

Director Qualifications:

Number: 3 or more [33-31-803] The articles may authorize a person or persons to exercise some or all of the powers which would otherwise be exercised by a board [33-31-801]
Residency: no
Age: no

Incorporator (Petitioner) Qualifications:

Residency: no
Age: no

Special Requirements: Articles must specify whether the corporation being formed is a public benefit, mutual benefit, or religious corporation. Most 501(c)(3)s are formed either as public benefit or religious corporations

Bylaws

Directors' Quorum: majority of the directors in office, or else as specified in articles or bylaws, but no fewer than 1/3 of the number in office or two directors, whichever is greater [33-31-824]

Members' Quorum: as specified in articles or bylaws, or else 10% of voting members [33-31-722]

Directors' Term of Office: as specified in articles or bylaws, but not to exceed 5 years except for designated or appointed board members; if not specified, then one year [33-31-805]

Officer Requirements: must designate president, secretary, and treasurer. One officer must be responsible for preparing minutes of meetings and authenticating corporate records. One person may hold one or more offices [33-31-840]

State Corporate Tax Exemption

Corporate Income or Franchise Tax: yes

State Agency to Contact:

South Carolina Department of Revenue, Columbia
www.sctax.org/default.htm

State Tax Exemption Requirements:

- Automatic with federal 501(c)(3) exemption
- Exempt organizations must file SC 990-T (Exempt Organization Business Tax Return), along with a copy of federal Form 990-T, to report and pay tax on any unrelated business income earned in the state
- Except for certain exemptions, 501(c)(3) nonprofits that intend to solicit contributions in the State of South Carolina, or have contributions solicited on their behalf, must file a registration statement with the secretary of state. Those that qualify for an exemption must file for an exemption with the secretary of state's office. For further information, go to the "Public Charities" section on the state corporate filing office website

South Dakota

Secretary of State Information

Secretary of State
State Capitol
500 East Capitol Ave.
Pierre, SD 57501
www.sdsos.gov/corporations
Phone number of the secretary of state's office:
  605-773-4845

Provides Articles of Incorporation: yes

Internet Forms: Fill-in-able nonprofit articles, plus other statutory forms, are available online at the state filing office website

The South Dakota Nonprofit Corporation Act, contained in Title 47 (Corporations), starting with Chapter 22 of the South Dakota Codified Laws, is browsable from the following website page (select South Dakota, then drill down through the folder headings in the left pane, as follows: "South Dakota Codified Laws," "Title 47," "Chapter 47-22"):
  www.michie.com

Corporate Name Requirements

Corporate Designator: not required

Articles of Incorporation

Director Qualifications:
Number: 3 or more [47-23-14]
Residency: no
Age: no

Incorporator Qualifications: [47-22-5]
Number: 3 or more
Residency:
Age: 18 or older

Bylaws

Directors' Quorum: majority of authorized number, unless a percentage is specified in the bylaws, which may not be less than 1/3 of the authorized number [47-23-20]

Members' Quorum: as specified in bylaws, or else 10% of voting members represented in person or by proxy [47-23-12]

Directors' Term of Office: as specified in the articles or bylaws, or else one year [47-23-16]

Officer Requirements: must designate president, vice president, secretary, and treasurer. Two or more offices may be held by the same person, except the offices of president and secretary. An officer's term may not exceed three years. If terms are not specified in the articles or bylaws, officers are appointed or elected by the board annually for one-year terms [47-23-24]

State Corporate Tax Exemption

Corporate Income or Franchise Tax: no

State Agency to Contact (for information about other taxes):
SD Dept. of Revenue, Pierre
www.state.sd.us/revenue/revenue.html

State Tax Exemption Requirements:
- no corporate income tax
- Application For Property Tax Exempt Status (SDCL 10-4-15) can be completed online from the Department of Revenue website (go to the Forms page section of the site)

Tennessee

Secretary of State Information

Secretary of State
Division of Business Services
Corporations Section
312 Eighth Avenue North
6th Floor, William R. Snodgrass Tower
Nashville, TN 37243
www.state.tn.us/sos/service.htm#corporations
Phone number for general corporate information:
  615-741-2286

Provides Articles of Incorporation: yes

Internet Forms: Fill-in-able Tennessee nonprofit corporation charter, plus other statutory forms, are available from the state office website. A *Filing Guide for Nonprofit Corporations* also is available for viewing and downloading

  The Tennessee Nonprofit Corporation Act is contained in Title 48 (Corporations and Associations), Chapters 51 through 68, starting with Section 48-51-101 of the Tennessee Code, and is browsable from the following website page (select Tennessee, then drill down through the folder headings in the left pane, as follows: "Tennessee Code," "Title 48," "Chapter 51" to view the first chapter of the Nonprofit Corporation Act—select other chapters to continue browsing the remaining sections of the Act):

  www.michie.com

Corporate Name Requirements

Corporate Designator: not required

Articles (Charter) of Incorporation

Director Qualifications:
  Number: 3 or more [48-58-103]
  Residency: no
  Age: no

Incorporator Qualifications:
  Residency: no
  Age: no

Special Requirements:

- After filing with the Secretary of State, Division of Business Services, a file-stamped copy of the charter must be filed with the Register of Deeds in the county in which the corporation has its principal office

- The corporation must be identified in the charter as a public benefit or mutual benefit corporation. (501(c)(3) tax-exempt nonprofit corporations are classified as public benefit corporations under the Tennessee Nonprofit Corporation Act). If the corporation is a religious corporation, this fact

also must be stated in the charter (a 501(c)(3) religious nonprofit is classified as a public benefit corporation *and* as a religious corporation under the Act). Most of the provisions of the Tennessee Nonprofit Corporation Act apply to a religious corporation. Exceptions are specified in Section 48-67-102 of the Act

Bylaws

Directors' Quorum: majority of the directors in office, or else as specified in bylaws, but no less than 1/3 of the number in office or two, whichever is greater [48-58-205]

Members' Quorum: unless the Nonprofit Act specifies a higher or lower requirement, 10% of the membership entitled to vote on a matter [48-57-203]

Directors' Term of Office: as specified in the charter or bylaws, but may not be more than five years except for designated or appointed directors; if not specified, then one year [48-58-105]

Officer Requirements: must designate president and secretary. One person may hold more than one office simultaneously, except for the offices of president and secretary [48-58-401]

State Corporate Tax Exemption

Corporate Income or Franchise Tax: yes

State Agency to Contact:
  Tennessee Dept. of Revenue, Nashville
  www.state.tn.us/revenue

State Tax Exemption Requirements:
  Automatic upon filing articles

Texas

Secretary of State Information
Secretary of State
Statutory Filings Division
Corporations Section
P.O. Box 13697
Austin, TX 78711
www.sos.state.tx.us/corp/index.shtml
Phone number for general corporate information:
512-463-5583
Provides Articles of Incorporation: yes
Internet Forms: Fill-in-able nonprofit articles of incorporation and other statutory forms are available for downloading on the state filing office website

The Texas Non-Profit Corporation Act is contained in Title 32 (Corporations), Chapter 9, of "Vernon's Texas Civil Statutes," starting with Article 1396–1.01, and is browsable from the following website page (select "Vernon's Texas Civil Statutes" at the bottom of the page, then select Title 32, Chapter 9):

www.capitol.state.tx.us/statutes/statutes.html

Corporate Name Requirements
Corporate Designator: not required. The Texas Education Code prohibits the use of the terms "college," "university," "seminary," "school of medicine," "medical school," "health science center," "school of law," "law school," and "law center." If a proposed name includes these terms, or terms of similar meaning, whether in English or another language, the corporation must obtain the prior approval of the Texas Higher Education Coordinating Board [Education Code Sec. 61.313]

Articles of Incorporation
Director Qualifications:
Number: 3 or more [1396-2.15]
Residency: no
Age: no
Incorporator Qualifications:
Residency: no
Age: 18 or older [1396-3.01]

Bylaws
Directors' Quorum: majority of the authorized number, or else as specified in the articles or bylaws, but a quorum may never be less than 3. Directors represented by proxy may not be counted towards a quorum (directors can vote by proxy if allowed by the articles or bylaws) [1396-2.17]
Members' Quorum: as specified in articles or bylaws, or else 10% of the voting membership [1396-2.12]

Directors' Term of Office: as specified in the articles or bylaws; if not specified, then one year [1396-2.15]
Officer Requirements: must designate president and secretary. One person may hold two or more offices except the office of president and secretary. Officers' term is limited to three years, and if not stated in the articles or bylaws, shall be one year. In the case of a corporation that is a church, officers are not required, but such duties and responsibilities may be vested in the board of directors or other designated body in any manner provided for in the articles of incorporation or the bylaws [1396-2.20]

State Corporate Tax Exemption
Corporate Income or Franchise Tax: yes
State Agency to Contact:
Comptroller of Public Accounts, Austin
www.window.state.tx.us
State Tax Exemption Requirements:
- Separate state application required but determination follows federal. Make application to Exempt Organizations Section, Comptroller of Public Accounts, Austin, Texas 78774-0100, 512-463-4600 or 800-252-1381. Obtain the appropriate exemption application form online from the state tax office website as follows:

  If your 501(c)(3) organization is applying for exemption:
  1. as a charitable organization...complete AP-205
  2. as a religious organization...complete AP-209
  3. as an educational organization...complete AP-207
  4. as any other 501(c)(3) exemption type...complete AP-204
- A federally exempt 501(c)(3) organization must send a copy of its federal determination letter to the Comptroller along with the proper application (see above) to receive state income tax exemption. Texas also has an annual corporate franchise tax, but new nonprofit organizations are not required to pay for their first 15 months of operation, or until they receive their federal exemption. A corporation that fails to receive an exemption will be liable for the postponed payment, but normally there is no additional penalty. See the tax office website for the latest and complete information

Utah

Secretary of State Information

Utah Division of Corporations and Commercial
Code
160 East 300 South, 2nd Floor
Box 146705
Salt Lake City, UT 84114-6705
www.commerce.state.ut.us/corporat/corpcoc.htm
Phone number of corporate filing section:
 801-530-4849 (toll free: 877-526-3994)

Provides Articles of Incorporation: yes (sample articles)

Internet Forms: Sample nonprofit articles of incorporation provided online

The Utah Revised Nonprofit Corporation Act is contained in Title 16, Chapter 6a, of the Utah Code, starting with Section 16-6a-101, and is browsable from the website page listed below (select search by "Keyword," then expand the left pane index to select Title 16, Chapter 6a):

 www.le.state.ut.us/Documents/code_const.htm

Corporate Name Requirements

Corporate Designator: not required, but may include "corporation," "incorporated," or "company"; or an abbreviation [16-6a-401]

Articles of Incorporation

Director (Trustee) Qualifications:
 Number: 3 or more [16-6a-803]
 Residency: no
 Age: 18 or older [16-6a-802]

Incorporator Qualifications:
 Residency: no
 Age: if an individual, must be 18 or over [16-6a-201]

Bylaws

Directors' (Trustees') Quorum: majority of the directors in office or else as specified in articles or bylaws, but no fewer than 1/3 the number of directors [16-6a-816]

Members' Quorum: as specified in the articles or bylaws; if not specified, then the number actually present in person or represented by proxy [16-6a-714]

Directors' (Trustees') Term of Office: as specified in bylaws; if not specified, one year [16-6a-805]

Officer Requirements: may have officers as specified in bylaws or designated by board consistent with bylaws. Must designate an officer to maintain records and keep minutes of meetings. More than one person may hold an office. Officers must be 18 years of age or older [16-6a-818]

State Corporate Tax Exemption

Corporate Income or Franchise Tax: yes

State Agency to Contact:
Utah State Tax Commission, Salt Lake City
www.tax.utah.gov

State Tax Exemption Requirements:
- Separate state application required but determination normally follows federal
- To apply for corporation franchise tax exemption, complete and file Form TC-161, "Utah Registration for Exemption from Corporate Franchise or Income Tax" (available on the tax office website under "Business and Corporate Income Tax Forms"). Include copy of federal determination letter as explained in instructions to the form
- Exempt organizations file Form TC-20 to report unrelated business income taxes earned within the state
- Exempt organizations file Form TC-20 UBI to report and pay taxes on unrelated business income earned in the state
- If your nonprofit will solicit funds in Utah contact the Division of Consumer Protection for information on state solicitation requirements (go online to www.commerce.utah.gov/dcp/index.html or call 801-530-6601)

Vermont

Secretary of State Information

Secretary of State
Corporations Division
81 River Street, Drawer 09
Montpelier, VT 05609-1104
www.sec.state.vt.us/corps/corpindex.htm
Phone number of Corporations Division:
802-828-2386

Provides Articles of Incorporation: yes, and model bylaws

Internet Forms: Vermont nonprofit corporation articles and other statutory forms are available for downloading from the state filing office website. A fill-in-able articles form can be completed online from your browser, then printed and mailed to the state filing office. The site includes a Nonprofit Center with additional nonprofit information and state links to nonprofit resources and information

The Vermont Nonprofit Corporation Act is contained in Title 11B of the Vermont Statutes, and is browsable from the following website page (select "Vermont Statutes," then "Title 11B"):
www.leg.state.vt.us

Corporate Name Requirements

Corporate Designator: name must include "corporation," "incorporated," "company," "limited," or an abbreviation; may not contain "cooperative" [4.01]

Articles of Incorporation

Director Qualifications:
Number: 3 or more [8.03]
Residency: no
Age: no

Incorporator Qualifications:
Residency: no
Age: of majority age (18 or older) [2.01]

Special Requirements: Articles must specify whether the corporation being formed is a public benefit or mutual benefit corporation. 501(c)(3)s (including 501(c)(3) religious nonprofits) are classified as public benefit corporations

Bylaws

Directors' Quorum: majority of the authorized number of directors, or a greater number as specified in the articles or bylaws [8.24]

Members' Quorum: as specified in articles or bylaws or else 10% of the voting membership. Unless one-third or more of the voting power is present in person or by proxy, the only matters that may be voted upon at an annual meeting of members are those matters that were described in the meeting notice [7.22]

Directors' Term of Office: as specified in articles or bylaws, but not to exceed 6 years except for designated or appointed directors; if not specified, then one year [8.05]

Officer Requirements: unless otherwise provided in articles or bylaws, must have a president, secretary, and treasurer. Person must be delegated to prepare maintain records and prepare minutes of meetings. One person may hold two or more offices, except the offices of president and secretary [8.40]

State Corporate Tax Exemption

Corporate Income or Franchise Tax: yes

State Agency to Contact:
Dept. of Taxes, Montpelier
www.state.vt.us/tax

State Tax Exemption Requirements:

- Separate state application required but determination follows federal
- For state tax exemptions (and to receive a state exempt organization number), complete and mail Form S-1, Application for Business Tax Account (available from the tax office website) together with a copy of federal tax-exemption determination letter (if you have not received a determination yet, send copies of articles and bylaws instead). This application applies to all state taxes (corporate income, sales and use, withholding, meals, and rooms)

Virginia

Secretary of State Information

Clerk of the State Corporation Commission
P.O. Box 1197
First Floor
Richmond, VA 23218
www.state.va.us/scc/division/clk/corp.htm
Phone number of corporate filing section:
 804-371-9733 (toll-free 1-866-SCC-CLK1)

Provides Articles of Incorporation: yes

Internet Forms: Virginia nonstock corporation articles are available for downloading from the state corporate filing office

The Virginia Nonstock Corporation Act is contained in Title 13.1 (Corporations) of the Virginia Code, Chapter 10, starting with Section 13.1-801, and is browsable from the following website page (click "Code of Virginia," then click "Table of Contents" on the search page; then select Title 13.1, then click Chapter 10 to see a list of the sections in the Act):

 http://legis.state.va.us/codecomm/codehome.htm

Corporate Name Requirements

Corporate Designator: not required

Articles of Incorporation

Director Qualifications:
Number: one or more [13.1-855]
Residency: no
Age: no

Incorporator Qualifications:
Residency: no
Age: no

Bylaws

Directors' Quorum: majority of the authorized number of directors, unless a percentage is specified in the articles or bylaws, which may not be less than 1/3 of the authorized number of directors [13.1-868]

Members' Quorum: as specified in the bylaws or else 10% of the membership entitled to vote [13.1-849]

Directors' Term of Office: as specified in articles; if not specified, then one year [13.1-857]

Officer Requirements: may have officers as specified in bylaws or by resolution of the board consistent with bylaws. One person may hold any two or more offices [13.1-872]

State Corporate Tax Exemption

Corporate Income or Franchise Tax: yes

State Agency to Contact:
Dept. of Taxation, Richmond
www.tax.state.va.us

State Tax Exemption Requirements:
- Automatic with federal 501(c)(3) exemption
- Exempt organizations must report any unrelated business income earned in the state on Form 500

Washington

Secretary of State Information

Secretary of State
Corporations Division
801 Capitol Way S.
P.O. Box 40234
Olympia, WA 98504
www.secstate.wa.gov/corps
Phone number for general corporate information:
360-753-7115

Provides Articles of Incorporation: yes

Internet Forms: Washington nonprofit corporation articles and other forms are available for downloading from the state office website

The Washington Nonprofit Corporation Act is contained in Title 24 of the Washington Code, starting with Section 24.03.005, and is browsable from the following website page (click "Revised Code of Washington," then "RCW by Title," then select "Title 24," then "Chapter 24.03"):
http://slc.leg.wa.gov/default.htm

Corporate Name Requirements

Corporate Designator: name cannot include or end with "incorporated," "company," "limited," or abbreviation thereof, but may have designation such as "association," "group," "club," "league," "services," "committee," "fund," "foundation," and so on [24.03.045]

Articles of Incorporation

Director Qualifications:
Number: one or more [24.03.100]
Residency: no
Age: no
Incorporator Qualifications:
Residency: no
Age: 18 or older if an individual [24.03.020]

Bylaws

Directors' Quorum: majority of the authorized number of directors, or else as stated in the articles or bylaws, provided the number or percentage so stated may not be less than 1/3 of the authorized number [24.03.110]

Members' Quorum: as specified in bylaws, or 10% of the voting members if not specified [24.03.090]

Directors' Term of Office: as specified in the articles or bylaws [24.03.100]

Officer Requirements: must designate president, vice president, secretary, and treasurer. One person may hold any two or more offices simultaneously if allowed by articles or bylaws, except for the offices of president and secretary. Unless the articles or bylaws provide otherwise, an officer's term is limited to one year [24.03.125]

State Corporate Tax Exemption

Corporate Income or Franchise Tax: no

State Agency to Contact (for information about other taxes):
Washington State Dept. of Revenue, Olympia
http://dor.wa.gov

State Tax Exemption Requirements:

- no corporate income tax, but state has a business tax based upon gross receipts that applies to all businesses including nonprofits. Income produced from the following nonprofit activities may be exempt from the business tax: fund-raising sales of certain nonprofit organizations (does not include the regular operation of a business enterprise, such as a bookstore, thrift shop, or restaurant); functions of the Red Cross; and child care provided by churches and child care resource and referral income. For business tax information and forms, go to the tax office website

- go to the "Charities" page on the state corporate filing office website to see information and registration and reporting forms if your nonprofit plans to solicit funds in Washington

West Virginia

Secretary of State Information

Secretary of State
Corporations Division
Bldg. 1, Suite 157-K
1900 Kanawha Blvd. East
Charleston, WV 25305-0770
www.wvsos.com
Phone number of corporate filing section:
  304-558-8000

Provides Articles of Incorporation: yes

Internet Forms: Provides articles of incorporation online (nonprofit and profit corporations use the same articles form)

The West Virginia Nonprofit Corporation Act is contained in Chapter 31E, of the West Virginia Code, beginning with Section 31E-1-101a, and is browsable from the following website page (select "State Code" from the WV Code folder in the left pane, then select "Browse by Chapter," then scroll down the browse box and select "Chapter 31E," then click "Go" to browse the Nonprofit Corporation Act):

www.legis.state.wv.us/legishp.html

Corporate Name Requirements

Corporate Designator: "corporation," "limited," "incorporated," "company," or abbreviation required in corporate name, or you may use "foundation" [31E-4-401]

Articles of Incorporation

Director Qualifications:
Number: 3 or more [31E-8-803]
Residency: no
Age: no

Incorporator Qualifications:
Residency: no
Age: no

Bylaws

Directors' Quorum: majority of the authorized number of directors, or else as stated in the articles or bylaws, which may not specify a number less than 1/3 of the authorized number [31E-8-824]

Members' Quorum: as specified in articles or bylaws; if not specified, the actual number of members present at a meeting constitute a quorum [31E-7-724]

Directors' Term of Office: one year between annual meetings to elect directors [31E-8-806]

Officer Requirements: as specified in the bylaws or as appointed by the board in accordance with the bylaws. One person may hold any two or more offices [31E-8-840]

State Corporate Tax Exemption

Corporate Income or Franchise Tax: yes

State Agency to Contact:
State Tax Department, Charleston
www.state.wv.us/taxdiv

State Tax Exemption Requirements:

- Automatic with federal 501(c)(3) exemption
- Federally exempt nonprofit corporations are exempt from paying the state business registration fee and business franchise tax (which normally applies to all forms of business), but must still complete and file Form WV/BUS-APP, file an initial application for a Business Registration Certificate (the state tax website tells nonprofits to file the business registration form after obtaining their federal tax exemption)
- 501(c) tax-exempt nonprofits also are exempt from the state corporate net income tax
- File unrelated business income tax on Form WV-CNF-120 with a copy of federal Form 990-T if your nonprofit earns unrelated business income in the state
- Register the 501(c)(3) nonprofit if your nonprofit plans to solicit funds within the state. The "Registration of Charitable Organization" form is available from the Charitable Organizations page on the state corporate filing office website

Wisconsin

Secretary of State Information
Department of Financial Institutions
Corporations Section, 3rd Floor
P.O. Box 7846
Madison, WI 53707-7846
www.wdfi.org/corporations/default.htm
Phone number of corporate filing section:
  608-261-7577
Provides Articles of Incorporation: yes
Internet Forms: Fill-in-able articles of nonstock
  corporation, plus other statutory forms, are avail-
  able online at the state filing office website
  The Wisconsin Nonprofit Corporation Act is
  contained in Chapter 181 of the Wisconsin Statutes,
  starting with Section 181.0103, and is browsable
  from the following website page (select "Statutes &
  Rules" on the left panel, then select "Nonstock
  Corporation"):
    www.wdfi.org/corporations/default.htm

Corporate Name Requirements
Corporate Designator: name must contain "corporation," "incorporated," "limited," or abbreviation
[181.0401]

Articles of Incorporation
Director Qualifications:
  Number: 3 or more [181.0803]
  Residency: no
  Age: no
Incorporator Qualifications:
  Residency: no
  Age: no

Bylaws
Directors' Quorum: majority of the directors in office
  or else as specified in the articles or bylaws
  [181.0824]
Members' Quorum: unless specified otherwise in the
  articles or bylaws, 10% of the voting membership
  [181.0722]
Directors' Term of Office: as specified in the articles
  or bylaws; if not specified, then one year [181.0805]
Officer Requirements: Unless otherwise provided in
  articles or bylaws, corporation must have president,
  secretary, and treasurer. One person may hold
  more than one office [181.0840]

State Corporate Tax Exemption
Corporate Income or Franchise Tax: yes
State Agency to Contact:
  Dept. of Revenue, Madison
  www.dor.state.wi.us
State Tax Exemption Requirements:
* Automatic with federal 501(c)(3) exemption
* Exempt organizations report unrelated business
  income earned in the state on Form 4T (to which
  federal Form 990-T must be attached)

Wyoming

Secretary of State Information

Secretary of State
Corporations Division
The Capitol Building, Room 110
200 W. 24th Street
Cheyenne, WY 82002-0020
soswy.state.wy.us/corporat/corporat.htm
Phone number of Corporations Division:
  307-777-7311

Provides Articles of Incorporation: yes

Internet Forms: Fill-in-able articles of incorporation
and other statutory forms are available from the
state filing office website

  The Wyoming Nonprofit Corporation Act is
contained in Title 17 of the Wyoming Statutes,
Chapter 19, starting with Section 17-19-101, and is
browsable from the following website page (click
the link to the "Nonprofit Corporation Act"; for special provisions that apply to churches, click
"Churches and Religious Societies Generally"):
  http://soswy.state.wy.us/corporat/statutes.htm

Corporate Name Requirements

Corporate Designator: not required

Articles of Incorporation

Director Qualifications:
  Number: 3 or more [17-19-803]
  Residency: no
  Age: no
Incorporator Qualifications:
  Residency: no
  Age: no
Special Requirements: articles must specify whether
the corporation being formed is a public benefit,
religious, or mutual benefit corporation. Most
501(c)(3)s incorporate as either public benefit or
religious corporations

Bylaws

Directors' Quorum: majority of the directors in office,
or else the percentage stated in the articles or
bylaws, which may not be less than 1/3 of the number in office or two directors, whichever is greater
[17-19-824]
Members' Quorum: unless specified otherwise in the
articles or bylaws, 10% of the voting members
[17-19-722]

Directors' Term of Office: as specified in the articles
or bylaws, but not to exceed 5 years except for designated or appointed directors; if not specified, then
one year [17-19-805]
Officer Requirements: unless provided otherwise in
articles or bylaws, must designate president, secretary, and treasurer. One person may hold any two
or more offices [17-19-840]

State Corporate Tax Exemption

Corporate Income or Franchise Tax: no
**State Agency to Contact (for information about other
taxes):**
  Secretary of State—see above address
State Tax Exemption Requirements: no corporate
income tax
  Dept. of Revenue, Cheyenne
  http://revenue.state.wy.us

Forms and Publications on CD-ROM

Corporate Form	File Name	Chapter
Incorporation Checklist	CHECKLIST.RTF	Intro, 9
Request for Nonprofit Corporation Information	CONTACT.RTF	6
Name Availability Letter	NAME.RTF	6
Application for Reservation of Corporate Name	RESERVE.RTF	6
Articles of Incorporation	ARTICLES.RTF	6
Articles Filing Letter	FILING.RTF	6
Bylaws (including Adoption of Bylaws and Membership Provisions)	BYLAWS.RTF	7
Waiver of Notice and Consent to Holding of First Meeting of Board of Directors	MINUTES.RTF	9
Minutes of First Meeting of Board of Directors	MINUTES.RTF	9

IRS Forms and Publications and Tax Articles	File Name	Chapter
*Asterisks indicate forms in portable document format (PDF) with fill-in text fields		
*Package 1023: Application for Recognition of Exemption (September 1998)	k1023.pdf	8
*Form 8718: User Fee for Exempt Organization Determination Letter Request (11/2003)	f8718.pdf	8
*Form SS-4: Application for Employer Identification Number (12/2001)	fss4.pdf	8
Instructions for Form SS-4 (12/2003)	iss4.pdf	8

IRS Forms and Publications and Tax Articles	File Name	Chapter
*Form 5768: Election/Revocation of Election by an Eligible Section 501(c)(3) Organization To Make Expenditures To Influence Legislation (12/1996)	f5768.pdf	3, 8
Publication 557: Tax Exempt Status for Your Organization (5/2003)	p557.pdf	3, 4, 8
Publication 578: Tax Information for Private Foundations and Foundation Managers (1/1989)	p578.pdf	3, 4, 8
IRS Revenue Procedure 75-50	IRS7550.RTF	3
IRC Section 4958, Taxes on Excess Benefit Transactions	IRS4958.RTF	3
IRS Regulations Section 53.4958-0, Table of Contents	IRS4958R.RTF	3
Public Charity or Private Foundation Status Issues Under IRC §§ 509(a)(1)-(4), 4942(j)(3), and 507	eotopicb03.pdf	4
Tax-Exempt Health Care Organizations Community Board and Conflicts of Interest Policy	topic-c.pdf	3
Tax-Exempt Health Care Organizations Revised Conflicts of Interest Policy	topice00.pdf	3, 8
Disclosure, FOIA and the Privacy Act	eotopicc03.pdf	3, 8
Update: The Final Regulations on the Disclosure Requirements for Annual Information Returns and Applications for Exemption	topico00.pdf	3
Education, Propaganda, and the Methodology Test	topic-h.pdf	3
Election Year Issues	topici02.pdf	3
Lobbying Issues	topic-p.pdf	3
Private School Update	topicn00.pdf	3
UBIT: Current Developments	topic-o.pdf	3, 5
Intermediate Sanctions (IRC 4958) Update	eotopice03.pdf	3

Appendix D

Information and Tear-Out Forms

Incorporation Checklist

Special Nonprofit Tax-Exempt Organizations

Request for Nonprofit Corporation Information

Name Availability Letter

Application for Reservation of Corporate Name

Articles of Incorporation

Articles Filing Letter

Bylaws

Adoptions of Bylaws

Membership Provisions of the Bylaws

Waiver of Notice and Consent to Holding of First Meeting of Board of Directors

Minutes of First Meeting of Board of Directors

IRS Package 1023: Application for Recognition of Exemption (9/1998)

IRS Form 8718: User Fee for Exempt Organization Determination Letter Request (11/2003)

IRS Form SS-4: Application for Employer Identification Number (12/2001)

Instructions for Form SS-4 (12/2003)

IRS Form 5768: Election/Revocation of Election by an Eligible Section 501(c)(3) Organization to Make Expenditures to Influence Legislation

Incorporation Checklist

Step	Location of Instructions
☐ Order Materials From Your Secretary of State	Chapter 6, Section A
☐ Choose a Corporate Name	Chapter 6, Section B
☐ Check Name Availability	Chapter 6, Section C
☐ Reserve Your Corporate Name	Chapter 6, Section E
☐ Perform a Name Search	Chapter 6, Section F
☐ Protect Your Name	Chapter 6, Section G
☐ Prepare Articles of Incorporation	Chapter 6, Section H
☐ File Articles of Incorporation	Chapter 6, Section I
☐ Prepare Bylaws	Chapter 7, Section C
☐ Prepare Membership Provisions	Chapter 7, Section D
☐ Prepare and File Your Federal Tax Exemption Application	Chapter 8, Section C
☐ Obtain State Corporate Income Tax Exemption	Chapter 9, Section A
☐ Set Up a Corporate Records Book	Chapter 9, Section B
☐ Prepare Minutes of First Board of Directors Meeting	Chapter 9, Section C
☐ Place Minutes and Attachments in Corporate Records Books	Chapter 9, Section D
☐ Prepare Assignments of Leases and Deeds	Chapter 9, Section F
☐ File Final Papers for Prior Organization (existing groups only)	Chapter 9, Section G
☐ Notify Others of Your Incorporation (existing groups only)	Chapter 9, Section H
☐ File Assumed Business Name Statement	Chapter 9, Section I
☐ Apply for Federal Nonprofit Mailing Permit	Chapter 9, Section J
☐ Apply for Property Tax Exemptions	Chapter 9, Section K
☐ File Corporate Report Form	Chapter 9, Section L
☐ Register With Attorney General	Chapter 9, Section M
☐ Comply With Political Reporting Requirements	Chapter 9, Section N

Special Nonprofit Tax-Exempt Organizations

of IRC §	Organization and Description	Application Form	Annual Return	Deductibility Contributions[1]
501(c)(1)	**Federal Corporations:** corporations organized under an Act of Congress as federal corporations specifically declared to be exempt from payment of federal income taxes.	No Form	None	Yes, if made for public purposes
501(c)(2)	**Corporations Holding Title to Property for Exempt Organizations:** corporations organized for the exclusive purpose of holding title to property, collecting income from property, and turning over this income, less expenses, to an organization which, itself, is exempt from payment of federal income taxes.	1024	990	No
501(c)(4)	**Civil Leagues, Social Welfare Organizations or Local Employee Associations:** civic leagues or organizations operated exclusively for the promotion of social welfare, or local associations of employees, the membership of which is limited to the employees of a particular employer within a particular municipality, and whose net earnings are devoted exclusively to charitable, educational or recreational purposes. Typical examples of groups which fall under this category are volunteer fire companies, home owners or real estate development associations or employee associations formed to further charitable community service.	1024	990	Generally, No[2]
501(c)(5)	**Labor, Agricultural or Horticultural Organizations:** organizations of workers organized to protect their interests in connection with their employment (e.g., labor unions) or groups organized to promote more efficient techniques in production or the betterment of conditions for workers engaged in agricultural or horticultural employment.	1024	990	No
501(c)(6)	**Business Leagues, Chambers of Commerce, Etc.:** business leagues, chambers of commerce, real estate boards or boards-of-trade organized for the purpose of improving business conditions in one or more lines of business.	1024	990	No
501(c)(7)	**Social and Recreational Clubs:** clubs organized for pleasure, recreation, and other nonprofit purposes, no part of the net earnings of which inure to the benefit of any member. Examples of such organizations are hobby clubs and other special interest social or recreational membership groups.	1024	990	No
501(c)(8)	**Fraternal Beneficiary Societies:** groups which operate under the lodge certain system for the exclusive benefit of their members, which provide benefits such as the payment of life, sick or accident insurance to members.	1024	990	Yes, if for 501(c)(3) purposes
501(c)(9)	**Volunteer Employee Beneficiary Associations:** associations of employees which provide benefits to their members, enrollment in which is strictly voluntary and none of the earnings of which inure to the benefit of any individual members except in accordance with the association's group benefit plan.	1024	990	No
501(c)(10)	**Domestic Fraternal Societies:** domestic fraternal organizations operating certain under the lodge system which devote their net earnings to religious, charitable, scientific, literary, educational or fraternal purposes and which do not provide for the payment of insurance or other benefits to members.	1024	990	Yes, if for 510(c)(3) purposes

Special Nonprofit Tax-Exempt Organizations

of IRC §	Organization and Description	Application Form	Annual Return	Deductibility Contributions[1]
501(c)(11)	**Local Teacher Retirement Fund Associations:** associations organized to receive amounts received from public taxation, from assessments on the teaching salaries of members or from income from investments, to devote solely to providing retirement benefits to its members.	No Form[3]	990	No
501(c)(12)	**Benevolent Life Insurance Associations, Mutual Water and Telephone Companies, Etc.:** organizations organized on a mutual or cooperative basis to provide the above and similar services to members, 85% of whose income is collected from members, and whose income is used solely to cover the expenses and losses of the organization.	1024	990	No
501(c)(13)	**Cemetery Companies:** companies owned and operated exclusively for the benefit of members solely to provide cemetery services to their members.	1024	990	Generally, Yes
501(c)(14)	**Credit Unions:** credit unions and other mutual financial organizations organized without capital stock for nonprofit purposes.	1024	990	No
501(c)(15)	**Mutual Insurance Companies:** certain mutual insurance companies whose gross receipts are from specific sources and are within certain statutory limits.	1024	990	No
501(c)(16)	**Farmers' Cooperatives:** associations organized and operated on a cooperative basis for the purpose of marketing the products of members or other products.	1024	990	No
501(c)(19)	**War Veteran Organizations:** posts or organizations whose members are war veterans and which are formed to provide benefits to their members.	1024	990	Generally, No
501(c)(20)	**Group Legal Service Organizations:** organizations created for the exclusive function of forming a qualified group legal service plan.	1024	990	No
510(d)	**Religious and Apostolic Organizations:** religious associations or corporations with a common treasury which engage in business for the common benefit of members. Each member's share of the net income of the corporation is reported on his individual tax return. This is a rarely used section of the Code used by religious groups which are ineligible for 501(c)(3) status because they engage in a communal trade or business.	No Form	1065	No
521(a)	**Farmers' Cooperative Associations:** farmers, fruit growers and like associations organized and operated on a cooperative basis for the purpose of marketing the products of members or other producers, or for the purchase of supplies and equipment for members at cost.	1028	990-C	No

For specific information on the requirements of several of these special-purpose tax exemption categories, see IRS publication 557, *Tax-Exempt Status for Your Organization.*

[1] An organization exempt under a subsection of IRC Section 501 other than (c)(3)—the type listed in this table—may establish a fund exclusively for 510(c)(3) purposes, contributions to which are deductible. Section 501(c)(3) tax-exempt status should be obtained for this separate fund of a non-501(c)(3) group. See IRS publication 557 for further details.

[2] Contributions to volunteer fire companies and similar organizations are deductible, but only if made for exclusively public purposes.

[3] Application is made by letter to the key District Director.

Date: _____

_____

_____

_____

_____

Re: Request for Nonprofit Corporation Information

I am in the process of forming a domestic nonprofit corporation. I would appreciate receiving the following forms, material and other information from your office:

- please correct the address of your corporate filings office above if it is incorrect or not completely current;

- the telephone number and contact person for inquiries related to incorporating a domestic nonprofit corporation;

- Articles of Incorporation and other corporate forms (with instructions) promulgated by your office for domestic nonprofit corporations. If your office reviews nonprofit Articles of Incorporation for correctness prior to filing, please advise me of the procedure I should follow to obtain this pre-filing review;

- the name and price of a publication which may be ordered from your office or from a commercial publisher which contains the corporate statutes regulating nonprofit corporations in this state;

- the telephone number or address of the division in your office which I can call to determine if a proposed corporate name is available for my use (plus any additional information available related to checking and reserving a proposed corporate name);

- a current schedule of fees for statutory filings, forms and publications;

- All other forms, statutes, publications and other materials available from your office detailing requirements for the formation, operation and dissolution of a domestic nonprofit corporation.

If there is a fee for any of the above material (such as the nonprofit corporation statutes), please advise. I enclose a stamped, self-addressed envelope for your reply. My name, address and telephone number are listed below if you wish to contact me regarding this request.

Name: _____

Address: _____

Phone: _____

Thank you for your assistance.

_____

Date:_____

_____

_____

_____

_____

Re: Corporate Name Availability

Please advise if the following proposed corporate names, listed in order of preference, are available for corporate use:

_____

_____

_____

_____

Enclosed is a stamped, self-addressed envelope for your reply. My name, address and phone number are included below if you wish to contact me regarding this request.

[I enclose a check for $_____ in payment of the fee for checking the availability of the above names.]

Name: _____

Address: _____

Phone: _____

Thank you for your assistance.

_____

Date:_____

_____

_____

_____

_____

Re: Corporate Name Reservation

Please reserve the following corporate name for my use for the allowable period specified under the state's corporation statutes.

_____

I enclose the required payment of $_____. My name, address and phone number are included below if you wish to contact me regarding this request.

Name: _____

Address: _____

Phone: _____

Thank you for your assistance.

_____

Articles of Incorporation

of

_____

A Nonprofit Corporation

Pursuant to the provision of the Nonprofit Corporation Act of this state, the undersigned incorporators hereby adopt the following Articles of Incorporation:

Article 1

The name of this corporation is: _____

_____

Article 2

The name and address of the registered agent and registered office of this corporation is: _____

_____

_____

Article 3

The purposes for which this corporation is organized are: _____

_____

_____

_____

_____

_____

_____

_____

_____

_____

_____

_____

Article 4

The number of initial directors of this corporation shall be _____ and the names and addresses of the initial directors are as follows: _____

_____

_____

_____

_____

Article 5

The name(s) and address(es) of the incorporator(s) of this corporation is/are: _____

_____

_____

Article 6

The period of the duration of this corporation is: _____.

Article 7

The classes, rights, privileges, qualifications and obligations of members of this corporation are as follows: _____

_____

_____

_____

Article 8

_____

_____

_____

_____

_____

_____

_____

_____

_____

_____

_____

_____

_____

_____

_____

_____

_____

_____

_____

_____

_____

_____

_____

_____

_____

_____

_____

_____

_____

_____

_____

The undersigned incorporators hereby declare under penalty of perjury that the statements made in the foregoing Articles of Incorporation are true.

Dated: _____

_____

_____

_____

_____

Name and Address of Incorporator: _____

_____

_____

Name and Address of Incorporator: _____

_____

_____

Name and Address of Incorporator: _____

_____

_____

Name and Address of Incorporator: _____

_____

_____

_____

_____

_____

_____

Date:_____

_____

_____

_____

_____

Re: Articles of Incorporation Filing

I enclose an original and _____ copies of the proposed Articles of Incorporation of

_____.

Please file the Articles of Incorporation and return a Certificate of Incorporation (or file-stamped copy of the original Articles) to me at the above address.

A check/money order in the amount of $_____, made payable to your office, for total filing and processing fees is enclosed.

The above corporate name was reserved for my use pursuant to reservation # _____ issued on _____.

Sincerely,

_____

_____, Incorporator

Bylaws

of

_____

Article 1
Offices

Section 1. Principal Office

The principal office of the corporation is located in _____ County,
State of _____.

Section 2. Change of Address

The designation of the county or state of the corporation's principal office may be changed by
amendment of these bylaws. The board of directors may change the principal office from one
location to another within the named county by noting the changed address and effective date
below, and such changes of address shall not be deemed, nor require, an amendment of these bylaws:

New Address: _____

Dated: _____, 20_____

New Address: _____

Dated: _____, 20_____

New Address: _____

Dated: _____, 20_____

Section 3. Other Offices

The corporation may also have offices at such other places, within or without its state of incorporation, where it is qualified to do business, as its business and activities may require, and as the board
of directors may, from time to time, designate.

Article 2
Nonprofit Purposes

Section 1. IRC Section 501(c)(3) Purposes

This corporation is organized exclusively for one or more of the purposes as specified in Section
501(c)(3) of the Internal Revenue Code, including, for such purposes, the making of distributions to
organizations that qualify as exempt organizations under Section 501(c)(3) of the Internal Revenue
Code.

Section 2. Specific Objectives and Purposes

The specific objectives and purposes of this corporation shall be: _____

_____

_____

_____

_____

_____

_____

_____

_____

_____

_____

_____

_____

_____

_____

_____

_____

_____

_____

_____

_____

_____

_____

_____

_____

_____

Article 3
Directors

Section 1. Number

The corporation shall have _____ directors and collectively they shall be known as the board of directors.

Section 2. Qualifications

Directors shall be of the age of majority in this state. Other qualifications for directors of this corporation shall be as follows: _____

_____

_____

_____

_____

_____

Section 3. Powers

Subject to the provisions of the laws of this state and any limitations in the articles of incorporation and these bylaws relating to action required or permitted to be taken or approved by the members, if any, of this corporation, the activities and affairs of this corporation shall be conducted and all corporate powers shall be exercised by or under the direction of the board of directors.

Section 4. Duties

It shall be the duty of the directors to:

a. Perform any and all duties imposed on them collectively or individually by law, by the articles of incorporation, or by these bylaws;

b. Appoint and remove, employ and discharge, and, except as otherwise provided in these bylaws, prescribe the duties and fix the compensation, if any, of all officers, agents and employees of the corporation;

c. Supervise all officers, agents and employees of the corporation to assure that their duties are performed properly;

d. Meet at such times and places as required by these bylaws;

e. Register their addresses with the secretary of the corporation, and notices of meetings mailed or telegraphed to them at such addresses shall be valid notices thereof.

Section 5. Term of Office

Each director shall hold office for a period of _____ and until his or her successor is elected and qualifies.

Section 6. Compensation

Directors shall serve without compensation except that a reasonable fee may be paid to directors for attending regular and special meetings of the board. In addition, they shall be allowed reasonable advancement or reimbursement of expenses incurred in the performance of their duties.

Section 7. Place of Meetings

Meetings shall be held at the principal office of the corporation unless otherwise provided by the board or at such other place as may be designated from time to time by resolution of the board of directors.

Section 8. Regular Meetings

Regular meetings of directors shall be held on _____ at _____ ____.M., unless such day falls on a legal holiday, in which event the regular meeting shall be held at the same hour and place on the next business day.

If this corporation makes no provision for members, then, at the regular meeting of directors held on _____, directors shall be elected by the board of directors. Voting for the election of directors shall be by written ballot. Each director shall cast one vote per candidate, and may vote for as many candidates as the number of candidates to be elected to the board. The candidates receiving the highest number of votes up to the number of directors to be elected shall be elected to serve on the board.

Section 9. Special Meetings

Special meetings of the board of directors may be called by the chairperson of the board, the president, the vice president, the secretary, by any two directors, or, if different, by the persons specifically authorized under the laws of this state to call special meetings of the board. Such meetings shall be held at the principal office of the corporation or, if different, at the place designated by the person or persons calling the special meeting.

Section 10. Notice of Meetings

Unless otherwise provided by the articles of incorporation, these bylaws, or provisions of law, the following provisions shall govern the giving of notice for meetings of the board of directors:

   a. **Regular Meetings.** No notice need be given of any regular meeting of the board of directors.

   b. **Special Meetings.** At least one week prior notice shall be given by the secretary of the corporation to each director of each special meeting of the board. Such notice may be oral or written, may be given personally, by first class mail, by telephone or by facsimile machine, and shall state the place, date and time of the meeting and the matters proposed to be acted upon at the meeting. In the case of facsimile notification, the director to be contacted shall acknowledge personal receipt of the facsimile notice by a return message or telephone call within twenty-four hours of the first facsimile transmission.

c. Waiver of Notice. Whenever any notice of a meeting is required to be given to any director of this corporation under provisions of the articles of incorporation, these bylaws or the law of this state, a waiver of notice in writing signed by the director, whether before or after the time of the meeting, shall be equivalent to the giving of such notice.

Section 11. Quorum for Meetings

A quorum shall consist of _____ of the members of the board of directors.

Except as otherwise provided under the articles of incorporation, these bylaws or provisions of law, no business shall be considered by the board at any meeting at which the required quorum is not present, and the only motion which the chair shall entertain at such meeting is a motion to adjourn.

Section 12. Majority Action As Board Action

Every act or decision done or made by a majority of the directors present at a meeting duly held at which a quorum is present is the act of the board of directors, unless the articles of incorporation, these bylaws or provisions of law require a greater percentage or different voting rules for approval of a matter by the board.

Section 13. Conduct of Meetings

Meetings of the board of directors shall be presided over by the chairperson of the board, or, if no such person has been so designated or, in his or her absence, the president of the corporation or, in his or her absence, by the vice president of the corporation or, in the absence of each of these persons, by a chairperson chosen by a majority of the directors present at the meeting. The secretary of the corporation shall act as secretary of all meetings of the board, provided that, in his or her absence, the presiding officer shall appoint another person to act as secretary of the meeting.

Meetings shall be governed by _____,

insofar as such rules are not inconsistent with or in conflict with the articles of incorporation, these Bylaws or with provisions of law.

Section 14. Vacancies

Vacancies on the board of directors shall exist (1) on the death, resignation or removal of any director, and (2) whenever the number of authorized directors is increased.

Any director may resign effective upon giving written notice to the chairperson of the board, the president, the secretary or the board of directors, unless the notice specifies a later time for the effectiveness of such resignation. No director may resign if the corporation would then be left without a duly elected director or directors in charge of its affairs, except upon notice to the Office of the Attorney General or other appropriate agency of this state.

Directors may be removed from office, with or without cause, as permitted by and in accordance with the laws of this state.

Unless otherwise prohibited by the articles of incorporation, these bylaws or provisions of law, vacancies on the board may be filled by approval of the board of directors. If the number of directors then in office is less than a quorum, a vacancy on the board may be filled by approval of a majority of the directors then in office or by a sole remaining director. A person elected to fill a vacancy on the board shall hold office until the next election of the board of directors or until his or her death, resignation or removal from office.

Section 15. Nonliability of Directors

The directors shall not be personally liable for the debts, liabilities or other obligations of the corporation.

Section 16. Indemnification by Corporation of Directors and Officers

The directors and officers of the corporation shall be indemnified by the corporation to the fullest extent permissible under the laws of this state.

Section 17. Insurance for Corporate Agents

Except as may be otherwise provided under provisions of law, the board of directors may adopt a resolution authorizing the purchase and maintenance of insurance on behalf of any agent of the corporation (including a director, officer, employee or other agent of the corporation) against liabilities asserted against or incurred by the agent in such capacity or arising out of the agent's status as such, whether or not the corporation would have the power to indemnify the agent against such liability under the articles of incorporation, these Bylaws or provisions of law.

Article 4
Officers

Section 1. Designation of Officers

The officers of the corporation shall be a president, a vice president, a secretary and a treasurer. The corporation may also have a chairperson of the board, one or more vice presidents, assistant secretaries, assistant treasurers and other such officers with such titles as may be determined from time to time by the board of directors.

Section 2. Qualifications

Any person may serve as officer of this corporation.

Section 3. Election and Term of Office

Officers shall be elected by the board of directors, at any time, and each officer shall hold office until he or she resigns or is removed or is otherwise disqualified to serve, or until his or her successor shall be elected and qualified, whichever occurs first.

Section 4. Removal and Resignation

Any officer may be removed, either with or without cause, by the board of directors, at any time. Any officer may resign at any time by giving written notice to the board of directors or to the president or secretary of the corporation. Any such resignation shall take effect at the date of receipt of such notice or at any later date specified therein, and, unless otherwise specified therein, the acceptance of such resignation shall not be necessary to make it effective. The above provisions of this section shall be superseded by any conflicting terms of a contract which has been approved or ratified by the board of directors relating to the employment of any officer of the corporation.

Section 5. Vacancies

Any vacancy caused by the death, resignation, removal, disqualification or otherwise, of any officer shall be filled by the board of directors. In the event of a vacancy in any office other than that of president, such vacancy may be filled temporarily by appointment by the president until such time as the board shall fill the vacancy. Vacancies occurring in offices of officers appointed at the discretion of the board may or may not be filled as the board shall determine.

Section 6. Duties of President

The president shall be the chief executive officer of the corporation and shall, subject to the control of the board of directors, supervise and control the affairs of the corporation and the activities of the officers. He or she shall perform all duties incident to his or her office and such other duties as may be required by law, by the articles of incorporation or by these bylaws or which may be prescribed from time to time by the board of directors. Unless another person is specifically appointed as chairperson of the board of directors, the president shall preside at all meetings of the board of directors and, if this corporation has members, at all meetings of the members. Except as otherwise expressly provided by law, by the articles of incorporation or by these bylaws, he or she shall, in the name of the corporation, execute such deeds, mortgages, bonds, contracts, checks or other instruments which may from time to time be authorized by the board of directors.

Section 7. Duties of Vice President

In the absence of the president, or in the event of his or her inability or refusal to act, the vice president shall perform all the duties of the president, and when so acting shall have all the powers of, and be subject to all the restrictions on, the president. The vice president shall have other powers and perform such other duties as may be prescribed by law, by the articles of incorporation or by these bylaws or as may be prescribed by the board of directors.

Section 8. Duties of Secretary

The secretary shall:

Certify and keep at the principal office of the corporation the original, or a copy, of these bylaws as amended or otherwise altered to date.

Keep at the principal office of the corporation or at such other place as the board may determine, a book of minutes of all meetings of the directors, and, if applicable, meetings of committees of directors and of members, recording therein the time and place of holding, whether regular or special, how called, how notice thereof was given, the names of those present or represented at the meeting and the proceedings thereof.

See that all notices are duly given in accordance with the provisions of these bylaws or as required by law.

Be custodian of the records and of the seal of the corporation and affix the seal, as authorized by law or the provisions of these bylaws, to duly executed documents of the corporation.

Keep at the principal office of the corporation a membership book containing the name and address of each and any members, and, in the case where any membership has been terminated, he or she shall record such fact in the membership book together with the date on which such membership ceased.

Exhibit at all reasonable times to any director of the corporation, or to his or her agent or attorney, on request therefor, the Bylaws, the membership book and the minutes of the proceedings of the directors of the corporation.

In general, perform all duties incident to the office of secretary and such other duties as may be required by law, by the articles of incorporation or by these bylaws or which may be assigned to him or her from time to time by the board of directors.

Section 9. Duties of Treasurer

The treasurer shall:

Have charge and custody of, and be responsible for, all funds and securities of the corporation, and deposit all such funds in the name of the corporation in such banks, trust companies or other depositories as shall be selected by the board of directors.

Receive, and give receipt for, monies due and payable to the corporation from any source whatsoever.

Disburse, or cause to be disbursed, the funds of the corporation as may be directed by the board of directors, taking proper vouchers for such disbursements.

Keep and maintain adequate and correct accounts of the corporation's properties and business transactions, including accounts of its assets, liabilities, receipts, disbursements, gains and losses.

Exhibit at all reasonable times the books of account and financial records to any director of the corporation, or to his or her agent or attorney, on request therefor.

Render to the president and directors, whenever requested, an account of any or all of his or her transactions as treasurer and of the financial condition of the corporation.

Prepare, or cause to be prepared, and certify, or cause to be certified, the financial statements to be included in any required reports.

In general, perform all duties incident to the office of treasurer and such other duties as may be required by law, by the articles of incorporation of the corporation or by these bylaws or which may be assigned to him or her from time to time by the board of directors.

Section 10. Compensation

The salaries of the officers, if any, shall be fixed from time to time by resolution of the board of directors. In all cases, any salaries received by officers of this corporation shall be reasonable and given in return for services actually rendered to or for the corporation.

Article 5
Committees

Section 1. Executive Committee

The board of directors may, by a majority vote of its members, designate an executive committee consisting of _____ board members and may delegate to such committee the powers and authority of the board in the management of the business and affairs of the corporation, to the extent permitted, and except as may otherwise be provided, by provisions of law.

By a majority vote of its members, the board may at any time revoke or modify any or all of the executive committee authority so delegated, increase or decrease but not below two (2) the number of the members of the executive committee and fill vacancies on the executive committee from the members of the board. The executive committee shall keep regular minutes of its proceedings, cause them to be filed with the corporate records and report the same to the board from time to time as the board may require.

Section 2. Other Committees

The corporation shall have such other committees as may from time to time be designated by resolution of the board of directors. These committees may consist of persons who are not also members of the board and shall act in an advisory capacity to the board.

Section 3. Meetings and Action of Committees

Meetings and action of committees shall be governed by, noticed, held and taken in accordance with the provisions of these bylaws concerning meetings of the board of directors, with such changes in the context of such bylaw provisions as are necessary to substitute the committee and its members for the board of directors and its members, except that the time for regular and special meetings of committees may be fixed by resolution of the board of directors or by the committee. The board of directors may also adopt rules and regulations pertaining to the conduct of meetings of committees to the extent that such rules and regulations are not inconsistent with the provisions of these bylaws.

Article 6
Execution of Instruments, Deposits and Funds

Section 1. Execution of Instruments

The board of directors, except as otherwise provided in these bylaws, may by resolution authorize any officer or agent of the corporation to enter into any contract or execute and deliver any instrument in the name of and on behalf of the corporation, and such authority may be general or confined to specific instances. Unless so authorized, no officer, agent or employee shall have any power or authority to bind the corporation by any contract or engagement or to pledge its credit or to render it liable monetarily for any purpose or in any amount.

Section 2. Checks and Notes

Except as otherwise specifically determined by resolution of the board of directors, or as otherwise required by law, checks, drafts, promissory notes, orders for the payment of money and other evidence of indebtedness of the corporation shall be signed by the treasurer and countersigned by the president of the corporation.

Section 3. Deposits

All funds of the corporation shall be deposited from time to time to the credit of the corporation in such banks, trust companies or other depositories as the board of directors may select.

Section 4. Gifts

The board of directors may accept on behalf of the corporation any contribution, gift, bequest or devise for the nonprofit purposes of this corporation.

Article 7
Corporate Records, Reports and Seal

Section 1. Maintenance of Corporate Records

The corporation shall keep at its principal office:

a. Minutes of all meetings of directors, committees of the board and, if this corporation has members, of all meetings of members, indicating the time and place of holding such meetings, whether regular or special, how called, the notice given and the names of those present and the proceedings thereof;

b. Adequate and correct books and records of account, including accounts of its properties and business transactions and accounts of its assets, liabilities, receipts, disbursements, gains and losses;

c. A record of its members, if any, indicating their names and addresses and, if applicable, the class of membership held by each member and the termination date of any membership;

d. A copy of the corporation's articles of incorporation and bylaws as amended to date, which shall be open to inspection by the members, if any, of the corporation at all reasonable times during office hours.

Section 2. Corporate Seal

The board of directors may adopt, use and at will alter, a corporate seal. Such seal shall be kept at the principal office of the corporation. Failure to affix the seal to corporate instruments, however, shall not affect the validity of any such instrument.

Section 3. Directors' Inspection Rights

Every director shall have the absolute right at any reasonable time to inspect and copy all books, records and documents of every kind and to inspect the physical properties of the corporation and shall have such other rights to inspect the books, records and properties of this corporation as may be required under the Articles of Incorporation, other provisions of these bylaws and provisions of law.

Section 4. Members' Inspection Rights

If this corporation has any members, then each and every member shall have the following inspection rights, for a purpose reasonably related to such person's interest as a member:

a. To inspect and copy the record of all members' names, addresses and voting rights, at reasonable times, upon written demand on the secretary of the corporation, which demand shall state the purpose for which the inspection rights are requested.

b. To obtain from the secretary of the corporation, upon written demand on, and payment of a reasonable charge to, the secretary of the corporation, a list of the names, addresses and voting rights of those members entitled to vote for the election of directors as of the most recent record date for which the list has been compiled or as of the date specified by the member subsequent to the date of demand. The demand shall state the purpose for which the list is requested. The membership list shall be made available within a reasonable time after the demand is received by the secretary of the corporation or after the date specified therein as of which the list is to be compiled.

c. To inspect at any reasonable time the books, records or minutes of proceedings of the members or of the board or committees of the board, upon written demand on the secretary of the corporation by the member, for a purpose reasonably related to such person's interests as a member.

Members shall have such other rights to inspect the books, records and properties of this corporation as may be required under the articles of incorporation, other provisions of these bylaws and provisions of law.

Section 5. Right to Copy and Make Extracts

Any inspection under the provisions of this article may be made in person or by agent or attorney and the right to inspection shall include the right to copy and make extracts.

Section 6. Periodic Report

The board shall cause any annual or periodic report required under law to be prepared and delivered to an office of this state or to the members, if any, of this corporation, to be so prepared and delivered within the time limits set by law.

Article 8
IRC 501(c)(3) Tax Exemption Provisions

Section 1. Limitations on Activities

No substantial part of the activities of this corporation shall be the carrying on of propaganda, or otherwise attempting to influence legislation (except as otherwise provided by Section 501(h) of the Internal Revenue Code), and this corporation shall not participate in, or intervene in (including the publishing or distribution of statements), any political campaign on behalf of, or in opposition to, any candidate for public office.

Notwithstanding any other provisions of these bylaws, this corporation shall not carry on any activities not permitted to be carried on (a) by a corporation exempt from federal income tax under Section 501(c)(3) of the Internal Revenue Code, or (b) by a corporation, contributions to which are deductible under Section 170(c)(2) of the Internal Revenue Code.

Section 2. Prohibition Against Private Inurement

No part of the net earnings of this corporation shall inure to the benefit of, or be distributable to, its members, directors or trustees, officers or other private persons, except that the corporation shall be authorized and empowered to pay reasonable compensation for services rendered and to make payments and distributions in furtherance of the purposes of this corporation.

Section 3. Distribution of Assets

Upon the dissolution of this corporation, its assets remaining after payment, or provision for payment, of all debts and liabilities of this corporation shall be distributed for one or more exempt purposes within the meaning of Section 501(c)(3) of the Internal Revenue Code or shall be distributed to the federal government, or to a state or local government, for a public purpose. Such distribution shall be made in accordance with all applicable provisions of the laws of this state.

Section 4. Private Foundation Requirements and Restrictions

In any taxable year in which this corporation is a private foundation as described in Section 509(a) of the Internal Revenue Code, the corporation 1) shall distribute its income for said period at such time and manner as not to subject it to tax under Section 4942 of the Internal Revenue Code; 2) shall not engage in any act of self-dealing as defined in Section 4941(d) of the Internal Revenue Code; 3) shall not retain any excess business holdings as defined in Section 4943(c) of the Internal Revenue Code; 4) shall not make any investments in such manner as to subject the corporation to tax under Section 4944 of the Internal Revenue Code; and 5) shall not make any taxable expenditures as defined in Section 4945(d) of the Internal Revenue Code.

Article 9
Amendment of Bylaws

Section 1. Amendment

Subject to the power of the members, if any, of this corporation to adopt, amend or repeal the bylaws of this corporation and except as may otherwise be specified under provisions of law, these bylaws, or any of them, may be altered, amended or repealed and new Bylaws adopted by approval of the board of directors.

Article 10
Construction and Terms

If there is any conflict between the provisions of these bylaws and the articles of Incorporation of this corporation, the provisions of the articles of incorporation shall govern.

Should any of the provisions or portions of these bylaws be held unenforceable or invalid for any reason, the remaining provisions and portions of these bylaws shall be unaffected by such holding.

All references in these bylaws to the articles of Incorporation shall be to the articles of incorporation, articles of organization, certificate of incorporation, organizational charter, corporate charter or other founding document of this corporation filed with an office of this state and used to establish the legal existence of this corporation.

All references in these bylaws to a section or sections of the internal revenue code shall be to such sections of the internal revenue code of 1986 as amended from time to time, or to corresponding provisions of any future federal tax code.

Adoption of Bylaws

We, the undersigned, are all of the initial directors or incorporators of this corporation, and we consent to, and hereby do, adopt the foregoing bylaws, consisting of _____ preceding pages, as the bylaws of this corporation.

Dated: _____

_____

_____

_____

_____

_____

[If you have chosen to adopt a membership structure for your corporation, you must attach Membership Bylaw Provisions before the "ADOPTION OF BYLAWS" clause at the end of this document. If you have decided to form a nonmembership corporation (as most nonprofits will), you should not include Membership Bylaw Provisions in your bylaws.]

[This document is for use in your bylaws if you have chosen to adopt a membership structure for your corporation. If you have decided to form a nonmembership corporation (as most nonprofits will), you should not include this document in your bylaws.]

Membership Provisions of the Bylaws

of

_____

Article 11
Members

Section 1. Determination and Rights of Members

The corporation shall have only one class of members. No member shall hold more than one membership in the corporation. Except as expressly provided in or authorized by the articles of incorporation, the bylaws of this corporation or provisions of law, all memberships shall have the same rights, privileges, restrictions and conditions.

Section 2. Qualifications of Members

The qualifications for membership in this corporation are as follows: _____

_____

_____

_____

_____

_____.

Section 3. Admission of Members

Applicants shall be admitted to membership_____

_____

_____

_____.

Section 4. Fees and Dues

a. The following fee shall be charged for making application for membership in the corporation:

_____.

b. The annual dues payable to the corporation by members shall be _____.

Section 5. Number of Members

There is no limit on the number of members the corporation may admit.

Section 6. Membership Book

The corporation shall keep a membership book containing the name and address of each member. Termination of the membership of any member shall be recorded in the book, together with the date of termination of such membership. Such book shall be kept at the corporation's principal office.

Section 7. Nonliability of Members

A member of this corporation is not, as such, personally liable for the debts, liabilities or obligations of the corporation.

Section 8. Nontransferability of Memberships

No member may transfer a membership or any right arising therefrom. All rights of membership cease upon the member's death.

Section 9. Termination of Membership

The membership of a member shall terminate upon the occurrence of any of the following events:

1. Upon his or her notice of such termination delivered to the president or secretary of the corporation personally or by mail, such membership to terminate upon the date of delivery of the notice or date of deposit in the mail.

2. If this corporation has provided for the payment of dues by members, upon a failure to renew his or her membership by paying dues on or before their due date, such termination to be effective thirty (30) days after a written notification of delinquency is given personally or mailed to such member by the secretary of the corporation. A member may avoid such termination by paying the amount of delinquent dues within a thirty (30) day period following the member's receipt of the written notification of delinquency.

3. After providing the member with reasonable written notice and an opportunity to be heard either orally or in writing, upon a determination by the board of directors that the member has engaged in conduct materially and seriously prejudicial to the interests or purposes of the corporation. Any person expelled from the corporation shall receive a refund of dues already paid for the current dues period.

All rights of a member in the corporation shall cease on termination of membership as herein provided.

Article 12
Meetings of Members

Section 1. Place of Meetings

Meetings of members shall be held at the principal office of the corporation or at such other place or places as may be designated from time to time by resolution of the board of directors.

Section 2. Regular Meetings

A regular meeting of members shall be held on _____, at _____ ____M., for the purpose of electing directors and transacting other business as may come before the meeting. The candidates receiving the highest number of votes up to the number of directors to be elected shall be elected. Each voting member shall cast one vote, with voting being by ballot only. The annual meeting of members for the purpose of electing directors shall be deemed a regular meeting.

Other regular meetings of the members shall be held on _____, at _____ ____M.,

If the day fixed for a regular meeting falls on a legal holiday, such meeting shall be held at the same hour and place on the next business day.

Section 3. Special Meetings of Members

Special meetings of the members shall be called by the board of directors, the chairperson of the board or the president of the corporation, or, if different, by the persons specifically authorized under the laws of this state to call special meetings of the members.

Section 4. Notice of Meetings

Unless otherwise provided by the articles of incorporation, these bylaws or provisions of law, notice stating the place, day and hour of the meeting and, in the case of a special meeting, the purpose or purposes for which the meeting is called, shall be delivered not less than ten (10) nor more than fifty (50) days before the date of the meeting, either personally or by mail, by or at the direction of the president, or the secretary, or the persons calling the meeting, to each member entitled to vote at such meeting. If mailed, such notice shall be deemed to be delivered when deposited in the United States mail addressed to the member at his or her address as it appears on the records of the corporation, with postage prepaid. Personal notification includes notification by telephone or by facsimile machine, provided however, in the case of facsimile notification, the member to be contacted shall acknowledge personal receipt of the facsimile notice by a return message or telephone call within twenty-four hours of the first facsimile transmission.

The notice of any meeting of members at which directors are to be elected shall also state the names of all those who are nominees or candidates for election to the board at the time notice is given.

Whenever any notice of a meeting is required to be given to any member of this corporation under provisions of the articles of incorporation, these bylaws or the law of this state, a waiver of notice in writing signed by the member, whether before or after the time of the meeting, shall be equivalent to the giving of such notice.

Section 5. Quorum for Meetings

A quorum shall consist of _____ of the voting members of the corporation.

Except as otherwise provided under the articles of incorporation, these bylaws or provisions of law, no business shall be considered by the members at any meeting at which the required quorum is not present, and the only motion which the chair shall entertain at such meeting is a motion to adjourn.

Section 6. Majority Action As Membership Action

Every act or decision done or made by a majority of voting members present in person or by proxy at a duly held meeting at which a quorum is present is the act of the members, unless the articles of incorporation, these bylaws or provisions of law require a greater number.

Section 7. Voting Rights

Each member is entitled to one vote on each matter submitted to a vote by the members. Voting at duly held meetings shall be by voice vote. Election of directors, however, shall be by written ballot.

Section 8. Action by Written Ballot

Except as otherwise provided under the articles of incorporation, these bylaws or provisions of law, any action which may be taken at any regular or special meeting of members may be taken without a meeting if the corporation distributes a written ballot to each member entitled to vote on the matter. The ballot shall:

1. set forth the proposed action;

2. provide an opportunity to specify approval or disapproval of each proposal;

3. indicate the number of responses needed to meet the quorum requirement and, except for ballots soliciting votes for the election of directors, state the percentage of approvals necessary to pass the measure submitted; and

4. shall specify the date by which the ballot must be received by the corporation in order to be counted. The date set shall afford members a reasonable time within which to return the ballots to the corporation.

Ballots shall be mailed or delivered in the manner required for giving notice of membership meetings as specified in these bylaws.

Approval of action by written ballot shall be valid only when the number of votes cast by ballot within the time period specified equals or exceeds the quorum required to be present at a meeting authorizing the action, and the number of approvals equals or exceeds the number of votes that would be required to approve the action at a meeting at which the total number of votes cast was the same as the number of votes cast by ballot.

Directors may be elected by written ballot. Such ballots for the election of directors shall list the persons nominated at the time the ballots are mailed or delivered.

Section 9. Conduct of Meetings

Meetings of members shall be presided over by the chairperson of the board, or, if there is no chairperson or, in his or her absence, by the president of the corporation or, in his or her absence, by the vice president of the corporation or, in the absence of all of these persons, by a chairperson chosen by a majority of the voting members present at the meeting. The secretary of the corporation shall act as secretary of all meetings of members, provided that, in his or her absence, the presiding off[...] shall appoint another person to act as secretary of the meeting.

Meetings shall be governed by _____, as suc[...] from time to time, insofar as such rules are not inconsistent with or in conflict w[...] incorporation, these bylaws or with provisions of law.

Waiver of Notice and Consent to Holding
of First Meeting of Board of Directors

of

_____

We, the undersigned, being all the directors of _____
_____, hereby waive notice of the first
meeting of the board of directors of the corporation and consent to the holding of said meeting at
_____,
on _____, 20_____, at _____ ____M., and consent to the
transaction of any and all business by the directors at the meeting, including, without limitation, the
adoption of bylaws, the election of officers and the selection of the place where the corporation's
bank accounts will be maintained.

Dated: _____

_____

_____, Director

_____

_____, Director

_____

_____, Director

_____

_____, Director

_____

_____, Director

_____

_____, Director

_____

_____, Director

NOLO
www.nolo.com
**Waiver of Notice and Consent to Holding
of First Meeting of Board of Directors**
Page 1 of 1

Minutes of First Meeting of Board of Directors

of

_____

The board of directors of _____
held its first meeting on _____, 20_____, at _____.
The following directors, constituting a quorum of the full board, were present at the meeting:

_____

_____

_____

_____

The following directors were absent:

_____

_____

_____

_____

On motion and by unanimous vote, _____
was elected temporary chairperson and then presided over the meeting. _____
_____ was elected temporary secretary of the meeting.

The chairperson announced that the meeting was held pursuant to written waiver of notice signed by each of the directors. Upon a motion duly made, seconded and unanimously carried, the waiver was made a part of the records of the meeting. It now precedes the minutes of this meeting in the corporate records book.

Articles of Incorporation

The chairperson announced that the articles of incorporation or similar organizing instrument of this corporation was filed with the office of _____
_____ on _____.

RESOLVED, that the secretary of this corporation is directed to see that a copy of the articles of incorporation or similar organizing instrument of this corporation, file-stamped or certified by the secretary of state or other appropriate state office or official, is kept at the corporation's principal office.

Bylaws

There was then presented to the meeting for adoption a proposed set of bylaws of the corporation. The bylaws were considered and discussed and, on motion duly made and seconded, it was unanimously

RESOLVED, that the bylaws presented to this meeting be and hereby are adopted as the bylaws of the corporation;

RESOLVED FURTHER, that the secretary of this corporation is directed to see that a copy of the bylaws is kept at the corporation's principal office.

Corporate Tax Exemptions

The chairperson announced that, upon application previously submitted to the Internal Revenue Service, the corporation was determined to be exempt from payment of federal corporate income taxes under Section 501(c)(3) of the Internal Revenue Code per Internal Revenue Service determination letter dated _____, 20_____. The chairperson then presented the federal tax exemption determination letter and the Secretary was instructed to insert this letter in the corporate records book.

The chairperson announced that the corporation was exempt from applicable state corporate income, franchise or similar taxes. The chairperson instructed the secretary to place a copy of any correspondence related to the corporation's state corporate tax exemption in the corporate records book.

Election of Officers

The chairperson then announced that the next item of business was the election of officers. Upon motion, the following persons were unanimously elected to the offices shown after their names:

_____ President

_____ Vice President

_____ Secretary

_____ Treasurer

Each officer who was present accepted his or her office. Thereafter, the president presided at the meeting as chairperson of the meeting, and the secretary of the corporation acted as secretary of the meeting.

Principal Office

After discussion as to the exact location of the corporation's principal office for the transaction of business in the county named in the bylaws, upon motion duly made and seconded, it was

RESOLVED, that the principal office of this corporation shall be located at

_____.

Bank Account

Upon motion duly made and seconded, it was

RESOLVED, that the funds of this corporation shall be deposited with

_____.

RESOLVED FURTHER, that the treasurer of this corporation be and hereby is authorized and directed to establish an account with said bank and to deposit the funds of this corporation therein.

RESOLVED FURTHER, that any officer, employee or agent of this corporation be and is authorized to endorse checks, drafts or other evidences of indebtedness made payable to this corporation, but only for the purpose of deposit.

RESOLVED FURTHER, that all checks, drafts and other instruments obligating this corporation to pay money shall be signed on behalf of this corporation by any of the following persons:

_____

_____

_____

_____

RESOLVED FURTHER, that said bank be and hereby is authorized to honor and pay all checks and drafts of this corporation signed as provided herein.

RESOLVED FURTHER, that the authority hereby conferred shall remain in force until revoked by the board of directors of this corporation and until written notice of such revocation shall have been received by said bank.

RESOLVED FURTHER, that the secretary of this corporation be and hereby is authorized to certify as to the continuing authority of these resolutions, the persons authorized to sign on behalf of this corporation and the adoption of said bank's standard form of resolution, provided that said form does not vary materially from the terms of the foregoing resolutions.

Compensation of Officers

There followed a discussion concerning the compensation to be paid by the corporation to its officers. Upon motion duly made and seconded, it was unanimously

RESOLVED, that the following annual salaries be paid to the officers of this corporation:

President	$_____
Vice President	$_____
Secretary	$_____
Treasurer	$_____

Corporate Seal

The secretary presented to the meeting for adoption a proposed form of seal of the corporation. Upon motion duly made and seconded, it was:

RESOLVED, that the form of corporate seal presented to this meeting be and hereby is adopted as the seal of this corporation, and the secretary of the corporation is directed to place an impression thereof in the space next to this resolution.

[Impress seal here]

Corporate Certificates

The secretary then presented to the meeting proposed director, sponsor, membership or other forms of corporate certificates for approval by the board. Upon motion duly made and seconded, it was

RESOLVED, that the form of certificates presented to this meeting are hereby adopted for use by this corporation and the secretary is directed to attach a copy of each form of certificate to the minutes of this meeting.

Since there was no further business to come before the meeting, on motion duly made and seconded, the meeting was adjourned.

Dated:_____

_____

_____, Secretary

Department of the Treasury
Internal Revenue Service

Application for Recognition of Exemption

Under Section 501(c)(3) of the Internal Revenue Code

Contents:
Form 1023 and
  Instructions
Form 872-C

Note: *For the addresses for filing* **Form 1023,** *see* **Form 8718,** *User Fee for Exempt Organization Determination Letter Request.*

For obtaining an employer identification number (EIN), see **Form SS-4,** *Application for Employer Identification Number.*

Package 1023
(Rev. September 1998)

Cat. No. 47194L

Department of the Treasury
Internal Revenue Service

Instructions for Form 1023

(Revised September 1998)

Application for Recognition of Exemption Under Section 501(c)(3) of the Internal Revenue Code

Note: *Retain a copy of the completed Form 1023 in the organization's permanent records. See **Public Inspection of Form 1023** regarding public inspection of approved applications.*

General Instructions

Section references are to the Internal Revenue Code unless otherwise noted.

User Fee.—Submit with the Form 1023 application for a determination letter, a **Form 8718,** User Fee for Exempt Organization Determination Letter Request, and the user fee called for in the Form 8718. You may obtain Form 8718, and additional forms and publications, through your local IRS office or by calling 1-800-829-3676 (1-800-TAX-FORM). User fees are subject to change on an annual basis. Therefore, be sure that you use the most current Form 8718.

Helpful information.—For additional information, see:
- **Pub. 557,** Tax-Exempt Status for Your Organization
- **Pub. 598,** Tax on Unrelated Business Income of Exempt Organizations
- **Pub. 578,** Tax Information for Private Foundations and Foundation Managers
- **Internet site,** www.irs.ustreas.gov/bus_info/eo/

Purpose of Form

1. Completed Form 1023 required for section 501(c)(3) exemption.—Unless it meets one of the exceptions in **2** below, any organization formed after October 9, 1969, must file a Form 1023 to qualify as a section 501(c)(3) organization.

The IRS determines if an organization is a private foundation from the information entered on a Form 1023.

2. Organizations not required to file Form 1023.—The following types of organizations may be considered tax-exempt under section 501(c)(3) even if they do not file Form 1023:

1. Churches,

2. Integrated auxiliaries of churches, and conventions or associations of churches, or

3. Any organization that:

(a) Is not a private foundation (as defined in section 509(a)), and

(b) Has gross receipts in each taxable year of normally not more than $5,000.

Even if the above organizations are not required to file Form 1023 to be tax-exempt, these organizations may choose to file Form 1023 in order to receive a determination letter that recognizes their section 501(c)(3) status.

Section 501(c)(3) status provides certain incidental benefits such as:
- Public recognition of tax-exempt status.
- Advance assurance to donors of deductibility of contributions.
- Exemption from certain state taxes.
- Exemption from certain Federal excise taxes.
- Nonprofit mailing privileges, etc.

3. Other organizations.—Section 501(e) and (f) cooperative service organizations, section 501(k) child care organizations, and section 501(n) charitable risk pools use Form 1023 to apply for a determination letter under section 501(c)(3).

4. Group exemption letter.—Generally, Form 1023 is not used to apply for a group exemption letter. See Pub. 557 for information on how to apply for a group exemption letter.

What To File

All applicants must complete pages 1 through 9 of Form 1023. These organizations must also complete the schedules or form indicated:

1. Churches . . . . Schedule A
2. Schools . . . . Schedule B
3. Hospitals and Medical Research . . . . . . Schedule C
4. Supporting Organizations (509(a)(3)) . . . . . Schedule D
5. Private Operating Foundations . . . . . . Schedule E
6. Homes for the Aged or Handicapped . . . . Schedule F
7. Child Care . . . . Schedule G
8. Scholarship Benefits or Student Aid . . . . . Schedule H
9. Organizations that have taken over or will take over a "for profit" institution . . . . Schedule I
10. Organizations requesting an advance ruling in Part III, Line 10 . . . . Form 872-C

Attachments.—For any attachments submitted with Form 1023.—
- Show the organization's name, address, and employer identification number (EIN).
- Identify the Part and line item number to which the attachment relates.
- Use 8½ x 11 inch paper for any attachments.
- Include any court decisions, rulings, opinions, etc., that will expedite processing of the application. Generally, attachments in the form of tape recordings are not acceptable unless accompanied by a transcript.

When To File

An organization formed after October 9, 1969, must file Form 1023 to be recognized as an organization described in section 501(c)(3). Generally, if an organization files its application within 15 months after the end of the month in which it was formed, and if the IRS approves the application, the effective date of the organization's section 501(c)(3) status will be the date it was organized.

Generally, if an organization does not file its application (Form 1023) within 15 months after the end of the month in which it was formed, it will not qualify for exempt status during the period before the date of its application. For exceptions and special rules, including automatic extensions in some cases, see Part III of Form 1023.

The date of receipt of the Form 1023 is the date of the U.S. postmark on the cover in which an exemption application is mailed or, if no postmark appears on the cover, the date the application is stamped as received by the IRS.

Private delivery services.—See the instructions for your income tax return for information on certain private delivery services designated by the IRS to meet the "timely mailing as timely filing/paying rule." The private delivery service can tell you how to get written proof of the mailing date.

Caution: *Private delivery services cannot deliver items to P.O. boxes. You must use the U. S. Postal Service to mail any item to an IRS P.O. box address. See the Form 8718 for the P.O. box address as well as the express mail or a delivery service address.*

Where To File

File the completed Form 1023 application, and all required information, with the IRS at the address shown in Form 8718.

The IRS will determine the organization's tax-exempt status and whether any annual returns must be filed.

Signature Requirements

An officer, a trustee who is authorized to sign, or another person authorized by a power of attorney, must sign the Form 1023 application. Attach a power of attorney to the application. You may use **Form 2848,** Power of Attorney and Declaration of Representative, for this purpose.

Deductibility of Contributions

Donors can take a charitable contribution deduction if their gift or bequest is made to a section 501(c)(3) organization.

The effective date of an organization's section 501(c)(3) status determines the date that contributions to it are deductible by donors. (See **When To File** on page 1.)

Contributions by U.S. residents to foreign organizations generally are not deductible. Tax treaties between the U.S. and certain foreign countries provide limited exceptions. Foreign organizations (other than those in Canada or Mexico) that claim eligibility to receive contributions deductible by U.S. residents must attach an English copy of the U.S. tax treaty that provides for such deductibility.

Appeal Procedures

The organization's application will be considered by the IRS which will either:

1. Issue a favorable determination letter;

2. Issue a proposed adverse determination letter denying the exempt status requested; or

3. Refer the case to the National Office.

If the IRS sends you a proposed adverse determination, it will advise you of your appeal rights at that time.

Language and Currency Requirements

Language requirements.—Prepare the Form 1023 and attachments in English. Provide an English translation if the organizational document or bylaws are in any other language.

You may be asked to provide English translations of foreign language publications that the organization produces or distributes and that are submitted with the application.

Financial requirements.—Report all financial information in U.S. dollars (specify the conversion rate used). Combine amounts from within and outside the United States and report the total for each item on the financial statements.

For example:

Gross Investment Income	
From U.S. sources	$4,000
From non-U.S. sources	1,000
Amount to report on income statement	$5,000

Annual Information Return

If an annual information return is due while the organization's application for recognition of exempt status is pending with the IRS (including any appeal of a proposed adverse determination), the organization should file at the following address:

Internal Revenue Service
Ogden Service Center
Ogden, Utah 84201-0027

● **Form 990,** Return of Organization Exempt From Income Tax, **or**

● **Form 990-EZ,** Short Form Return of Organization Exempt From Income Tax, **and,**

● **Schedule A (Form 990),** Organization Exempt Under Section 501(c)(3), **or**

● **Form 990-PF,** Return of Private Foundation, if the organization acknowledges it is a private foundation, **and**

Indicate that an application is pending.

If an organization has unrelated business income of more than $1,000, file **Form 990-T,** Exempt Organization Business Income Tax Return.

Public Inspection of Form 1023

Caution: *Note the discussion below for the potential effect of the Taxpayer Bill of Rights 2 (TBOR2) on these instructions.*

IRS responsibilities for public inspection.—If the organization's application for section 501(c)(3) status is approved, the following items will be open to public inspection in any District office and at the National Office of the IRS (section 6104):

1. The organization's application and any supporting documents.

2. Any letter or other document issued by the IRS with regard to the application.

Note that the following items are not available for public inspection:

1. Any information relating to a trade secret, patent, style of work, or apparatus that, if released, would adversely affect the organization, or

2. Any other information that would adversely affect the national defense.

IMPORTANT: Applicants must identify this information by clearly marking it, "NOT SUBJECT TO PUBLIC INSPECTION," and must attach a statement to explain why the organization asks that the information be withheld. If the IRS agrees, the information will be withheld.

Organization's responsibilities for public inspection.—The organization must make available a copy of its approved application and supporting documents, along with any document or letter issued by the IRS for public inspection.

These documents must be available during regular business hours at the organization's principal office and at each of its regional or district offices having at least three paid employees. See Notice 88-120,1988-2 C.B. 454.

A penalty of $20 a day will be imposed on any person under a duty to comply with the public inspection requirements for each day a failure to comply continues.

Furnishing copies of documents under TBOR2.—The Taxpayer Bill of Rights 2 (TBOR2), enacted July 30, 1996, modified prospectively the section 6685 penalty and the rules for the public inspection of returns and exemption applications. An organization must furnish a copy of its Form 990, Form 990-EZ, or exemption application, and certain related documents, if a request is made in writing or in person.

For a request made in person, the organization must make an immediate response.

For a response to a written request, the organization must provide the requested copies within 30 days.

The organization must furnish copies of its Forms 990, or Forms 990-EZ, for any of its 3 most recent taxable years. No charge is to be made other than charging a reasonable fee for reproduction and actual postage costs.

An organization need not provide copies if:

1. The organization has made the requested documents widely available in a manner provided in Treasury regulations, or

2. The Secretary of the Treasury determined, upon application by the organization, that the organization was subject to a harassment campaign such that a waiver of the obligation to provide copies would be in the public interest.

Penalty for failure to allow public inspection or provide copies.—The section 6685 penalty for willful failure to allow public inspections or provide copies is increased from the present-law level of $1,000 to $5,000 by TBOR2.

Effective date of TBOR2.—These public inspection provisions governing tax-exempt organizations under TBOR2 generally apply to requests made no earlier than 60 days after the date on which the Treasury Department publishes the regulations required under the provisions. However, Congress, in the legislative history of TBOR2, indicated that organizations would comply voluntarily with the public inspection provisions prior to the issuance of such regulations.

Special Rule for Canadian Colleges and Universities

A Canadian college or university that received **Form T2051,** Notification of Registration, from Revenue Canada (Department of National Revenue, Taxation) and whose registration has not been revoked, does not need to complete all parts of Form 1023.

Such an organization must complete only Part I of Form 1023 and Schedule B (Schools, Colleges, and Universities). It must attach a copy of its **Form T2050,** Application for Registration, together with all the required attachments submitted to Revenue Canada. It must furnish an English translation if any attachments were prepared in French.

Other Canadian organizations.—Other Canadian organizations that seek a determination of section 501(c)(3) status must complete Form 1023 in the same manner as U.S. organizations.

Specific Instructions

The following instructions are keyed to the line items on the application form:

Part I. Identification of Applicant

Line 1. Full name and address of organization.—Enter the organization's name exactly as it appears in its creating document including amendments. Show the other name in parentheses, if the organization will be operating under another name.

For a foreign address, enter the information in the following order: city, province or state, and country. Follow the country's practice in placing the postal code in the address. **Do not** abbreviate the country name.

Line 2. Employer identification number (EIN).—All organizations must have an EIN. Enter the nine-digit EIN the IRS assigned to the organization. See **Form SS-4,** Application for Employer Identification Number, for information on how to obtain an EIN immediately by telephone, if the organization does not have an EIN. Enter, "applied for," if the organization has applied for an EIN number previously. Attach a statement giving the date of the application and the office where it was filed. **Do not** apply for an EIN more than once.

Line 3. Person to contact.—Enter the name and telephone number of the person to contact during business hours if more information is needed. The contact person should be an officer, director, or a person with power of attorney who is familiar with the organization's activities and is authorized to act on its behalf. Attach Form 2848 or other power of attorney.

Line 4. Month the annual accounting period ends.—Enter the month the organization's annual accounting period ends. The accounting period is usually the 12-month period that is the organization's tax year. The organization's first tax year depends on the accounting period chosen. The first tax year could be less than 12 months.

Line 5. Date formed.—Enter the date the organization became a legal entity. For a corporation, this is the date that the articles of incorporation were approved by the appropriate state official. For an unincorporated organization, it is the date its constitution or articles of association were adopted.

Line 6.—Indicate if the organization is one of the following:

- 501(e) Cooperative hospital service organization
- 501(f) Cooperative service organization of operating educational organization
- 501(k) Organization providing child care
- 501(n) Charitable risk pool

If none of the above applies, make no entry on line 6.

Line 7.—Indicate if the organization has ever filed a Form 1023 or **Form 1024,** Application for Recognition of Exemption Under Section 501(a), with the IRS.

Line 8.—If the organization for which this application is being filed is a private foundation, answer "N/A." If the organization is not required to file Form 990 (or Form 990-EZ) and is not a private foundation, answer "No" and attach an explanation. See the Instructions for Form 990 and Form 990-EZ for a discussion of organizations not required to file Form 990 (or Form 990-EZ). Otherwise, answer "Yes."

Line 9.—Indicate if the organization has ever filed Federal income tax returns as a taxable organization or filed returns as an exempt organization (e.g., Form 990, 990-EZ, 990-PF, or 990-T).

Line 10. Type of organization and organizational documents.— Organizing instrument.—Submit a conformed copy of the organizing instrument. If the organization does not have an organizing instrument, it will not qualify for exempt status.

A conformed copy is one that agrees with the original and all amendments to it. The conformed copy may be:

- A photocopy of the original signed and dated organizing document, OR

- A copy of the organizing document that is unsigned but is sent with a written declaration, signed by an authorized individual, that states that the copy is a complete and accurate copy of the original signed and dated document.

Corporation.—In the case of a corporation, a copy of the articles of incorporation, approved and dated by an appropriate state official, is sufficient by itself.

If an unsigned copy of the articles of incorporation is submitted, it must be accompanied by the written declaration discussed above.

Signed, or unsigned, copies of the articles of incorporation must be accompanied by a declaration stating that the original copy of the articles was filed with, and approved by, the state. The date filed must be specified.

Unincorporated association.—In the case of an unincorporated association, the conformed copy of the constitution, articles of association, or other organizing document must indicate, in the document itself, or in a written declaration, that the organization was formed by the adoption of the document by two or more persons.

Bylaws.—If the organization has adopted bylaws, include a current copy. The bylaws do not need to be signed if they are submitted as an attachment to the Form 1023 application. The bylaws of an organization alone are not an organizing instrument. They are merely the internal rules and regulations of the organization.

Trust.—In the case of a trust, a copy of the signed and dated trust instrument must be furnished.

Dissolution clause.—For an organization to qualify for exempt status, its organizing instrument must contain a proper dissolution clause, or state law must provide for distribution of assets for one or more section 501(c)(3) purposes upon dissolution. If the organization is relying on state law, provide the citation for the law and briefly state the law's provisions in an attachment. Foreign organizations must provide the citation for the foreign statute and attach a copy of the statute along with an English language translation.

See Pub. 557 for a discussion of dissolution clauses under the heading, **Articles of Organization, Dedication and Distribution of Assets.** Examples of dissolution clauses are shown in the sample organizing instruments given in that publication.

Organizational purposes.—The organizing instrument must specify the organizational purposes of the organization. The purposes specified must be limited to one or more of those given in section 501(c)(3). See Pub. 557 for detailed instructions and for sample organizing instruments that satisfy the requirements of section 501(c)(3) and the related regulations.

Part II. Activities and Operational Information

Line 1.—It is important that you report all activities carried on by the organization to enable the IRS to make a proper determination of the organization's exempt status.

Line 2.—If it is anticipated that the organization's principal sources of support will increase or decrease substantially in relation to the organization's total support, attach a statement describing anticipated changes and explaining the basis for the expectation.

Line 3.—For purposes of providing the information requested on line 3, "fundraising activity" includes the solicitation of contributions and both functionally related activities and unrelated business activities. Include a description of the nature and magnitude of the activities.

Line 4a.—Furnish the mailing addresses of the organization's principal officers, directors, or trustees. Do not give the address of the organization.

Line 4b.—The annual compensation includes salary, bonus, and any other form of payment to the individual for services while employed by the organization.

Line 4c.—Public officials include anyone holding an elected position or anyone appointed to a position by an elected official.

Line 4d.—For purposes of this application, a "disqualified person" is any person who, if the applicant organization were a private foundation, is:

1. A "substantial contributor" to the foundation (defined below);

2. A foundation manager;

3. An owner of more than 20% of the total combined voting power of a corporation that is a substantial contributor to the foundation;

4. A "member of the family" of any person described in **1, 2,** or **3** above;

5. A corporation, partnership, or trust in which persons described in **1, 2, 3,** or **4** above, hold more than 35% of the combined voting power, the profits interest, or the beneficial interests; and

6. Any other private foundation that is effectively controlled by the same persons who control the first-mentioned private foundation or any other private foundation substantially all of whose contributions were made by the same contributors.

A substantial contributor is any person who gave a total of more than $5,000 to the organization, and those contributions are more than 2% of all the contributions and bequests received by the organization from the date it was created up to the end of the year the contributions by the substantial contributor were received. A creator of a trust is treated as a substantial contributor regardless of the amount contributed by that person or others.

See Pub. 578 for more information on "disqualified persons."

Line 5.—If your organization controls or is controlled by another exempt organization or a taxable organization, answer "Yes." "Control" means that:

1. Fifty percent (50%) or more of the filing organization's officers, directors, trustees, or key employees are also officers, directors, trustees, or key employees of the second organization being tested for control;

2. The filing organization appoints 50% or more of the officers, directors, trustees, or key employees of the second organization; or

3. Fifty percent (50%) or more of the filing organization's officers, directors, trustees, or key employees are appointed by the second organization.

Control exists if the 50% test is met by any one group of persons even if collectively the 50% test is not met. Examples of special relationships are common officers and the sharing of office space or employees.

Line 6.—If the organization conducts any financial transactions (either receiving or distributing cash or other assets), or nonfinancial activities with an exempt organization (other than a 501(c)(3) organization), or with a political organization, answer "Yes," and explain.

Line 7.—If the organization must report its income and expense activity to any other organization (tax-exempt or taxable entity), answer "Yes."

Line 8.—Examples of assets used to perform an exempt function are: land, building, equipment, and publications. Do not include cash or property producing investment income. If you have no assets used in performing the organization's exempt function, answer "N/A."

Line 10a.—If the organization is managed by another exempt organization, a taxable organization, or an individual, answer "Yes."

Line 10b.—If the organization leases property from anyone or leases any of its property to anyone, answer "Yes."

Line 11.—A membership organization for purposes of this question is an organization that is composed of individuals or organizations who:

1. Share in the common goal for which the organization was created;

2. Actively participate in achieving the organization's purposes; and

3. Pay dues.

Line 12.—Examples of benefits, services, and products are: meals to homeless people, home for the aged, a museum open to the public, and a symphony orchestra giving public performances.

Note: *Organizations that provide low-income housing should see Rev. Proc. 96-32, 1996-1 C.B. 717, for a "safe harbor" and an alternative facts and circumstances test to be used in completing line 12.*

Line 13.—An organization is attempting to influence legislation if it contacts or urges the public to contact members of a legislative body, for the purpose of proposing, supporting, or opposing legislation, or if it advocates the adoption or rejection of legislation.

If you answer "Yes," you may want to file **Form 5768,** Election/Revocation of Election by an Eligible Section 501(c)(3) Organization To Make Expenditures To Influence Legislation.

Line 14.—An organization is intervening in a political campaign if it promotes or opposes the candidacy or prospective candidacy of an individual for public office.

Part III. Technical Requirements

Line 1.—If you check "Yes," proceed to line 7. If you check "No," proceed to line 2.

Line 2a.—To qualify as an integrated auxiliary, an organization must not be a private foundation and must satisfy the affiliation and support tests of Regulations section 1.6033-2(h).

Line 3.—Relief from the 15-month filing requirement is granted automatically if the organization submits a completed Form 1023 within 12 months from the end of the 15-month period.

To get this extension, an organization must add the following statement at the top of its application: "Filed Pursuant to Section 301.9100-2." No request for a letter ruling is required to obtain an automatic extension.

Line 4.—See Regulation sections 301.9100-1 and 301.9100-3 for information about a discretionary extension beyond the 27-month period. Under these regulations, the IRS will allow an organization a reasonable extension of time to file a Form 1023 if it submits evidence to establish that:

(a) It acted reasonably and in good faith, and

(b) Granting relief will not prejudice the interests of the government.

Showing reasonable action and good faith.—An organization acted reasonably and showed good faith if at least one of the following is true.

1. The organization filed its application before the IRS discovered its failure to file.

2. The organization failed to file because of intervening events beyond its control.

3. The organization exercised reasonable diligence but was not aware of the filing requirement.

To determine whether the organization exercised reasonable diligence, it is necessary to take into account the complexity of filing and the organization's experience in these matters.

4. The organization reasonably relied upon the written advice of the IRS.

5. The organization reasonably relied upon the advice of a qualified tax professional who failed to file or advise the organization to file Form 1023. An organization cannot rely on the advice of a qualified tax professional if it knows or should know that he or she is not competent to render advice on filing exemption applications or is not aware of all the relevant facts.

Not acting reasonably and in good faith.—An organization has not acted reasonably and in good faith if it chose not to file after being informed of the requirement to file and the consequences of failure to do so. Furthermore, an organization has not acted reasonably and in good faith if it used hindsight to request an extension of time to file. That is, if after the original deadline to file passes, specific facts have changed so that filing an application becomes advantageous to an organization, the IRS will not ordinarily grant an extension. To qualify for an extension in this situation, the organization must prove that its decision to file did not involve hindsight.

No prejudice to the interest of the government.—Prejudice to the interest of the government results if granting an extension of time to file to an organization results in a lower total tax liability for the years to which the filing applies than would have been the case if the organization had applied on time. Before granting an extension, the IRS may require the organization requesting it to submit a statement from an independent auditor certifying that no prejudice will result if the extension is granted.

Procedure for requesting extension.—To request a discretionary extension, an organization must submit the following with its Form 1023:

● A statement showing the date Form 1023 should have been filed and the date it was actually filed.

● An affidavit describing in detail the events that led to the failure to apply and to the discovery of that failure. If the organization relied on a qualified tax professional's advice, the affidavit must describe the engagement and responsibilities of the professional and the extent to which the organization relied on him or her.

● All documents relevant to the election application.

● A dated declaration, signed by an individual authorized to act for the organization, that includes the following statement: "Under penalties of perjury, I declare that I have examined this request, including accompanying documents, and, to the best of my knowledge and belief, the request contains all the relevant facts relating to the request, and such facts are true, correct, and complete."

● A detailed affidavit from individuals having knowledge or information about the events that led to the failure to make the application and to the discovery of that failure. These individuals include accountants or attorneys knowledgeable in tax matters who advised the organization concerning the application. Any affidavit from a tax professional must describe the engagement and responsibilities of the professional as well as the advice that the professional provided to the organization. The affidavit must also include the name, current address, and taxpayer identification number of the individual making the affidavit (the affiant). The affiant must also forward with the affidavit a dated and signed declaration that states: "Under penalties of perjury, I declare that I have examined this request, including accompanying documents, and, to the best of my knowledge and belief, the request contains all the relevant facts relating to the request, and such facts are true, correct, and complete."

The reasons for late filing should be specific to your particular organization and situation. Regulation section 301.9100-3 (see above) lists the factors the IRS will consider in determining if good cause exists for granting a discretionary extension of time to file the application. To address these factors, your response for line 4 should provide the following information:

1. Whether the organization consulted an attorney or accountant knowledgeable in tax matters or communicated with a responsible IRS employee (before or after the organization was created) to ascertain the organization's Federal filing requirements and, if so, the names and occupations or titles of the persons contacted, the approximate dates, and the substance of the information obtained;

2. How and when the organization learned about the 15-month deadline for filing Form 1023;

3. Whether any significant intervening circumstances beyond the organization's control prevented it from submitting the application timely or within a reasonable period of time after it learned of the requirement to file the application within the 15-month period; and

4. Any other information that you believe may establish reasonable action and good faith and no prejudice to the interest of the government for not filing timely or otherwise justify granting the relief sought.

A request for relief under this section is treated as part of the request for the exemption determination letter and is covered by the user fee submitted with Form 8718.

Line 5.—If you answer "No," the organization may receive an adverse letter limiting the effective date of its exempt status to the date its application was received.

Line 6.—The organization may still be able to qualify for exemption under section 501(c)(4) for the period preceding the effective date of its exemption as a section 501(c)(3) organization. If the organization is qualified under section 501(c)(4) and page 1 of Form 1024 is filed as directed, the organization will not be liable for income tax returns as a taxable entity. Contributions to section 501(c)(4) organizations are generally not deductible by donors as charitable contributions.

Line 7.—Private foundations are subject to various requirements, restrictions, and excise taxes under Chapter 42 of the Code that do not apply to public charities. Also, contributions to private foundations may receive less favorable treatment than contributions to public charities. See Pub. 578. Therefore, it is usually to an organization's advantage to show that it qualifies as a public charity rather than as a private foundation if its activities or sources of support permit it to do so. Unless an organization meets one of the exceptions below, it is a private foundation. In general, an organization is **not** a private foundation if it is:

1. A church, school, hospital, or governmental unit;

2. A medical research organization operated in conjunction with a hospital;

3. An organization operated for the benefit of a college or university that is owned or operated by a governmental unit;

4. An organization that normally receives a substantial part of its support in the form of contributions from a governmental unit or from the general public as provided in section 170(b)(1)(A)(vi);

5. An organization that normally receives not more than one-third of its support from gross investment income and more than one-third of its support from contributions, membership fees, and gross receipts related to its exempt functions (subject to certain exceptions) as provided in section 509(a)(2);

6. An organization operated solely for the benefit of, and in connection with, one or more organizations described above (or for the benefit of one or more of the organizations described in section 501(c)(4), (5), or (6) of the Code and also described in **5** above), but not controlled by disqualified persons other than foundation managers, as provided in section 509(a)(3); or

7. An organization organized and operated to test for public safety as provided in section 509(a)(4).

Line 8.—Basis for private operating foundation status: (Complete this line **only** if you answered "Yes" to the question on line 7.)

A "private operating foundation" is a private foundation that spends substantially all of its adjusted net income or its minimum investment return, whichever is less, directly for the active conduct of the activities constituting the purpose or function for which it is organized and operated.

The foundation must satisfy the income test and one of the three supplemental tests: **(1)** the assets test; **(2)** the endowment test; or **(3)** the support test. For additional information, see Pub. 578.

Line 9.—Basis for nonprivate foundation status: Check the box that shows why your organization is not a private foundation.

Box (a). A church or convention or association of churches.

Box (b). A school.—See the definition in the instructions for Schedule B.

Box (c). A hospital or medical research organization.—See the instructions for Schedule C.

Box (d). A governmental unit.—This category includes a state, a possession of the United States, or a political subdivision of any of the foregoing, or the United States, or the District of Columbia.

Box (e). Organizations operated in connection with or solely for organizations described in (a) through (d) or (g), (h), and (i).—The organization must be organized and operated for the benefit of, to perform the functions of, or to carry out the purposes of one or more specified organizations described in section 509(a)(1) or (2). It must be operated, supervised, or controlled by or in connection with one or more of the organizations described in the instructions for boxes **(a)** through **(d)** or **(g), (h),** and **(i).** It must not be controlled directly or indirectly by disqualified persons (other than foundation managers or organizations described in section 509(a)(1) or (2)). To show whether the organization satisfies these tests, complete Schedule D.

Box (f). An organization testing for public safety.—An organization in this category is one that tests products to determine their acceptability for use by the general public. It does not include any organization testing for the benefit of a manufacturer as an operation or control in the manufacture of its product.

Box (g). Organization for the benefit of a college or university owned or operated by a governmental unit.—The organization must be organized and operated exclusively for the benefit of a college or university that:

● Is an educational organization within the meaning of section 170(b)(1)(A)(ii) and is an agency or instrumentality of a state or political subdivision of a state;

● Is owned or operated by a state or political subdivision of a state; OR

● Is owned or operated by an agency or instrumentality of one or more states or political subdivisions.

The organization must also normally receive a substantial part of its support from a state or any state or political subdivision of a state, or from direct or indirect contributions from the general public or from a combination of these sources.

An organizaton described in section 170(b)(1)(A)(iv) will be subject to the same publicly supported rules that are applicable to 170(b)(1)(A)(vi) organizations described in box (h) below.

Box (h). Organization receiving support from a governmental unit or from the general public.—The organization must receive a substantial part of its support from the United States or any state or political subdivision, or from direct or indirect contributions from the general public, or from a combination of these sources.

The organization may satisfy the support requirement in either of two ways.

(1) It will be treated as publicly supported if the support it normally receives from the above-described governmental units and the general public equals at least one-third of its total support.

(2) It will also be treated as publicly supported if the support it normally receives from governmental or public sources equals at least 10% of total support and the organization is set up to attract new and additional public or governmental support on a continuous basis.

If the organization's governmental and public support is at least 10%, but not over one-third of its total support, the questions on lines 1 through 14 of Part II will apply to determine both the organization's claim of exemption and whether it is publicly supported. Preparers should exercise care to assure that those questions are answered in detail.

Box (i). Organization described in section 509(a)(2).—The organization must satisfy the support test under section 509(a)(2)(A) and the gross investment income test under section 509(a)(2)(B).

To satisfy the support test, the organization must normally receive more than one-third of its support from: **(a)** gifts, grants, contributions, or membership fees, and **(b)** gross receipts from admissions, sales of merchandise, performance of services, or furnishing of facilities, in an activity that is not an unrelated trade or business (subject to certain limitations discussed below).

This one-third of support must be from organizations described in section 509(a)(1), governmental sources, or persons other than disqualified persons.

In computing gross receipts from admissions, sales of merchandise, performance of services, or furnishing of facilities in an activity that is not an unrelated trade or business, the gross receipts from any one person or from any bureau or similar agency of a governmental unit are includible only to the extent they do not exceed the greater of $5,000 or 1% of the organization's total support.

To satisfy the gross investment income test, the organization must not receive more than one-third of its support from gross investment income.

Box (j).—If you believe the organization meets the public support test of section 170(b)(1)(A)(vi) or 509(a)(2) but are uncertain as to which public support test it satisfies, check box **(j).** By checking this box, you are claiming that the organization is not a private foundation and are agreeing to let the IRS compute the public support of your organization and determine the correct foundation status.

Line 10.—An organization must complete a tax year consisting of at least 8 months to receive a definitive (final) ruling under sections 170(b)(1)(A)(vi) and 509(a)(1), or under section 509(a)(2).

However, organizations that checked box **(h), (i),** or **(j)** on line 9 that do not meet the 8-month requirement must request an advance ruling that covers their first 5 tax years instead of requesting a definitive ruling.

An organization that meets the 8-month requirement has two options:

1. It may request a definitive ruling. The organization's public support computation will be based on the support the organization has received to date; or

2. It may request an advance ruling. The organization's public support computation will be based on the support it receives during its first 5 tax years.

An organization should consider the advance ruling option if it has not received significant public support during its first tax year or during its first and second tax years, but it reasonably expects to receive such support by the end of its fifth tax year.

An organization that receives an advance ruling is treated, during the 5-year advance ruling period, as a public charity (rather than a private foundation) for certain purposes, including those relating to the deductibility of contributions by the general public.

Line 11.—For definition of an unusual grant, see instructions for Part IV-A, line 12.

Line 12.—Answer this question only if you checked box **(g), (h),** or **(j)** on line 9.

Line 13.—Answer the question on this line only if you checked box **(i)** or **(j)** on line 9 and are requesting a definitive ruling on line 10.

Line 14.—Answer "Yes" or "No" on each line. If "Yes," you must complete the appropriate schedule. Each schedule is included in this application package with accompanying instructions. For a brief definition of each type of organization, see the appropriate schedule.

Part IV. Financial Data

Complete the Statement of Revenue and Expenses for the current year and each of the 3 years immediately before it (or the years the organization has existed, if less than 4).

Any applicant that has existed for less than 1 year must give financial data for the current year and proposed budgets for the following 2 years.

The IRS may request financial data for more than 4 years if necessary.

All financial information for the current year must cover the period beginning on the first day of the organization's established annual accounting period and ending on any day that is within 60 days of the date of this application.

If the date of this application is less than 60 days after the first day of the current accounting period, no financial information is required for the current year.

Financial information is required for the 3 preceding years regardless of the current year requirements. Please note that if no financial information is required for the current year, the preceding year's financial information can end on any day that is within 60 days of the date of this application.

Prepare the statements using the method of accounting and the accounting period (entered on line 4 of Part I) the organization uses in keeping its books and records. If the organization uses a method other than the cash receipts and disbursements method, attach a statement explaining the method used.

A. Statement of Revenue and Expenses

Line 1.—Do not include amounts received from the general public or a governmental unit for the exercise or performance of the organization's exempt function. However, include payments made by a governmental unit to enable the organization to provide a service to the general public.

Do not include unusual grants. See the explanation for unusual grants in Line 12 of this section.

Line 2.—Include amounts received from members for the purpose of providing support to the organization. These are considered as contributions. Do not include payments to purchase admissions, merchandise, services, or use of facilities.

Line 3.—Include on this line the income received from dividends, interest, and payments received on securities loans, rents, and royalties.

Line 4.—Enter the organization's net income from any activities that are regularly carried on and are not related to the organization's exempt purposes.

Examples of such income include fees from the commercial testing of products; income from renting office equipment or other personal property; and income from the sale of advertising in an exempt organization's periodical. See Pub. 598 for information about unrelated business income and activities.

Line 5.—Enter the amount collected by the local tax authority from the general public that has been allocated for your organization.

Line 6.—To report the value of services and/or facilities furnished by a governmental unit, use the fair market value at the time the service/facility was furnished to your organization. Do not include any other donated services or facilities in Part IV.

Line 7.—Enter the total income from all sources that is not reported on lines 1 through 6, or lines 9, 11, and 12. Attach a schedule that lists each type of revenue source and the amount derived from each.

Line 9.—Include income generated by the organization's exempt function activities (charitable, educational, etc.) and its nontaxable fundraising events (excluding any contributions received).

Examples of such income include the income derived by a symphony orchestra from the sale of tickets to its performances; and raffles, bingo, or other fundraising-event income that is not taxable as unrelated business income because the income-producing activities are not regularly carried on or because they are conducted with substantially all (at least 85%) volunteer labor. Record related cost of sales on line 22, Other.

Line 11.—Attach a schedule that shows a description of each asset, the name of the person to whom sold, and the amount received. In the case of publicly traded securities sold through a broker, the name of the purchaser is not required.

Line 12.—Unusual grants generally consist of substantial contributions and bequests from disinterested persons that:

1. Are attracted by reason of the publicly supported nature of the organization;

2. Are unusual and unexpected as to the amount; and

3. Would, by reason of their size, adversely affect the status of the organization as normally meeting the support test of section 170(b)(1)(A)(vi) or section 509(a)(2), as the case may be.

If the organization is awarded an unusual grant and the terms of the granting instrument provide that the organization will receive the funds over a period of years, the amount received by the organization each year under the grant may be excluded. See the regulations under sections 170 and 509.

Line 14.—Fundraising expenses represent the total expenses incurred in soliciting contributions, gifts, grants, etc.

Line 15.—Attach a schedule showing the name of the recipient, a brief description of the purposes or conditions of payment, and the amount paid. The following example shows the format and amount of detail required for this schedule:

Recipient	Purpose	Amount
Museum of Natural History	General operating budget	$29,000
State University	Books for needy students	14,500
Richard Roe	Educational scholarship	12,200

Colleges, universities, and other educational institutions and agencies subject to the Family Educational Rights and Privacy Act (20 U.S.C. 1232g) are not required to list the names of individuals who were provided scholarships or other financial assistance where such disclosure would violate the privacy provisions of the law. Instead, such organizations should group each type of financial aid provided, indicate the number of individuals who received the aid, and specify the aggregate dollar amount.

Line 16.—Attach a schedule showing the name of each recipient, a brief description of the purposes or condition of payment, and amount paid. Do not include any amounts that are on line 15. The schedule should be similar to the schedule shown in the line 15 instructions above.

Line 17.—Attach a schedule that shows the name of the person compensated; the office or position; the average amount of time devoted to the organization's affairs per week, month, etc.; and the amount of annual compensation. The following example shows the format and amount of detail required:

Name	Position	Time devoted	Annual salary
Philip Poe	President and general manager	16 hrs. per wk.	$27,500

Line 18.—Enter the total of employees' salaries not reported on line 17.

Line 19.—Enter the total interest expense for the year, excluding mortgage interest treated as if an occupancy expense on line 20.

Line 20.—Enter the amount paid for the use of office space or other facilities, heat, light, power, and other utilities, outside janitorial services, mortgage interest, real estate taxes, and similar expenses.

Line 21.—If your organization records depreciation, depletion, and similar expenses, enter the total.

Line 22.—Attach a schedule listing the type and amount of each **significant** expense for which a separate line is not provided. Report other miscellaneous expenses as a single total if not substantial in amount.

B. Balance Sheet

Line 1.—Enter the total cash in checking and savings accounts, temporary cash investments (money market funds, CDs, treasury bills, or other obligations that mature in less than 1 year), change funds, and petty cash funds.

Line 2.—Enter the total accounts receivable that arose from the sale of goods and/or performance of services, less any reserve for bad debt.

Line 3.—Enter the amount of materials, goods, and supplies purchased or manufactured by the organization and held to be sold or used in some future period.

Line 4.—Attach a schedule that shows the name of the borrower, a brief description of the obligation, the rate of return on the principal indebtedness, the due date, and the amount due. The following example shows the format and amount of detail required:

Name of borrower	Description of obligation	Rate of return	Due date	Amount
Hope Soap Corporation	Debenture bond (no senior issue outstanding)	8%	Jan. 2004	$37,500
Big Spool Company	Collateral note secured by company's fleet of 20 delivery trucks	10%	Jan. 2003	262,000

Line 5.—Attach a schedule listing the organization's corporate stock holdings.

For stock of closely held corporations, the statement should show the name of the corporation, a brief summary of the corporation's capital structure, and the number of shares held and their value as carried on the organization's books. If such valuation does not reflect current fair market value, also include fair market value.

For stock traded on an organized exchange or in substantial quantities over the counter, the statement should show the name of the corporation, a description of the stock and the principal exchange on which it is traded, the number of shares held, and their value as carried on the organization's books.

The following example shows the format and the amount of detail required:

Name of corporation	Capital structure (or exchange on which traded)	Shares	Book amount	Fair market value
Little Spool Corporation	100 shares nonvoting preferred issued and outstanding, no par value; 50 shares common issued and outstanding, no par value.			
	Preferred shares:	50	$20,000	$24,000
	Common shares:	10	25,000	30,000
Flintlock Corporation	Class A common N.Y.S.E.	80	6,000	6,500

Line 6.—Report each loan separately, even if more than one loan was made to the same person. Attach a schedule that shows the borrower's name, purpose of loan, repayment terms, interest rate, and original amount of loan.

Line 7.—Enter the book value of government securities held (U.S., state, or municipal). Also enter the book value of buildings and equipment held for investment purposes. Attach a schedule identifying and reporting the book value of each.

Line 8.—Enter the book value of buildings and equipment **not** held for investment. This includes plant and equipment used by the organization in conducting its exempt activities. Attach a schedule listing these assets held at the end of the current tax year/period and the cost or other basis.

Line 9.—Enter the book value of land **not** held for investment.

Line 10.—Enter the book value of each category of assets not reported on lines 1 through 9. Attach a schedule listing each.

Line 12.—Enter the total of accounts payable to suppliers and others, such as salaries payable, accrued payroll taxes, and interest payable.

Line 13.—Enter the unpaid portion of grants and contributions that the organization has made a commitment to pay to other organizations or individuals.

Line 14.—Enter the total of mortgages and other notes payable outstanding at the end of the current tax year/period. Attach a schedule that shows each item separately and the lender's name, purpose of loan, repayment terms, interest rate, and original amount.

Line 15.—Enter the amount of each liability not reported on lines 12 through 14. Attach a separate schedule.

Line 17.—Under fund accounting, an organization segregates its assets, liabilities, and net assets into separate funds according to restrictions on the use of certain assets. Each fund is like a separate entity in that it has a self-balancing set of accounts showing assets, liabilities, equity (fund balance), income, and expenses. If the organization does not use fund accounting, report only the "net assets" account balances, such as: capital stock, paid-in capital, and retained earnings or accumulated income.

Procedural Checklist

Make sure the application is complete.

If you do not complete all applicable parts or do not provide all required attachments, we may return the incomplete application to your organization for resubmission with the missing information or attachments. This will delay the processing of the application and may delay the effective date of your organization's exempt status. The organization may also incur additional user fees.

Have you . . .

_____ Attached **Form 8718** (User Fee for Exempt Organization Determination Letter Request) and the appropriate fee?

_____ Prepared the application for mailing? (See **Where To File** addresses on Form 8718.) Do **not** file the application with your local Internal Revenue Service Center.

_____ Completed Parts I through IV and any other schedules that apply to the organization?

_____ Shown the organization's **Employer Identification Number (EIN)?**

    a. If your organization has an EIN, write it in the space provided.

    b. If this is a newly formed organization and does not have an Employer Identification Number, obtain an EIN by telephone. (See Specific Instructions, Part I, Line 2, on page 3.)

_____ Described your organization's **specific activities** as directed in Part II, line 1, of the application?

_____ Included a **conformed copy** of the complete organizing instrument? (See Specific Instructions, Part I, Line 10, on page 3.)

_____ Had the application signed by one of the following?

    a. An officer or trustee who is authorized to sign (e.g., president, treasurer); **or**

    b. A person authorized by a power of attorney (Submit Form 2848, or other power of attorney.)

_____ Enclosed **financial statements** (Part IV)?

    a. Current year (must include period up to within 60 days of the date the application is filed) and 3 preceding years.

    b. Detailed breakdown of revenue and expenses (no lump sums).

    c. If the organization has been in existence less than 1 year, you must also submit proposed budgets for 2 years showing the amounts and types of receipts and expenditures anticipated.

Note: _During the technical review of a completed application, it may be necessary to contact the organization for more specific or additional information._

Do not send this checklist with the application.

Form **1023**
(Rev. September 1998)
Department of the Treasury
Internal Revenue Service

Application for Recognition of Exemption
Under Section 501(c)(3) of the Internal Revenue Code

OMB No. 1545-0056

Note: *If exempt status is approved, this application will be open for public inspection.*

Read the instructions for each Part carefully.
A User Fee must be attached to this application.
If the required information and appropriate documents are not submitted along with Form 8718 (with payment of the appropriate user fee), the application may be returned to you.
Complete the Procedural Checklist on page 8 of the instructions.

Part I   **Identification of Applicant**

1a Full name of organization (as shown in organizing document)

2 Employer identification number (EIN)
(If none, see page 3 of the **Specific Instructions.**)

1b c/o Name (if applicable)

3 Name and telephone number of person to be contacted if additional information is needed

1c Address (number and street)   Room/Suite

(   )

1d City, town, or post office, state, and ZIP + 4. If you have a foreign address, see **Specific Instructions** for Part I, page 3.

4 Month the annual accounting period ends

5 Date incorporated or formed

1e Web site address

6 Check here if applying under section:
a ☐ 501(e) **b** ☐ 501(f) **c** ☐ 501(k) **d** ☐ 501(n)

7 Did the organization previously apply for recognition of exemption under this Code section or under any other section of the Code? . . . . ☐ **Yes** ☐ **No**
If "Yes," attach an explanation.

8 Is the organization required to file Form 990 (or Form 990-EZ)? . . . . ☐ **N/A** ☐ **Yes** ☐ **No**
If "No," attach an explanation (see page 3 of the **Specific Instructions**).

9 Has the organization filed Federal income tax returns or exempt organization information returns? . . ☐ **Yes** ☐ **No**
If "Yes," state the form numbers, years filed, and Internal Revenue office where filed.

10 Check the box for the type of organization. ATTACH A CONFORMED COPY OF THE CORRESPONDING ORGANIZING DOCUMENTS TO THE APPLICATION BEFORE MAILING. (See **Specific Instructions** for Part I, Line 10, on page 3.) See also Pub. 557 for examples of organizational documents.)

a ☐ Corporation—Attach a copy of the Articles of Incorporation (including amendments and restatements) showing approval by the appropriate state official; also include a copy of the bylaws.

b ☐ Trust—   Attach a copy of the Trust Indenture or Agreement, including all appropriate signatures and dates.

c ☐ Association— Attach a copy of the Articles of Association, Constitution, or other creating document, with a declaration (see instructions) or other evidence the organization was formed by adoption of the document by more than one person; also include a copy of the bylaws.

If the organization is a corporation or an unincorporated association that has not yet adopted bylaws, check here ▶ ☐

I declare under the penalties of perjury that I am authorized to sign this application on behalf of the above organization and that I have examined this application, including the accompanying schedules and attachments, and to the best of my knowledge it is true, correct, and complete.

Please Sign Here ▶

_____   _____   _____
(Signature)   (Type or print name and title or authority of signer)   (Date)

For Paperwork Reduction Act Notice, see page 7 of the instructions.   Cat. No. 17133K

Part II   Activities and Operational Information

1 Provide a detailed narrative description of all the activities of the organization—past, present, and planned. **Do not merely refer to or repeat the language in the organizational document.** List each activity separately in the order of importance based on the relative time and other resources devoted to the activity. Indicate the percentage of time for each activity. Each description should include, as a minimum, the following: **(a)** a detailed description of the activity including its purpose and how each acitivity furthers your exempt purpose; **(b)** when the activity was or will be initiated; and **(c)** where and by whom the activity will be conducted.

2 What are or will be the organization's sources of financial support? List in order of size.

3 Describe the organization's fundraising program, both actual and planned, and explain to what extent it has been put into effect. Include details of fundraising activities such as selective mailings, formation of fundraising committees, use of volunteers or professional fundraisers, etc. Attach representative copies of solicitations for financial support.

Part II Activities and Operational Information *(Continued)*

4 Give the following information about the organization's governing body:

a Names, addresses, and titles of officers, directors, trustees, etc.	**b** Annual compensation

c Do any of the above persons serve as members of the governing body by reason of being public officials or being appointed by public officials? . . . . ☐ **Yes** ☐ **No**
If "Yes," name those persons and explain the basis of their selection or appointment.

d Are any members of the organization's governing body "disqualified persons" with respect to the organization (other than by reason of being a member of the governing body) or do any of the members have either a business or family relationship with "disqualified persons"? (See **Specific Instructions** for Part II, Line 4d, on page 3.) . . . . ☐ **Yes** ☐ **No**
If "Yes," explain.

5 Does the organization control or is it controlled by any other organization? . . . . ☐ **Yes** ☐ **No**
Is the organization the outgrowth of (or successor to) another organization, or does it have a special relationship with another organization by reason of interlocking directorates or other factors? . . . . ☐ **Yes** ☐ **No**
If either of these questions is answered "Yes," explain.

6 Does or will the organization directly or indirectly engage in any of the following transactions with any political organization or other exempt organization (other than a 501(c)(3) organization): **(a)** grants; **(b)** purchases or sales of assets; **(c)** rental of facilities or equipment; **(d)** loans or loan guarantees; **(e)** reimbursement arrangements; **(f)** performance of services, membership, or fundraising solicitations; or **(g)** sharing of facilities, equipment, mailing lists or other assets, or paid employees? . . . . ☐ **Yes** ☐ **No**
If "Yes," explain fully and identify the other organizations involved.

7 Is the organization financially accountable to any other organization? . . . . ☐ **Yes** ☐ **No**
If "Yes," explain and identify the other organization. Include details concerning accountability or attach copies of reports if any have been submitted.

Part II   **Activities and Operational Information** (Continued)

8   What assets does the organization have that are used in the performance of its exempt function? (Do not include property producing investment income.) If any assets are not fully operational, explain their status, what additional steps remain to be completed, and when such final steps will be taken. If none, indicate "N/A."

---

9   Will the organization be the beneficiary of tax-exempt bond financing within the next 2 years?. . . . ☐ **Yes** ☐ **No**

10a Will any of the organization's facilities or operations be managed by another organization or individual under a contractual agreement?. . . . . ☐ **Yes** ☐ **No**

  b Is the organization a party to any leases? . . . . ☐ **Yes** ☐ **No**
      If either of these questions is answered "Yes," attach a copy of the contracts and explain the relationship between the applicant and the other parties.

---

11 Is the organization a membership organization? . . . . ☐ **Yes** ☐ **No**
      If "Yes," complete the following:
  a Describe the organization's membership requirements and attach a schedule of membership fees and dues.

  b Describe the organization's present and proposed efforts to attract members and attach a copy of any descriptive literature or promotional material used for this purpose.

  c What benefits do (or will) the members receive in exchange for their payment of dues?

12a If the organization provides benefits, services, or products, are the recipients required, or will they be required, to pay for them? . . . . ☐ **N/A** ☐ **Yes** ☐ **No**
      If "Yes," explain how the charges are determined and attach a copy of the current fee schedule.

  b Does or will the organization limit its benefits, services, or products to specific individuals or classes of individuals? . . . . ☐ **N/A** ☐ **Yes** ☐ **No**
      If "Yes," explain how the recipients or beneficiaries are or will be selected.

---

13 Does or will the organization attempt to influence legislation?. . . . . ☐ **Yes** ☐ **No**
      If "Yes," explain. Also, give an estimate of the percentage of the organization's time and funds that it devotes or plans to devote to this activity.

---

14 Does or will the organization intervene in any way in political campaigns, including the publication or distribution of statements? . . . . ☐ **Yes** ☐ **No**
      If "Yes," explain fully.

Part III   Technical Requirements

1 Are you filing Form 1023 within 15 months from the end of the month in which your organization was
created or formed? . . . . ☐ **Yes** ☐ **No**
If you answer "Yes," do not answer questions on lines 2 through 6 below.

2 If one of the exceptions to the 15-month filing requirement shown below applies, check the appropriate box and proceed
to question 7.

Exceptions—You are not required to file an exemption application within 15 months if the organization:

☐ **a** Is a church, interchurch organization of local units of a church, a convention or association of churches, or an
integrated auxiliary of a church. See **Specific Instructions,** Line 2a, on page 4;

☐ **b** Is not a private foundation and normally has gross receipts of not more than $5,000 in each tax year; or

☐ **c** Is a subordinate organization covered by a group exemption letter, but only if the parent or supervisory organization
timely submitted a notice covering the subordinate.

3 If the organization does not meet any of the exceptions on line 2 above, are you filing Form 1023 within
27 months from the end of the month in which the organization was created or formed?. . . . . . ☐ **Yes** ☐ **No**

If "Yes," your organization qualifies under Regulation section 301.9100-2, for an automatic 12-month
extension of the 15-month filing requirement. Do not answer questions 4 through 6.

If "No," answer question 4.

4 If you answer "No" to question 3, does the organization wish to request an extension of time to apply
under the "reasonable action and good faith" and the "no prejudice to the interest of the government"
requirements of Regulations section 301.9100-3? . . . . ☐ **Yes** ☐ **No**

If "Yes," give the reasons for not filing this application within the 27-month period described in question 3.
See **Specific Instructions,** Part III, Line 4, before completing this item. Do not answer questions 5 and 6.

If "No," answer questions 5 and 6.

5 If you answer "No" to question 4, your organization's qualification as a section 501(c)(3) organization can
be recognized only from the date this application is filed. Therefore, do you want us to consider the
application as a request for recognition of exemption as a section 501(c)(3) organization from the date
the application is received and not retroactively to the date the organization was created or formed? . ☐ **Yes** ☐ **No**

6 If you answer "Yes" to question 5 above and wish to request recognition of section 501(c)(4) status for the period beginning
with the date the organization was formed and ending with the date the Form 1023 application was received (the effective
date of the organization's section 501(c)(3) status), check here ▶ ☐   and attach a completed page 1 of Form 1024 to this
application.

Part III   **Technical Requirements** (*Continued*)

7   Is the organization a private foundation?
- ☐ **Yes** (Answer question 8.)
- ☐ **No** (Answer question 9 and proceed as instructed.)

8   If you answer "Yes" to question 7, does the organization claim to be a private operating foundation?
- ☐ **Yes** (Complete Schedule E.)
- ☐ **No**

After answering question 8 on this line, go to line 14 on page 7.

9   If you answer "No" to question 7, indicate the public charity classification the organization is requesting by checking the box below that most appropriately applies:

THE ORGANIZATION IS NOT A PRIVATE FOUNDATION BECAUSE IT QUALIFIES:

a ☐	As a church or a convention or association of churches (CHURCHES MUST COMPLETE SCHEDULE A.)	Sections 509(a)(1) and 170(b)(1)(A)(i)
b ☐	As a school (MUST COMPLETE SCHEDULE B.)	Sections 509(a)(1) and 170(b)(1)(A)(ii)
c ☐	As a hospital or a cooperative hospital service organization, or a medical research organization operated in conjunction with a hospital (These organizations, except for hospital service organizations, MUST COMPLETE SCHEDULE C.)	Sections 509(a)(1) and 170(b)(1)(A)(iii)
d ☐	As a governmental unit described in section 170(c)(1).	Sections 509(a)(1) and 170(b)(1)(A)(v)
e ☐	As being operated solely for the benefit of, or in connection with, one or more of the organizations described in **a** through **d, g, h,** or **i** (MUST COMPLETE SCHEDULE D.)	Section 509(a)(3)
f ☐	As being organized and operated exclusively for testing for public safety.	Section 509(a)(4)
g ☐	As being operated for the benefit of a college or university that is owned or operated by a governmental unit.	Sections 509(a)(1) and 170(b)(1)(A)(iv)
h ☐	As receiving a substantial part of its support in the form of contributions from publicly supported organizations, from a governmental unit, or from the general public.	Sections 509(a)(1) and 170(b)(1)(A)(vi)
i ☐	As normally receiving not more than one-third of its support from gross investment income and more than one-third of its support from contributions, membership fees, and gross receipts from activities related to its exempt functions (subject to certain exceptions).	Section 509(a)(2)
j ☐	The organization is a publicly supported organization but is not sure whether it meets the public support test of **h** or **i.** The organization would like the IRS to decide the proper classification.	Sections 509(a)(1) and 170(b)(1)(A)(vi) or Section 509(a)(2)

If you checked one of the boxes a through f in question 9, go to question 14. If you checked box g in question 9, go to questions 11 and 12. If you checked box h, i, or j, in question 9, go to question 10.

Part III   **Technical Requirements** (*Continued*)

10   If you checked box **h, i,** or **j** in question 9, has the organization completed a tax year of at least 8 months?

☐ **Yes**—Indicate whether you are requesting:

☐ A definitive ruling. (Answer questions 11 through 14.)

☐ An advance ruling. (Answer questions 11 and 14 and attach two Forms 872-C completed and signed.)

☐ **No—You must request an advance ruling by completing and signing two Forms 872-C and attaching them to the Form 1023.**

11   If the organization received any unusual grants during any of the tax years shown in Part IV-A, **Statement of Revenue and Expenses,** attach a list for each year showing the name of the contributor; the date and the amount of the grant; and a brief description of the nature of the grant.

12   If you are requesting a definitive ruling under section 170(b)(1)(A)(iv) or (vi), check here ▶ ☐   and:

a Enter 2% of line 8, column (e), Total, of Part IV-A . . . . _____

b Attach a list showing the name and amount contributed by each person (other than a governmental unit or "publicly supported" organization) whose total gifts, grants, contributions, etc., were more than the amount entered on line **12a** above.

13   If you are requesting a definitive ruling under section 509(a)(2), check here ▶ ☐   and:

a For each of the years included on lines 1, 2, and 9 of Part IV-A, attach a list showing the name of and amount received from each "disqualified person." (For a definition of "disqualified person," see **Specific Instructions,** Part II, Line 4d, on page 3.)

b For each of the years included on line 9 of Part IV-A, attach a list showing the name of and amount received from each payer (other than a "disqualified person") whose payments to the organization were more than $5,000. For this purpose, "payer" includes, but is not limited to, any organization described in sections 170(b)(1)(A)(i) through (vi) and any governmental agency or bureau.

14 Indicate if your organization is one of the following. If so, complete the required schedule. (Submit only those schedules that apply to your organization. **Do not submit blank schedules.**)	Yes	No	If "Yes," complete Schedule:
Is the organization a church?			A
Is the organization, or any part of it, a school?			B
Is the organization, or any part of it, a hospital or medical research organization?			C
Is the organization a section 509(a)(3) supporting organization?			D
Is the organization a private operating foundation?			E
Is the organization, or any part of it, a home for the aged or handicapped?			F
Is the organization, or any part of it, a child care organization?			G
Does the organization provide or administer any scholarship benefits, student aid, etc.?			H
Has the organization taken over, or will it take over, the facilities of a "for profit" institution? . . .			I

Part IV Financial Data

Complete the financial statements for the current year and for each of the 3 years immediately before it. If in existence less than 4 years, complete the statements for each year in existence. **If in existence less than 1 year, also provide proposed budgets for the 2 years following the current year.**

A. Statement of Revenue and Expenses

		Current tax year	3 prior tax years or proposed budget for 2 years			(e) TOTAL
		(a) From .... to	**(b)**	**(c)**	**(d)**	
Revenue	**1** Gifts, grants, and contributions received (not including unusual grants—see page 6 of the instructions)					
	2 Membership fees received . .					
	3 Gross investment income (see instructions for definition) . .					
	4 Net income from organization's unrelated business activities not included on line 3					
	5 Tax revenues levied for and either paid to or spent on behalf of the organization					
	6 Value of services or facilities furnished by a governmental unit to the organization without charge (not including the value of services or facilities generally furnished the public without charge)					
	7 Other income (not including gain or loss from sale of capital assets) (attach schedule) . .					
	8 **Total** (add lines 1 through 7)					
	9 Gross receipts from admissions, sales of merchandise or services, or furnishing of facilities in any activity that is not an unrelated business within the meaning of section 513. Include related cost of sales on line 22					
	10 **Total** (add lines 8 and 9) . .					
	11 Gain or loss from sale of capital assets (attach schedule) . . .					
	12 Unusual grants					
	13 **Total** revenue (add lines 10 through 12)					
Expenses	**14** Fundraising expenses . . .					
	15 Contributions, gifts, grants, and similar amounts paid (attach schedule)					
	16 Disbursements to or for benefit of members (attach schedule) .					
	17 Compensation of officers, directors, and trustees (attach schedule)					
	18 Other salaries and wages . .					
	19 Interest					
	20 Occupancy (rent, utilities, etc.) .					
	21 Depreciation and depletion . .					
	22 Other (attach schedule) . . .					
	23 **Total** expenses (add lines 14 through 22)					
	24 Excess of revenue over expenses (line 13 minus line 23)					

Part IV	Financial Data *(Continued)*

B. Balance Sheet (at the end of the period shown)		Current tax year Date ....
Assets		
1 Cash	1	
2 Accounts receivable, net	2	
3 Inventories	3	
4 Bonds and notes receivable (attach schedule)	4	
5 Corporate stocks (attach schedule)	5	
6 Mortgage loans (attach schedule)	6	
7 Other investments (attach schedule)	7	
8 Depreciable and depletable assets (attach schedule)	8	
9 Land	9	
10 Other assets (attach schedule)	10	
11 **Total assets** (add lines 1 through 10)	11	
Liabilities		
12 Accounts payable	12	
13 Contributions, gifts, grants, etc., payable	13	
14 Mortgages and notes payable (attach schedule)	14	
15 Other liabilities (attach schedule)	15	
16 **Total liabilities** (add lines 12 through 15)	16	
Fund Balances or Net Assets		
17 Total fund balances or net assets	17	
18 **Total liabilities and fund balances or net assets** (add line 16 and line 17)	18	

If there has been any substantial change in any aspect of the organization's financial activities since the end of the period shown above, check the box and attach a detailed explanation . . . . ▶ ☐

Form **872-C**	**Consent Fixing Period of Limitation Upon Assessment of Tax Under Section 4940 of the Internal Revenue Code**	OMB No. 1545-0056
(Rev. September 1998) Department of the Treasury Internal Revenue Service	(See instructions on reverse side.)	**To be used with Form 1023. Submit in duplicate.**

Under section 6501(c)(4) of the Internal Revenue Code, and as part of a request filed with Form 1023 that the organization named below be treated as a publicly supported organization under section 170(b)(1)(A)(vi) or section 509(a)(2) during an advance ruling period,

----
(Exact legal name of organization as shown in organizing document)

(Number, street, city or town, state, and ZIP code)

and the

District Director of Internal Revenue, or Assistant Commissioner (Employee Plans and Exempt Organizations)

consent and agree that the period for assessing tax (imposed under section 4940 of the Code) for any of the 5 tax years in the advance ruling period will extend 8 years, 4 months, and 15 days beyond the end of the first tax year.

However, if a notice of deficiency in tax for any of these years is sent to the organization before the period expires, the time for making an assessment will be further extended by the number of days the assessment is prohibited, plus 60 days.

Ending date of first tax year --
(Month, day, and year)

Name of organization (as shown in organizing document)	Date
Officer or trustee having authority to sign	Type or print name and title
Signature ▶	

For IRS use only

District Director or Assistant Commissioner (Employee Plans and Exempt Organizations)	Date

By ▶

For Paperwork Reduction Act Notice, see page 7 of the Form 1023 Instructions.   Cat. No. 16905Q

You must complete Form 872-C and attach it to the Form 1023 if you checked box **h, i,** or **j** of Part III, question 9, and the organization has not completed a tax year of at least 8 months.

For example: If the organization incorporated May 15 and its year ends December 31, it has completed a tax year of only 7½ months. Therefore, Form 872-C must be submitted.

(a) Enter the name of the organization. This must be entered exactly as it appears in the organizing document. Do not use abbreviations unless the organizing document does.

(b) Enter the current address.

(c) Enter the ending date of the first tax year.

For example:

(1) If the organization was formed on June 15 and it has chosen December 31 as its year end, enter December 31, ...

(2) If the organization was formed June 15 and it has chosen June 30 as its year end, enter June 30, ... In this example, the organization's first tax year consists of only 15 days.

(d) The form must be signed by an authorized officer or trustee, generally the president or treasurer. The name and title of the person signing must be typed or printed in the space provided.

(e) Enter the date that the form was signed.

DO NOT MAKE ANY OTHER ENTRIES.

Schedule A. Churches

1   Provide a brief history of the development of the organization, including the reasons
       for its formation.

2   Does the organization have a written creed or statement of faith?. . . . ☐ **Yes**   ☐ **No**

       If "Yes," attach a copy.

3   Does the organization require prospective members to renounce other
       religious beliefs or their membership in other churches or religious orders
       to become members? . . . . ☐ **Yes**   ☐ **No**

4   Does the organization have a formal code of doctrine and discipline for
       its members? . . . . ☐ **Yes**   ☐ **No**

       If "Yes," describe.

5   Describe the form of worship and attach a schedule of worship services.

6   Are the services open to the public?. . . . . ☐ **Yes**   ☐ **No**

       If "Yes," describe how the organization publicizes its services and explain the criteria for
       admittance.

7   Explain how the organization attracts new members.

8   **(a)** How many active members are currently enrolled in the church?

       (b) What is the average attendance at the worship services?

9   In addition to worship services, what other religious services (such as baptisms, weddings,
       funerals, etc.) does the organization conduct?

Schedule A. Churches *(Continued)*

10 Does the organization have a school for the religious instruction of the young? . . . . ☐ **Yes** ☐ **No**

11 Were the current deacons, minister, and/or pastor formally ordained after a prescribed course of study? . . . . ☐ **Yes** ☐ **No**

12 Describe the organization's religious hierarchy or ecclesiastical government.

13 Does the organization have an established place of worship? . . . . . . ☐ **Yes** ☐ **No**

If "Yes," provide the name and address of the owner or lessor of the property and the address and a description of the facility.

If the organization has no regular place of worship, state where the services are held and how the site is selected.

14 Does (or will) the organization license or otherwise ordain ministers (or their equivalent) or issue church charters? . . . . ☐ **Yes** ☐ **No**

If "Yes," describe in detail the requirements and qualifications needed to be so licensed, ordained, or chartered.

15 Did the organization pay a fee for a church charter? . . . . ☐ **Yes** ☐ **No**

If "Yes," state the name and address of the organization to which the fee was paid, attach a copy of the charter, and describe the circumstances surrounding the chartering.

16 Show how many hours a week the minister/pastor and officers each devote to church work and the amount of compensation paid to each of them. If the minister or pastor is otherwise employed, indicate by whom employed, the nature of the employment, and the hours devoted to that employment.

Schedule A. Churches (Continued)

17 Will any funds or property of the organization be used by any officer, director, employee, minister, or pastor for his or her personal needs or convenience? ☐ **Yes**   ☐ **No**

If "Yes," describe the nature and circumstances of such use.

18 List any officers, directors, or trustees related by blood or marriage.

19 Give the name of anyone who has assigned income to the organization or made substantial contributions of money or other property. Specify the amounts involved.

Instructions

Although a church, its integrated auxiliaries, or a convention or association of churches is not required to file Form 1023 to be exempt from Federal income tax or to receive tax-deductible contributions, such an organization may find it advantageous to obtain recognition of exemption. In this event, you should submit information showing that your organization is a church, synagogue, association or convention of churches, religious order or religious organization that is an integral part of a church, and that it is carrying out the functions of a church.

In determining whether an admittedly religious organization is also a church, the IRS does not accept any and every assertion that such an organization is a church. Because beliefs and practices vary so widely, there is no single definition of the word "church" for tax purposes. The IRS considers the facts and circumstances of each organization applying for church status.

The IRS maintains two basic guidelines in determining that an organization meets the religious purposes test:

1. That the particular religious beliefs of the organization are truly and sincerely held, and

2. That the practices and rituals associated with the organization's religious beliefs or creed are not illegal or contrary to clearly defined public policy.

In order for the IRS to properly evaluate your organization's activities and religious purposes, it is important that all questions in Schedule A be answered.

The information submitted with Schedule A will be a determining factor in granting the "church" status requested by your organization. In completing the schedule, consider the following points:

1. The organization's activities in furtherance of its beliefs must be exclusively religious, and

2. An organization will not qualify for exemption if it has a substantial nonexempt purpose of serving the private interests of its founder or the founder's family.

Schedule B. Schools, Colleges, and Universities

1 Does, or will, the organization normally have: **(a)** a regularly scheduled curriculum, **(b)** a regular faculty of qualified teachers, **(c)** a regularly enrolled student body, and **(d)** facilities where its educational activities are regularly carried on? . . . . ☐ **Yes** ☐ **No**
If "No," do not complete the rest of Schedule B.

2 Is the organization an instrumentality of a state or political subdivision of a state? . . . . ☐ **Yes** ☐ **No**
If "Yes," document this in Part II and do not complete items 3 through 10 of Schedule B. (See instructions on the back of Schedule B.)

3 Does or will the organization (or any department or division within it) discriminate in any way on the basis of race with respect to:
a Admissions? . . . . ☐ **Yes** ☐ **No**
b Use of facilities or exercise of student privileges? . . . . ☐ **Yes** ☐ **No**
c Faculty or administrative staff? . . . . ☐ **Yes** ☐ **No**
d Scholarship or loan programs? . . . . ☐ **Yes** ☐ **No**
If "Yes" for any of the above, explain.

4 Does the organization include a statement in its charter, bylaws, or other governing instrument, or in a resolution of its governing body, that it has a racially nondiscriminatory policy as to students? . . . . ☐ **Yes** ☐ **No**

Attach whatever corporate resolutions or other official statements the organization has made on this subject.

5a Has the organization made its racially nondiscriminatory policies known in a manner that brings the policies to the attention of all segments of the general community that it serves? . . . . ☐ **Yes** ☐ **No**

If "Yes," describe how these policies have been publicized and how often relevant notices or announcements have been made. If no newspaper or broadcast media notices have been used, explain.

b If applicable, attach clippings of any relevant newspaper notices or advertising, or copies of tapes or scripts used for media broadcasts. Also attach copies of brochures and catalogs dealing with student admissions, programs, and scholarships, as well as representative copies of all written advertising used as a means of informing prospective students of the organization's programs.

6 Attach a numerical schedule showing the racial composition, as of the current academic year, and projected to the extent feasible for the next academic year, of: **(a)** the student body, and **(b)** the faculty and administrative staff.

7 Attach a list showing the amount of any scholarship and loan funds awarded to students enrolled and the racial composition of the students who have received the awards.

8a Attach a list of the organization's incorporators, founders, board members, and donors of land or buildings, whether individuals or organizations.

b State whether any of the organizations listed in **8a** have as an objective the maintenance of segregated public or private school education, and, if so, whether any of the individuals listed in **8a** are officers or active members of such organizations.

9a Enter the public school district and county in which the organization is located.

b Was the organization formed or substantially expanded at the time of public school desegregation in the above district or county? . . . . ☐ **Yes** ☐ **No**

10 Has the organization ever been determined by a state or Federal administrative agency or judicial body to be racially discriminatory? . . . . ☐ **Yes** ☐ **No**

If "Yes," attach a detailed explanation identifying the parties to the suit, the forum in which the case was heard, the cause of action, the holding in the case, and the citations (if any) for the case. Also describe in detail what changes in the organization's operation, if any, have occurred since then.

For more information, see back of Schedule B.

Instructions

A "school" is an organization that has the primary function of presenting formal instruction, normally maintains a regular faculty and curriculum, normally has a regularly enrolled student body, and has a place where its educational activities are carried on.

The term generally corresponds to the definition of an "educational organization" in section 170(b)(1)(A)(ii). Thus, the term includes primary, secondary, preparatory and high schools, and colleges and universities. The term does not include organizations engaged in both educational and noneducational activities unless the latter are merely incidental to the educational activities. A school for handicapped children is included within the term, but an organization merely providing handicapped children with custodial care is not.

For purposes of Schedule B, "Sunday schools" that are conducted by a church are not included in the term "schools," but separately organized schools (such as parochial schools, universities, and similar institutions) are included in the term.

A private school that otherwise meets the requirements of section 501(c)(3) as an educational institution will not qualify for exemption under section 501(a) unless it has a racially nondiscriminatory policy as to students.

This policy means that the school admits students of any race to all the rights, privileges, programs, and activities generally accorded or made available to students at that school and that the school does not discriminate on the basis of race in the administration of its educational policies, admissions policies, scholarship and loan programs, and athletic or other school-administered programs.

The IRS considers discrimination on the basis of race to include discrimination on the basis of color and national or ethnic origin. A policy of a school that favors racial minority groups in admissions, facilities, programs, and financial assistance will not constitute discrimination on the basis of race when the purpose and effect is to promote the establishment and maintenance of that school's racially nondiscriminatory policy as to students.

See Rev. Proc. 75-50, 1975-2 C.B. 587, for guidelines and recordkeeping requirements for determining whether private schools that are applying for recognition of exemption have racially nondiscriminatory policies as to students.

Line 2

An instrumentality of a state or political subdivision of a state may qualify under section 501(c)(3) if it is organized as a separate entity from the governmental unit that created it and if it otherwise meets the organizational and operational tests of section 501(c)(3). See Rev. Rul. 60-384, 1960-2 C.B. 172. Any such organization that is a school is not a private school and, therefore, is not subject to the provisions of Rev. Proc. 75-50.

Schools that incorrectly answer "Yes" to line 2 will be contacted to furnish the information called for by lines 3 through 10 in order to establish that they meet the requirements for exemption. To prevent delay in the processing of your application, be sure to answer line 2 correctly and complete lines 3 through 10, if applicable.

Schedule C. Hospitals and Medical Research Organizations

☐ Check here if claiming to be a hospital; complete the questions in Section I of this schedule; and write "N/A" in Section II.
☐ Check here if claiming to be a medical research organization operated in conjunction with a hospital; complete the questions in Section II of this schedule; and write "N/A" in Section I.

Section I   Hospitals

1a How many doctors are on the hospital's courtesy staff?. . . . . **1a** _____

  b Are all the doctors in the community eligible for staff privileges? . . . . ☐ **Yes** ☐ **No**
    If "No," give the reasons why and explain how the courtesy staff is selected.

2a Does the hospital maintain a full-time emergency room?. . . . . ☐ **Yes** ☐ **No**
  b What is the hospital's policy on administering emergency services to persons without apparent means to pay?

  c Does the hospital have any arrangements with police, fire, and voluntary ambulance services for the delivery or admission of emergency cases? . . . . ☐ **Yes** ☐ **No**
    Explain.

3a Does or will the hospital require a deposit from persons covered by Medicare or Medicaid in its admission practices? . . . . ☐ **Yes** ☐ **No**
    If "Yes," explain.

  b Does the same deposit requirement, if any, apply to all other patients?. . . . . ☐ **Yes** ☐ **No**
    If "No," explain.

4 Does or will the hospital provide for a portion of its services and facilities to be used for charity patients? ☐ **Yes** ☐ **No**
Explain the policy regarding charity cases. Include data on the hospital's past experience in admitting charity patients and arrangements it may have with municipal or government agencies for absorbing the cost of such care.

5 Does or will the hospital carry on a formal program of medical training and research?. . . . . . . ☐ **Yes** ☐ **No**
If "Yes," describe.

6 Does the hospital provide office space to physicians carrying on a medical practice? . . . . ☐ **Yes** ☐ **No**
If "Yes," attach a list setting forth the name of each physician, the amount of space provided, the annual rent, the expiration date of the current lease and whether the terms of the lease represent fair market value.

Section II   Medical Research Organizations

1 Name the hospitals with which the organization has a relationship and describe the relationship.

2 Attach a schedule describing the organization's present and proposed (indicate which) medical research activities; show the nature of the activities, and the amount of money that has been or will be spent in carrying them out. (Making grants to other organizations is not direct conduct of medical research.)

3 Attach a statement of assets showing their fair market value and the portion of the assets directly devoted to medical research.

For more information, see back of Schedule C.

Additional Information

Hospitals

To be entitled to status as a "hospital," an organization must have, as its principal purpose or function, the providing of medical or hospital care or medical education or research. "Medical care" includes the treatment of any physical or mental disability or condition, the cost of which may be taken as a deduction under section 213, whether the treatment is performed on an inpatient or outpatient basis. Thus, a rehabilitation institution, outpatient clinic, or community mental health or drug treatment center may be a hospital if its principal function is providing the above-described services.

On the other hand, a convalescent home or a home for children or the aged is not a hospital. Similarly, an institution whose principal purpose or function is to train handicapped individuals to pursue some vocation is not a hospital. Moreover, a medical education or medical research institution is not a hospital, unless it is also actively engaged in providing medical or hospital care to patients on its premises or in its facilities on an inpatient or outpatient basis.

Cooperative Hospital Service Organizations

Cooperative hospital service organizations (section 501(e)) should not complete Schedule C.

Medical Research Organizations

To qualify as a medical research organization, the principal function of the organization must be the direct, continuous, and active conduct of medical research in conjunction with a hospital that is described in section 501(c)(3), a Federal hospital, or an instrumentality of a governmental unit referred to in section 170(c)(1).

For purposes of section 170(b)(1)(A)(iii) only, the organization must be set up to use the funds it receives in the active conduct of medical research by January 1 of the fifth calendar year after receipt. The arrangement it has with donors to assure use of the funds within the 5-year period must be legally enforceable.

As used here, "medical research" means investigations, experiments, and studies to discover, develop, or verify knowledge relating to the causes, diagnosis, treatment, prevention, or control of human physical or mental diseases and impairments.

For further information, see Regulations section 1.170A-9(c)(2).

Schedule D. Section 509(a)(3) Supporting Organizations

1a Organizations supported by the applicant organization: Name and address of supported organization	**b** Has the supported organization received a ruling or determination letter that it is not a private foundation by reason of section 509(a)(1) or (2)?	
--	☐ Yes	☐ No
--	☐ Yes	☐ No
--	☐ Yes	☐ No
--	☐ Yes	☐ No
--	☐ Yes	☐ No

c If "No" for any of the organizations listed in **1a,** explain.

2 Does the supported organization have tax-exempt status under section 501(c)(4), 501(c)(5), or 501(c)(6)? ☐ Yes ☐ No
If "Yes," attach: **(a)** a copy of its ruling or determination letter, and **(b)** an analysis of its revenue for the current year and the preceding 3 years. (Provide the financial data using the formats in Part IV-A (lines 1–13) and Part III (lines 11, 12, and 13).)

3 Does your organization's governing document indicate that the majority of its governing board is elected or appointed by the supported organizations? . . . . ☐ Yes ☐ No
If "Yes," skip to line 9.
If "No," you must answer the questions on lines 4 through 9.

4 Does your organization's governing document indicate the common supervision or control that it and the supported organizations share? . . . . ☐ Yes ☐ No
If "Yes," give the article and paragraph numbers. If "No," explain.

5 To what extent do the supported organizations have a significant voice in your organization's investment policies, in the making and timing of grants, and in otherwise directing the use of your organization's income or assets?

6 Does the mentioning of the supported organizations in your organization's governing instrument make it a trust that the supported organizations can enforce under state law and compel to make an accounting? ☐ Yes ☐ No
If "Yes," explain.

7a What percentage of your organization's income does it pay to each supported organization?

b What is the total annual income of each supported organization?

c How much does your organization contribute annually to each supported organization?

For more information, see back of Schedule D.

Schedule D. Section 509(a)(3) Supporting Organizations *(Continued)*

8 To what extent does your organization conduct activities that would otherwise be carried on by the supported organizations? Explain why these activities would otherwise be carried on by the supported organizations.

9 Is the applicant organization controlled directly or indirectly by one or more "disqualified persons" (other than one who is a disqualified person solely because he or she is a manager) or by an organization that is not described in section 509(a)(1) or (2)? . . . . ☐ **Yes** ☐ **No**
If "Yes," explain.

Instructions

For an explanation of the types of organizations defined in section 509(a)(3) as being excluded from the definition of a private foundation, see Pub. 557, Chapter 3.

Line 1

List each organization that is supported by your organization and indicate in item **1b** if the supported organization has received a letter recognizing exempt status as a section 501(c)(3) public charity as defined in section 509(a)(1) or 509(a)(2). If you answer "No" in **1b** to any of the listed organizations, please explain in **1c.**

Line 3

Your organization's governing document may be articles of incorporation, articles of association, constitution, trust indenture, or trust agreement.

Line 9

For a definition of a "disqualified person," see **Specific Instructions,** Part II, Line 4d, on page 3 of the application's instructions.

Schedule E. Private Operating Foundations

		Most recent tax year
Income Test		
1a Adjusted net income, as defined in Regulations section 53.4942(a)-2(d)	**1a**	
b Minimum investment return, as defined in Regulations section 53.4942(a)-2(c)	**1b**	
2 Qualifying distributions:		
a Amounts (including administrative expenses) paid directly for the active conduct of the activities for which organized and operated under section 501(c)(3) (attach schedule)	**2a**	
b Amounts paid to acquire assets to be used (or held for use) directly in carrying out purposes described in section 170(c)(1) or 170(c)(2)(B) (attach schedule)	**2b**	
c Amounts set aside for specific projects that are for purposes described in section 170(c)(1) or 170(c)(2)(B) (attach schedule).	**2c**	
d **Total** qualifying distributions (add lines 2a, b, and c).	**2d**	
3 Percentages:		
a Percentage of qualifying distributions to adjusted net income (divide line 2d by line 1a)	**3a**	%
b Percentage of qualifying distributions to minimum investment return (divide line 2d by line 1b). . . (Percentage must be at least 85% for 3a or 3b)	**3b**	%
Assets Test		
4 Value of organization's assets used in activities that directly carry out the exempt purposes. Do not include assets held merely for investment or production of income (attach schedule)	**4**	
5 Value of any stock of a corporation that is controlled by applicant organization and carries out its exempt purposes (attach statement describing corporation)	**5**	
6 Value of all qualifying assets (add lines 4 and 5)	**6**	
7 Value of applicant organization's total assets	**7**	
8 Percentage of qualifying assets to total assets (divide line 6 by line 7—percentage must exceed 65%)	**8**	%
Endowment Test		
9 Value of assets not used (or held for use) directly in carrying out exempt purposes:		
a Monthly average of investment securities at fair market value.	**9a**	
b Monthly average of cash balances.	**9b**	
c Fair market value of all other investment property (attach schedule).	**9c**	
d **Total** (add lines 9a, b, and c).	**9d**	
10 Acquisition indebtedness related to line 9 items (attach schedule)	**10**	
11 Balance (subtract line 10 from line 9d)	**11**	
12 Multiply line 11 by 3⅓% (⅔ of the percentage for the minimum investment return computation under section 4942(e)). Line 2d above must equal or exceed the result of this computation	**12**	
Support Test		
13 Applicant organization's support as defined in section 509(d)	**13**	
14 Gross investment income as defined in section 509(e)	**14**	
15 Support for purposes of section 4942(j)(3)(B)(iii) (subtract line 14 from line 13)	**15**	
16 Support received from the general public, five or more exempt organizations, or a combination of these sources (attach schedule).	**16**	
17 For persons (other than exempt organizations) contributing more than 1% of line 15, enter the total amounts that are more than 1% of line 15	**17**	
18 Subtract line 17 from line 16.	**18**	
19 Percentage of total support (divide line 18 by line 15—must be at least 85%)	**19**	%

20 Does line 16 include support from an exempt organization that is more than 25% of the amount of line 15? . . . . ☐ **Yes** ☐ **No**

21 Newly created organizations with less than 1 year's experience: Attach a statement explaining how the organization is planning to satisfy the requirements of section 4942(j)(3) for the income test and one of the supplemental tests during its first year's operation. Include a description of plans and arrangements, press clippings, public announcements, solicitations for funds, etc.

22 Does the amount entered on line 2a above include any grants that the applicant organization made?   ☐ **Yes** ☐ **No**
If "Yes," attach a statement explaining how those grants satisfy the criteria for "significant involvement" grants described in section 53.4942(b)-1(b)(2) of the regulations.

For more information, see back of Schedule E.

Instructions

If the organization claims to be an operating foundation described in section 4942(j)(3) and—

a. Bases its claim to private operating foundation status on normal and regular operations over a period of years; or

b. Is newly created, set up as a private operating foundation, and has at least 1 year's experience;

provide the information under the **income test and under one of the three supplemental tests** (assets, endowment, or support). If the organization does not have at least 1 year's experience, provide the information called for on line 21. If the organization's private operating foundation status depends on its normal and regular operations as described in **a** above, attach a schedule similar to Schedule E showing the data in tabular form for the 3 years preceding the most recent tax year. (See Regulations section 53.4942(b)-1 for additional information before completing the "Income Test" section of this schedule.) Organizations claiming section 4942(j)(5) status must satisfy the income test and the endowment test.

A "private operating foundation" described in section 4942(j)(3) is a private foundation that spends substantially all of the smaller of its adjusted net income (as defined below) or its minimum investment return directly for the active conduct of the activities constituting the purpose or function for which it is organized and operated. The foundation must satisfy the income test under section 4942(j)(3)(A), as modified by Regulations section 53.4942(b)-1, and one of the following three supplemental tests: **(1)** the assets test under section 4942(j)(3)(B)(i); **(2)** the endowment test under section 4942(j)(3)(B)(ii); or **(3)** the support test under section 4942(j)(3)(B)(iii).

Certain long-term care facilities described in section 4942(j)(5) are treated as private operating foundations for purposes of section 4942 only.

"Adjusted net income" is the excess of gross income determined with the income modifications described below for the tax year over the sum of deductions determined with the deduction modifications described below. Items of gross income from any unrelated trade or business and the deductions directly connected with the unrelated trade or business are taken into account in computing the organization's adjusted net income.

Income Modifications

The following are income modifications (adjustments to gross income):

1. Section 103 (relating to interest on certain governmental obligations) does not apply. Thus, interest that otherwise would have been excluded should be included in gross income.

2. Except as provided in **3** below, capital gains and losses are taken into account only to the extent of the net short-term gain. Long-term gains and losses are disregarded.

3. The gross amount received from the sale or disposition of certain property should be included in gross income to the extent that the acquisition of the property constituted a qualifying distribution under section 4942(g)(1)(B).

4. Repayments of prior qualifying distributions (as defined in section 4942(g)(1)(A)) constitute items of gross income.

5. Any amount set aside under section 4942(g)(2) that is "not necessary for the purposes for which it was set aside" constitutes an item of gross income.

Deduction Modifications

The following are deduction modifications (adjustments to deductions):

1. Expenses for the general operation of the organization according to its charitable purposes (as contrasted with expenses for the production or collection of income and management, conservation, or maintenance of income-producing property) should not be taken as deductions. If only a portion of the property is used for production of income subject to section 4942 and the remainder is used for general charitable purposes, the expenses connected with that property should be divided according to those purposes. Only expenses related to the income-producing portion should be taken as deductions.

2. Charitable contributions, deductible under section 170 or 642(c), should not be taken into account as deductions for adjusted net income.

3. The net operating loss deduction prescribed under section 172 should not be taken into account as a deduction for adjusted net income.

4. The special deductions for corporations (such as the dividends-received deduction) allowed under sections 241 through 249 should not be taken into account as deductions for adjusted net income.

5. Depreciation and depletion should be determined in the same manner as under section 4940(c)(3)(B).

Section 265 (relating to the expenses and interest connected with tax-exempt income) should not be taken into account.

You may find it easier to figure adjusted net income by completing column (c), Part 1, Form 990-PF, according to the instructions for that form.

An organization that has been held to be a private operating foundation will continue to be such an organization only if it meets the income test and either the assets, endowment, or support test in later years. See Regulations section 53.4942(b) for additional information. No additional request for ruling will be necessary or appropriate for an organization to maintain its status as a private operating foundation. However, data related to the above tests must be submitted with the organization's annual information return, Form 990-PF.

Schedule F. Homes for the Aged or Handicapped

1 What are the requirements for admission to residency? Explain fully and attach promotional literature and application forms.

2 Does or will the home charge an entrance or founder's fee? . . . . ☐ **Yes** ☐ **No**
If "Yes," explain and specify the amount charged.

3 What periodic fees or maintenance charges are or will be required of its residents?

4a What established policy does the home have concerning residents who become unable to pay their regular charges?

b What arrangements does the home have or will it make with local and Federal welfare units, sponsoring organizations, or others to absorb all or part of the cost of maintaining those residents?

5 What arrangements does or will the home have to provide for the health needs of its residents?

6 In what way are the home's residential facilities designed to meet some combination of the physical, emotional, recreational, social, religious, and similar needs of the aged or handicapped?

7 Provide a description of the home's facilities and specify both the residential capacity of the home and the current number of residents.

8 Attach a sample copy of the contract or agreement the organization makes with or requires of its residents.

For more information, see back of Schedule F.

Instructions

Line 1

Provide the criteria for admission to the home and submit brochures, pamphlets, or other printed material used to inform the public about the home's admissions policy.

Line 2

Indicate whether the fee charged is an entrance fee or a monthly charge, etc. Also, if the fee is an entrance fee, is it payable in a lump sum or on an installment basis?

Line 4

Indicate the organization's policy regarding residents who are unable to pay. Also, indicate whether the organization is subsidized for all or part of the cost of maintaining those residents who are unable to pay.

Line 5

Indicate whether the organization provides health care to the residents, either directly or indirectly, through some continuing arrangement with other organizations, facilities, or health personnel. If no health care is provided, indicate "N/A."

Schedule G. Child Care Organizations

1 Is the organization's primary activity the providing of care for children away from their homes?. . . . . ☐ **Yes**   ☐ **No**

2 How many children is the organization authorized to care for by the state (or local governmental unit), and what was the average attendance during the past 6 months, or the number of months the organization has been in existence if less than 6 months?

3 How many children are currently cared for by the organization?

4 Is substantially all (at least 85%) of the care provided for the purpose of enabling parents to be gainfully employed or to seek employment? . . . ☐ **Yes**   ☐ **No**

5 Are the services provided available to the general public?. . . . . ☐ **Yes**   ☐ **No**
   If "No," explain.

6 Indicate the category, or categories, of parents whose children are eligible for the child care services (check as many as apply):

   ☐ low-income parents

   ☐ any working parents (or parents looking for work)

   ☐ anyone with the ability to pay

   ☐ other (explain)

Instructions

Line 5

If your organization's services are not available to the general public, indicate the particular group or groups that may utilize the services.

REMINDER—If this organization claims to operate a school, then it must also fill out Schedule B.

Schedule H. Organizations Providing Scholarship Benefits, Student Aid, etc., to Individuals

1a Describe the nature and the amount of the scholarship benefit, student aid, etc., including the terms and conditions governing its use, whether a gift or a loan, and how the availability of the scholarship is publicized. If the organization has established or will establish several categories of scholarship benefits, identify each kind of benefit and explain how the organization determines the recipients for each category. Attach a sample copy of any application the organization requires individuals to complete to be considered for scholarship grants, loans, or similar benefits. (Private foundations that make grants for travel, study, or other similar purposes are required to obtain advance approval of scholarship procedures. See Regulations sections 53.4945-4(c) and (d).)

b If you want this application considered as a request for approval of grant procedures in the event we determine that the organization is a private foundation, check here . . . . ▶ ☐

c If you checked the box in **1b** above, check the box(es) for which you wish the organization to be considered.

☐ 4945(g)(1)   ☐ 4945(g)(2)   ☐ 4945(g)(3)

2 What limitations or restrictions are there on the class of individuals who are eligible recipients? Specifically explain whether there are, or will be, any restrictions or limitations in the selection procedures based upon race or the employment status of the prospective recipient or any relative of the prospective recipient. Also indicate the approximate number of eligible individuals.

3 Indicate the number of grants the organization anticipates making annually . . . . ▶

4 If the organization bases its selections in any way on the employment status of the applicant or any relative of the applicant, indicate whether there is or has been any direct or indirect relationship between the members of the selection committee and the employer. Also indicate whether relatives of the members of the selection committee are possible recipients or have been recipients.

5 Describe any procedures the organization has for supervising grants (such as obtaining reports or transcripts) that it awards and any procedures it has for taking action if the terms of the grant are violated.

Additional Information

Private foundations that make grants to individuals for travel, study, or other similar purposes are required to obtain advance approval of their grant procedures from the IRS. Such grants that are awarded under selection procedures that have not been approved by the IRS are subject to a 10% excise tax under section 4945. (See Regulations sections 53.4945-4(c) and (d).)

If you are requesting advance approval of the organization's grant procedures, the following sections apply to line **1c:**

4945(g)(1)— The grant constitutes a scholarship or fellowship grant that meets the provisions of section 117(a) prior to its amendment by the Tax Reform Act of 1986 and is to be used for study at an educational organization (school) described in section 170(b)(1)(A)(ii).

4945(g)(2)— The grant constitutes a prize or award that is subject to the provisions of section 74(b), if the recipient of such a prize or award is selected from the general public.

4945(g)(3)— The purpose of the grant is to achieve a specific objective, produce a report or other similar product, or improve or enhance a literary, artistic, musical, scientific, teaching, or other similar capacity, skill, or talent of the grantee.

Schedule I. Successors to "For Profit" Institutions

1 What was the name of the predecessor organization and the nature of its activities?

2 Who were the owners or principal stockholders of the predecessor organization? (If more space is needed, attach schedule.)

Name and address	Share or interest

3 Describe the business or family relationship between the owners or principal stockholders and principal employees of the predecessor organization and the officers, directors, and principal employees of the applicant organization.

4a Attach a copy of the agreement of sale or other contract that sets forth the terms and conditions of sale of the predecessor organization or of its assets to the applicant organization.

b Attach an appraisal by an independent qualified expert showing the fair market value at the time of sale of the facilities or property interest sold.

5 Has any property or equipment formerly used by the predecessor organization been rented to the applicant organization or will any such property be rented? . . . . ☐ **Yes** ☐ **No**
If "Yes," explain and attach copies of all leases and contracts.

6 Is the organization leasing or will it lease or otherwise make available any space or equipment to the owners, principal stockholders, or principal employees of the predecessor organization? . . . . . ☐ **Yes** ☐ **No**
If "Yes," explain and attach a list of these tenants and a copy of the lease for each such tenant.

7 Were any new operating policies initiated as a result of the transfer of assets from a profit-making organization to a nonprofit organization? . . . . ☐ **Yes** ☐ **No**
If "Yes," explain.

Additional Information

A "for profit" institution for purposes of Schedule I includes any organization in which a person may have a proprietary or partnership interest, hold corporate stock, or otherwise exercise an ownership interest. The institution need not have operated for the purpose of making a profit.

Form 8718
(Rev. November 2003)
Department of the Treasury
Internal Revenue Service

User Fee for Exempt Organization Determination Letter Request

▶ Attach this form to determination letter application.
(Form 8718 is NOT a determination letter application.)

For
IRS
Use
Only

OMB No. 1545-1798

Control number _____

Amount paid _____

User fee screener

1 Name of organization	2 Employer Identification Number

Caution: *Do not attach Form 8718 to an application for a pension plan determination letter. Use Form 8717 instead.*

3   Type of request   **Fee**

a ☐   Initial request for a determination letter for:
- An exempt organization that has had annual gross receipts averaging not more than $10,000 during the preceding 4 years, or
- A new organization that anticipates gross receipts averaging not more than $10,000 during its first 4 years ▶ $150

Note: *If you checked box 3a, you must complete the Certification below.*

Certification

I certify that the annual gross receipts of ....
name of organization

have averaged (or are expected to average) not more than $10,000 during the preceding 4 (or the first 4) years of operation.

Signature ▶   Title ▶

b ☐   Initial request for a determination letter for:
- An exempt organization that has had annual gross receipts averaging more than $10,000 during the preceding 4 years or
- A new organization that anticipates gross receipts averaging more than $10,000 during its first 4 years   .   ▶ $500

c ☐   Group exemption letters   .   .   .   .   ▶ $500

Instructions

The law requires payment of a user fee with each application for a determination letter. The user fees are listed on line 3 above. For more information, see Rev. Proc. 2003-8, 2003-1, I.R.B. 236, or latest annual update.

Check the box or boxes on line 3 for the type of application you are submitting. If you check box 3a, you must complete and sign the certification statement that appears under line 3a.

Attach to Form 8718 a check or money order payable to the "United States Treasury" for the full amount of the user fee. If you do not include the full amount, your application will be returned. Attach Form 8718 to your determination letter application.

Generally, the user fee will be refunded only if the Internal Revenue Service declines to issue a determination.

Where To File

Send the determination letter application and Form 8718 to:

Internal Revenue Service
P.O. Box 192
Covington, KY 41012-0192

If you are using express mail or a delivery service, send the application and Form 8718 to:

Internal Revenue Service
201 West Rivercenter Blvd.
Attn: Extracting Stop 312
Covington, KY 41011

Paperwork Reduction Act Notice. We ask for the information on this form to carry out the Internal Revenue laws of the United States. If you want your organization to be recognized as tax-exempt by the IRS, you are required to give us this information. We need it to determine whether the organization meets the legal requirements for tax-exempt status.

You are not required to provide the information requested on a form that is subject to the Paperwork Reduction Act unless the form displays a valid OMB control number. Books or records relating to a form or its instructions must be retained as long as their contents may become material in the administration of any Internal Revenue law. The rules governing the confidentiality of Form 8718 are covered in Code section 6104.

The time needed to complete and file this form will vary depending on individual circumstances. The estimated average time is 5 minutes. If you have comments concerning the accuracy of this time estimate or suggestions for making this form simpler, we would be happy to hear from you. You can write to the Tax Products Coordinating Committee, Western Area Distribution Center, Rancho Cordova, CA 95743-0001. **Do not** send this form to this address. Instead, see **Where To File** above.

Attach Check or Money Order Here

Cat. No. 64728Z   Form **8718** (Rev. 11-2003)

Form **SS-4**	**Application for Employer Identification Number**	EIN	
(Rev. December 2001)	(For use by employers, corporations, partnerships, trusts, estates, churches, government agencies, Indian tribal entities, certain individuals, and others.)		
Department of the Treasury Internal Revenue Service	▶ See separate instructions for each line. ▶ Keep a copy for your records.	OMB No. 1545-0003	

Type or print clearly.

1 Legal name of entity (or individual) for whom the EIN is being requested

2 Trade name of business (if different from name on line 1)

3 Executor, trustee, "care of" name

4a Mailing address (room, apt., suite no. and street, or P.O. box)

5a Street address (if different) (Do not enter a P.O. box.)

4b City, state, and ZIP code

5b City, state, and ZIP code

6 County and state where principal business is located

7a Name of principal officer, general partner, grantor, owner, or trustor

7b SSN, ITIN, or EIN

8a Type of entity (check only one box)

- ☐ Sole proprietor (SSN) _____
- ☐ Partnership
- ☐ Corporation (enter form number to be filed) ▶ _____
- ☐ Personal service corp.
- ☐ Church or church-controlled organization
- ☐ Other nonprofit organization (specify) ▶ _____
- ☐ Other (specify) ▶

- ☐ Estate (SSN of decedent) _____
- ☐ Plan administrator (SSN) _____
- ☐ Trust (SSN of grantor) _____
- ☐ National Guard   ☐ State/local government
- ☐ Farmers' cooperative   ☐ Federal government/military
- ☐ REMIC   ☐ Indian tribal governments/enterprises
- Group Exemption Number (GEN) ▶ _____

8b If a corporation, name the state or foreign country (if applicable) where incorporated

State

Foreign country

9 **Reason for applying** (check only one box)

- ☐ Started new business (specify type) ▶ _____
- ☐ Hired employees (Check the box and see line 12.)
- ☐ Compliance with IRS withholding regulations
- ☐ Other (specify) ▶

- ☐ Banking purpose (specify purpose) ▶ _____
- ☐ Changed type of organization (specify new type) ▶ _____
- ☐ Purchased going business
- ☐ Created a trust (specify type) ▶ _____
- ☐ Created a pension plan (specify type) ▶ _____

10 Date business started or acquired (month, day, year)

11 Closing month of accounting year

12 First date wages or annuities were paid or will be paid (month, day, year). **Note:** If applicant is a withholding agent, enter date income will first be paid to nonresident alien. (month, day, year) . . . . ▶

13 Highest number of employees expected in the next 12 months. **Note:** If the applicant does not expect to have any employees during the period, enter "-0-." . . . . ▶

Agricultural	Household	Other

14 Check **one** box that best describes the principal activity of your business.

- ☐ Construction   ☐ Rental & leasing   ☐ Transportation & warehousing
- ☐ Real estate   ☐ Manufacturing   ☐ Finance & insurance
- ☐ Health care & social assistance   ☐ Wholesale–agent/broker
- ☐ Accommodation & food service   ☐ Wholesale–other   ☐ Retail
- ☐ Other (specify)

15 Indicate principal line of merchandise sold; specific construction work done; products produced; or services provided.

16a Has the applicant ever applied for an employer identification number for this or any other business? . . . . ☐ Yes ☐ No

Note: If "Yes," please complete lines 16b and 16c.

16b If you checked "Yes" on line 16a, give applicant's legal name and trade name shown on prior application if different from line 1 or 2 above.

Legal name ▶   Trade name ▶

16c Approximate date when, and city and state where, the application was filed. Enter previous employer identification number if known.

Approximate date when filed (mo., day, year)   City and state where filed   Previous EIN

Third Party Designee

Complete this section **only** if you want to authorize the named individual to receive the entity's EIN and answer questions about the completion of this form.

Designee's name   Designee's telephone number (include area code) ( )

Address and ZIP code   Designee's fax number (include area code) ( )

Under penalties of perjury, I declare that I have examined this application, and to the best of my knowledge and belief, it is true, correct, and complete.

Applicant's telephone number (include area code) ( )

Name and title (type or print clearly) ▶

Applicant's fax number (include area code) ( )

Signature ▶   Date ▶

For Privacy Act and Paperwork Reduction Act Notice, see separate instructions.   Cat. No. 16055N   Form **SS-4** (Rev. 12-2001)

Do I Need an EIN?

File Form SS-4 if the applicant entity does not already have an EIN but is required to show an EIN on any return, statement, or other document.[1] **See also the separate instructions for each line on Form SS-4.**

IF the applicant...	AND...	THEN...
Started a new business	Does not currently have (nor expect to have) employees	Complete lines 1, 2, 4a–6, 8a, and 9–16c.
Hired (or will hire) employees, including household employees	Does not already have an EIN	Complete lines 1, 2, 4a–6, 7a–b (if applicable), 8a, 8b (if applicable), and 9–16c.
Opened a bank account	Needs an EIN for banking purposes only	Complete lines 1–5b, 7a–b (if applicable), 8a, 9, and 16a–c.
Changed type of organization	Either the legal character of the organization or its ownership changed (e.g., you incorporate a sole proprietorship or form a partnership)[2]	Complete lines 1–16c (as applicable).
Purchased a going business[3]	Does not already have an EIN	Complete lines 1–16c (as applicable).
Created a trust	The trust is other than a grantor trust or an IRA trust[4]	Complete lines 1–16c (as applicable).
Created a pension plan as a plan administrator[5]	Needs an EIN for reporting purposes	Complete lines 1, 2, 4a–6, 8a, 9, and 16a–c.
Is a foreign person needing an EIN to comply with IRS withholding regulations	Needs an EIN to complete a Form W-8 (other than Form W-8ECI), avoid withholding on portfolio assets, or claim tax treaty benefits[6]	Complete lines 1–5b, 7a–b (SSN or ITIN optional), 8a–9, and 16a–c.
Is administering an estate	Needs an EIN to report estate income on Form 1041	Complete lines 1, 3, 4a–b, 8a, 9, and 16a–c.
Is a withholding agent for taxes on non-wage income paid to an alien (i.e., individual, corporation, or partnership, etc.)	Is an agent, broker, fiduciary, manager, tenant, or spouse who is required to file **Form 1042,** Annual Withholding Tax Return for U.S. Source Income of Foreign Persons	Complete lines 1, 2, 3 (if applicable), 4a–5b, 7a–b (if applicable), 8a, 9, and 16a–c.
Is a state or local agency	Serves as a tax reporting agent for public assistance recipients under Rev. Proc. 80-4, 1980-1 C.B. 581[7]	Complete lines 1, 2, 4a–5b, 8a, 9, and 16a–c.
Is a single-member LLC	Needs an EIN to file **Form 8832,** Classification Election, for filing employment tax returns, **or** for state reporting purposes[8]	Complete lines 1–16c (as applicable).
Is an S corporation	Needs an EIN to file **Form 2553,** Election by a Small Business Corporation[9]	Complete lines 1–16c (as applicable).

[1] For example, a sole proprietorship or self-employed farmer who establishes a qualified retirement plan, or is required to file excise, employment, alcohol, tobacco, or firearms returns, must have an EIN. **A partnership, corporation, REMIC (real estate mortgage investment conduit), nonprofit organization (church, club, etc.), or farmers' cooperative must use an EIN for any tax-related purpose even if the entity does not have employees.**

[2] However, **do not** apply for a new EIN if the existing entity only **(a)** changed its business name, **(b)** elected on Form 8832 to change the way it is taxed (or is covered by the default rules), or **(c)** terminated its partnership status because at least 50% of the total interests in partnership capital and profits were sold or exchanged within a 12-month period. (The EIN of the terminated partnership should continue to be used. See Regulations section 301.6109-1(d)(2)(iii).)

[3] Do not use the EIN of the prior business unless you became the "owner" of a corporation by acquiring its stock.

[4] However, IRA trusts that are required to file **Form 990-T,** Exempt Organization Business Income Tax Return, must have an EIN.

[5] A plan administrator is the person or group of persons specified as the administrator by the instrument under which the plan is operated.

[6] Entities applying to be a Qualified Intermediary (QI) need a QI-EIN even if they already have an EIN. **See Rev. Proc. 2000-12.**

[7] See also Household employer on page 4. (**Note:** State or local agencies may need an EIN for other reasons, e.g., hired employees.)

[8] Most LLCs **do not** need to file Form 8832. See **Limited liability company (LLC)** on page 4 for details on completing Form SS-4 for an LLC.

[9] An existing corporation that is electing or revoking S corporation status should use its previously-assigned EIN.

Instructions for Form SS-4
(Rev. September 2003)

Department of the Treasury
Internal Revenue Service

For use with Form SS-4 (Rev. December 2001)
Application for Employer Identification Number.
Section references are to the Internal Revenue Code unless otherwise noted.

General Instructions

Use these instructions to complete **Form SS-4,** Application for Employer Identification Number. Also see **Do I Need an EIN?** on page 2 of Form SS-4.

Purpose of Form

Use Form SS-4 to apply for an employer identification number (EIN). An EIN is a nine-digit number (for example, 12-3456789) assigned to sole proprietors, corporations, partnerships, estates, trusts, and other entities for tax filing and reporting purposes. The information you provide on this form will establish your business tax account.

*An EIN is for use in connection with your business activities only. Do **not** use your EIN in place of your social security number (SSN).*

Items To Note

Apply online. You can now apply for and receive an EIN online using the internet. See **How To Apply** below.

File only one Form SS-4. Generally, a sole proprietor should file only one Form SS-4 and needs only one EIN, regardless of the number of businesses operated as a sole proprietorship or trade names under which a business operates. However, if the proprietorship incorporates or enters into a partnership, a new EIN is required. Also, each corporation in an affiliated group must have its own EIN.

EIN applied for, but not received. If you do not have an EIN by the time a return is due, write "Applied For" and the date you applied in the space shown for the number. **Do not** show your SSN as an EIN on returns.

If you do not have an EIN by the time a tax deposit is due, send your payment to the Internal Revenue Service Center for your filing area as shown in the instructions for the form that you are filing. Make your check or money order payable to the "United States Treasury" and show your name (as shown on Form SS-4), address, type of tax, period covered, and date you applied for an EIN.

How To Apply

You can apply for an EIN online, by telephone, by fax, or by mail depending on how soon you need to use the EIN. Use only one method for each entity so you do not receive more than one EIN for an entity.

Online. You can receive your EIN by internet and use it immediately to file a return or make a payment. Go to the IRS website at **www.irs.gov/businesses** and click on **Employer ID Numbers** under **topics.**

Telephone. You can receive your EIN by telephone and use it immediately to file a return or make a payment. Call the IRS at **1-800-829-4933.** (International applicants must call 215-516-6999.) The hours of operation are 7:00 a.m. to 10:00 p.m. The person making the call must be authorized to sign the form or be an authorized designee. See **Signature** and **Third Party Designee** on page 6. Also see the **TIP** below.

If you are applying by telephone, it will be helpful to complete Form SS-4 before contacting the IRS. An IRS representative will use the information from the Form SS-4 to establish your account and assign you an EIN. Write the number you are given on the upper right corner of the form and sign and date it. Keep this copy for your records.

If requested by an IRS representative, mail or fax (facsimile) the signed Form SS-4 (including any Third Party Designee authorization) within 24 hours to the IRS address provided by the IRS representative.

*Taxpayer representatives can apply for an EIN on behalf of their client and request that the EIN be faxed to their **client** on the same day. **Note:** By using this procedure, you are authorizing the IRS to fax the EIN without a cover sheet.*

Fax. Under the Fax-TIN program, you can receive your EIN by fax within 4 business days. Complete and fax Form SS-4 to the IRS using the Fax-TIN number listed on page 2 for your state. A long-distance charge to callers outside of the local calling area will apply. Fax-TIN numbers can only be used to apply for an EIN. **The numbers may change without notice.** Fax-TIN is available 24 hours a day, 7 days a week.

Be sure to provide your fax number so the IRS can fax the EIN back to you. **Note:** By using this procedure, you are authorizing the IRS to fax the EIN without a cover sheet.

Mail. Complete Form SS-4 at least 4 to 5 weeks before you will need an EIN. Sign and date the application and mail it to the service center address for your state. You will receive your EIN in the mail in approximately 4 weeks. See also **Third Party Designee** on page 6.

Call 1-800-829-4933 to verify a number or to ask about the status of an application by mail.

Where To Fax or File

If your principal business, office or agency, or legal residence in the case of an individual, is located in:	Call the Fax-TIN number shown or file with the "Internal Revenue Service Center" at:
Connecticut, Delaware, District of Columbia, Florida, Georgia, Maine, Maryland, Massachusetts, New Hampshire, New Jersey, New York, North Carolina, Ohio, Pennsylvania, Rhode Island, South Carolina, Vermont, Virginia, West Virginia	Attn: EIN Operation P. O. Box 9003 Holtsville, NY 11742-9003 Fax-TIN 631-447-8960
Illinois, Indiana, Kentucky, Michigan	Attn: EIN Operation Cincinnati, OH 45999 Fax-TIN 859-669-5760
Alabama, Alaska, Arizona, Arkansas, California, Colorado, Hawaii, Idaho, Iowa, Kansas, Louisiana, Minnesota, Mississippi, Missouri, Montana, Nebraska, Nevada, New Mexico, North Dakota, Oklahoma, Oregon, Puerto Rico, South Dakota, Tennessee, Texas, Utah, Washington, Wisconsin, Wyoming	Attn: EIN Operation Philadelphia, PA 19255 Fax-TIN 215-516-3990
If you have no legal residence, principal place of business, or principal office or agency in any state:	Attn: EIN Operation Philadelphia, PA 19255 Telephone 215-516-6999 Fax-TIN 215-516-3990

How To Get Forms and Publications

Phone. You can order forms, instructions, and publications by phone 24 hours a day, 7 days a week. Call 1-800-TAX-FORM (1-800-829-3676). You should receive your order or notification of its status within 10 workdays.

Personal computer. With your personal computer and modem, you can get the forms and information you need using the IRS website at **www.irs.gov** or File Transfer Protocol at **ftp.irs.gov.**

CD-ROM. For small businesses, return preparers, or others who may frequently need tax forms or publications, a CD-ROM containing over 2,000 tax products (including many prior year forms) can be purchased from the National Technical Information Service (NTIS).

To order **Pub. 1796,** Federal Tax Products on CD-ROM, call **1-877-CDFORMS** (1-877-233-6767) toll free or connect to **www.irs.gov/cdorders.**

Tax Help for Your Business

IRS-sponsored Small Business Workshops provide information about your Federal and state tax obligations.

For information about workshops in your area, call 1-800-829-4933.

Related Forms and Publications

The following **forms** and **instructions** may be useful to filers of Form SS-4:
- **Form 990-T,** Exempt Organization Business Income Tax Return
- **Instructions for Form 990-T**
- **Schedule C (Form 1040),** Profit or Loss From Business
- **Schedule F (Form 1040),** Profit or Loss From Farming
- **Instructions for Form 1041 and Schedules A, B, D, G, I, J, and K-1,** U.S. Income Tax Return for Estates and Trusts
- **Form 1042,** Annual Withholding Tax Return for U.S. Source Income of Foreign Persons
- **Instructions for Form 1065,** U.S. Return of Partnership Income
- **Instructions for Form 1066,** U.S. Real Estate Mortgage Investment Conduit (REMIC) Income Tax Return
- **Instructions for Forms 1120 and 1120-A**
- **Form 2553,** Election by a Small Business Corporation
- **Form 2848,** Power of Attorney and Declaration of Representative
- **Form 8821,** Tax Information Authorization
- **Form 8832,** Entity Classification Election
    For more **information** about filing Form SS-4 and related issues, see:
- **Circular A,** Agricultural Employer's Tax Guide (Pub. 51)
- **Circular E,** Employer's Tax Guide (Pub. 15)
- **Pub. 538,** Accounting Periods and Methods
- **Pub. 542,** Corporations
- **Pub. 557,** Exempt Status for Your Organization
- **Pub. 583,** Starting a Business and Keeping Records
- **Pub. 966,** Electronic Choices for Paying ALL Your Federal Taxes
- **Pub. 1635,** Understanding Your EIN
- **Package 1023,** Application for Recognition of Exemption Under Section 501(c)(3) of the Internal Revenue Code
- **Package 1024,** Application for Recognition of Exemption Under Section 501(a)

Specific Instructions

Print or type all entries on Form SS-4. Follow the instructions for each line to expedite processing and to avoid unnecessary IRS requests for additional information. Enter "N/A" (nonapplicable) on the lines that do not apply.

Line 1—Legal name of entity (or individual) for whom the EIN is being requested. Enter the legal name of the entity (or individual) applying for the EIN exactly as it appears on the social security card, charter, or other applicable legal document.

Individuals. Enter your first name, middle initial, and last name. If you are a sole proprietor, enter your individual name, not your business name. Enter your business name on line 2. Do not use abbreviations or nicknames on line 1.

Trusts. Enter the name of the trust.

Estate of a decedent. Enter the name of the estate.

Partnerships. Enter the legal name of the partnership as it appears in the partnership agreement.

Corporations. Enter the corporate name as it appears in the corporation charter or other legal document creating it.

Plan administrators. Enter the name of the plan administrator. A plan administrator who already has an EIN should use that number.

Line 2—Trade name of business. Enter the trade name of the business if different from the legal name. The trade name is the "doing business as " (DBA) name.

 *Use the full legal name shown on line 1 on all tax returns filed for the entity. (However, if you enter a trade name on line 2 and choose to use the trade name instead of the legal name, enter the trade name on **all returns** you file.) To prevent processing delays and errors, **always** use the legal name only (or the trade name only) on **all** tax returns.*

Line 3—Executor, trustee, "care of" name. Trusts enter the name of the trustee. Estates enter the name of the executor, administrator, or other fiduciary. If the entity applying has a designated person to receive tax information, enter that person's name as the "care of" person. Enter the individual's first name, middle initial, and last name.

Lines 4a-b—Mailing address. Enter the mailing address for the entity's correspondence. If line 3 is completed, enter the address for the executor, trustee or "care of" person. Generally, this address will be used on all tax returns.

 *File **Form 8822**, Change of Address, to report any subsequent changes to the entity's mailing address.*

Lines 5a-b—Street address. Provide the entity's physical address **only** if different from its mailing address shown in lines 4a-b. **Do not** enter a P.O. box number here.

Line 6—County and state where principal business is located. Enter the entity's primary **physical** location.

Lines 7a-b—Name of principal officer, general partner, grantor, owner, or trustor. Enter the first name, middle initial, last name, and SSN of **(a)** the principal officer if the business is a corporation, **(b)** a general partner if a partnership, **(c)** the owner of an entity that is disregarded as separate from its owner (disregarded entities owned by a corporation enter the corporation's name and EIN), or **(d)** a grantor, owner, or trustor if a trust.

If the person in question is an **alien individual** with a previously assigned individual taxpayer identification number (ITIN), enter the ITIN in the space provided and submit a copy of an official identifying document. If

necessary, complete **Form W-7,** Application for IRS Individual Taxpayer Identification Number, to obtain an ITIN.

You are **required** to enter an SSN, ITIN, or EIN unless the only reason you are applying for an EIN is to make an entity classification election (see Regulations sections 301.7701-1 through 301.7701-3) and you are a nonresident alien with no effectively connected income from sources within the United States.

Line 8a—Type of entity. Check the box that best describes the type of entity applying for the EIN. If you are an alien individual with an ITIN previously assigned to you, enter the ITIN in place of a requested SSN.

 *This is not an election for a tax classification of an entity. See **Limited liability company (LLC)** on page 4.*

Other. If not specifically listed, check the "Other" box, enter the type of entity and the type of return, if any, that will be filed (for example, "Common Trust Fund, Form 1065" or "Created a Pension Plan"). Do not enter "N/A." If you are an alien individual applying for an EIN, see the **Lines 7a-b** instructions above.

● **Household employer.** If you are an individual, check the "Other" box and enter "Household Employer" and your SSN. If you are a state or local agency serving as a tax reporting agent for public assistance recipients who become household employers, check the "Other" box and enter "Household Employer Agent." If you are a trust that qualifies as a household employer, you do not need a separate EIN for reporting tax information relating to household employees; use the EIN of the trust.

● **QSub.** For a qualified subchapter S subsidiary (QSub) check the "Other" box and specify "QSub."

● **Withholding agent.** If you are a withholding agent required to file Form 1042, check the "Other" box and enter "Withholding Agent."

Sole proprietor. Check this box if you file Schedule C, C-EZ, or F (Form 1040) and have a qualified plan, or are required to file excise, employment, alcohol, tobacco, or firearms returns, or are a payer of gambling winnings. Enter your SSN (or ITIN) in the space provided. If you are a nonresident alien with no effectively connected income from sources within the United States, you do not need to enter an SSN or ITIN.

Corporation. This box is for any corporation **other than a personal service corporation.** If you check this box, enter the income tax form number to be filed by the entity in the space provided.

 *If you entered "**1120S**" after the "Corporation" checkbox, the corporation **must** file Form 2553 **no later than the 15th day of the 3rd month of the tax year the election is to take effect.** Until Form 2553 has been received and approved, you will be considered a Form 1120 filer. See the Instructions for Form 2553.*

Personal service corp. Check this box if the entity is a personal service corporation. An entity is a personal service corporation for a tax year only if:

- The principal activity of the entity during the testing period (prior tax year) for the tax year is the performance of personal services substantially by employee-owners, and
- The employee-owners own at least 10% of the fair market value of the outstanding stock in the entity on the last day of the testing period.

Personal services include performance of services in such fields as health, law, accounting, or consulting. For more information about personal service corporations, see the Instructions for Forms 1120 and 1120-A and Pub. 542.

Other nonprofit organization. Check this box if the nonprofit organization is other than a church or church-controlled organization and specify the type of nonprofit organization (for example, an educational organization).

 *If the organization also seeks tax-exempt status, you **must** file either Package 1023 or Package 1024. See Pub. 557 for more information.*

If the organization is covered by a group exemption letter, enter the four-digit **group exemption number (GEN).** (Do not confuse the GEN with the nine-digit EIN.) If you do not know the GEN, contact the parent organization. Get Pub. 557 for more information about group exemption numbers.

Plan administrator. If the plan administrator is an individual, enter the plan administrator's SSN in the space provided.

REMIC. Check this box if the entity has elected to be treated as a real estate mortgage investment conduit (REMIC). See the Instructions for Form 1066 for more information.

Limited liability company (LLC). An LLC is an entity organized under the laws of a state or foreign country as a limited liability company. For Federal tax purposes, an LLC may be treated as a partnership or corporation or be disregarded as an entity separate from its owner.

By **default,** a domestic LLC with only one member is **disregarded** as an entity separate from its owner and must include all of its income and expenses on the owner's tax return (e.g., **Schedule C (Form 1040)**). Also by default, a domestic LLC with two or more members is treated as a partnership. A domestic LLC may file Form 8832 to avoid either default classification and elect to be classified as an association taxable as a corporation. For more information on entity classifications (including the rules for foreign entities), see the instructions for Form 8832.

 Do not** file Form 8832 if the LLC accepts the default classifications above. **However, if the LLC will be electing S Corporation status, it must timely file both Form 8832 and Form 2553.

Complete Form SS-4 for LLCs as follows:
- A single-member domestic LLC that accepts the default classification (above) does not need an EIN and generally should not file Form SS-4. Generally, the LLC

should use the name and EIN of its **owner** for all Federal tax purposes. However, the reporting and payment of employment taxes for employees of the LLC may be made using the name and EIN of **either** the owner or the LLC as explained in Notice 99-6. You can find Notice 99-6 on page 12 of Internal Revenue Bulletin 1999-3 at **www.irs.gov/pub/irs-irbs/irb99-03.pdf. (Note:** If the LLC applicant indicates in box 13 that it has employees or expects to have employees, the owner (whether an individual or other entity) of a single-member domestic LLC will also be assigned its own EIN (if it does not already have one) even if the LLC will be filing the employment tax returns.)
- A single-member, domestic LLC that accepts the default classification (above) and wants an EIN for filing employment tax returns (see above) or non-Federal purposes, such as a state requirement, must check the "Other" box and write "Disregarded Entity" or, when applicable, "Disregarded Entity—Sole Proprietorship" in the space provided.
- A multi-member, domestic LLC that accepts the default classification (above) must check the "Partnership" box.
- A domestic LLC that will be filing Form 8832 to elect corporate status must check the "Corporation" box and write in "Single-Member" or "Multi-Member" immediately below the "form number" entry line.

Line 9—Reason for applying. Check only **one** box. Do not enter "N/A."

Started new business. Check this box if you are starting a new business that requires an EIN. If you check this box, enter the type of business being started. **Do not** apply if you already have an EIN and are only adding another place of business.

Hired employees. Check this box if the existing business is requesting an EIN because it has hired or is hiring employees and is therefore required to file employment tax returns. **Do not** apply if you already have an EIN and are only hiring employees. For information on employment taxes (e.g., for family members), see Circular E.

 You may be required to make electronic deposits of all depository taxes (such as employment tax, excise tax, and corporate income tax) using the Electronic Federal Tax Payment System (EFTPS). See section 11, Depositing Taxes, of Circular E and Pub. 966.

Created a pension plan. Check this box if you have created a pension plan and need an EIN for reporting purposes. Also, enter the type of plan in the space provided.

 Check this box if you are applying for a trust EIN when a new pension plan is established. In addition, check the "Other" box in line 8a and write "Created a Pension Plan" in the space provided.

Banking purpose. Check this box if you are requesting an EIN for banking purposes only, and enter the banking purpose (for example, a bowling league for depositing dues or an investment club for dividend and interest reporting).

Changed type of organization. Check this box if the business is changing its type of organization. For example, the business was a sole proprietorship and has been incorporated or has become a partnership. If you check this box, specify in the space provided (including available space immediately below) the type of change made. For example, "From Sole Proprietorship to Partnership."

Purchased going business. Check this box if you purchased an existing business. **Do not** use the former owner's EIN unless you became the "owner" of a corporation by acquiring its stock.

Created a trust. Check this box if you created a trust, and enter the type of trust created. For example, indicate if the trust is a nonexempt charitable trust or a split-interest trust.

Exception. Do **not** file this form for certain grantor-type trusts. The trustee does not need an EIN for the trust if the trustee furnishes the name and TIN of the grantor/owner and the address of the trust to all payors. See the Instructions for Form 1041 for more information.

 Do not check this box if you are applying for a trust EIN when a new pension plan is established. Check "Created a pension plan."

Other. Check this box if you are requesting an EIN for any other reason; and enter the reason. For example, a newly-formed state government entity should enter "Newly-Formed State Government Entity" in the space provided.

Line 10—Date business started or acquired. If you are starting a new business, enter the starting date of the business. If the business you acquired is already operating, enter the date you acquired the business. If you are changing the form of ownership of your business, enter the date the new ownership entity began. Trusts should enter the date the trust was legally created. Estates should enter the date of death of the decedent whose name appears on line 1 or the date when the estate was legally funded.

Line 11—Closing month of accounting year. Enter the last month of your accounting year or tax year. An accounting or tax year is usually 12 consecutive months, either a calendar year or a fiscal year (including a period of 52 or 53 weeks). A calendar year is 12 consecutive months ending on December 31. A fiscal year is either 12 consecutive months ending on the last day of any month other than December or a 52-53 week year. For more information on accounting periods, see Pub. 538.

Individuals. Your tax year generally will be a calendar year.

Partnerships. Partnerships must adopt one of the following tax years:
• The tax year of the majority of its partners,
• The tax year common to all of its principal partners,
• The tax year that results in the least aggregate deferral of income, or
• In certain cases, some other tax year.

See the Instructions for Form 1065 for more information.

REMICs. REMICs must have a calendar year as their tax year.

Personal service corporations. A personal service corporation generally must adopt a calendar year unless:
• It can establish a business purpose for having a different tax year, or
• It elects under section 444 to have a tax year other than a calendar year.

Trusts. Generally, a trust must adopt a calendar year except for the following:
• Tax-exempt trusts,
• Charitable trusts, and
• Grantor-owned trusts.

Line 12—First date wages or annuities were paid or will be paid. If the business has or will have employees, enter the date on which the business began or will begin to pay wages. If the business does not plan to have employees, enter "N/A."

Withholding agent. Enter the date you began or will begin to pay income (including annuities) to a nonresident alien. This also applies to individuals who are required to file Form 1042 to report alimony paid to a nonresident alien.

Line 13—Highest number of employees expected in the next 12 months. Complete each box by entering the number (including zero ("-0-")) of "Agricultural," "Household," or "Other" employees expected by the applicant in the next 12 months. For a definition of agricultural labor (farmwork), see Circular A.

Lines 14 and 15. Check the **one** box in line 14 that best describes the principal activity of the applicant's business. Check the "Other" box (and specify the applicant's principal activity) if none of the listed boxes applies.

Use line 15 to describe the applicant's principal line of business in more detail. For example, if you checked the "Construction" box in line 14, enter additional detail such as "General contractor for residential buildings" in line 15.

Construction. Check this box if the applicant is engaged in erecting buildings or other structures, (e.g., streets, highways, bridges, tunnels). The term "Construction" also includes special trade contractors, (e.g., plumbing, HVAC, electrical, carpentry, concrete, excavation, etc. contractors).

Real estate. Check this box if the applicant is engaged in renting or leasing real estate to others; managing, selling, buying or renting real estate for others; or providing related real estate services (e.g., appraisal services).

Rental and leasing. Check this box if the applicant is engaged in providing tangible goods such as autos, computers, consumer goods, or industrial machinery and equipment to customers in return for a periodic rental or lease payment.

Manufacturing. Check this box if the applicant is engaged in the mechanical, physical, or chemical transformation of materials, substances, or components into new products. The assembling of component parts of manufactured products is also considered to be manufacturing.

Transportation & warehousing. Check this box if the applicant provides transportation of passengers or cargo; warehousing or storage of goods; scenic or sight-seeing transportation; or support activities related to these modes of transportation.

Finance & insurance. Check this box if the applicant is engaged in transactions involving the creation, liquidation, or change of ownership of financial assets and/or facilitating such financial transactions; underwriting annuities/insurance policies; facilitating such underwriting by selling insurance policies; or by providing other insurance or employee-benefit related services.

Health care and social assistance. Check this box if the applicant is engaged in providing physical, medical, or psychiatric care using licensed health care professionals or providing social assistance activities such as youth centers, adoption agencies, individual/ family services, temporary shelters, etc.

Accommodation & food services. Check this box if the applicant is engaged in providing customers with lodging, meal preparation, snacks, or beverages for immediate consumption.

Wholesale–agent/broker. Check this box if the applicant is engaged in arranging for the purchase or sale of goods owned by others or purchasing goods on a commission basis for goods traded in the wholesale market, usually between businesses.

Wholesale–other. Check this box if the applicant is engaged in selling goods in the wholesale market generally to other businesses for resale on their own account.

Retail. Check this box if the applicant is engaged in selling merchandise to the general public from a fixed store; by direct, mail-order, or electronic sales; or by using vending machines.

Other. Check this box if the applicant is engaged in an activity not described above. Describe the applicant's principal business activity in the space provided.

Lines 16a-c. Check the applicable box in line 16a to indicate whether or not the entity (or individual) applying for an EIN was issued one previously. Complete lines 16b and 16c **only** if the "Yes" box in line 16a is checked. If the applicant previously applied for **more than one** EIN, write "See Attached" in the empty space in line 16a and attach a separate sheet providing the line 16b and 16c information for each EIN previously requested.

Third Party Designee. Complete this section **only** if you want to authorize the named individual to receive the entity's EIN and answer questions about the completion of Form SS-4. The designee's authority terminates at the time the EIN is assigned and released to the designee. **You must complete the signature area for the authorization to be valid.**

Signature. When required, the application must be signed by **(a)** the individual, if the applicant is an individual, **(b)** the president, vice president, or other principal officer, if the applicant is a corporation, **(c)** a responsible and duly authorized member or officer having knowledge of its affairs, if the applicant is a partnership, government entity, or other unincorporated organization, or **(d)** the fiduciary, if the applicant is a trust or an estate. Foreign applicants may have any duly-authorized person, (e.g., division manager), sign Form SS-4.

Privacy Act and Paperwork Reduction Act Notice. We ask for the information on this form to carry out the Internal Revenue laws of the United States. We need it to comply with section 6109 and the regulations thereunder which generally require the inclusion of an employer identification number (EIN) on certain returns, statements, or other documents filed with the Internal Revenue Service. If your entity is required to obtain an EIN, you are required to provide all of the information requested on this form. Information on this form may be used to determine which Federal tax returns you are required to file and to provide you with related forms and publications.

We disclose this form to the Social Security Administration for their use in determining compliance with applicable laws. We may give this information to the Department of Justice for use in civil and criminal litigation, and to the cities, states, and the District of Columbia for use in administering their tax laws. We may also disclose this information to Federal and state agencies to enforce Federal nontax criminal laws and to combat terrorism.

We will be unable to issue an EIN to you unless you provide all of the requested information which applies to your entity. Providing false information could subject you to penalties.

You are not required to provide the information requested on a form that is subject to the Paperwork Reduction Act unless the form displays a valid OMB control number. Books or records relating to a form or its instructions must be retained as long as their contents may become material in the administration of any Internal Revenue law. Generally, tax returns and return information are confidential, as required by section 6103.

The time needed to complete and file this form will vary depending on individual circumstances. The estimated average time is:

Recordkeeping	6 min.
Learning about the law or the form	22 min.
Preparing the form	46 min.
Copying, assembling, and sending the form to the IRS	20 min.

If you have comments concerning the accuracy of these time estimates or suggestions for making this form simpler, we would be happy to hear from you. You can write to the Tax Products Coordinating Committee, Western Area Distribution Center, Rancho Cordova, CA 95743-0001. **Do not** send the form to this address. Instead, see **How To Apply** on page 1.

Form **5768**

(Rev. December 1996)

Department of the Treasury
Internal Revenue Service

Election/Revocation of Election by an Eligible Section 501(c)(3) Organization To Make Expenditures To Influence Legislation

(Under Section 501(h) of the Internal Revenue Code)

For IRS
Use Only ▶

Name of organization	Employer identification number

Number and street (or P.O. box no., if mail is not delivered to street address)	Room/suite

City, town or post office, and state	ZIP + 4

1 Election—As an eligible organization, we hereby elect to have the provisions of section 501(h) of the Code, relating to expenditures to influence legislation, apply to our tax year ending..and all subsequent tax years until revoked.

(Month, day, and year)

Note: *This election must be signed and postmarked within the first taxable year to which it applies.*

2 Revocation—As an eligible organization, we hereby revoke our election to have the provisions of section 501(h) of the Code, relating to expenditures to influence legislation, apply to our tax year ending..

(Month, day, and year)

Note: *This revocation must be signed and postmarked before the first day of the tax year to which it applies.*

Under penalties of perjury, I declare that I am authorized to make this (check applicable box) ▶ ☐ election ☐ revocation on behalf of the above named organization.

(Signature of officer or trustee)	(Type or print name and title)	(Date)

General Instructions

Section references are to the Internal Revenue Code.

Section 501(c)(3) states that an organization exempt under that section will lose its tax-exempt status and its qualification to receive deductible charitable contributions if a substantial part of its activities are carried on to influence legislation. Section 501(h), however, permits certain eligible 501(c)(3) organizations to elect to make limited expenditures to influence legislation. An organization making the election will, however, be subject to an excise tax under section 4911 if it spends more than the amounts permitted by that section. Also, the organization may lose its exempt status if its lobbying expenditures exceed the permitted amounts by more than 50% over a 4-year period. For any tax year in which an election under section 501(h) is in effect, an electing organization must report the actual and permitted amounts of its lobbying expenditures and grass roots expenditures (as defined in section 4911(c)) on its annual return required under section 6033. See Schedule A (Form 990). Each electing member of an affiliated group must report these amounts for both itself and the affiliated group as a whole.

To make or revoke the election, enter the ending date of the tax year to which the election or revocation applies in item **1** or **2,** as applicable, and sign and date the form in the spaces provided.

Eligible Organizations.—A section 501(c)(3) organization is permitted to make the election if it is not a disqualified organization (see below) and is described in:

1. Section 170(b)(1)(A)(ii) (relating to educational institutions),

2. Section 170(b)(1)(A)(iii) (relating to hospitals and medical research organizations),

3. Section 170(b)(1)(A)(iv) (relating to organizations supporting government schools),

4. Section 170(b)(1)(A)(vi) (relating to organizations publicly supported by charitable contributions),

5. Section 509(a)(2) (relating to organizations publicly supported by admissions, sales, etc.), or

6. Section 509(a)(3) (relating to organizations supporting certain types of public charities other than those section 509(a)(3) organizations that support section 501(c)(4), (5), or (6) organizations).

Disqualified Organizations.—The following types of organizations are not permitted to make the election:

a. Section 170(b)(1)(A)(i) organizations (relating to churches),

b. An integrated auxiliary of a church or of a convention or association of churches, or

c. A member of an affiliated group of organizations if one or more members of such group is described in **a** or **b** of this paragraph.

Affiliated Organizations.—Organizations are members of an affiliated group of organizations only if **(1)** the governing instrument of one such organization requires it to be bound by the decisions of the other organization on legislative issues, or **(2)** the governing board of one such organization includes persons (i) who are specifically designated representatives of another such organization or are members of the governing board, officers, or paid executive staff members of such other organization, and (ii) who, by aggregating their votes, have sufficient voting power to cause or prevent action on legislative issues by the first such organization.

For more details, see section 4911 and section 501(h).

Note: *A private foundation (including a private operating foundation) is not an eligible organization.*

Where To File.—Mail Form 5768 to the Internal Revenue Service Center, Ogden, UT 84201-0027.

Cat. No. 12125M

Form **5768** (Rev. 12-96)

Index

V

W

■

NONPROFIT CORPORATE KITS

Nolo, in cooperation with Julius Blumberg, Inc. offers two superior corporate kits. The kits are fully described in Chapter 9.
The Ex Libris® and Centennial® kits include:

• A corporate records book with minute paper and index dividers for Articles of Incorporation, Bylaws, Minutes and Corporate Certificates.
We are partial to the Centennial book which features a handcrafted, red and black simulated leather binder with your corporate name embossed in gold on the spine.

• A metal corporate seal designed to emboss your corporate name and year of incorporation on important corporate documents.

• 20 lithographed Director Certificates printed with your corporate name. An option is provided for you to add 20 Sponsor Certificates.

• An option is included to order membership materials consisting of a membership index and roll sheets, plus 40 lithographed membership certificates.

Ex Libris® and Centennial® are registered trademarks of Julius Blumberg, Inc.

ORDER COUPON *How to Form a Nonprofit Corporation [NNP]*

Name of Corporation (print exactly as on Articles of Incorporation). Put one character per space (including punctuation and spaces).
BE SURE CAPITAL AND LOWER CASE LETTERS ARE CLEAR AND SPELLING IS ACCURATE. CORPORATE KITS ARE NONREFUNDABLE.

|45*|

Year of Incorporation: _____   State of Incorporation: _____

❑ Ex Libris Kit $109.95 (100 DRNL)   ❑ Centennial Kit $129.95 (930 DRNL) .... $_____
Each kit includes 20 Director Certificates

❑ Ex Libris Kit $119.95 (100 DRSP)   ❑ Centennial Kit $139.95 (930 DRSP) .... $_____
Each kit includes 20 Director Certificates plus 20 Sponsor Certificates

❑ Membership Materials including 40 Membership Certificates—add $40.00 (9MEMNL) .... $_____

❑ Extra Corporate Seal $30.00 .... $_____

* Long corporate names (over 45 characters) cost an additional $25.00 .... $_____

California Sales Tax (Add Your Local Sales Tax) .... $_____

Shipping Charges   ❑ $10.00 *or* ❑ $25.00 .... $_____

Regular $10.00 shipping within 12 - 15 business days/Rush $25 shipping within 4 business days**

TOTAL ENCLOSED .... $_____

METHOD OF PAYMENT   ❑ Check enclosed   ❑ VISA   ❑ Mastercard   ❑ Discover Card   ❑ American Express
NAME _____

STREET ADDRESS (NO PO BOXES) _____

CITY _____ STATE _____ ZIP _____ PHONE _____

SIGNATURE _____ ACCOUNT # _____ EXP. DATE _____

**All delivery dates are calculated from the day we receive your order. Before submitting your order, please call 1-800-728-3555 for current prices.

Sorry, we do not accept telephone orders for corporate kits. Prices are subject to change without notice.

CATALOG

...more from Nolo

	PRICE	CODE

BUSINESS

	PRICE	CODE
Buy-Sell Agreement Handbook:		
Plan Ahead for Changes in the Ownership of Your Business (Book w/CD-ROM)	$49.99	BSAG
The CA Nonprofit Corporation Kit (Binder w/CD-ROM)	$59.95	CNP
Consultant & Independent Contractor Agreements (Book w/CD-ROM)	$29.99	CICA
The Corporate Minutes Book (Book w/CD-ROM)	$69.99	CORMI
Create Yor Own Employee Handbook	$49.99	EMHA
Dealing With Problem Employees	$44.99	PROBM
Drive a Modest Car & 16 Other Keys to Small Business Success	$24.99	DRIV
The Employer's Legal Handbook	$39.99	EMPL
Everyday Employment Law	$29.99	ELBA
Federal Employment Laws	$49.99	FELW
Form Your Own Limited Liability Company (Book w/CD-ROM)	$44.99	LIAB
Hiring Independent Contractors: The Employer's Legal Guide (Book w/CD-ROM)	$34.99	HICI
How to Create a Noncompete Agreement	$44.95	NOCMP
How to Form a California Professional Corporation (Book w/CD-ROM)	$59.95	PROF
How to Form a Nonprofit Corporation (Book w/CD-ROM)—National Edition	$44.99	NNP
How to Form a Nonprofit Corporation in California (Book w/CD-ROM)	$44.99	NON
How to Form Your Own California Corporation (Binder w/CD-ROM)	$59.99	CACI
How to Form Your Own California Corporation (Book w/CD-ROM)	$34.99	CCOR
How to Get Your Business on the Web	$29.99	WEBS
How to Write a Business Plan	$34.99	SBS
Incorporate Your Business	$49.95	NIBS
The Independent Paralegal's Handbook	$29.95	PARA
Leasing Space for Your Small Business	$34.95	LESP

Prices subject to change.

	PRICE	CODE
Legal Guide for Starting & Running a Small Business	$34.99	RUNS
Legal Forms for Starting & Running a Small Business (Book w/CD-ROM)	$29.99	RUNS2
Marketing Without Advertising	$24.00	MWAD
Music Law (Book w/CD-ROM)	$34.99	ML
Nolo's Guide to Social Security Disability	$29.99	QSS
Nolo's Quick LLC	$24.99	LLCQ
Nondisclosure Agreements	$39.95	NAG
The Small Business Start-up Kit (Book w/CD-ROM)	$29.99	SMBU
The Small Business Start-up Kit for California (Book w/CD-ROM)	$34.99	OPEN
The Partnership Book: How to Write a Partnership Agreement (Book w/CD-ROM)	$39.99	PART
Sexual Harassment on the Job	$24.95	HARS
Starting & Running a Successful Newsletter or Magazine	$29.99	MAG
Take Charge of Your Workers' Compensation Claim	$34.99	WORK
Tax Savvy for Small Business	$36.99	SAVVY
Working for Yourself: Law & Taxes for the Self-Employed	$39.99	WAGE
Your Crafts Business: A Legal Guide	$26.99	VART
Your Limited Liability Company: An Operating Manual (Book w/CD-ROM)	$49.99	LOP
Your Rights in the Workplace	$29.99	YRW

CONSUMER

	PRICE	CODE
How to Win Your Personal Injury Claim	$29.99	PICL
Nolo's Encyclopedia of Everyday Law	$29.99	EVL
Nolo's Guide to California Law	$24.95	CLAW
Trouble-Free Travel...And What to Do When Things Go Wrong	$14.95	TRAV

ESTATE PLANNING & PROBATE

	PRICE	CODE
8 Ways to Avoid Probate	$19.99	PRO8
9 Ways to Avoid Estate Taxes	$29.95	ESTX

	PRICE	CODE
Estate Planning Basics	$21.99	ESPN
How to Probate an Estate in California	$49.99	PAE
Make Your Own Living Trust (Book w/CD-ROM)	$39.99	LITR
Nolo's Simple Will Book (Book w/CD-ROM)	$36.99	SWIL
Plan Your Estate	$44.99	NEST
Quick & Legal Will Book	$16.99	QUIC

FAMILY MATTERS

	PRICE	CODE
Child Custody: Building Parenting Agreements That Work	$29.99	CUST
The Complete IEP Guide	$24.99	IEP
Divorce & Money: How to Make the Best Financial Decisions During Divorce	$34.99	DIMO
Do Your Own California Adoption: Nolo's Guide for Stepparents and Domestic Partners (Book w/CD-ROM)	$34.99	ADOP
Get a Life: You Don't Need a Million to Retire Well	$24.99	LIFE
The Guardianship Book for California	$39.99	GB
A Legal Guide for Lesbian and Gay Couples	$29.99	LG
Living Together: A Legal Guide (Book w/CD-ROM)	$34.99	LTK
Medical Directives and Powers of Attorney in California	$19.99	CPOA
Using Divorce Mediation: Save Your Money & Your Sanity	$29.95	UDMD

GOING TO COURT

	PRICE	CODE
Beat Your Ticket: Go To Court and Win! (National Edition)	$19.99	BEYT
The Criminal Law Handbook: Know Your Rights, Survive the System	$34.99	KYR
Everybody's Guide to Small Claims Court (National Edition)	$26.99	NSCC
Everybody's Guide to Small Claims Court in California	$26.99	CSCC
Fight Your Ticket ... and Win! (California Edition)	$29.99	FYT
How to Change Your Name in California	$34.95	NAME
How to Collect When You Win a Lawsuit (California Edition)	$29.99	JUDG

	PRICE	CODE
How to Seal Your Juvenile & Criminal Records (California Edition)	$34.95	CRIM
The Lawsuit Survival Guide	$29.99	UNCL
Nolo's Deposition Handbook	$29.99	DEP
Represent Yourself in Court: How to Prepare & Try a Winning Case	$34.99	RYC
Sue in California Without a Lawyer	$34.99	SLWY

HOMEOWNERS, LANDLORDS & TENANTS

	PRICE	CODE
California Tenants' Rights	$27.99	CTEN
Deeds for California Real Estate	$24.99	DEED
Dog Law	$21.95	DOG
Every Landlord's Legal Guide (National Edition, Book w/CD-ROM)	$44.99	ELLI
Every Tenant's Legal Guide	$29.99	EVTEN
For Sale by Owner in California	$29.99	FSBO
How to Buy a House in California	$34.99	BHCA
The California Landlord's Law Book: Rights & Responsibilities (Book w/CD-ROM)	$44.99	LBRT
The California Landlord's Law Book: Evictions (Book w/CD-ROM)	$44.99	LBEV
Leases & Rental Agreements	$29.99	LEAR
Neighbor Law: Fences, Trees, Boundaries & Noise	$26.99	NEI
The New York Landlord's Law Book (Book w/CD-ROM)	$39.99	NYLL
New York Tenants' Rights	$27.99	NYTEN
Renters' Rights (National Edition)	$24.99	RENT
Stop Foreclosure Now in California	$29.95	CLOS

HUMOR

	PRICE	CODE
Poetic Justice	$9.95	PJ

IMMIGRATION

	PRICE	CODE
Becoming A U.S. Citizen: A Guide to the Law, Exam and Interview	$24.99	USCIT
Fiancé & Marriage Visas	$44.99	IMAR

	PRICE	CODE
How to Get a Green Card	$29.99	GRN
Student & Tourist Visas	$29.99	ISTU
U.S. Immigration Made Easy	$44.99	IMEZ

MONEY MATTERS

	PRICE	CODE
101 Law Forms for Personal Use (Book w/CD-ROM)	$29.99	SPOT
Bankruptcy: Is It the Right Solution to Your Debt Problems?	$19.99	BRS
Chapter 13 Bankruptcy: Repay Your Debts	$34.99	CH13
Creating Your Own Retirement Plan	$29.99	YROP
Credit Repair (Book w/CD-ROM)	$24.99	CREP
Getting Paid: How to Collect From Bankrupt Debtors	$29.99	CRBNK
How to File for Chapter 7 Bankruptcy	$34.99	HFB
IRAs, 401(k)s & Other Retirement Plans: Taking Your Money Out	$34.99	RET
Money Troubles: Legal Strategies to Cope With Your Debts	$29.99	MT
Stand Up to the IRS	$24.99	SIRS
Surviving an IRS Tax Audit	$24.95	SAUD
Take Control of Your Student Loan Debt	$26.95	SLOAN

PATENTS AND COPYRIGHTS

	PRICE	CODE
The Copyright Handbook: How to Protect and Use Written Works (Book w/CD-ROM)	$39.99	COHA
Copyright Your Software	$34.95	CYS
Domain Names	$26.95	DOM
Getting Permission: How to License and Clear Copyrighted Materials Online and Off (Book w/CD-ROM)	$34.99	RIPER
How to Make Patent Drawings Yourself	$29.99	DRAW
Inventor's Guide to Law, Business and Taxes	$34.99	ILAX
The Inventor's Notebook	$24.99	INOT
Nolo's Patents for Beginners	$29.99	QPAT
Patent Pending in 24 Hours	$29.99	PEND

	PRICE	CODE
License Your Invention (Book w/CD-ROM)	$39.99	LICE
Patent, Copyright & Trademark	$39.99	PCTM
Patent It Yourself	$49.99	PAT
Patent Searching Made Easy	$29.95	PATSE
The Public Domain	$34.95	PUBL
Trademark: Legal Care for Your Business and Product Name	$39.99	TRD
Web and Software Development: A Legal Guide (Book w/ CD-ROM)	$44.95	SFT

RESEARCH & REFERENCE

	PRICE	CODE
Legal Research: How to Find & Understand the Law	$39.99	LRES

SENIORS

	PRICE	CODE
Choose the Right Long-Term Care: Home Care, Assisted Living & Nursing Homes	$21.99	ELD
The Conservatorship Book for California	$44.99	CNSV
Social Security, Medicare & Goverment Pensions	$29.99	SOA

SOFTWARE

**Call or check our website at www.nolo.com
for special discounts on Software!**

	PRICE	CODE
LeaseWriter CD—Windows	$129.95	LWD1
LLC Maker—Windows	$89.95	LLP1
PatentPro Plus—Windows	$399.99	PAPL
Personal RecordKeeper 5.0 CD—Windows	$59.95	RKD5
Quicken Legal Business Pro 2005—Windows	$109.99	SBQB5
Quicken WillMaker Plus 2005—Windows	$79.99	WQP5

Special Upgrade Offer

Save 35% on the latest edition of your Nolo book

Because laws and legal procedures change often, we update our books regularly. To help keep you up-to-date, we are extending this special upgrade offer. Cut out and mail the title portion of the cover of your old Nolo book and we'll give you **35% off** the retail price of the NEW EDITION of that book when you purchase directly from Nolo. This offer is to individuals only.

Call us today at 1-800-728-3555

Prices and offer subject to change without notice.

Order Form

Name _____

Address _____

City _____

State, Zip _____

Daytime Phone _____

E-mail _____

Our "No-Hassle" Guarantee

Return anything you buy directly from Nolo for any reason and we'll cheerfully refund your purchase price. No ifs, ands or buts.

☐ Check here if you do not wish to receive mailings from other companies

Item Code	Quantity	Item	Unit Price	Total Price

Method of payment

☐ Check   ☐ VISA   ☐ MasterCard
☐ Discover Card   ☐ American Express

Subtotal	
Add your local sales tax (California only)	
Shipping: RUSH $9, Basic $5 (See below)	
"I bought 3, ship it to me FREE!"(Ground shipping only)	
TOTAL	

Account Number _____

Expiration Date _____

Signature _____

Shipping and Handling

Rush Delivery—Only $9

We'll ship any order to any street address in the U.S. by UPS 2nd Day Air* for only $9!

* Order by noon Pacific Time and get your order in 2 business days. Orders placed after noon Pacific Time will arrive in 3 business days. P.O. boxes and S.F. Bay Area use basic shipping. Alaska and Hawaii use 2nd Day Air or Priority Mail.

Basic Shipping—$5

Use for P.O. Boxes, Northern California and Ground Service.

Allow 1-2 weeks for delivery. U.S. addresses only.

For faster service, use your credit card and our toll-free numbers

**Call our customer service group
Monday thru Friday 7am to 7pm PST**

Phone   1-800-728-3555

Fax   1-800-645-0895

Mail   Nolo
                950 Parker St.
                Berkeley, CA 94710

Order 24 hours a day @
www.nolo.com

Remember:

Little publishers have big ears.
We really listen to you.

Take 2 Minutes & Give Us Your 2 cents

Your comments make a big difference in the development and revision of Nolo books and software. Please take a few minutes and register your Nolo product—and your comments—with us. Not only will your input make a difference, you'll receive special offers available only to registered owners of Nolo products on our newest books and software. Register now by:

PHONE
1-800-728-3555

FAX
1-800-645-0895

EMAIL
cs@nolo.com

or **MAIL** us
this registration card

fold here

NOLO Registration Card

NAME _____ DATE _____

ADDRESS _____

_____

CITY _____ STATE _____ ZIP _____

PHONE _____ E-MAIL _____

WHERE DID YOU HEAR ABOUT THIS PRODUCT? _____

WHERE DID YOU PURCHASE THIS PRODUCT? _____

DID YOU CONSULT A LAWYER? (PLEASE CIRCLE ONE) YES NO NOT APPLICABLE

DID YOU FIND THIS BOOK HELPFUL? (VERY) 5 4 3 2 1 (NOT AT ALL)

COMMENTS _____

_____

_____

WAS IT EASY TO USE? (VERY EASY) 5 4 3 2 1 (VERY DIFFICULT)

We occasionally make our mailing list available to carefully selected companies whose products may be of interest to you.

❑ If you do not wish to receive mailings from these companies, please check this box.

❑ You can quote me in future Nolo promotional materials.
    Daytime phone number _____.

NNP 6.0

Nolo
in the
NEWS

"Nolo helps lay people perform legal tasks without the aid—or fees—of lawyers."

—USA TODAY

Nolo books are ..."written in plain language, free of legal mumbo jumbo, and spiced with witty personal observations."

—ASSOCIATED PRESS

"...Nolo publications...guide people simply through the how, when, where and why of law."

—WASHINGTON POST

"Increasingly, people who are not lawyers are performing tasks usually regarded as legal work... And consumers, using books like Nolo's, do routine legal work themselves."

—NEW YORK TIMES

"...All of [Nolo's] books are easy-to-understand, are updated regularly, provide pull-out forms...and are often quite moving in their sense of compassion for the struggles of the lay reader."

—SAN FRANCISCO CHRONICLE

- - - - - - - - - - - - - - - - - fold here - - - - - - - - - - - - - - - - -

Place
stamp here

Nolo
950 Parker Street
Berkeley, CA 94710-9867

Attn: NNP 6.0